Good Housekeeping

The **Essential** Book of

Parenting

Good Housekeeping

The **Essential** Book of

Parenting

Everything you need to know to care for your child,
from before birth to age five

TED SMART

Random House Australia (Pty) Limited
20 Alfred Street, Milsons Point, Sydney, New South Wales 2061, Australia

Random House New Zealand Limited
18 Poland Road, Glenfield, Auckland 10, New Zealand

Random House South Africa (Pty) Limited
Endulini, 5a Jubilee Road, Parktown 2193, South Africa

Random House UK Limited Reg. No. 954009

A catalogue record for this book is available from the British Library

The material in this book has also been published as part of
Good Housekeeping The Complete Book of Parenting.

General Medical Editor: Dr Nicola McClure
Good Housekeeping Editor: Linda Gray
Editors: Anne Yelland, Nicky Adamson

Design and Art Direction: Martin Lovelock
Photography: Jo Foord
Photographic Stylists: Hilary Guy, Kay McGlone
Illustrations: Raymond Turvey

Printed and bound by Oriental Press in Dubai

Foreword

'When will *Good Housekeeping* bring out a baby book?', readers have been pleading for years. Well, I'm delighted to announce that *Good Housekeeping's* new baby has arrived. This is a childcare book with a difference, because it recognizes that parenting is not as easy as some people claim. Packed with practical advice, sensitively given, this is the one book you need to take you through pregnancy, and those all-absorbing months with your new baby, to nursery age.

Written by a panel of leading specialists in health and child development, it combines a wealth of up-to-date information (including an invaluable A-Z of baby health which you will refer to again and again) with an emphasis on your child's emotional needs. What you will not find anywhere is an unrealistic emphasis on perfection. Being a 'good enough' parent is all that is required and all that any child needs. I hope this book will help to make that easier and more enjoyable for you.

LINDA GRAY, ASSOCIATE EDITOR, *Good Housekeeping*

THE CONTRIBUTORS

Nikki Bradford (Pregnancy / Your Baby at Home) was formerly Health Correspondent for *Good Housekeeping* magazine and Health Editor of *Essentials*. She is the Honorary Secretary of the Guild of Health Writers and initiated the Men's Healthline counselling service in 1995. Her many previous books include *The Well Woman's Self Help Directory*, *Pain Relief in Childbirth* and *Men's Health Matters*.

Dr Dorothy Einon (Giving Birth / The First Year / Toddlerhood and Beyond) is a lecturer in Psychology at University College, London. She also contributes to newspapers and magazines and has broadcast on radio and TV. Her previous books are *Creative Play*, *Parenthood* and, with Jane Asher, *Time for Play*.

Jennie Lindon (Learning Through Play / Help with Your Child) is a chartered psychologist who works as a freelance consultant on training and other issues for various professional bodies. She writes extensively on children and families and three of her previous books include *Your Child from 5-11*, *Help Your Child through School* and *Child Development from Birth to 8 Years*. She has written for many magazines, including *Nursery World* and *Practical Parenting*.

Dr Nicola McClure (General medical editor) is a GP in a busy West London practice. She was the medical consultant and main contributor to the *Good Housekeeping Family Health Encyclopedia* and her other publications include *The Century Book of Pregnancy and Birth* and *A Baby's Story*.

June Thompson (Your Baby's Health) is a medical journalist who is also a qualified nurse, midwife and health visitor. Her freelance work has included the preparation of professional handbooks and research reports for the Department of Health and the Health Education Authority, and she has also been published in many professional and consumer magazines. She is the author of numerous childcare and parenting books.

Heather Welford (Feeding Your Baby) is a freelance journalist and author who has written for a wide range of newspapers and magazines including *Parents*, the *Guardian* and *The Times Educational Supplement*. She is an NCT breastfeeding counsellor and tutor. Her previous books include *The Illustrated Dictionary of Pregnancy and Birth*, *Sleep and Wakefulness* and *Feeding Your Child from 0-3*.

Contents

1 PREGNANCY

Before Your Baby's Birth   10
Before You Conceive   10
What Happens in Conception   12
Your Pregnancy Week by Week   14
Your Antenatal Care   19
Working in Pregnancy   28
What You Will Need   30
Discomforts in Pregnancy   34
More Serious Problems   37
Having Twins   39
The Baby that Was Not to Be   41

2 GIVING BIRTH

Birth and Your Newborn Baby   44
Becoming a Parent   44
What Happens in Labour   45
The Three Stages of Labour   47
What to Do During Labour   49
Coping with Pain   51
Special Cases   54
The Father's Role   57
First Impressions   58
Your Changing Baby   61
Bonding   62
Reflexes   62
Babies with Problems   63
First Days   65

3 FEEDING YOUR BABY

Breast or Bottle?   70
Birth to Six Weeks   70
Six Weeks to Four Months   81
Introducing Solid Food   83
Continuing to Breastfeed   87
Weaning   89

4 YOUR BABY AT HOME

First Days with a Newborn   92
Taking Care of Your Baby   92
Keeping Your Baby Clean   97
Babies and Crying   101
Sleepless Babies, Exhausted Parents   104
What About You?   108
Postnatal Exercises   112
Care after a Caesarean   114
The Six-week Check   116
Sex and Contraception   118
Going It Alone   120

5 THE FIRST YEAR

Your Baby's Development   124
Your Baby's Growth   125
Your Baby's Body   127
Your Baby's Physical Development   130
How Your Baby's Senses Develop   135
Learning to Talk   140
Learning about Relationships   144
Learning about Feelings   146
Learning to Remember   148

6 YOUR BABY'S HEALTH

Your Baby's Well-being   152
Who Can Help?   152
Regular Health Checks   154
Immunization   157
A–Z of Baby Health   160
Is Your Child Safe?   168
Children with Special Needs   173

7 TODDLERHOOD AND BEYOND

The Preschool Years   178
Growing Up   178
From Baby to Child   180
How Children Grow   185
The Developing Senses   190
Learning to Talk   192
Learning to Think   194
Learning Who She Is   197
Learning to Feel   198
Learning Right from Wrong   199
Spreading Her Wings   201
Having a Second Child   202

8 LEARNING THROUGH PLAY

The Importance of Play   206
How Children Learn through Play   206
Word Play   208
Encouraging Your Child   209
Physical Play   209
Around the Home   211
Imaginative Play   213
Creative Play   214
Sand and Water   217
Fun with Music and Song   218
Learning to Love Books   220
Play and Technology   224
Playing with Other Children   225
Why Play Counts   227

9 HELP WITH YOUR CHILD

Sharing the Care   230
What Babies Need   230
Taking a Break   231
Child Care   234
Care Outside Your Home   240
Preschool Activities   244
The Importance of Home   247

Useful Contacts   248

Index   252

Acknowledgments   256

CHAPTER ONE

Pregnancy

Becoming pregnant, particularly for the first time, is an overwhelming and thoroughly absorbing experience, colouring every aspect of your life and every moment you are awake. This chapter details what you can expect during a normal pregnancy, how the baby grows, the decisions you will have to make and the items that you will need to acquire to make the first few weeks with a newborn easier.

Before your baby's birth

Having a baby can be so fulfilling that it can be hard to find words to express how you feel. It gives your life a whole new focus – from now on, you have somebody else to think of, somebody who affects almost everything you do. But along with the excitement comes a certain amount of apprehension. Will I love my baby? How will we cope? Will the baby be all right?

The good news is that mothers and babies are healthier and birth is safer than ever before. And although that is partly due to the ability of doctors to intervene in difficult or premature births, it is also due to increased knowledge of how babies develop in the womb, and to a better understanding of the importance of pre-conceptual care.

BEFORE YOU CONCEIVE

Most doctors now believe that it is important for both partners to be as fit and healthy as possible to maximize their chances of having a healthy baby. Being fit before you try to conceive increases your chances of doing so (one in six couples in the UK has trouble conceiving) and of carrying the pregnancy to term. Estimates suggest that as many as half of all pregnancies end in miscarriage (although often so early that you're aware only of a late period); 25 per cent of confirmed pregnancies are miscarried before the end of the twelfth week.

Ideally, you should both start planning for pregnancy at least three (preferably six) months before you want to conceive. It is important you both do so, because a healthy baby results from a healthy sperm fertilizing a healthy egg – a healthy egg fertilized by unhealthy sperm increases the risk of miscarriage – and it takes up to three months for new sperm cells to be made.

What you can both do

Give up smoking
Many studies suggest that tobacco reduces both men's and women's fertility. An American study found that female non-smokers were more than three times more likely to conceive than smokers; a Finnish study that smoking affected the speed at which sperm moved, making it move more slowly.

This advice applies to recreational drugs, in addition to tobacco.

Give up alcohol
Alcohol affects sperm production, not depressing the amount the body makes but increasing the proportion that is dead, damaged or in some way deformed. It has also been implicated in early miscarriage and is thought to affect the action of the cilia – the tiny hairs lining the fallopian tubes, the action of which helps the passage of the egg from the ovary to the womb.

Check for infections
Ask your GP to test for symptomless genito-urinary infections, as these can make both miscarriage and premature labour more likely. Chlamydia, in particular, is important to detect since it can affect a newborn baby.

Reduce your stress levels
Trying to become pregnant – especially if it takes longer than you hoped it would – can become stressful in itself.

In women, stress is believed to induce spasms in the fallopian tubes, which can interfere with ovulation, affect the womb lining and inhibit egg implantation. In men, stress hormones are known to affect sperm production.

Eat a healthy diet

Eat as much fresh food, wholegrain bread and cereals, fish, meat and pasteurized dairy produce as possible, to ensure that you get plenty of vitamins, minerals and essential fatty acids. Iron-rich foods, such as red and white meat, fish, lentils, green leafy vegetables and beans are also important.

Make love often

Although timing affects whether you conceive or not, the regularity with which you make love can be as important. Making love regularly two or three times a week will maximize your chances of conception. There is a 'window' of three or four days in the middle of your cycle when conception is likely, so don't feel you have to make love on the day you ovulate – this can become stressful in itself.

Monitor drug use

Let your GP know that you are trying to conceive in case your doctor is planning to prescribe any medicine for you. Some prescription drugs – including certain antibiotics and steroids for asthma in men – can affect fertility. Other drugs may harm a developing embryo. Try to avoid over-the-counter drugs for three months before trying to conceive, and during pregnancy.

Both men and women should avoid street drugs. In particular, cannabis is known to reduce sperm production significantly , and the effect can take a long time to wear off.

What men can do

Keep your testicles cool

Their optimum temperature is a degree or two cooler than the rest of your body. Avoid tight briefs and trousers and sitting for long periods with your legs crossed; turn the central heating down.

What women can do

Stop using contraceptives

You should stop taking the contraceptive pill at least three months before you plan to conceive and use a barrier method of contraception in the meantime. If you have an IUCD (intra-uterine contraceptive device or "coil"), have it removed at least one month before you start trying for a baby.

Check your immunity to rubella

If you have never had German measles, a blood test can check your immunity. Wait at least three months before trying to conceive after immunization.

Take extra folic acid

Insufficient folic acid in the diet can increase the risk of having a baby with spina bifida or other neural tube defects. You should try to increase your intake of folic acid at least three months before trying to conceive and continue through the first three months of pregnancy. Folic acid is found in dark green vegetables, beans, peas, pulses, bananas, grapefruit and oranges, and some breads and cereals. You can also buy folic acid supplements.

Wear gloves when gardening

This reduces the risk of toxoplasmosis, caused by an organism sometimes found in cats' faeces, which can cause miscarriage and birth defects. Wear gloves when handling cat litter and wash your hands afterwards.

Take regular exercise

Do not start anything new and strenuous, but keep up any exercise you are taking and try to walk or swim more often (see also pp. 25–7).

Avoid X-rays

Do not have an X-ray of your lower back, abdomen or pelvis if you are or are planning to become pregnant. If your dentist wishes to give you an X-ray,

How long will it take?

Women are at their peak fertility in their mid-twenties, after which it starts slowly to decline. This decline is accelerated after the age of 35. Men's fertility levels remain unchanged until their fifties, and men are biologically able to father children into their eighties.

As a general guide, about half of all couples trying to conceive do so within six months, a further 35 per cent within a year. The remaining 15 per cent may have problems.

If you are in your early thirties and have not conceived after a year of trying, ask to be referred to a fertility clinic.

see if it can be postponed; otherwise you should be given a lead-lined apron to be placed over your abdomen. If you are not, ask for one.

Watch what you eat

Infections such as listeria which in non-pregnant people cause food poisoning, can result in miscarriage or birth defects if you eat affected products when you are pregnant. Avoid if you can: raw and partially cooked meat and fish; unpasteurized milk and cheeses or yogurt made from it; soft, mould-ripened cheeses such as Brie and Camembert; soft-boiled eggs; pâtés; soft, whipped ice-cream from machines; and ready-made, prepacked salads and sandwiches. Women are also now being advised to avoid liver since veterinary feeds contain large quantities of vitamin A, which builds up in animal livers. High levels of this vitamin can cause foetal abnormalities. And caffeine prevents the absorption of certain vitamins and minerals.

When you cannot conceive

Infertility affects one British couple in six at some time, but the good news is that new fertility treatments and approaches to preconceptual care have made it more likely than ever before that they will become parents.

If you have not conceived within a year of trying, you can ask to be referred for infertility treatment. Since in 40 per cent of cases the 'problem' involves both partners, you will both be examined and interviewed, together and separately, in order to find out if the problem might be associated with your lifestyle – if you are smoking or drinking too much alcohol, for example – or whether further medical investigation is called for. Once the problem is identified, treatment can be carried out.

Sometimes minor surgery or treatment with drugs may be required; if the problem is more serious, one of the many variation of IVF (in vitro fertilization) now available may be considered, although these are time-consuming and you will almost certainly have to pay. Take heart if you are having trouble becoming pregnant – more than half of all couples treated professionally for infertility do become parents.

WHAT HAPPENS IN CONCEPTION

For most couples becoming pregnant poses no problems and results in a normal, healthy baby. Looked at in detail, however, the process is complex and if anything goes wrong along the way, there will be no pregnancy. Knowing what happens when will help you to do the best for yourself and your child.

Successful pregnancy

Pregnancy depends on the following events happening in the right order and at the right time.

- The man must produce healthy, normal sperm and ensure that they are placed by the entrance to the woman's cervix (neck of the womb). From here the sperm must get through the barrier of mucus which protects the cervix from bacteria and viruses. Around the middle of the woman's menstrual cycle, the mucus is watery so sperm can swim through it more easily. At other times of the month, it is quite thick.
- The woman needs to have ripened and released a healthy egg from one of her ovaries. This travels down one of her two fallopian tubes, stroked along its length by the tiny, finger-like cilia fronds which line the tubes.
- Sperm then swim past the cervix, through the womb and up into the fallopian tubes to meet the descending egg. Eggs can live about 24 hours and sperm may live for two to three days, so they need to find each other within this fairly brief period.
- Several sperm may reach the egg at about the same time, but one needs to be able to break through the egg's protective shell and get inside.
- Once this has happened, the nucleus of the sperm fuses with that of the egg and the egg's wall becomes impenetrable to other sperm. The egg spends the next two or three days passing down the remainder of the fallopian tube, then reaches the womb cavity, where it floats free for two or three days. Conception has now taken place.
- Inside the fertilized egg, the combined ball of egg and sperm nuclei have been dividing, first in two, then four, eight, sixteen and so on, to develop into a cluster of cells called an embryo.

Boy or girl?

When a sperm cell fuses with an egg cell, the result is a ball of their nuclei. Sperm and egg each donate 23 chromosomes, making a set of 23 pairs in all. These form the genetic blueprint for your future baby, and cover everything from hair and eye colour to blood group. However, it is the father who determines a baby's gender. Women's cells have two X chromosomes, so egg cells always contribute an X chromosome; whereas sperm cells may contain either one X or one Y. When a Y chromosome combines with an X, it results in a male baby. If an X-carrying sperm fertilizes the egg, the baby will be a girl.

- The embryo embeds itself in the blood-rich lining of the womb. You are now technically pregnant. However, it is believed that as many as 40 per cent of pregnancies are lost at this stage because the embryo does not implant itself properly.
- The womb lining is kept in place (rather than being shed in a normal monthly period) by extra progesterone produced by your ovaries. It is the major upsurge in the amount of this hormone in the body that makes many pregnant women feel nauseous in the first few weeks of pregnancy.

This entire process, made to look so easy by couples who conceive quickly, or accidentally, is very finely balanced throughout. It is thought that perhaps as many as 20 per cent of embryos which do implant are lost in what seems to be a late period.

Finding out you are pregnant

Some women know almost immediately that they are pregnant – they simply feel it, especially if they have been trying to conceive for some time. Others appear to be having periods and retain fairly flat tummies and are oblivious, in the most extreme cases for several months. It is possible to continue to bleed a little for a couple of months after you conceive. This is because your body may be producing enough progesterone to maintain most of your thick womb lining and the embryo in it, but not enough to prevent a little of it being shed.

The first signs
Early signs that you may be pregnant include:
- A missed period, or one which is lighter than usual.
- Tender, larger or tingling breasts, perhaps with darkened nipples.
- Nausea and vomiting.
- Changing tastes and a heightened or altered sense of smell.
- A need to urinate frequently.
- Feeling more emotional.
- Constipation.

Pregnancy tests

Most pregnancy tests are done on a sample of your urine, by checking for increased levels of one of the hormones produced in pregnancy called human chorionic gonadotrophin (HCG). Hospitals and some specialist clinics can do a more sensitive test on a blood sample.

Your GP may no longer do free routine pregnancy tests; many GPs who continue to offer tests charge for doing so. You can also get a test done for a fee by your local pharmacist. Or you can buy a home pregnancy testing kit. These can generally be used from the first day after your period should have started. Manufacturers claim such kits are 99 per cent accurate, but you must follow the instructions to the letter. It is worth doing a back-up test a day or so later.

How do you feel?

Emotional reactions to a positive test can vary enormously. Obviously if you had not planned to become pregnant, you will probably feel shock, surprise and, perhaps, disbelief. Even if you have been trying for some time, you may – along with the delight – feel panic, relief, anxiety, or even have second thoughts. Some people want to rush out and tell the whole world immediately; others want to take some time to get used to the idea themselves (it can be difficult keeping a secret like this from prospective grandparents, particularly if they have been waiting a long time for a grandchild). Often, several conflicting emotions are at work, until one or two start to dominate. Whatever you feel is perfectly natural.

Your partner's reactions are also likely to vary widely. Disbelief, pride and anxiety are all common.

Many men are surprised by the almost immediate change in their partners who, long before there are any visible signs she is pregnant, may prefer not to drive to a dinner party and sit up talking half the night, but stay at home and get an early night.

If there are no physical signs of pregnancy, you may find the first few months rather unreal. Often it is seeing the baby move on a scan (see pp. 23–4) that brings the reality that you are going to have a baby home to you. And if you are nauseous almost from the start and working outside the home, perhaps in a situation in which you do not want everyone to know immediately, the first few weeks can make you feel so wretched that you have almost no time for any real thoughts about the fact that you are going to be a mother and your partner a father.

Broadly speaking, there are three areas where you are likely to find your outlook changing.

Finance

Babies and children are expensive. No one believes the surveys that compute the cost of raising a child to the age of 18, until they have a child of their own.

Going it alone

Whether you intended to have a child on your own or not, you are likely to go through the same emotions as other women. Do not feel, because you do not have a partner, that you need to face everything alone. Groups such as Gingerbread and the National Council for One-Parent Families (see Useful Contacts, pp. 248–51) may have local support groups – people in your area who can share their experiences of single parenthood with you. Your health visitor (see pp. 152–3) is there for you, as is your GP. You have the same rights as anyone else to have a partner of your choice – friend, relative – with you at antenatal appointments and classes, and during the birth (see p. 21).

Bringing up a baby is not easy, even when two share the care and the responsibility. There is no doubt, however, that it is less difficult to raise your child alone than to do so with an uncooperative, uninvolved – or perhaps even hostile – partner.

One of you may lose some or most of your income for a few months, and even if you return to full-time employment while your baby is still small, there are the costs of child care to consider (see Help with Your Child, pp. 230–47).

Security

Women often feel very vulnerable when pregnant, not only is your body changing – at times almost on what seems like a daily basis – in a way over which you have no control, but you may feel sick and tired, and your emotions may be haywire. A warm, stable relationship becomes of paramount importance in such circumstances.

Responsibility

You and your partner are going to be completely responsible for another person, in a way that neither of you has been before. This can be a tremendously exciting and thrilling prospect; it can also be unnerving and even frightening.

Many parents are glad that pregnancy lasts 40 weeks – it gives you plenty of time to sort out your feelings about moving into a radically different phase of your life. There is no rule that says you must be delighted on day one and have worked out how you will manage to cope with a tiny baby on top of everything else in your lives by day two. The overwhelming majority of parents simply sort it out as they go along.

YOUR PREGNANCY WEEK BY WEEK

Pregnancy is measured from the first day of your last period, so that although you are four weeks pregnant, it is only two weeks since conception. Pregnancy usually lasts for 37 to 42 weeks from the first day of your last period: the average is 40 weeks.

In the early weeks of pregnancy, the developing baby is referred to as an 'embryo'; from about eight weeks, the term 'foetus' (meaning 'young one' is used). Technically, the foetus is not called a baby until birth. However, once your abdomen starts to bulge and you feel the baby's movement, it is almost impossible for you to think of the foetus as anything other than your baby.

Weeks 4–5

Your baby

This period ends with the implantation of the fertilized egg in the womb lining (see p. 13). The outer cells of the egg link up with the mother's blood supply. The inner cells form into two, and later into three layers, each of which will become a different part of your baby's body. One forms the brain and nervous system, skin, eyes and ears; another the lungs, stomach and gut; and the third the heart, blood, bones and muscles. At around 4–5 weeks your baby's heart starts to beat.

You

This is about the time that you will miss your first period but you may not even realize you are pregnant, although you may have some of the early signs.

Weeks 6–7

Your baby

All the major organs are now in place, although they are still rudimentary. Your baby's facial features are beginning to form and the first movements are being made. The heartbeat may be seen on a transvaginal scan as a pinprick of light blinking on and off. Your baby is now around 25 mm (1 in) long.

You

You may feel more tired than usual, or nauseous, or you may vomit; you may feel none of these. A test will confirm that you are pregnant.

Weeks 8–9

Your baby

Fingers, toes and tear ducts are present and the face is recognizable with eyes (which have some colour), nose, mouth (with tongue) and ears. The soft cartilage of the skeleton begins to turn to bone.

You

There is a rapid rise in the production of hormones from the placenta and ovary to adapt for pregnancy, so you may feel nauseous and/or vomit. Your womb is sufficiently large for a doctor to confirm that you are pregnant by an internal examination.

Sex in pregnancy

In a normal pregnancy, there is no reason why you should not continue to make love as often or as little as you wish. Many pregnant women report a higher libido than at any other time of their lives; others – particularly if they are tired and nauseous – don't. Both are perfectly natural.

If you have had a previous miscarriage, ask your GP for advice. Some doctors think it safest to avoid penetrative sex in the early months in these circumstances.

You may need to experiment with different positions for lovemaking, since what is comfortable at one stage may not be a few weeks later. Be assured that whatever you do cannot harm your developing baby. Later in pregnancy, an orgasm may set off contractions, but these will pass if you relax.

Finally, you should avoid sex once your waters have broken because of the risks of introducing infection (see p. 46).

10 weeks

Your baby

Eyelids and fingernails have formed, as have the external genitalia so that it is possible to tell whether you will have a boy or a girl. Your baby is now about 56 mm (2¼ in) long.

You

You may start to notice that you are putting on weight, and your breasts in particular may be getting heavier. Buy a good support bra (see p. 33).

12 weeks

Your baby

Limbs, hands, feet and internal organs are fully formed. Your baby is now feeding via the umbilical cord and placenta and moving around, although you will not be able to feel this yet. She can swallow and move her upper lip in an early sucking reflex. She will also react if her forehead is touched, by turning away and frowning. At this stage, she measures some 87 cm (3½ in) long and weighs more than 30 g (1 oz).

You

You have now missed two periods and have no doubts that you are pregnant. You may notice increased skin pigmentation in various parts of your body (see p. 36) and a brown line may appear up the midline of your abdomen. You may still be nauseous and vomiting, although this will start to subside over the next couple of weeks.

Your first antenatal appointment (or 'booking in', see pp. 22–3) will probably take place now and you may be offered a routine ultrasound scan at around this time (see pp. 23–4). Make enquiries, too, about antenatal classes (see p. 25) so that you can be sure of a place at the ones you want.

16 weeks

Your baby

Now weighing around 150 g (5 oz), your baby is some 150 mm (6 in) long. There is fine, downy hair, known as lanugo, all over her and a greasy white substance (vernix) is beginning to cover the body; vernix is believed to protect the unborn baby's very thin skin. Your baby can suck her thumb.

You

This is the stage of pregnancy at which many tests for abnormalities are carried out (see p. 24) and you may have another ultrasound scan. All morning sickness will normally have disappeared as you enter the stage at which most women start to feel and look their best, with clear skin, glossy hair and a renewed sense of energy and well-being.

Your pregnancy may now start to show, although if you have good abdominal muscles and are on the small side, it may be another couple of weeks before your pregnancy is obvious to strangers. Your tightest-fitting clothes will no longer fit.

20 weeks

Your baby

Her skin is now a deep reddish colour and the head is approximately half the size of the body. The limbs are still very thin but growing stronger and bigger and your baby may be able to hear your voice.

You

If this is your first pregnancy, you will probably feel your baby move for the first time (you will notice these movements a couple of weeks earlier with subsequent babies, largely because you know what to expect). Initially this is like a fluttering or bubbling sensation, but as your pregnancy progresses, these movements become definite kicks and you will be able to tell whether the elbow, bottom or foot is doing the 'kicking'. Tell your midwife or GP when you first feel a movement – this can also help in dating the pregnancy.

Your breasts, which have been changing in size and shape since you were first pregnant may now have reached their final, pre-breastfeeding size.

Foetal development

Although as your pregnancy becomes more advanced, the changes in your body are increasingly apparent, it can be difficult to visualize how your baby is developing. Broadly speaking, babies' vital organs and body parts form early in pregnancy, after which the baby grows in length and weight. From around week 32, most are head down all the time.

12 WEEKS   **16 WEEKS**

24 weeks

Your baby

Her skin is now translucent and pinkish-red and her eyelashes and eyebrows are recognizable. Simple behavioural experiments suggest that your baby is capable of learning; certainly she reacts to loud noises by kicking or jumping. She is swallowing tiny amounts of the amniotic fluid in which she is floating and passing small amounts of urine back into the fluid. She may hiccup, which you will be able to feel. She is now about 225–250 mm (9–10 in) long and weighs about 450 g (1 lb).

Some babies born at this age have, with skilled medical care, lived and thrived.

You

Your abdomen is getting progressively larger and you may start to develop stretch marks. A doctor may be able to hear your baby's heartbeat with a foetal stethoscope – ask to listen.

The increasing size and weight of your womb will also affect your posture, and you will throw back your shoulders and stick out your bottom, arching your lower back. To avoid back problems, try to tuck your bottom in and relax your shoulders. It also helps if you have been taking regular exercise.

This is the time when you gain weight most rapidly and your feet and ankles may start to feel the strain. Make sure that your shoes are comfortable and try to spend some time each day with your feet up.

26 weeks

Your baby

Your baby will respond to bright light from outside the womb: she will know, for example, if you are sunbathing in a bikini. Experiments suggest that she will also respond to music, remembering after birth themes played repeatedly.

Her eyes are now open and blue; although a few babies are born with brown eyes, the majority have blue eyes which remain blue until a few weeks after birth. She also has fingerprints.

You

Your heart and lungs are now doing 50 per cent more work than they did before you were pregnant. Make sure that you are eating well (see pp. 27–8).

28 weeks

Your baby

Now 350 mm (14 in) long and weighing about 900 g (2 lb), your baby has a 75 per cent chance of survival if born at this stage. She would cry weakly and breathe with difficulty. Subcutaneous fat gives her skin more of a flesh tone than previously.

You

You will probably start having antenatal appointments every two weeks from now on. This is the earliest at which you can begin your maternity

28 WEEKS   **36 WEEKS**   **40 WEEKS**

leave, if you work (see Your rights and benefits, pp. 28–30). Consider when you might want to stop working: remember you must give 21 days' notice.

If you wish to travel by plane, from now on you will need a letter from your doctor stating that you are fit to do so.

Make sure that you are getting plenty of rest and enough sleep.

30 weeks

Your baby

If she is born now, your baby has an 85–90 per cent chance of survival. She is around 400 mm (16 in) long and weighs about 1.5 kg (3½ lb). Her head is now more in proportion to the rest of the body, but she is still very wrinkled and thin.

You

You will probably start attending antenatal or parentcraft classes about now. Do not put off any of the larger purchases you intend to make for the baby or your home much longer – you may soon be too tired to shop.

32 weeks

Your baby

Most babies have now turned head down and are likely to stay that way since there is more room in the upper womb for the bulkier bottom and legs.

You

The upward pressure on your diaphragm may make it more difficult for you to breathe properly.

If you have other children, make arrangements now for their care while you are in hospital. Even if you plan a home birth, someone must be on hand to care for them, and it is best to be prepared in case something goes wrong and you have to go into hospital.

34 weeks

Your baby

The kidneys and lungs are now fully mature, she is some 430 mm (17 in) long and weighs around 2.5 kg (5½ lb). If she is born at this stage, she has a 95 per cent chance of survival.

You

Kicks and punches will now be very clear. If you have stopped work, spend the time relaxing – read a book, go for a walk, rest. Make sure you get plenty of sleep and eat well.

36 weeks

Your baby

The head may now have 'engaged' – dropped down into the birth canal, which eases pressure on your diaphragm. Do not worry if the head does not engage: some don't until nearer 40 weeks, others until well into labour.

You

The pressure of the head on your bladder may make you want to urinate frequently, including at night, so that getting a good night's sleep may be difficult. Try to catch up by resting during the day.

You will not be permitted to travel by plane, even for a short, internal flight. From now on, your antenatal appointments will be every week. Pack your bag for hospital (see box opposite) and keep important phone numbers – hospital labour ward, midwife – handy. Make sure you can always contact your partner if you need him. You may now feel quite strong contractions of your abdomen. Known as Braxton–Hicks contractions, these occur throughout pregnancy, but it is only in the last few weeks that you become aware of them. It is a good idea to practise your breathing techniques on them.

38 weeks

Your baby

She is now fully mature, with a rounded plump body. Most of the lanugo has dropped off although the hair on her head may be up to 40 mm (1¾ in) long. Finger and toe nails reach the ends of her fingers and toes.

40 weeks

Your baby

The birth may be at any time, but only 5 per cent of first babies arrive on the due date, so don't be anxious. Her movements decrease as space gets more limited, but you will still be able to see and feel kicks and jabs.

You

Get plenty of rest; cat nap during the day to make up for lost sleep at night. If you feel up to it, walk or swim. If not, try a relaxing bath. Many women get an overwhelming urge to 'spring clean' – tidying out cupboards, cleaning windows and so on – as the time for the birth nears, which has been attributed to a 'nesting instinct'; others do not.

If you do have a surge of energy, use it profitably but sensibly. Don't stand on ladders to reach high windows or top shelves, and if you have not finished decorating the baby's room, ask someone else to do so or leave it (the baby will not notice!). Similarly avoid kneeling or sitting on the floor working on low cupboards for any length of time – you may find yourself unable to get up again. It is a good idea, however, to stock up on necessities for when you come out of hospital – nappies (if you intend to use disposables) and other baby essentials such as wipes, cottonwool, soap or babybath and cream, washing powder and other cleaning materials, toilet rolls, sanitary pads. Avoid lifting anything heavy.

If you like cooking and find it relaxing, make some meals to freeze so that neither you nor your partner has to think about shopping for the first few days.

YOUR ANTENATAL CARE

Although the physical and emotional aspects of being pregnant can be overwhelming, with all the changes that are happening to you and to your relationship with your partner, there are a number of practical decisions to make too: what type of antenatal care would you like? what sort of birth? It makes sense to think about these and other practicalities as early as possible so that you have ample time to investigate your options.

Where to have your baby

You can choose to have your baby at home or in hospital (not necessarily the closest to your home), and you have a right to maternity care, whatever you choose to do. Take the time to look into the choices with your partner, with a midwife and with your GP. Ask other mothers in your area where they had their babies, and what sort of care they received.

Some women feel more comfortable in a hospital where emergency equipment is to hand, others are happiest in their own home, where they are able to feel in control. It is up to you.

Packing your bag for hospital

It makes sense to do this well before you will need it in case your baby arrives suddenly.
- wash bag and towel
- small sponge (for sips of water and sponging your face) and a larger one (to sponge you down)
- two clean nightdresses, with front openings
- dressing gown, slippers
- underwear, including nursing bras if you intend to breastfeed
- money or a card for the telephone
- earplugs (to block out the sound of other people's babies)
- bran tablets (constipation is uncomfortable and if you have had stitches, painful)
- a child's inflatable swimming ring (if you have had stitches it can help to sit 'in' one of these and there are rarely enough in hospital)
- glucose or dextrose tablets (you may need the energy)

- a tennis ball in a sock (for backache in labour)
- socks, shawl or cardigan (in case you start to shiver)
- something to wear in labour (if you don't want to give birth in a hospital gown)
- clothes to wear home (something that fitted when you were about six months pregnant should be about right)
- clothes and nappies for the baby
- a book, cassettes and personal stereo, writing paper, knitting, needlepoint (or anything else that relaxes you)
- camera and film
- pillows or cushions for the car

At the last minute, add:
- food for your partner
- ice packs (keep them in the freezer until you are ready to go)

Giving birth in hospital

Depending on where you live and where your health authority has contracts for its deliveries, you may be able to choose between different local hospitals, all within reasonably easy reach of your home.

Most women today have the majority of their antenatal care with their GP or community midwife and you may only visit the hospital once or twice during your pregnancy. It is becoming more common for the 'booking in' appointment – the first antenatal appointment that 'books' you a place for delivery (see pp. 22–3) – to be done at home. You are likely to have most of your care at the hospital if there is any problem with your pregnancy, since you may need to see a consultant obstetrician regularly; if a problem develops while you are pregnant, you will also probably be asked to see the consultant too.

The majority of babies – even if they are born in hospitals – are delivered by midwives. Normally doctors only intervene if forceps are needed or if a caesarean is necessary.

There are a number of issues which might affect your choice of hospital or decision to choose home rather than a hospital. All hospitals now say that they treat every mother and baby as individuals and they are anxious to get away from the idea that procedures take precedence over a mother's wishes. You may, however, want to ask specific questions to reassure yourself that you will be welcome to express your preferences (see also Making a birth plan, opposite).

The Patient's Charter

The Department of Health has a free leaflet entitled Maternity Services, which sets out the standards and rights included in the Patient's Charter regarding maternity services. Among your rights are:

- the right to a named midwife
- the right to see and keep your records
- you should be given a time for antenatal appointments and seen within 30 minutes of that time
- the right to keep your baby with you at all times, unless there are medical reasons not to.

Your GP or midwife should be able to give you a copy of this leaflet.

Some mothers prefer to give birth in a midwife-led unit or, in the few areas in which these are available, a ward or wards called a 'community' or 'GP unit'. Many of these are in fact attached to maternity hospitals, but staffed separately.

Consider the following questions:

- Can you have a domino delivery? This means that the community midwife comes to your home and stays with you until she thinks it is time to go to hospital. She then takes you to hospital, delivers the baby and takes you home a few hours after the birth. She will continue to visit you at home.
- Will you have the chance to meet the midwives who are likely to deliver the baby? Most hospitals operate a team midwifery system for antenatal, delivery and postnatal care. This means that the same midwives look after you before, during and after the birth.
- If you prefer a woman doctor, will it always be possible to see one?
- Can your birth companion be with you at all times if that is what you want?
- Can you talk over your birth choices and have a record of them put in your notes?
- Will you be able to move around in labour and is there a variety of equipment so that you can give birth in the position that you find comfortable?
- Can you use a water pool during labour if that is what you would like?
- Do you have a choice in the way your baby is monitored?
- How long might you be expected to stay in hospital after the birth (you can discharge yourself whenever you wish, but it may help to know the average length of stay)?
- Is there good breastfeeding support?
- What are the visiting hours?
- Will there be a chance to talk about the birth afterwards with the midwife who delivered your baby and ask any questions about the birth?

Having a baby at home

You can arrange for a home birth through your GP, or via your local community midwives. Many GPs are reluctant to support first-time mothers in having a home birth, because there is no way of telling how difficult a birth is going to be (your experience the first

Making a birth plan

Wherever you choose to have your baby (including at home), it is a good idea to talk through your options for care and any treatment, preferably with at least one of the midwives who is likely to be with you during labour. This discussion can then be formalized into a birth plan, which is written down and held with your notes.

Some hospital maternity departments have their own forms for birth plans but you do not have to stick to theirs if you don't want to. In any case your midwife is likely to point out that it is best to be flexible: your birth plan does not commit you to anything and circumstances and preferences can change even at the last minute.

The birth plan is really an aid to communication between you and your carers and it is better to compile it with a midwife than to present her with one that you have already drawn up. She may well think of issues you have missed, and will know what facilities are available in your area (not all hospitals have water pools, for example).

- **Who do you want with you?**
You will probably want to have your partner with you, but you may also want more than one person, such as a friend or relative, or no one. If you do not want anyone you know, but do want some extra support, ask for someone to be with you: a midwife or student midwife will be happy to be there for you, while her colleague delivers the baby.

- **What sort of position might you find comfortable?**
Ideally you should give birth in a room that offers a range of options: cushions, chair, bed, a covered area on the floor, so that you can move between them as and when you feel like it.

- **Can you opt for an epidural at any point?**
This may become particularly important if you need a caesarean. A general anaesthetic takes effect more quickly, but not all 'emergency' caesareans need to be done immediately.

- **Do you want an electronic foetal monitor all or only some of the time?** See p. 48.

- **Do you wish to avoid an episiotomy? Or induction? Other intervention?** See pp. 53–4.

- **Do you want your waters broken or would you prefer them to go naturally?**

- **Do you want your birth companion with you at all times, including when you are being examined?**

- **How long might you have to stay in hospital?**

- **See pp. 51–4 for options in pain relief.**

time gives some indication of the ease with which you will give birth subsequently). However, if you have young children at home already and do not wish to disrupt them, or feel that the birth will be more relaxed at home, you may decide that this is for you. You have the right to a home birth if that is what you want.

Your GP may be able to offer you antenatal care. If not, contact your local FHSA for the address of a GP who has an interest in childbirth. And contact your local supervisor of midwives who will arrange your antenatal care, delivery and postnatal care.

You will see the community midwife for all your antenatal checks, and she is the one to call when you think your labour has started. She will stay with you through labour and, perhaps with another midwife, deliver the baby. She will call a doctor or ambulance if you need to get to hospital in an emergency.

Antenatal appointments

In order to ensure that you and your baby are fit and that the baby is developing as she should, throughout your pregnancy you will have regular check-ups under the care of either a hospital antenatal clinic, or your GP or a community midwife. Who looks after you depends largely on where you are going to have the baby. If the baby is going to be born in hospital, your antenatal appointments are likely to be split between the hospital antenatal clinic and your GP or community midwife (this is known as 'shared care'). If you are having the baby at home or in a community or GP unit, your GP and community midwife will look after you throughout your pregnancy, although you may be asked to go to the hospital for a scan.

When is it due?

You can assess when your baby is due from the chart on the right, although it is important to remember that very few babies actually arrive on the date on which they are technically 'due'. This is because due dates are calculated on the basis that women have a regular 28-day menstrual cycle, and that conception takes place right in the middle of that, neither of which is necessarily true. Most doctors agree that pregnancy lasts between 39 and 41 weeks; induction will normally be advised if your pregnancy has lasted more than 42 weeks.

The important date to remember is that of the start of your last menstrual period. These are given in pink in each column. The date at which your baby can be expected is given in blue.

January / October	February / November	March / December	April / January	May / February	June / March	July / April	August / May	September / June	October / July	November / August	December / September
1 8	1 8	1 6	1 6	1 5	1 8	1 7	1 8	1 8	1 8	1 8	1 7
2 9	2 9	2 7	2 7	2 6	2 9	2 8	2 9	2 9	2 9	2 9	2 8
3 10	3 10	3 8	3 8	3 7	3 10	3 9	3 10	3 10	3 10	3 10	3 9
4 11	4 11	4 9	4 9	4 8	4 11	4 10	4 11	4 11	4 11	4 11	4 10
5 12	5 12	5 10	5 10	5 9	5 12	5 11	5 12	5 12	5 12	5 12	5 11
6 13	6 13	6 11	6 11	6 10	6 13	6 12	6 13	6 13	6 13	6 13	6 12
7 14	7 14	7 12	7 12	7 11	7 14	7 13	7 14	7 14	7 14	7 14	7 13
8 15	8 15	8 13	8 13	8 12	8 15	8 14	8 15	8 15	8 15	8 15	8 14
9 16	9 16	9 14	9 14	9 13	9 16	9 15	9 16	9 16	9 16	9 16	9 15
10 17	10 17	10 15	10 15	10 14	10 17	10 16	10 17	10 17	10 17	10 17	10 16
11 18	11 18	11 16	11 16	11 15	11 18	11 17	11 18	11 18	11 18	11 18	11 17
12 19	12 19	12 17	12 17	12 16	12 19	12 18	12 19	12 19	12 19	12 19	12 18
13 20	13 20	13 18	13 18	13 17	13 20	13 19	13 20	13 20	13 20	13 20	13 19
14 21	14 21	14 19	14 19	14 18	14 21	14 20	14 21	14 21	14 21	14 21	14 20
15 22	15 22	15 20	15 20	15 19	15 22	15 21	15 22	15 22	15 22	15 22	15 21
16 23	16 23	16 21	16 21	16 20	16 23	16 22	16 23	16 23	16 23	16 23	16 22
17 24	17 24	17 22	17 22	17 21	17 24	17 23	17 24	17 24	17 24	17 24	17 23
18 25	18 25	18 23	18 23	18 22	18 25	18 24	18 25	18 25	18 25	18 25	18 24
19 26	19 26	19 24	19 24	19 23	19 26	19 25	19 26	19 26	19 26	19 26	19 25
20 27	20 27	20 25	20 25	20 24	20 27	20 26	20 27	20 27	20 27	20 27	20 26
21 28	21 28	21 26	21 26	21 25	21 28	21 27	21 28	21 28	21 28	21 28	21 27
22 29	22 29	22 27	22 27	22 26	22 29	22 28	22 29	22 29	22 29	22 29	22 28
23 30	23 30	23 28	23 28	23 27	23 30	23 29	23 30	23 30	23 30	23 30	23 29
24 31	24 1	24 29	24 29	24 28	24 31	24 30	24 31	24 1	24 31	24 31	24 30
25 1	25 2	26 30	25 30	25 1	25 1	25 1	25 1	25 2	25 1	25 1	25 1
26 2	26 3	26 31	26 31	26 2	26 2	26 2	26 2	26 3	26 2	26 2	26 2
27 3	27 4	27 1	27 1	27 3	27 3	27 3	27 3	27 4	27 3	27 3	27 3
28 4	28 5	28 2	28 2	28 4	28 4	28 4	28 4	28 5	28 4	28 4	28 4
29 5		29 3	29 3	29 5	29 5	29 5	29 5	29 6	29 5	29 5	29 5
30 6		30 4	30 4	30 6	30 6	30 6	30 6	30 7	30 6	30 6	30 6
31 7		31 5		31 7		31 7	31 7		31 7		31 7

Column footers: January / November · February / December · March / January · April / February · May / March · June / April · July / May · August / June · September / July · October / August · November / September · December / October

Medical checks

Your first major antenatal appointment – the 'booking in' appointment – is done at home, at the health centre or at the hospital antenatal clinic, usually when you are between 8 and 14 weeks pregnant. You will be asked questions about your general health, your family history, any medical problems, any previous pregnancies and how you feel that this pregnancy is going. You will be asked the date of your last period so that the baby's due date can be worked out (see chart above). Your heart will be listened to for signs of its overall health and your blood pressure may be measured. Routine internal examinations are no longer common, unless there are doubts about the duration of your pregnancy, but you will have a cervical smear if you have not had one in the last three years.

You will be asked to give a blood sample, which is then sent to the lab for testing. The lab identifies your blood group; checks your haemoglobin levels (to make sure you are not anaemic); looks for signs of immunity to rubella; and checks whether you have been exposed to hepatitis B or syphilis. If you live in a high-risk area (usually classed as the metropolitan areas, and in particular London and Glasgow), you may be asked if you wish your blood sample to be tested for HIV antibodies. This is done routinely and anonymously at certain hospitals which are part of a national programme to measure how widespread HIV is in the community – if your hospital is part of the scheme, you will be told. If you are not asked, but would like an HIV test, request it. Whatever the result, DoH guidelines lay down that you should be told face to face.

If your pregnancy is going well, the usual routine is for your antenatal checks to take place every month until you are 28 weeks pregnant, then every two weeks until 36 weeks, and once a week thereafter. Local practices vary, however, so you may be seen less frequently; you will be seen more often if you have problems, if you have had a previous pregnancy that was complicated, or if your GP or anyone at the clinic feels that it is appropriate for you.

Routine checks

The same checks are made at each appointment, wherever the appointment takes place.

Urine

You will be asked either to bring a sample with you or to produce one at the time. This will be checked on the spot for signs of infection, diabetes and pre-eclampsia (see p. 38).

Blood pressure

Raised blood pressure is one of the telltale signs of pre-eclampsia.

Weight

Research has shown that monitoring your weight is an inefficient way to tell whether the baby is growing as she should and is a poor indicator of your general health. As a result, you may not be weighed, although it is still common practice in many areas.

Abdomen

The midwife may measure your girth and she will check (by feeling) the position of the baby and the height of your uterus.

The baby's heartbeat

This will be felt using a stethoscope, or – depending on hospital policy – using a foetal monitor.

Your legs, feet and hands

For swelling (another sign of pre-eclampsia) or varicose veins.

It is a good idea to use your appointments to bring up any questions or problems you have (write them down in advance so that you cover everything you want to). If you prefer, sit up so that you can talk to your doctor or midwife face to face – having a conversation is difficult when you are lying down and someone is feeling your tummy. If you have something sensitive to talk about, ask if you can have time after your examination to do so when you have your clothes back on.

SCANS

You will have an ultrasound scan in early pregnancy. You will be asked to make sure that your bladder is full, so that your womb is more clearly visible, then a scanner is passed over your abdomen. Ask for help in 'interpreting' the picture.

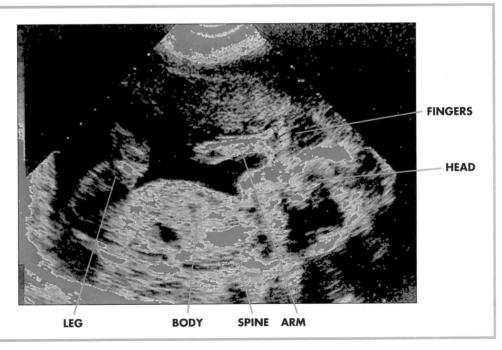

FINGERS

HEAD

LEG   BODY   SPINE   ARM

You may also be offered an ultrasound scan. It is very common for a scan to be done in early pregnancy (around 12-14 weeks) and perhaps another later on. The main reasons for a scan are: to help date the pregnancy; to check for more than one baby; to check the baby's growth and development; to monitor the placenta. Ultrasound is increasingly efficient at diagnosing abnormalities, notably spina bifida and Down's syndrome. Practices vary, but if you want your partner there he should be able to accompany you, and you may be offered an instant photograph of the scan, although you will probably have to pay for it.

Other tests

Depending on your age and your family's medical history, you may also be offered other tests. If you are not, and would like them, ask.

The nuchal scan

Done at 11-13 weeks, an ultrasound scan measures the thickness of the nuchal pad (fluid) in the baby's neck. A thicker than average pad may indicate abnormal chromosomes, so you may be offered an amniocentesis.

The AFP (alphafetoprotein) test

This is done at 16–18 weeks. A blood sample is checked for high or low levels of AFP, which may be associated with spina bifida or Down's syndrome. An ultrasound scan can rule out or confirm the diagnosis.

The triple test

Sometimes called the Bart's test or serum screening, this is done at about 15 weeks. A blood sample is tested for chemicals that help to calculate the risks of Down's syndrome or spina bifida. You may then be offered a diagnostic scan or amniocentesis.

Chorionic villus sampling (CVS)

This is done at around 10–11 weeks and involves removing a tiny frond of the tissue that forms the placenta and examining it for chromosomal abnormalities, especially Down's syndrome.

Amniocentesis

Carried out at around 18 weeks, amniocentesis involves having a needle inserted in your abdomen to draw off a sample of amniotic fluid. The sample is then checked for abnormalities, especially Down's syndrome, but also spina bifida, muscular dystrophy, cystic fibrosis and haemophilia. It will also determine the sex of the baby: if you do not want to know, say so.

Getting the results

None of these tests is perfect. Both CVS and amniocentesis carry a small risk of miscarriage and any test could increase your anxiety (although, since the results usually show that there is nothing to worry about, some women are more reassured by them). None of the tests offers a totally certain diagnosis and even routine ultrasound has its critics.

If a test shows that your baby is likely to have an abnormality, you may want to consider a termination. You should be given a chance to talk this through before you have the test (contact SATFA for advice, see Useful Contacts, pp. 248–51). Even if you know you could not consider a termination, you may want the time to prepare for having a baby with special needs.

Depending on where you live, your ethnic origin and family history, you may also be offered other, less common tests. You should be given the chance to discuss the associated risks and benefits before you decide whether to go ahead.

The risk of Down's syndrome

Down's syndrome is an abnormality that affects a baby very soon after conception. Affected children have a characteristic appearance: a flatter than usual face, slanting eyes, snub nose and a large and protruding tongue. They may suffer from heart disease. The degree of learning disability varies enormously. All children with the syndrome are mentally and physically affected, but most will learn to speak and many can read and write. Down's children are usually loving and affectionate.

The risk of having a child who is affected rises sharply according to the age of the mother.

At 25 years	1 in 1,500 births
At 30 years	1 in 800 births
At 35 years	1 in 300 births
At 38 years	1 in 180 births
At 40 years	1 in 100 births
At 45 years	1 in 30 births

Antenatal classes

Many maternity units and health centres run classes for expectant parents. They may be called antenatal classes or parentcraft classes. These classes are free and usually taken by midwives and health visitors with perhaps one class including a contribution from a hospital doctor, probably about pain relief, caesarean section or special care facilities for babies who are sick or premature.

The major non-NHS classes are run by the National Childbirth Trust (see Useful Contacts, pp. 248–51), with courses taken by their own specially trained teachers in most areas of the UK. There is usually a charge for NCT classes, although in some areas subsidized places are available for those who cannot afford to pay.

NCT classes are often less formal than NHS ones, with teachers concerned to encourage class members to support each other and to use the class as a safe, welcoming environment in which to explore feelings and fears, as well as a forum for information giving. NHS classes vary enormously – some are excellent, others patchy – but there is usually not the same emphasis on group support. NHS classes usually offer you the opportunity to visit the labour ward and the special care baby unit (although you can always ask to do this if you intend to have your baby in hospital, even if you do not attend the classes).

A typical course of antenatal classes consists of between seven and ten two-hour sessions and you can expect to start going when you are around seven months pregnant. Good classes cover:

- what to expect during labour and birth and afterward, with time for questions and discussion so that you go into the birth confident that you are making the right decisions for you
- you may be shown a video of childbirth
- options in pain relief (see pp. 51–4)
- relaxation techniques to help with pain in labour
- exercises to keep fit and to help in labour
- advice on caring for your baby
- advice on looking after yourself after the birth.

If you know other women with children, ask them which classes they found most useful. You may also be influenced by the timing and location of classes. Some classes are primarily for couples, others for women only. You can of course go to more than one set. Local classes (particularly if you have not been working locally) can be a good place to meet other mothers-to-be with whom you can perhaps stay in touch after your baby's birth.

Ask your community or hospital midwife about the availability of classes; in some cases you may have to book in advance.

Exercise in pregnancy

If you are wondering whether you should exercise while you are pregnant, the answer is an unequivocal 'yes'. If you are fit, you are far more likely to get through the tiring last weeks of pregnancy and cope more easily with the hard work of labour than if you are not. If you are used to regular exercise, keep it up as long as you feel able. You will probably be advised at antenatal classes to avoid sports that carry a risk of falling or rough contact with other players, such as martial arts, squash, skiing or riding. If you are not used to exercise, pregnancy can be a good time to start, as long as you do it gradually.

Whatever you do, be responsive to your own body and do not push yourself too far. Total, physical exhaustion is not a good idea. Stop and rest more than you would normally. Also, avoid taking on anything strenuous when it is hot – you are more likely to faint or become dizzy – and be sure to drink plenty of fluids to avoid dehydration. If you attend exercise classes of any sort, tell your instructor that you are pregnant: she may suggest that you miss some exercises out, or do them in a different way. High-impact aerobics involving heavy bouncing are best avoided, since all your muscles and ligaments are softer in pregnancy (so that they stretch to enable you to give birth). This means that they are more easily damaged than at other times. Your extra weight could also mean that you put undue strain on your back.

Swimming and walking are great exercise and suitable right to the end of your pregnancy. In some areas aquanatal classes – which combine swimming with body toning and stretching to focus on the muscles used in pregnancy and childbirth – may be available. Some antenatal classes include toning and stretching exercises. If you do not usually exercise, try to choose antenatal classes that include a simple fitness programme.

Pelvic floor exercises

You will hear several times during your pregnancy and afterward how important it is that you do your pelvic floor exercises. The muscles of the pelvic floor support the internal organs, including your womb, bladder and back passage. Keeping these muscles in good tone will, therefore, help you during and after the birth – as they have to stretch sufficiently to allow your baby to come out and then go back to their normal state afterward. If these muscles are weak, you run the risk of stress incontinence – leaking of small amounts of urine from your bladder when you cough, run, laugh or sneeze. This can occur in the last few weeks of pregnancy (see p. 35) but is more common after the birth.

The basic pelvic floor exercise is very simple and you can do it anywhere, sitting, standing or lying. For most women, the problem is remembering to do the sequence often enough. You need to tighten the muscles of your front passage as if you were trying to hold on to urine when you are 'bursting' to go. Keep tightening, first vaginal area, then rectum, hold for four seconds, and then relax. Repeat several times, and repeat the whole sequence several times a day.

Relaxation techniques

If you have already tried yoga or other meditation techniques, you will find that they are particularly useful in pregnancy. If you have not, learning basic relaxation will help you while you are pregnant, during the birth and afterward.

The easiest way to start learning to relax is to make space in your day for 10 minutes' uninterrupted, quiet time. Lie down, and starting at your toes and feet, alternately tense and relax each part of your body, right up to your head. Don't forget your shoulders, arms and hands, or your face (frown, screw up your face and then let it go). Keep your eyes gently closed as you are doing this. Some people find it helps to have some soothing music playing; others to focus on a beautiful image. In time, you will be able to use this technique whenever you feel stressed to help you regain your physical and mental equilibrium.

This technique is particularly useful in childbirth. Coping with contractions is easier if you are relaxed; it also conserves your energy.

Of course, there are other ways to relax. Simply making some time for yourself, even once a day, is

Antenatal exercises

Regular exercise, including stretching, in the months before you become pregnant and in pregnancy itself, will stand you in good stead to face the hard work of labour. The exercises illustrated here will all help with labour and delivery, but are no substitute for a structured session of antenatal exercise, either as part of your antenatal classes, or on the advice of your local sports centre or gym. Warm up before you begin.

Sit with your feet together and forearms along your inner calves. Gently press your knees toward the floor. Hold for 10 seconds.

Stand with your feet shoulder width apart and slowly ease down into a squatting position. Repeat as often as you can.

Squatting is not easy if your muscles are tight and you may find it helps to support yourself on a chair or the end of the bed.

important. In late pregnancy, you may be advised to rest with your feet up to help combat mild oedema (swelling or puffiness). You can even do this at work in the middle of the day. Take some time to have a proper lunch break, away from your desk, rather than rushing around the shops and grabbing a sandwich. Ask your partner to do the shopping.

Take care to look after your other physical needs. Many women find their skin and hair look better than ever before in pregnancy – especially from about four or five months. If you have a tendency to oiliness, this is likely to lessen while you are pregnant to give you that healthy bloom that makes you look and feel good. If you find that your skin is dry, add oil to your bath and be generous with the moisturizer. Treat yourself to a good haircut shortly before the baby is born. It may make you feel better in the days immediately after the birth if your hair looks good, and you will find it difficult to make time for an appointment for weeks afterward.

Don't be afraid to ask for help, particularly in the later stages. If asking a neighbour to pick up your toddler from playgroup – when he or she is probably going for their own child in any case – gives you ten minutes to put your feet up, then do so. Most people are only too willing to help. Remember that toddlers do not always need to be running around: after a busy morning at playgroup or with friends in the park, she may be quite happy to cuddle up on the sofa with you while you look at a book or watch a video or TV programme together.

What to eat

Good-quality food, low in sugar and high in carbohydrate from a variety of sources should be the basis of a healthy diet at all times, not only when you are pregnant. Opinions differ as to how many extra calories you actually need when you are pregnant (certainly you should not be 'eating for two'), but the metabolism does change at this time – both to cope with the extra demands on your heart and lungs, and later while you are breastfeeding – so it is likely you will feel hungrier than usual once any morning sickness has passed.

Follow your appetite, without heading for instant 'junk' foods. Snack on fresh and dried fruits if you are hungry between meals, and drink plenty of water. As

Lift your right shoulder forward and up, then back and down. Repeat with your left arm.

Aerobic fitness helps you cope with the extra demands on your heart. Try rhythmic marching.

When you have a good marching pace, lift your right knee and touch with your left hand.

Repeat right hand to left knee. Try to keep the pace even, and aim to get your knees high.

a general guide, most women gain 10–12.5 kg (22–28 lb) during pregnancy and, although it is difficult to get rid of excess weight after the birth, it is usually more of a worry to your GP and midwife if you put on too little rather than too much weight while you are pregnant.

Make sure you have plenty of fresh fruit and vegetables, carbohydrates such as bread, cereals, pasta and rice, plus proteins such as eggs, pulses, meat and fish. A high-fibre diet, with plenty of fluid, may help combat constipation, which is common in pregnancy. Milk is a convenient source of many nutrients, including calcium and protein but if you do not like it, it is not essential. Everything found in milk can be obtained from other foods too.

There have been few studies into the effects of alcohol on foetuses after the first 13 weeks, when all the major organs have been formed. As a result, there is no recommended 'safe' limit on the amount you can drink without harming your baby. For this reason, many doctors advise you not to drink alcohol at all while you are pregnant. Equally, there is no real evidence that the odd glass of wine or beer does any harm. But binge drinking and heavy habitual drinking do harm babies. See also p. 10.

WORKING IN PREGNANCY

Many mothers-to-be work until quite late in pregnancy and feel fine doing so. It is normal, however, to want to reduce the pace of your working life, particularly during the most physically demanding times. For many women, this means the first three months and the last six to eight weeks.

In early pregnancy, sickness and tiredness may mean that you want to avoid the rush, fumes and pressure of early-morning travelling. Think about negotiating a later start time in return for a later finishing time. Later on, the sheer exhaustion of being heavier and more uncomfortable can make travelling stressful. Again, try to change your hours, even temporarily, to suit how you feel. If you anticipate that your employer might be unsympathetic, ask your GP or the antenatal clinic to back up your request.

You have certain rights regarding hazardous working conditions (see below). If appropriate, ask to move to a non-smoking area and make sure you sit in such an area in the canteen. Don't skip lunch – you and the baby both need it. If you do not feel like sitting, go for a walk or swim, but do take a break.

Standing for long stretches of the day can cause tiredness, backache and swelling. If your job involves long periods of standing, see if you can sit for some of the time in a chair that supports your back). Again, if you anticipate problems, ask your GP for support.

Your rights and benefits

There are three broad classes of state benefit to which you may be entitled: those for which everyone can apply as of right; those for parents or their partners on low incomes; and those which apply if you are (or have been) in employment.

Benefits for all
- Free dental treatment and prescriptions for you during your pregnancy and for a year afterward, and for your child until she is 16.
- Child benefit: a weekly tax-free flat-rate benefit paid directly to the mother for every child until she is 16, or 19 if still in full-time education, with additional benefit for those on Income Support or Family Credit.
- One-parent family benefit, plus advice, training and help to find work and childcare facilities.

Benefits if you are on a low income

You may be entitled to some of the following benefits as the size of your family increases; amounts usually vary and are dependent on several factors, including income, savings, size of your family, whether any member of your family has special needs and whether you or your partner is working. Call the DSS free telephone enquiry line for up-to-date information on benefits to which you may be entitled.

Income Support
This is payable to anyone who does nor have enough money to live on. Income Support 'tops up' earnings and other benefits so the amount to which you may be entitled varies. If you have a mortgage, Income Support may help toward your interest payments, which may be paid direct to your mortgage lender.

Family Credit

Working families on low incomes may be eligible for this tax-free benefit but one partner must work at least 16 hours a week and you must have one child.

Maternity payments

A flat-rate payment to help you to buy things for the baby; you must claim within three months of the birth.

Housing Benefit

Amounts vary, but Housing Benefit is paid direct to the council if you are a council tenant and to you if you are a private tenant.

Council tax

You may be entitled to help with paying this tax; amounts vary but you could get your whole bill paid.

Free milk and vitamins

If you are entitled to Income Support, you will get tokens for a pint of milk a day for you and each child under five (they can be exchanged at the baby clinic for formula for under-ones); vitamins are available free at baby and child health clinics for you while you are pregnant and breastfeeding, and for your children until they are five.

For working women

If you are pregnant and in employment, you have certain legal rights to time off and, sometimes, to pay during that time. Current rights are detailed below, but it is advisable to contact the DSS Helpline, your trade union, the Citizen's Advice Bureau, local law centre or the Maternity Alliance (see Useful Contacts, pp. 248–51) for up-to-date information and advice as early in your pregnancy as possible. Some benefits depend on your telling your employer your intentions before a certain stage in your pregnancy.

Classes and appointments

You are entitled to time off without loss of pay to attend antenatal appointments and antenatal classes, including relaxation and parentcraft classes. Your employer is entitled to ask for a letter from your GP, midwife or health visitor to say that these classes are necessary and has the right to ask to see your appointment card.

The nature of your work

If you cannot do your job while you are pregnant, have given birth in the past six months or are breast-feeding (if it involves heavy lifting, for example, or working with X-rays), your employer must offer you a suitable alternative, if one is available; if not, you are entitled to be suspended on full pay. If you refuse a suitable alternative, you lose the right to full pay.

Unfair dismissal

You cannot be dismissed because you are pregnant, nor can you be dismissed during your maternity leave. If your employers wish to make you redundant, they must wait until you apply to return to work after the birth.

Maternity leave

You are entitled to 14 weeks off work (18 weeks from 2000), regardless of how many hours a week you work, or how long you have worked for your employer. You must write to your employer at least 21 days before you intend to start your leave. You can start up to 11 weeks before the baby is due, or work right until the due date. If you return after your full maternity leave, you do not have to give your employer any notice that you are returning; if you want to go back before the full leave has elapsed, you must give your employer seven days' notice. You should return to your own job.

Benefits for fathers

There is as yet no statutory requirement on employers to offer paternity leave, although European Union regulations mean that the situation is changing and some employers do already offer a few days' leave. Most give time off for you to be at the birth, but you may be expected to take a holiday to cover the period when the baby comes home.

It is, however, important that you are there for as long as possible. If your partner is in hospital for a few days, try to work then so that you can be at home when mother and baby come out.

As well as the practical support that you can give, changing nappies, bathing, spending time with the baby while your partner rests, shopping and so on, you need time with your partner and baby, simply learning to be a family.

Maternity leave does not count as 'time off', so that pension rights, holiday entitlement and company car are unaffected by this break.

Extended maternity leave

If you have worked for your employer for two years (one year from 2000) by the 12th week before your baby is due and your employer has more than five employees, you are entitled to additional maternity leave to your 14 weeks, until the end of the 29th week after your baby is born. This extra leave is usually unpaid, but many companies do pay something so it is worth enquiring.

To qualify you must notify your employer 21 days before you leave that it is your intention to return; you must also notify your employer at least 21 days before you intend to return to work. Your employer is entitled to write to you at any time after 11 weeks from the start of your leave, asking if you intend to return, and you must answer within 14 days. If you are not sure at this stage, follow the procedure until the final stage (21 days before your return).

Other benefits

Statutory maternity pay (SMP)

If you have worked for your employer for at least 26 weeks by the end of the 15th week before your baby is due, you are entitled to statutory maternity pay.

SMP is paid for any 18 weeks between week 11 before the birth and week 11 after the birth. For the first six weeks, you get 90 per cent of your average pay; for the next 12 weeks you will get the basic rate SMP. To qualify you must write to your employer claiming SMP 21 days before you stop work

Maternity allowance

This is paid to women who are not eligible to receive SMP (including the self-employed); to qualify you must have paid NI contributions for 26 of the 66 weeks before the week the baby is due. Like SMP, this is paid for 18 weeks. If you are unsure, claim anyway: the DSS will work out whether you are entitled or not.

Sickness benefit

If you have paid NI in the last three years, but have not paid enough contributions to claim maternity allowance, you may be entitled to sick pay, paid from six weeks before the baby is born to two weeks after.

WHAT YOU WILL NEED

It is a good idea to get most of the basic equipment and clothes for your baby before she is born. Shopping for major purchases will be difficult once she is with you. But try to resist the temptation to rush out and buy lots of clothes and bedding, especially if you have generous family and friends, and have friends with children who may pass outgrown clothes on to you.

Choose machine-washable items only and avoid anything with long, trailing ribbons and trimmings that could come loose.

The list here is of the basic items you will need for the first few weeks. Gifts will still be welcome, since this is the minimum – you will be washing very frequently if this is all you have.

Somewhere for the baby to sleep

This could be a cot, carrycot or crib. You might find it easier to use a pram top, carrycot or cradle as your baby's sleeping place for the first few weeks, since all are portable and can easily be carried from room to room and even up and down stairs. Check that the mattress is fits correctly. Depending on how quickly she grows, you will need a proper cot within around six months.

You will also need two or three sets of bedding – sheets and machine-washable blankets (see pp. 168–9).

Transport

Your pram or pushchair is one of the most expensive single purchases of your baby's first year, so it makes sense to take time over choosing one.

Full-size, traditional 'coach-built' prams are extremely hard-wearing, beautiful-looking and very warm and comfortable for your baby. They are, however, very expensive (although they seem to keep their value secondhand, even if you have used them for more than a couple of children of your own). Sometimes they cannot be used inside shops, they take up a lot of room and it is impossible to travel with them by car or public transport.

Many parents today opt for a pram which comes in two parts – a fold-down frame and a top which can be used as a carrycot with handles. It's difficult to get this on a bus (although you can on most trains), and

Hood protects from wind and rain; sunshade needed in summer

Check handle is at a comfortable height

Carrycot lifts off; can be replaced by pushchair

Swivel wheels aid manoeuvrability

Tray for bag, shopping is useful

Sturdy brake essential

seat, keeping the same basic frame.) Buggies which fold up like an umbrella are lightweight and easy to handle, excellent if you are on and off buses a lot. These are, however, not really warm or sufficiently well sprung for a tiny baby and are best for toddlers who need less support.

You may also want to buy a rain cover, sunshade, shopping basket or tray for the pram or pushchair.

Car seat
Read the advice on car seats given on p. 172.

For bathing
You can bath your baby with you in the ordinary bath, as can your partner, but it may not be convenient at all times, so a baby bath or large washing-up bowl is a good idea. You will also need toiletries (baby soap and shampoo) and two towels.

Clothing for a newborn
- two shawls or wraps
- four vests
- four stretchsuits
- two cardigans or matinee jackets
- one outer garment, such as a snowsuit
- socks (unless all your stretchsuits have feet)
- a pair of mittens
- a hat (against the sun or the cold, or both, depending on when the baby is born)

folding it down after separating top and frame, then carrying the frame and baby is often a two-person job so it cannot be used on escalators. Most car boots and hatchbacks will hold both frame and top.

A popular alternative is a pushchair which folds flat, with a seat that tips into different positions from lie-flat to sitting. (You may find this comes as an extra to a frame and carrycot model, so that you use the carrycot when the baby is small, then graduate to the

Front opening and poppers down leg make nappy changing easier

Wide or envelope neck makes it easier to get vest over baby's head

Warm hat vital for winter baby; sunhat essential in summer

Mitts vital in winter and may stop baby scratching her face

Socks essential unless all sleepsuits have feet

Front opening makes dressing easier; choose close-knit patterns

For changing

You can change a baby on a waterproof sheet over an old towel, but a plastic changing mat with raised edges is a good idea. It is safest to put the mat on the floor; if you want it at waist weight, keep one hand on the baby at all times. You will also need:

- nappies (new babies get through at least six a day, see Nappies, pp. 93–6)
- baby lotion and cottonwool balls, or baby wipes
- barrier cream
- (if you are using terries) a bucket with a lid

For feeding

If you are going to breastfeed:

- two nursing bras (these are not essential, but they are comfortable and convenient)

If you are going to bottlefeed:

- bottles
- sterilizing kit
- formula milk

You may also want to buy a breast pump (although expressing by hand is a useful skill, see p. 77) and breast pads (or cotton hankies). You will also need sanitary pads for up to six weeks after the birth.

Wipe clean tray; rim prevents scraps spilling on floor

Chair that sits in frame can be used as low table and chair later

Harness essential; use shoulder harness too

Check that base is secure

You may want to add these items:

Baby chair

▶ Some of these double as car seats, others consist of a fabric seat on a lightweight frame which hold your baby in a semi-upright position. Both are ideal for when your baby is awake but don't put them on a raised surface. Babies love being able to see what is going on, which is impossible in a carrycot.

Baby carrier

◀ Choose one that supports the baby's head if you are buying one for use from birth. This is an essential if you have to use public transport a lot, and a good way of keeping your baby close to you. Many fretful babies are soothed by the contact and movement they get in this way.

Later on in the baby's first year (remember to budget for these items), you will need:

More clothing

Babies grow out of first clothes by the time they are three to four months old.

Padded head rest supports neck and head

Secure harness over shoulders and around back for comfort

Feeding chair

◀ This will be useful from about four months. Feeding chairs do not have to be 'high'. You can buy chairs which fit on to your table, which are also useful for when you are out and about. Some high chairs convert later into a low chair and table, which can prolong their usefulness. If space is short, consider a foldaway chair, but choose and site carefully – some are not as stable as more traditional models. Think carefully about how easy a chair is going to be to keep clean: some look beautiful but collect food scraps in impossible crannies.

You will also need a safety harness, bibs, feeding utensils and, of course, food.

Larger car seat

Stage One seats only last until the baby is around eight months (see also Buying a car seat, p. 172).

Toys

Babies appreciate colours, textures and sounds from very early on; most can hold a rattle by around six to eight weeks and a small cuddly toy in the cot or crib may quickly become a trusted friend.

And, if you are using disposables

More and more nappies (see pp. 93–6).

Padded cushion supports baby's head

Clip-on toy adds to play value

Gentle rocking can be soothing

Strong sling essential

Buying secondhand

Accepting hand-me-downs and buying large items secondhand makes sense as long as you are happy with the safety of the item. The exception to this is a car seat, since any impact can cause perhaps invisible damage (see also p. 172). Check prams, pushchairs and cots carefully for loose bolts, nuts and fixings, torn fabric or chipped paint.

Avoid anything that looks very old, even if it appears to be in good condition – it may have been made before modern manufacturing standards ensured a high degree of safety.

Clothes for you

Depending on your usual wardrobe, you may be able to wear your ordinary clothes for the first five or six months of your pregnancy, although obviously if you generally choose tailored suits or tight jeans, these will not fit for that long. It does not make sense to buy lots of new clothes for just a few months' wear, but a couple of new outfits can be a morale booster and will be useful after the birth (remember it can take several months to get into all your pre-pregnancy clothes again: some women never do).

The most important factor in choosing clothes to wear while you are pregnant is comfort. Avoid anything tight or restricting, including belts, and tights and socks with tight ribbing. Baggy tops, trousers and leggings with drawstring waists and loose pinafore dresses are all ideal. Natural fibres such as cotton are preferable to synthetics. Tops with low front openings may make breastfeeding easier, though teeshirts and sweaters will do just as well and may be more discreet when you're out.

A well-fitting bra is a must: by the end of your pregnancy you may be at least two cup sizes bigger than usual. In the last month, if you intend to breastfeed, you will need to buy a couple of nursing bras (take them into hospital with you, in case you are still there when your milk 'comes in').

High heels are not a good idea, neither are flat shoes. Choose styles with a small heel to avoid putting strain on your back and ankles. After about seven months you may find bending down to tie laces difficult.

DISCOMFORTS IN PREGNANCY

You may go through pregnancy having never felt better in your life, but most women feel at least some twinges now and then. Many of these discomforts come and go, so you are unlikely to be uncomfortable with any one of them throughout your pregnancy. In almost all cases, too, there is something you can do about it.

Pregnant women are still entitled to free prescriptions, so it makes sense to go to your doctor, rather than buy over-the-counter preparations.

Anaemia

- Have a blood test to check that you are anaemic and not tired for any other reason.
- Eat iron-rich foods: eggs, whole grains, lean meat, kelp, wheatgerm.
- On your GP's advice, take iron supplements in conjunction with vitamin C (iron on its own is not absorbed well).

Backache

- Take care when lifting and bending – bend your knees and keep your back straight. This is particularly important when you lift your other children (see p. 37); it is all too easy to swing them up, which can cause problems.
- If your feet don't reach the floor when you sit, sit with them on a couple of heavy books.

- Ask the hospital physiotherapist for advice about your posture.
- Discard your high heels, but wear shoes with a small heel for support.
- Swim regularly to strengthen your back and also to take the stress off it for a time.
- Try yoga and do some gentle stretches.
- Place a cushion in the small of your back when you are sitting or driving.
- Try a maternity panty girdle for extra support.

Bleeding gums and gum disease

- Dental care is free on the NHS while you are pregnant and until your baby is a year old. Make the most of it.
- Use a softer toothbrush than normal.
- Rinse with an anti-plaque mouthwash before brushing your teeth.
- Floss your teeth daily.

Breathlessness

- Take slow deep breaths.
- Sit as straight as possible.
- Prop your head and shoulders with several pillows at night (see below).

Cramps

- Massage and flex the affected area.
- Make sure you get plenty of calcium in your diet: milk, cheese, leafy green vegetables, nuts, seeds, peas, beans and pulses.

How to lie

Increased weight and your expanding waistline mean that some of the movements you make on a day-to-day basis are uncomfortable or difficult, particularly as your pregnancy advances. Often a change of position or the addition of some cushions for support is all that is needed.

You will find it uncomfortable to lie on your front, so sleep or rest on your side or back. A cushion under your thigh prevents you rolling on to your tummy.

Feeling faint, or fainting

- Eat protein- or carbohydrate-rich snacks mid-morning and mid-afternoon (unsalted nuts, banana, rice cakes).
- Lie on your side with your feet raised, or sit with your head between your knees.
- Avoid lying on your back, prolonged standing and tight clothing.
- Tell your doctor.

Fluid retention

- Spend at least 15 minutes twice a day lying on the sofa with your feet raised slightly higher than your head.
- Avoid long periods of standing; do not wear tight socks or elasticated hold-up stockings; avoid salty foods (read food labels for added salt).
- Try lying on your left side.
- Massage the affected areas regularly.

Frequent urination

- Avoid diuretic drinks such as tea and coffee, but do not cut down on your overall fluid intake.
- Always empty your bladder fully.
- Empty your bladder last thing at night and before you go out.

Haemorrhoids

- Eat a high-fibre diet and drink plenty of water so that you do not become constipated. If you do, try a small bowl of prunes, a drink of prune juice or nibble dried prunes.
- Avoid very hot baths. Soaking in a warm bath can help ease discomfort. Alternatively apply an ice pack for about 10 minutes.
- Ask your GP to prescribe a cream to shrink them.

Heartburn

- Eat little and often.
- Avoid hot, spicy foods.
- Eat your evening meal at least two hours before you go to bed.
- Try antacid tablets – ask your GP for advice.

High blood pressure

Your blood pressure will be measured at all your antenatal appointments as a rise in blood pressure could indicate the onset of pre-eclampsia (see p. 38).

- Take regular daily naps, or complete bed rest, depending on what the doctor suggests.
- Try gentle exercise such as swimming.
- Do relaxation exercises, or go to yoga or relaxation classes. If these are not specifically for pregnant women, tell the instructor that you are pregnant – you may need to make some movements differently from other class members.

Incontinence

- Do your pelvic floor exercises (see p. 26).
- Empty your bladder frequently.
- Avoid lifting on a full stomach.

Lying well propped with pillows and cushions may make you more comfortable.

To get up from lying, roll on to your side, and use your arms to push yourself up.

Insomnia

- Take a warm, relaxing bath before bed. Add a drop or two of lavender aromatherapy oil.
- Relaxation techniques or a massage, again with soothing oil, before bed may help.
- Try sleeping with a pillow supporting your stomach, another supporting your back and one under your knees.

Morning sickness

This is inaptly named since it can occur at any time. It is caused by the upsurge of hormonal activity in your body and affects four out of five women.
- Eat a plain biscuit or slice of dry toast before you get out of bed in the morning.
- Do not rush about, especially in the morning.
- Ginger capsules or drinks may help. These are available from health food shops; follow the directions for preparation on the packet.
- Eat small meals every two to three hours.

Pelvic pain

- Rest with your body supported on a pillow.
- Try a warm bath, or hold a warm hot-water bottle over the painful area.
- Gently rock to and fro.
- Call your doctor or midwife if the pain is intense and/or persistent. In early pregnancy, it could be the start of a miscarriage (although it is more likely to be caused by the ligaments of your womb stretching); later it may be that the baby's head is pressing on your pelvic nerve; toward the end of pregnancy, it could be a sign of early labour.

Skin darkening

- Avoid strong sun and sunbathing – use a sun block or a face-shading hat. The pregnancy hormones cause more melanin to be produced by the skin (this is the pigment that gives you a suntan). In pregnancy, this can be deposited under the skin in a, literally, butterfly shaped mask over the cheeks and nose. It disappears after delivery.

Stretch marks

- Try not to put on too much weight.
- Rich oils may help, although there is no proof that they do (likewise expensive stretch mark creams are not scientifically proven to work).
- Consult a qualified aromatherapist over which essential oils to add to the oil – some should not be used during pregnancy.

Thrush

To prevent thrush:
- Keep your vulva area cool, wear cotton underwear, and skirts rather than trousers. Avoid tights.

How to sit

Sitting cross-legged can aggravate varicose veins and should be avoided while you are pregnant. Make sure any chair you sit on regularly (in an office, for example) supports your back – use a cushion if necessary – and allows you to place both feet flat on the floor. Try to avoid lounging unsupported, even in an armchair.

Sitting with your back straight, shoulders back and legs apart is good for the spine and stretches your inner thighs.

Sit cross-legged with your back straight and shoulders back to gently stretch your inner thighs.

- Wipe your bottom from front to back.
- Wash your vulva with a cool, gentle shower spray after lovemaking.

If you get it:

- Sitting in a warm bath gives temporary relief.
- Consult your GP and ask for a prescription for a fungicidal cream or pessaries.

Tiredness

- Rest whenever you get the chance.
- Delegate as much housework as possible.
- Eat little and often.

Varicose veins

- Wear support tights.
- Raise your feet higher than your head as often as possible. Always read or watch TV like this.
- Avoid standing for long periods.
- Swimming and low-impact aerobics improve the circulation, which may help.

How to lift

It is even more important than usual to keep your back straight and bend your knees when you are lifting. Take special care when you lift children, who tend to 'hurl' themselves at you. Try to make sure his weight is evenly distributed and do not move him from side to side. Avoid heavy shopping bags altogether if you possibly can.

MORE SERIOUS PROBLEMS

Most pregnancies progress completely normally but occasionally there are complications. Thanks to thorough antenatal checks, any difficulties can usually be detected early, which means that they can either be put right, or at least, managed effectively.

In early pregnancy

Early pregnancy is classed as referring to the first 12–14 weeks.

Bleeding

This is very common and may have a completely harmless cause, such as the slight bleeding or spotting which occurs due to erosion of the ripe cervix. It may, however, also suggest more serious problems and is one of the signs of miscarriage.

Don't panic, or assume that you are having a miscarriage. Phone your doctor straight away. He or she may suggest you go to hospital as a precaution.

Ectopic or tubal pregnancy

This is the term used when the embryo has implanted itself outside the womb, usually in one of the fallopian tubes. Many such pregnancies cause no special problems – the embryo dies at six to eight weeks and is reabsorbed back into the body.

In other cases, however, the pregnancy stretches and finally ruptures the tube wall, causing sudden and severe abdominal pain. This is an emergency, which may cause heavy haemorrhaging. You will need surgery straight away.

Gestational diabetes

This affects about one woman is 25 and simply means diabetes that develops while you are pregnant and disappears after the birth (you will be checked for signs of this at each antenatal appointment). It can be very mild or more serious.

If you have a slight predisposition to diabetes – if someone in your immediate family suffers from it, for example – pregnancy can tip the balance. One of its effects can be to make the baby put on weight which makes a caesarean more likely (if you have already delivered a baby of 4.5 kg/10 lb, you will be monitored especially closely).

Depending on its severity, you may initially be given a high-fibre diet to follow. If that does not control it, or if it is severe, insulin tablets will be prescribed.

The overwhelming majority of babies born to women with gestational diabetes are healthy and normal, although there is a higher risk of prematurity.

Rhesus incompatibility

The red blood cells of most Caucasians contain a substance called the Rhesus factor and are said to be Rhesus positive (+). If you do not have it, you are Rhesus negative (–). Problems only arise when Rh– women with Rh+ partners carry Rh+ babies. Routine blood tests reveal your status and if there is any risk your partner will be tested too.

Difficulties in first pregnancies are rare. In subsequent ones, however, some of the first baby's Rh+ cells, which entered the mother's body during delivery, can cause the mother to produce antibodies to fight them.

If this is left untreated, during a second pregnancy these antibodies cross the placenta and start to damage the red blood cells of a Rh+ baby, leading to rhesus haemolytic disease. Amniocentesis will show the degree to which the baby is affected. If he is too young to be born, he can be given a blood transfusion from around 22 weeks. He may need others before the pregnancy comes to term. If he is sufficiently mature to survive, delivery is induced or a caesarean carried out. He may need another transfusion at birth.

Problems later in pregnancy

Once the first 12–14 weeks are over, most pregnancies are relatively problem free. The most common difficulties are listed here (although rest assured that all are rare).

Bleeding

This may be minor, but could have more serious consequences. Let your doctor know immediately if you start to bleed. In later pregnancy, bleeding may be caused by problems with the placenta. The two most common are:

Placenta praevia

This means that the placenta is attached at the bottom of the womb, either partially or wholly blocking the baby's way out. As the baby gets bigger, it takes up more space and the bottom of the womb, in particular, stretches to accommodate the extra growth. If the placenta is low down, it may start to peel away from the wall of the womb, which causes it to bleed intermittently.

If placenta praevia is suspected you will have regular scans to monitor its position (it can edge its way up the side of the womb, out of the way). If it stays at the bottom of the womb, it will cut off your baby's food and oxygen supply once labour starts so you will usually be given a caesarean.

Placental abruption

This is when a normally attached placenta starts to detach itself from the wall of the womb. If this happens with one or two tiny sections, it causes no problem, but in some cases as much as a third can come away. In mild cases no treatment is necessary; in moderate cases, you will probably be admitted to hospital to rest for the remainder of your pregnancy. In severe cases, you may need a transfusion and your baby will be delivered by caesarean.

Pre-eclampsia

This is a potentially dangerous condition that only occurs in pregnancy, usually after the 20th week. If undetected it may lead to eclampsia, which can be fatal for mother and baby. Raised blood pressure and protein in the urine are signs of pre-eclampsia, which is why both are checked regularly at the antenatal clinic. If you have pre-eclampsia, you will be closely monitored either in hospital or at a day centre, depending on the seriousness of the condition, as it may be necessary to deliver the baby early. Delivery of the baby reverses all the effects.

Polyhydramnios

This means having too much amniotic fluid, so that your abdomen feels like a balloon tightly filled with water. It is at best uncomfortable and can be extremely painful. This may develop slowly at any time between 22 and 32 weeks, or it may come quickly at the end of the pregnancy. It is often associated with a multiple pregnancy. Treatment usually involves rest (not necessarily in hospital), draining of small amounts of fluid with a syringe and, if the condition causes a great deal of pain, sedation.

HAVING TWINS

Twin – or supertwin – pregnancies are becoming more common, a fact that is usually attributed to the use of fertility treatments, particularly the use of drugs to stimulate ovulation. About one in 80 pregnancies results in a multiple birth; as recently as 15 years ago, the figure was one in 100.

You may sail through a multiple pregnancy – there are no medical reasons why you should not. Carrying two babies is, however, harder on your body and the births will be subject to closer medical supervision. Your doctor is unlikely to agree to anything other than a hospital birth.

Twins can be fraternal, resulting from two different eggs fertilized by two different sperm, in which case they are no more alike than any other siblings. If they are the result of a single, fertilized egg splitting in half at a very early stage, the babies will be identical.

Around a third of twins born in Britain are identical, evenly divided between boy and girl pairs. About half of non-identical pairs are boy and girl; the remainder are equally split between dissimilar girls and dissimilar boys.

Your pregnancy

If you carry twins or triplets, you are likely to gain weight more rapidly than a woman carrying a single baby, and to gain more since you have the weight of two babies, two placentas and two amniotic sacs. Your total gain may be up to half your normal weight. You will feel very cumbersome toward the end of your

The likelihood of twins

The chances that you will have twins increase if:
- you are taking fertility drugs
- you have several children already
- you have a family history of twins
- you are in your early 30s: the likelihood increases to 35, then starts to fall
- you are of African origin (you are twice as likely as a European to have twins)

pregnancy and may also experience what in other women are minor discomforts, such as nausea and tiredness, far more acutely.

Multiple pregnancies are, however, usually shorter than single ones, at around 35–37 weeks and the average weight for each baby is lower (some 2.5 kg/ 5½ lb as opposed to 3.1 kg/7 lb).

What you can do

- Get as much rest as you can. Sleeping, particularly from around six months onward can be difficult – you cannot find a comfortable position. Nap little and often.
- Think carefully, well in advance, about how long you want to carry on working. At 30 weeks, you may have gained as much weight as a woman pregnant with a single baby at 40 weeks. Try to negotiate reduced hours if at all possible, and be prepared to be flexible about when you start your maternity leave.
- Try to exercise – swimming is excellent since your extra weight is supported, as are aquarobics, if you can find a class at your local leisure centre. Yoga is also good exercise.
- Be sure to do your pelvic floor exercises (see p. 26) – these are even more important if you are carrying two babies. If you find it difficult to do them standing as your pregnancy advances, lie on the floor with your feet up on a chair to 'tip' the weight of the babies and your womb off your pelvic floor.
- Take extra care when lifting; follow the advice on p. 37. And try to stand properly – avoid arching your back as far as possible. Always roll on to your side when getting up from lying down (see p. 35).

How twins lie

In the womb, twins usually lie so that either both are head down (or vertex, below left) or one is vertex and one breech (below right).

- Go to all your antenatal checks. You will probably be asked to attend more frequently than for a single pregnancy (perhaps weekly from 30 weeks), and not be able to have shared care for as long. It is important to keep appointments, however, so that any problems can be monitored effectively.
- Go to antenatal classes. Hospital classes tend to be geared to single births which are, by and large, straightforward: twins are more likely to be premature or delivered by caesarean or both. It is still, however, worth going. Your local twins support group may be able to help you find the most suitable classes. Tell the course leader that you are expecting twins. You should also arrange to attend classes earlier than normal, otherwise you risk not completing the full course if your babies arrive early.
- Eat well: two babies need more food than one. Eat regularly and get lots of fresh foods. Women carrying more than one baby can be prone to anaemia (see p. 34), so get plenty of iron-rich foods such as spinach and other leafy green vegetables, lean red meat (but not liver), dried fruit and nuts. Drink plenty of water to help combat constipation.
- Contact your local twins or superbirth support groups (see Useful Contacts, pp. 248–51).

Potential problems

Some problems are more common in twin pregnancies, but good antenatal care should mean early identification and effective treatment.

- One baby may grow more slowly than the other, perhaps because one placenta is working more effectively than the other.
- High blood pressure is more common in twin than single pregnancies, as is pre-eclampsia.
- Reabsorption of one embryo can happen: a scan shows twins, but later there is only one baby. This presumably has always happened but in the days before ultrasound was common, women did not realize they were carrying twins until much later in pregnancy than they do today.
- Premature birth is common: technically babies born before 37 weeks are premature.
- Miscarriage involving the loss of one baby while the other continues to term may occur.

The birth

How straightforward the birth of twins is depends on two factors: their maturity at birth and their position in the womb.

Pre-term twins and triplets can be very small and need careful handling during birth. This often means a caesarean which, if planned, can be done by epidural so that you are awake, but does not put them through the trauma of being pushed into the world. They may still need time in a special baby care unit.

It is not easy for both twins to get into the correct position to be born. In only 50 per cent of cases are they both head down so that they can be born normally. Often one twin is head down and one breech, but sometimes one is lying transverse, blocking the way out. In this case, your obstetrician may try to turn the baby, but usually you will have a caesarean. The more complex their positions, the more likely that they will be delivered by caesarean.

What you will need

Twins, obviously, need more clothes and equipment than single babies. In most cases, double up on what is suggested on pp. 30–3.

- **Sleeping**
  You may prefer to buy one cot for them to sleep in together to start with, then add a second as they grow. If not, you will need two cribs, carrycots or Moses baskets.
- **Transport**
  A double carriage pram is costly. A double pram with two carrycots, which converts to a double pushchair, is a good alternative. (If your babies are sleeping in the carrycots at night, check the mattresses are suitable – some are not.) A double folding buggy is useful later, but not stable or warm enough for newborns. You will need two car seats.
- **Clothes**
  Later on, it helps twins to see themselves as individuals if you dress them differently. That may not be possible when they are tiny, when the most important thing is a clean, dry sleepsuit, regardless of colour. But try to keep at least one outfit personal to each baby.

THE BABY THAT WAS NOT TO BE

Miscarriage is the loss of a pregnancy before the end of its 24th week; the loss of a baby after that date is classed as a stillbirth.

If you have suffered three miscarriages in a row, you will be investigated and treated. If this does not happen automatically, contact the Miscarriage Alliance for advice (see Useful Contacts, pp. 248–51).

Many factors are known to be involved in miscarriage, but in only about half of all miscarriages can a specific and almost certain cause – usually a chromosomal abnormality – be identified. If you have suffered a miscarriage, take special note of any information the hospital can give you when you plan a second pregnancy.

Are you miscarrying?

Signs that you may be about to miscarry include:
- bleeding, from spotting to a period-like flow
- passing clots of blood
- cramping, period-like pains
- backache
- feeling generally unwell.

You may have no symptoms at all; on the other hand, having any of the above symptoms does not mean that you are about to miscarry. Do not panic, but contact your doctor or midwife immediately.

Coming to terms with your loss

It is important that you are allowed to grieve for the loss of your pregnancy. It can help to cry as much as you feel you need to, and talk about what has happened as much as you wish, with anyone who will listen kindly. Some people find that it helps to know as much as possible about the miscarriage. Can your doctor give you a reason why it happened? What sex was the baby? After a couple of weeks, write down all the questions you would like to ask and arrange to go and see the gynaecologist who was caring for you.

After a stillbirth, many parents find it comforting to see and hold their baby. Even if there was some deformity, it is seldom as marked as you might have imagined. If you do not want to see the baby, most hospitals take photographs of the baby, which you can ask to have to keep (later if you do not want them straight away). Naming her and having a blessing, memorial service or burial may all help you to acknowledge your baby as special, as an individual.

Facing the future

The stages of recovery tend to follow a pattern: shock or denial; intense distress; feelings of loss, loneliness, guilt; and depression, for varying periods of time. You may find the date that the baby should have been born difficult to get through for a couple of years at least.

If you are feeling well there is no medical reason why you should not try to become pregnant again after you have had your first period following a miscarriage. But obviously emotionally you may need more time. Don't rush it if you are not ready.

Termination for abnormality

If your unborn baby is diagnosed as having an abnormality, you face a difficult decision. Do you continue with the pregnancy and care for a child with special needs, or do you have the pregnancy that you were so happy about terminated?

If you are more than 14 weeks pregnant (and many test results do only come through after this time), you will probably undergo an induced labour which could be long and painful. The baby, though small, is likely to be fully formed.
- Do you want to know as much as possible about the baby and the diagnosed disorder?
- Talk to the staff about tranquillizers, pain relief, epidurals, anything that might help you.
- Tell them what you want of the delivery. This should take place with dignity. Would you like a photograph of the baby? Do you want to see and hold her? Either, or both, may help you come to terms with her individuality and death.
- A post-mortem can help determine what went wrong. Consider asking for one since results can be valuable for genetic counselling when you are deciding about another pregnancy.
- A blessing, burial or memorial service can be comforting. Speak to the hospital chaplain.

If you have to consider, or have undergone, a termination in such circumstances, contact SATFA (see Useful Contacts, pp. 248–51) for information, advice and support.

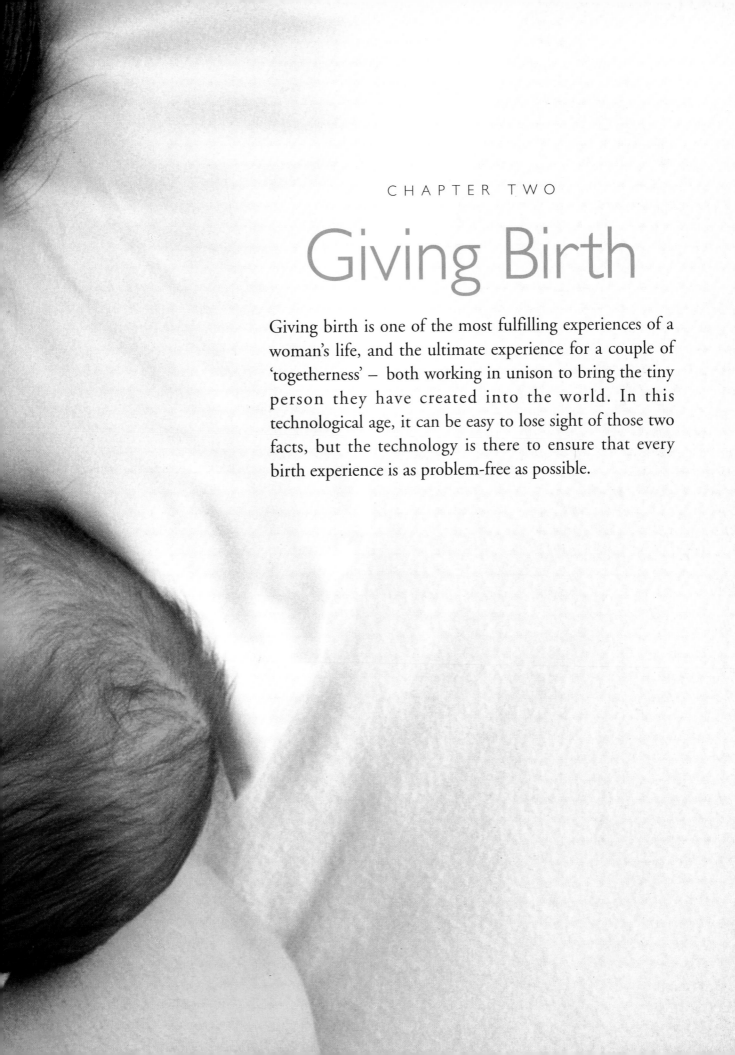

CHAPTER TWO

Giving Birth

Giving birth is one of the most fulfilling experiences of a woman's life, and the ultimate experience for a couple of 'togetherness' – both working in unison to bring the tiny person they have created into the world. In this technological age, it can be easy to lose sight of those two facts, but the technology is there to ensure that every birth experience is as problem-free as possible.

Birth and your newborn baby

BECOMING A PARENT

It is surprisingly difficult to think beyond the actual birth to parenthood. It is as if you need to know what the baby looks like before you can fit him into your dreams. You take out the layette and try to imagine how your baby will look in the clothes you have bought, but the reality of parenthood is elusive. It is hard to believe that the physical aspects of giving birth or nursing a child will ever seem insignificant. But they will.

Because most couples prepare for birth rather than parenthood, getting the birth 'right' seems important. But really it is not. The older and more organized you are, the more likely you are to want it to go to plan. It is easy to lose sight of the fact that birth is just day one of parenthood. There are thousands more days to follow. The most important aspect of giving birth is to deliver a healthy child as safely and as easily as possible. Plans should be flexible.

A month before

During the final month before your expected delivery date, you should:

- Make sure you and your partner know how to get to the hospital and where you can park your car.
- Put the telephone number of the hospital and a taxi company by the phone. You will usually be entitled to call an ambulance in an emergency, but it may not be possible (you may not feel up to driving yourself). Keep the taxi fare handy.
- If you don't have a phone arrange with neighbours to use theirs. Check which local pay or card phones are in working order. Remember that you may have to call the hospital or taxi company at night. Keep some change and a phonecard handy.

- Make arrangements to keep in touch with your partner. If you cannot always contact him by phone, make sure he can contact you. Pagers and mobile phones can be hired for short periods of time. Check advertisements in child-care magazines for details.
- Pack your bag (see p. 19).

If you are having a home birth

- Keep your midwife's and doctor's telephone numbers pinned up permanently beside the telephone.
- Make sure you have everything you need at home ready well in advance. Discuss this with your midwife in good time (see below). She will supply quite a lot of the equipment herself.
- As with a hospital birth, in the month before the baby is due, when your partner is not at home, make sure you know exactly where he is going to be at all times.
- Make sure you have a close friend or relation who can come round quickly to be with you until your midwife or partner arrives if you go into labour when you are on your own at home.

Your bed for a home birth

Your midwife will discuss the layout of the room in which you give birth with you – she will need to have access to both sides of the bed, for example. As soon as you are sure you are in labour, make up the bed with clean sheets, then cover the whole with a large sheet of strong plastic. Cover that with newspapers, then clean, old sheets. After the birth, you can strip off the soiled sheets and protection to leave you with a clean, fresh bed.

WHAT HAPPENS IN LABOUR

Labour is the hardest work known to man or woman (save the superhuman efforts needed to face disasters). Your body will be working for hour after hour but you cannot stop or pause for breath. It is easy to feel out of control, especially if you are unprepared for labour or do not understand what is happening to you.

How you give birth

If you pucker your lips to whistle, your mouth is in a similar position to the cervix before labour begins. If you open as wide as possible it is in the position reached at the end of labour.

To whistle, the lip muscles are small and tight. They have contracted. The cheeks are long and thin because the muscles are extended. You can feel this if you put a thumb in your mouth and a finger on your cheek and pinch.

Now open your mouth as wide as you can. Look at and feel the change in the muscles. The lips have narrowed and expanded. The cheeks have bulged and

Above: The end of pregnancy is a time for physical closeness and relaxation, sharing the last few days of being a couple, before you are transformed into a family.

The end of pregnancy

Towards the end of your pregnancy, some of the following may occur:

- Lightening or engagement: 2–4 weeks before birth the baby begins to descend into the pelvis thus lightening the pressure on the diaphragm.
- Groin pain and cramp (this is rare in first pregnancies).
- Loss of about 0.9–1.3 kg (2–3 lb) in weight.
- A change in energy level, either up or down. You may feel an overwhelming urge to clean all the kitchen cupboards or alternatively a sudden feeling of being utterly fatigued.
- Increase and thickening of vaginal discharge.
- Strong and more frequent Braxton–Hicks (see p. 18) contractions.
- Diarrhoea (this is often a sign labour is just about to begin).
- The loss of the mucus plug – a pinkish 'show'.
- Backache.

shortened. As you force your mouth to its widest possible position, you can feel the tightness extending far beyond your lips. Now move your lips from the whistling to the fully wide position. See how much the cheek and neck muscles must work to achieve the open position.

At the beginning of labour the cervix is closed and low in the vagina like lips which are puckered to whistle. By the end of labour it is wide open. In the course of labour, you will feel the tugs of each contraction as they pull the cervix open. Like the feeling in the neck and cheeks as you begin to open your mouth, the sensation of those early contractions is some distance from the opening: in the lower abdomen and back.

What to do if your waters break

Membranes can tear at any stage of pregnancy. If this happens some amniotic fluid will be lost. Sometimes there is a gush of fluid, at other times there is just a trickle. You may think you have wet yourself – many women experience stress incontinence during the latter stages of pregnancy (see p. 35) but amniotic fluid can be distinguished from urine by its pale straw colour and sweet smell. Because amniotic fluid is constantly replaced, unless there has been an almost complete loss, the baby continues to be bathed in fluid. Babies whose heads are engaged will act as a plug to the flow of amniotic fluid, so you may only be conscious of a slight leakage.

If your waters break you should:
- If it is just a trickle, inform your midwife, doctor or the hospital; if it is a gush – which is unmistakable – go straight to the hospital.
- Avoid sexual intercourse.
- Do not swim.
- Do not take a bath.
- Keep the vaginal area as clean as possible.
- Use a sanitary towel to absorb the flow.
- Be especially careful to wipe front to back after using the toilet.
- If the fluid trickles and then stops the membrane may simply have torn and repaired itself, but you should tell your doctor.
- If the fluid gushes or continues to flow, contact the hospital. Provided you are near term, labour is normally induced if it does not begin within 24 hours of the membranes breaking.

Recognizing that labour has started

With a first baby, in particular, it can be quite difficult to determine whether this really is 'it'.

You are probably *not* in labour if:
- The 'show' was brown.
- You feel contractions in the lower abdomen.
- Foetal movements increase with contractions.
- Contractions are irregular.
- Contractions do not increase in severity.
- Contractions do not increase in frequency.
- Contractions die down if you walk about.

You probably *are* in labour if:
- You have a pinkish 'show'.
- The membranes rupture, particularly if they gush.
- Your contractions feel as if they start in the lower back and spread to the lower abdomen.
- Contractions feel more or less the same whether you sit or stand.
- As time passes contractions become more regular.
- As time passes contractions become longer.
- As time passes contractions feel stronger.

When to worry

The following symptoms could indicate serious problems for you or the baby. Try not to panic, but do not ignore them.

Cord prolapse
If the waters break, the umbilical cord occasionally drops into the neck of the uterus or out through the vagina. Because pressure on the cord can cut off the baby's oxygen supply, you must act immediately.
- Get on your hands and knees and remain there (this reduces the pressure).
- Support any cord which protrudes from the vagina with a warm wet sanitary pad.
- Avoid any pressure on the cord. Do not try to push it back.
- If you are travelling by car, get on your hands and knees in the back seat.
- Call your hospital, doctor or midwife straight away – if possible get someone else to do this for you. If there is no one available, call an ambulance to take you to hospital.

Greenish brown liquid leaks from your vagina
Occasionally amniotic fluid is greenish brown because it contains meconium. This is present in the gut of all babies at birth. Passing meconium, which then leaks from your vagina prior to the birth, may be an indication that the baby is in distress.
- Ring the hospital immediately.

Vaginal bleeding
The early stages of labour are often accompanied by slight spotting or bleeding. Bleeding can also occur after lovemaking.

- Heavy bleeding should never be ignored. Call an ambulance or get someone to rush you to hospital at once.
- Pinkish or red-streaked mucus (a 'show') which does not persist should be reported at your next appointment, but otherwise can be ignored. If it is accompanied by contractions, ring the hospital: labour has begun.
- Brownish-tinged mucus or slight spotting which occurs 24–48 hours after intercourse or vaginal examination and then stops is quite normal. Tell your doctor at the next examination. If it persists call the doctor.
- Bright red bleeding or persistent spotting can indicate problems with the placenta. Call the doctor or go to hospital at once.

THE THREE STAGES OF LABOUR

Birth has three stages. In the first stage (which is sometimes itself divided into three phases) the cervix is opened, in the second the baby is pushed out of the womb. In the final stage the placenta is detached from the wall of the womb, and like the baby is pushed out through the cervix, vagina and perineum (the area between the anus and the vagina). All of these stages are under hormonal control. At the beginning of labour hormones, released into the mother's bloodstream, set labour in motion; as labour advances hormones maintain it.

The first stage

For most women labour begins with the onset of fairly regular and widely spaced contractions. These continue until the cervix is fully dilated and the baby born. The early stages of labour may be marked by nothing more than odd twinges or strong Braxton–Hicks contractions (see p. 18). More typically contractions occur at increasingly regular intervals. Women often describe them as similar to cramps, period pains, or twinges of backache. Sometimes a tightening feeling starts in the back and moves around to the lower abdomen then stops. Typically contractions occur once every 20 minutes and last about 30 seconds. Between contractions there is no discomfort.

Over the next hours contractions intensify until they last about 45 seconds, occur every five to ten minutes and have quite distinct peaks. As labour progresses the tightly puckered cervix relaxes and a gap opens up. At the end of the first phase labour has usually been in progress for two to six hours but the gap is only about 3 cm wide. Now things begin to move faster. The next 4 cm of dilatation takes only two to three hours on average, although all these phases tend to be longer for first babies. Contractions feel more intense and are more predictable. The space between them shortens. They feel as if something is being pulled hard, then harder, then unbelievably hard before it is slowly relaxed. Contractions dominate, taking your entire attention and making you feel increasingly uncomfortable. It becomes harder to relax or keep up the breathing exercises. Labour begins to feel endless.

Transition

Any remaining feelings of being in control are likely to disappear as the final or transitional phase is entered. Some women don't experience this as a separate phase at all; a lucky few cope. For the majority, the best that can be said of transition is that it is usually short. Contractions suddenly speed up, and may tumble together in an endless stream. The last 1–3 cm of dilatation can take less than 15 minutes. Most women now feel irritable, and exhausted.

The slow, steady building of contractions during the early stages of labour gives many the confidence to cope without drugs. For some transition is no more than a speeding up of these contractions. For others a range of problems arise which undermine confidence and undo all preparation. You may find it impossible to predict when or if a contraction will subside or whether there will be a pause before the next.

In addition, you may vomit and/or your body temperature may begin to go haywire. You may run a temperature, sweat and thrash about restlessly. You may feel cold, shiver and tremble uncontrollably. You may do one, then the other. As if this was not enough the flow of oxygen to the muscles of the cervix can often leave the brain a little short. When this happens you feel befuddled, irritable and sleepy.

Toward the end of this phase the baby's head begins to press down on the back passage and lower back. This causes some women to soil themselves which can be distressing but is normal. Your midwife will be quite used to dealing with it so try not to be embarrassed. As the cervix is pulled back to its full extent blood vessels are broken and vaginal bleeding which has previously been slight may increase.

Not coping in these circumstances is understandable. If you scream, shout and swear you will not be the first. Coping is a matter of luck, not simply preparation.

The second stage

In the second stage the baby passes through the fully opened cervix, into the vagina and out through the perineum. This takes about an hour with a first baby,

rather less with subsequent children. If the second stage seems to be extended the doctor may feel that it is necessary to monitor the baby's health electronically. (Practices vary: in some hospitals, electronic foetal monitoring at intervals or even constantly throughout labour is normal. If this means that your movement is restricted and you are not happy, say so.) If all goes well the baby can be delivered vaginally even if the second stage is two hours or more. If however the baby shows any signs of distress the delivery will probably be assisted by forceps or suction (see pp. 54–5). If you are having your baby at home and your midwife or doctor feels that labour is delayed you will be admitted to hospital for an assisted delivery.

The second stage usually begins with an urge to start pushing. Although pushing or bearing down

Stages of labour

In the first stage of labour, the cervix thins, and the cervical canal is eliminated, or fully effaced. At that stage, further contractions dilate the cervix.

When you are 7 cm dilated, the midwife can feel only the front and sides of the cervix round the baby's head. When it has disappeared, you are fully dilated.

You are now ready to start pushing the baby down the birth canal. With each contraction, the head moves nearer to your vaginal opening.

As the anus and perineum bulge, the vaginal tissues are stretched so thin that the nerves are blocked. The baby's head finally emerges.

helps to expel the baby, most of the work is still done by the contractions. The more upright you are, the easier it is to push the baby out. If you lie on your back the route is uphill, if you squat it is straight down. Most hospitals are now flexible about birth positions, and have birthing stools, cushions and floor mats so that mothers can choose what feels most comfortable. Your antenatal classes (see p. 25) should include advice on this, since support helps to avoid excess pressure on the perineum and unnecessary tearing.

The contractions at this stage are more widely spaced, often less intense and last from 60 to 90 seconds. In one of these contractions the baby's head first comes into sight. It will slip back from the vulva before reappearing in the entrance at the next contraction. Watching the head through the vulva gives the impression of a battering ram pushing, retreating, pushing, and retreating once more. This is basically what is happening. Each time the head comes forward the vulva opens a little wider, and stays wide until the head approaches again. The feeling has been described as like trying to pass a large melon when you're extremely constipated! You feel the baby move into the birth channel, then forward and back with each contraction. The pushing continues until the head can squeeze through the wide open vulva.

As the head is crowned you may feel a stinging sensation if you have not had local anaesthesia such as an epidural block (see p. 54). As soon as you feel this you should stop pushing and pant. (To get an idea of how the stinging feels try pulling your mouth wide at the corners until it hurts, and then pull wider still.) Once the head is born the rest is easy and quick. Your midwife will turn the baby's head to the side and ease out first one shoulder then the other. In two or three contractions the baby is born.

The third stage

The final task is to deliver the placenta. The birth has pulled it from the uterine wall, and contractions (helped by bearing down once more) push it quickly out through the cervix. Many doctors administer an injection of a synthetic version of oxytocin (the hormone which induces contractions) just after the birth of the baby to speed up the delivery of the placenta. There is controversy about whether this is always necessary, and many natural birth proponents

recommend putting the baby to the breast immediately after the birth as the same hormone, oxytocin, is involved in the 'let down' reflex – the release of milk into the milk sacs behind the areola (see p. 71). The contractions of the third stage can be felt, and are very similar to severe period pains or cramps. But they do not last and most women do not find them at all troublesome. If you have had an episiotomy or have torn, you will be stitched.

WHAT TO DO DURING LABOUR

In the first phase of dilatation you should:
- Call your partner.
- Pack your bag if it is not already packed.
- Keep moving about.
- Time your contractions.
- Practise your breathing: even if you do not need it yet, it makes sense to remind yourself what to do.
- Unless contractions have obvious peaks, have a drink and a light meal (it may be ages before you eat again).
- Try to urinate at least once an hour.
- Call the hospital.
- Have a warm bath (but not if your waters have broken – if they have, take a shower).
- Try to relax. It will speed up labour.
- Make a snack to eat after the birth. Put champagne on ice.

In the second phase of dilatation you should:
- Keep up your breathing pattern.
- Go to hospital.
- Try to stay relaxed.
- Try to keep moving for as long as possible.
- Use your partner, the midwife or the wall for support during contractions.
- Do not eat or drink.
- Try to urinate if you can, on the hour every hour. Get your partner to remind you.
- If you need pain relief, ask for it. It gets worse before it gets better.

In transition:
- Hang on.
- Try to relax between and during contractions.

How long does labour last?

First stage: dilatation of the cervix

- The first 3 cm: dilatation starts slowly and imperceptibly. The first 3 cm can take days – even weeks. You are unlikely to be aware of any sensations that this is happening until the last two to six hours (perhaps the last 1 cm), but significantly longer for first babies.

- From 3 to 7 cm dilatation: some women remain unaware of labour for much of this stage too, although toward the end there is no doubt of what is happening. For most it lasts two to three hours during which contractions get longer, stronger and more frequent.

- From 7 to 10 cm: about 15 minutes to one hour of strong and frequent contractions – longer for first babies.

Second stage: birth of the baby

- 15 minutes to one hour; occasionally it can take up to two hours, but any longer is rare – most doctors intervene to avoid a long and tiring second stage.

Third stage: birth of the placenta or afterbirth

- About 10 to 15 minutes, or up to half an hour, depending on whether an injection has been administered or not.

- Adjust your breathing pattern to find one which helps you at this stage. Abandon them all if they do not help. Try to distract yourself from pain.
- Don't worry if you cannot cope: very few can.
- Take deep breaths between contractions: but don't hyperventilate.
- Say exactly what you want.
- If you feel like pushing, pant and hold back until the midwife has checked the cervix is fully dilated.

In the second stage:

- Push with your pelvic floor muscles during contractions.

- Stop pushing and pant when the midwife tells you to. Pushing once a contraction has finished is a waste of effort – save it for the next one.
- Do not worry if you feel as if you are soiling yourself – or if you do.

What your birth companion can do to help:

- Time contractions.
- Stay calm.
- Keep a sense of humour.
- Help to distract her – watch a video, play cards, go for a walk. Try to remember the names of all the shops in the High Street, the counties of England,

Comfortable labour positions

If you want to bear down before the cervix is fully dilated, kneel and lean forward on your hands to slow the baby down.

In the early stages, keep upright with your back straight and knees apart. It often helps to use the back of a chair for support.

the states of the USA, last year's hit songs – anything which will keep her mind off labour.

- Offer reassurance, support and comfort and mediate with the medical staff.
- Just be there.
- Breathe with her if it helps. Remind her if she forgets. Massage if it's needed. Hold her hand.
- Stop all of the above if she asks you to.
- If she shows signs of hyperventilation (dizziness, numbness, becoming light-headed) cup your hands over her mouth and get her to take a few shallow breaths. Breathe with her if it helps.
- Never criticize. Stay calm even if the medical staff irritate you.
- Remind her to urinate every hour, give her ice to suck (take it with you) or moisten her lips with a damp sponge.
- Use a cool flannel to wash her when she is hot. Cover her up if she feels cold.
- Take the photos and open the champagne when it is all over.
- Stay as long as you can after the birth.
- Phone everyone and let them know.
- Prepare for the homecoming.

COPING WITH PAIN

Most women interpret the huge muscular effort their body engages in during labour as pain. Some feel pain in the earliest stages of labour. Others do not make this interpretation until much later.

There is nothing fixed about feeling pain. It is known for example that those involved in road accidents can be unaware of their own serious injuries while they fight to save the lives of others. Pain catches up with them as soon as the emergency has passed.

Those who do research into how we perceive pain suggest that between the body and the brain there is something rather like a gate. This gate is usually partly open. When pain signals arrive only a few can get through at a time. If there is an emergency we can almost shut the gate. This blocks out most of the pain. At other times (when we are on the look out for danger) we can open it very wide and we become sensitive to the smallest pain.

This makes a lot of sense. In a real emergency no one wants the pain from a small cut to interfere with survival. At other times the exaggeration of pain might add a necessary note of caution. Although for the vast majority of women painless childbirth is a myth, managed pain is a possibility.

Pain control in childbirth

The following methods of pain control are often used by women in labour. One or more may work for you.

Relaxation

Tension makes pain feel worse but relaxation raises the threshold for pain. The more relaxed you feel, the less something hurts. Women report that the following help them to relax in labour:

Use your partner as a support as much as you want to. If you sit on the end of the bed with your feet on a chair (far left) and lean into him, you take some pressure off your lower back and have a feeling of closeness. If you prefer to stand (left), let him take your weight. Try to stay upright, but if you need to rest, do so.

Partners who assist in this way are also able to monitor signs of tension and help to reduce it before it becomes a problem.

Emergency delivery

If you think that the baby is coming quickly and have no time to get to hospital, this is what you should do:

1 Call 999 for an ambulance.

2 Pant and avoid bearing down for as long as possible.

3 Find someone to help.

4 Wash your hands and the perineal area.

5 Spread some clean towels or newspapers on the floor and lie down. Raise your buttocks with cushions or pillows to slow the birth down.

6 If the baby starts to arrive, move your buttock support. Sit in a semi-upright position or crouch. Push with each contraction. Pant or blow as the head appears. Let it emerge gradually. Never pull. As the head emerges, you (or a companion if you have found one) should reach for the baby and feel whether the cord is around the neck.

7 If it is round the neck, hook a finger under the cord and gently work it over the baby's head. Pant as this is done to avoid pushing.

8 Stroke the baby's nose downward and under the chin upward to help expel mucus.

9 Your companion should take the head gently in both hands. As the next contraction arrives, push as your companion presses the baby's head slightly downward while the first shoulder is delivered. As the arm appears lift the head slightly to free the other shoulder.

10 Quickly place the baby on your stomach and cover both of you with something warm. Do not tug the cord.

11 If the placenta arrives wrap it in newspaper; check you have all the bits: throw nothing away.

12 Keep the placenta higher than the baby but do not cut the cord. Leave that to the experts.

- Keeping moving for as long as possible.
- Being at home for as long as possible.
- Instruction in relaxation techniques (see p. 26).
- Having a birth companion.
- Music and soft lights.
- Foot massage.
- A warm bath.

Breathing exercises

Drawing in breath rapidly makes you tense; doing so repeatedly can make you hyperventilate. Controlled breathing, on the other hand, lowers tension and helps maintain a feeling of relaxation. To help:

- Take classes; they are run in most areas (see p. 25).
- Deep slow breathing, concentrating on the out breath will help relaxation in early labour.
- High chest breathing (blow as if trying to bend a candle flame without blowing it out) helps at the top of a contraction.
- By concentrating on breathing out during contractions, you can avoid clenching your teeth and taking a swift intake of breath.

Delivery positions

Squatting is an ideal position in which to give birth, since gravity helps, but most Western women find this difficult unaided. Let your partner take your weight in his arms (right). Alternatively, sit in between his legs (far right). He can feel contractions coming in this position and you can lean back on him and relax between pushes.

Distraction

Having something to do while in pain reduces its perceived intensity.

- Tap out a rhythm or sing a song.
- Recite a poem.

Gas and air (Entonox)

Entonox is a mixture of anaesthetic gases and air, breathed in through a face mask. It takes about 30 seconds to work. It works well during transition because not only does it reduce pain, it can also return a sense of being in control. Grabbing the mask and putting it to your face feels as if you are doing something to help.

TENS

This is not available at all hospitals, so it is worth asking beforehand if you would like to try it. TENS stands for transcutaneous electrical nerve stimulation and is believed to work by stimulating the body to produce endorphins, its own natural painkillers. Electrodes are taped to your back, connected by wires to a hand-held battery-powered stimulator. As you feel the need, you press the stimulator, giving yourself small amounts of current. There are no side effects on you or the baby.

Some women find TENS does lessen the pain; others that it makes no difference.

Pethidine

This is an analgesic, usually given by injection, which has the effect of continuing your present mood. If you are feeling good it will make you feel better. If you are feeling bad it makes you feel worse. Many women find it does not help with pain. Some like the woozy feeling it gives. It can be passed to the baby, making her sleepy and slow to respond after the birth.

Epidural

See box on p. 54.

Episiotomy

This is a small cut in the perineum, usually made under local anaesthetic, to ease the passage of the baby's head. It does not hurt at the time it is made but can be painful afterward. The cut is made along the midline toward the anus or slanting to one side. The intention is to prevent tearing, but this is controversial: some doctors feel it increases the likelihood of tearing and the healing process is slower and can interfere with lovemaking. As a result the practice of giving routine episiotomies has declined. However, they are needed for forceps deliveries and when babies need to be removed from the vagina quickly.

Cuts have to be stitched after the birth under local anaesthetic. Each layer of the perineum must be stitched separately, which is why it takes so long.

If you want to avoid an episiotomy, tell the hospital that you do not want one unless it is essential and ask your partner to make this clear when you are in labour. You can also reduce the risk of tearing or episiotomy by stretching your perineum in the last months of pregnancy. To do this, first wash your hands thoroughly. Take some cocoa butter or oil and massage your labia, vaginal entrance and perineum

Breathing

Practise breathing for labour with your partner beforehand – he must be able to feel the different effects on your body of deep and shallow breaths. At the beginning and end of contractions, breathe deeply so that your ribcage expands (far left); at the height of contractions, take shallow breaths, just enough to raise your shoulder blades slightly (left).

Episiotomy is a cut in your perineum, usually from the back of the vagina out to the side; it can also be made toward the anus, or a combination of the two.

until the oil is absorbed. Then, put more cream on your fingers and insert them into your vagina and stretch the outer lips. Continue until you feel the burn and hold at this point for a few minutes. Your aim is to be able to open the vagina to about 7–8 cm (2¾–3 in) before the burning begins. It takes about a month to work up to this point. Regular pelvic floor exercises (see p. 26) will also help. This procedure, however, is not recommended for anyone who is at risk from miscarriage.

SPECIAL CASES

Not all births are straightforward, but fortunately few problems these days are life threatening to the mother or child. Here is a list of the most frequent problems. If you are reading this before you go into labour do remember that they are all the exception rather than the rule.

Forceps delivery

Since the 16th century forceps have been used to turn babies who are poorly aligned with the birth canal or who need lifting out of the vagina because the second stage of labour fails to progress quickly enough. Forceps look like a pair of shiny coal tongs which can be separated. They are used to:
- Protect the baby's head from the pressure of the vaginal wall.
- Enable the baby's head to be manipulated.
- Enable the baby to be gently manipulated and then lifted from the vagina – the baby is definitely not pulled or dragged out.

Epidural and other nerve blocks

Nerve blocks are local anaesthetics injected along the course of a nerve. They deaden sensation. The two most often used in labour and delivery are the pudendal block and the epidural block.

The pudendal block is used for forceps deliveries and stitches to the perineum. An anaesthetic is injected into the vagina. Once the area is deadened, you will feel pressure but not pain.

The epidural block is used for vaginal and caesarean deliveries. It is the only means of ensuring a completely pain-free labour. A very fine tube is inserted beside your spine. Anaesthetic is delivered into the tube and topped up as required. You will still feel pressure, but not pain. Very, very occasionally after an epidural women suffer from severe headaches which can persist for a couple of days. Even more occasionally numbness is felt in the legs for a few days.

Site of epidural

Area numbed

What happens in a forceps delivery

- Your legs will be put into stirrups.
- A local anaesthetic will be injected into the vagina.
- An episiotomy will be cut.
- One by one the two curved blades of the forceps will be slipped into the vagina and placed on either side of the baby's head and locked into position.

After a forceps delivery

You will have a certain amount of bruising and also stitches to contend with. The soreness should not last more than a week.

Ventouse

Sometimes a vacuum extractor is used instead of forceps. One advantage of ventouse is that it doesn't usually need an episiotomy, but the baby's head must be in the birth canal. A vacuum cup is attached to the baby's head by suction. The head is then drawn out in much the same way as it would be by forceps. The suction cup often leaves a bump on the head, which may look alarming but the swelling is superficial and should disappear within a week.

Breech delivery

Many babies spend much of pregnancy in an upright position. Most are, however, born head first and facing backward. If a baby is still upright (in a breech position) at 32–34 weeks an external cephalic version (ECV) may be carried out. The doctor will attempt to turn the baby by the use of gentle pressure. Few babies turn after 36 weeks.

There are three breech positions:

- A frank breech is most common. In this position the baby's legs are folded flat up against his body, so that they touch the face or tuck under the chin. Babies enter the birth channel in this folded position. A frank breech is the easiest of breech deliveries. Many will be delivered vaginally and without major complications.
- In a complete breech the baby's feet are tucked up beside the bottom.
- In a footling breech one leg is extended downward from the breech position so that the foot is born before the buttocks.

How babies lie

Most babies are head down by the end of pregnancy (top left) and delivered vaginally. Others lie across the exit (centre). A complete breech (above) occurs when the baby 'sits' across the exit. In a frank breech (far left) the baby's bottom, but not legs, is first into the birth canal; in a footling breech, one foot appears first.

Vaginal delivery of breech babies

This is usually only possible if:
- The baby is expected to weigh less than 4 kg (8½ lb)
- It is a frank breech.
- There are no obstetric complications.
- The presenting part is engaged.
- The baby's head is tucked down toward the chest.

- Both complete and footling breech babies are difficult to deliver. An elective (a planned) caesarean section is normally carried out.

Coping with a posterior birth

Most babies are born facing your back, and during labour the baby's bottom is pressing on the abdominal wall. Occasionally the baby is the other way around. This does not necessarily make labour more difficult but it can mean that there is pressure on the mother's back, which produces painful backache throughout labour. Babies born face first may progress rather slowly in the second stage.

Do not lie on your back during labour. Keep walking for as long as possible and then crouch or squat. You might find that getting down on all fours is the most comfortable position. If you feel you must lie down to rest, lie on one side and keep your back well rounded.
- A hot-water bottle soothes the back.
- An ice pack numbs the pain.
- Strong counter pressure or fairly aggressive massage applied to the lower back helps ease the pain. Your partner can use his knuckles, the heel of his hand or a tennis ball wrapped in a sock. The pressure needs to be quite intense in order to work. Expect bruising! Some women find that direct pressure works best, others that a firm circular motion brings more relief.
- Apply strong finger pressure just below the centre of the ball of the foot. This is the acupuncture point for backache.
- A forceps delivery is more likely, after which most women are sore. The baby's head may also be bruised and temporarily misshapen.

Birth by caesarean section

A caesarean section is a safe and quick operation. The actual birth only takes about five minutes, but stitching the wound is a longer process, and can take 15 to 20 minutes. In the past a caesarean was carried out under general anaesthetic, but today most are carried out using epidural anaesthesia. This is safer for mother and baby and makes recovery more straightforward. A planned caesarean under epidural is less dangerous than having your tonsils out.

Watching your baby born by caesarean section is not as alarming as it seems: you do not see the cut being made or even have to watch the baby being lifted out. Your view is blocked by a screen.

Reasons for caesarean section

Caesarean sections are usually performed in the following circumstances:
- Breech births (see p. 55).
- Problems associated with the placenta (placenta praevia or placental abruption, see p. 38) or cord.
- Women who have had one or more earlier sections.
- Where the maternal pelvis is too small for normal delivery (this is rare).
- Where the baby's head has not lined up correctly in the birth channel.
- Where pre-eclampsia has not responded to treatment (see p. 38).
- If there are complications. These include active vaginal herpes; maternal diabetes (see p. 37); hypertension or kidney disease; pre-term maternal or foetal distress.
- If a foetus is more than two weeks overdue and/or placental function has diminished.
- If labour has failed to progress after 16 hours.
- Multiple births, especially if the first baby is breech.

What happens during a caesarean section

Before the operation your pubic hair will be shaved, a catheter inserted into your bladder and a glucose drip inserted into your arm. If you are having a general anaesthetic the smallest dose possible is used to avoid any anaesthetic passing to the baby. You will be unconscious for a very short time.

If you have an epidural the needle will be inserted into your lower back. You will feel numb from the waist down, but you will feel pressure during the procedure. A screen is put up so you cannot see the operation taking place.

A small cut is made in the lower abdomen (at about the bikini line). You will feel this being made but it will not hurt. A second cut is then made in the lower part of the womb. The membranes are ruptured and the waters drained. (This sounds as if someone is eating soup rather noisily.) Next the baby is eased out by hand, or hand and forceps. You will feel a pulling or tugging sensation as this is carried out, but again it will not hurt. You will then be given an injection of the hormone oxytocin to help the womb contract.

Next the placenta is removed, and the cord cut and the surgeon will stitch you up. Because each layer is stitched separately, this takes a little time. You will hear the suction tubes draining blood and fluids before the abdominal wall is closed.

The surgeon should explain what he or she is doing at each stage of the operation and may warn you how it will feel. In many hospitals a partner can watch the operation. You or your partner can hold the baby while you are being stitched.

There will be a paediatrician in attendance at the operation, and most babies delivered by caesarean section spend the first hours in intensive care. Do not be alarmed. This is standard procedure in many hospitals and does not mean anything is wrong.

Twins

About one in 80 pregnancies results in a multiple birth – most of them twins, but about one in 90 multiple births are triplets. Carrying more than one baby puts both mother and baby under strain so there is a higher incidence of birth complications and prematurity among twin births. The risk of delivering prematurely is highest between 28 and 32 weeks and mothers should be particularly careful at this time. Rest is vital and you should avoid lifting. Once past 32 weeks the likelihood of premature delivery declines, but in any case few twin pregnancies go to full 40 weeks' term.

The actual delivery need be no more complicated than the delivery of one baby. Twins may both lie head down in the normal birth position, or one or both of them may be breech (see p. 39). Birth is most straightforward if both enter the world head first. If the second baby is breech, forceps are generally used

to lift this baby out after the normal delivery of the first. Both babies are normally delivered by caesarean section if the first-born baby is breech.

Because twins are more likely to be small (either due to prematurity or because they are small for dates) there is a higher probability that they will both spend the early weeks in intensive care. Sometimes the way they lie in the uterus means that one twin has taken the lion's share of the nourishment. As a result, one baby comes home and the other remains in intensive care, which can be particularly difficult for you and your partner.

Coping with two babies is difficult, especially if they are both small. You will need plenty of help in the early weeks and you may need to review your priorities. Remember, babies do not have to be breast-fed, or bathed every day, and it is also perfectly acceptable to leave them in the same clothes for 24 hours occasionally.

THE FATHER'S ROLE

Today, most fathers are present at their child's birth and many describe it as among the most joyous experiences life has to offer. At the time, however, that joy may be clouded by anxiety. It is hard to watch someone you love in pain, especially when there seems to be so little you can do about it. However, women are almost unanimous in saying that having their partners there helped. Pain is a movable feast: our perception of it depends on so many things that we do not fully understand. Sharing the birth with her partner makes a woman feel more secure and reduces the anxiety of giving birth in a strange place. Because it reduces anxiety, it almost certainly reduces the perception of the pain of childbirth too.

Being at the birth may be an anxious time for men, but the anxiety is not reduced by waiting outside. It is easy to imagine the worst. Where studies have been carried out men seem to be more anxious if they wait outside, and whereas a man's anxiety is reduced by seeing and holding the child he watched being born, the absent father's anxiety seems to persist for longer. Once he stops worrying about his partner he starts worrying about the child. A newborn baby looks rather alarming when you have not observed the blood and gore of birth!

Men who attend the birth feel more united with their partners and more in tune with the caring side of their natures. But watching the birth also may make them feel more physically vulnerable. Men's view of their vulnerability is at odds with women's views of them. Those whose partners were present at birth are more likely to see their man as strong, competent and dependable.

Men who are absent from the birth are often those who see children as badges of their manhood; women whose partners choose not to attend the birth are more likely to see them as someone to worry about rather than depend upon. (If your partner will not be there, choose another companion, see p. 21.)

Birth changes the dynamics of a couple's relationship. The shared experience of childbirth reinforces the feelings of being a couple as well as a family. It undoubtedly brings those who share the experience closer together.

FIRST IMPRESSIONS

Your baby can begin to breathe before his body is completely born. Most breathe within two or three minutes of birth though some need their airways cleared first, and others need the stimulation of a slap. Not all babies cry; some gasp or splutter into independent life. It does not matter how they start as long as they are breathing well within the first couple of minutes.

The condition of your baby is assessed at birth according to a checklist known as the APGAR score (see box). You may be unaware of staff doing this.

Babies make breathing movements before birth, but it is amniotic fluid rather than air which is drawn in and out at this stage. Without air the lungs remain flat and sticky. They need the first breath of air to inflate them. They expand and stretch with each breath like a shrivelled-up plant given water. As the lungs expand blood rushes into the capillaries which surround the spongy tissue. The blood gathers the oxygen and transports it to all parts of the body. A new and separate life has begun.

The first minutes

In the first minutes most babies are alert. He may seem smaller than you expected, puffy eyed, rather red, with an oversized head, large genitals, a round abdomen and rather puny looking arms and legs. He is of course beautiful. You will smile and look your baby in the eye – he can focus quite clearly on you when held 20–25cm (8–10in) from your face. Then hands begin to explore, and words of endearment are

APGAR scores

SIGN	POINTS		
	0	1	2
Appearance	Pale or blue	Body pink extremities blue	Pink
Pulse	Not detectable	Below 100	Over 100
Grimace (reflex irritability)	No response to stimulation	Grimace	Lusty cry
Activity (muscle tone)	Flaccid	Some movement of extremities	A lot of movement
Respiration (breathing)	None	Slow irregular	Good (cries)

Babies who score 4–6 often need resuscitation; those who score under 4 need life-saving techniques. A score of 7 or more at five minutes is a good prognosis. Not all babies who have scores lower than this have later problems but some do.

interspersed with questions and comments on how the baby looks. Greeting the baby, parents often behave rather like lovers do after a separation.

In the first minutes mothers often comment how similar the child is to the father. It is as if they wish to draw the father into the relationship but it is rarely necessary. Although some men are nervous of holding the baby and may be at a loss how to behave, most describe watching the birth of their child in a way that shows something is too deeply felt and personal to be put into words: they say things like 'amazing' or 'unbelievable'. For both of you, the exhilaration of birth is overwhelming.

The alert baby

In the first hour most babies are wide awake. You may notice that he looks closely at your face, focusing on your eyes. He may pull faces, poke out his tongue and make little snuffling noises. More alarmingly he may shiver and shudder and may even suddenly stop breathing for a few seconds. All this is quite normal, as is the sleepiness that follows. Having viewed the world most babies curl up and retreat from it. It may be days before he has that look of wide-eyed wonder again. Most babies spend the first few days sleeping.

A small baby's breathing is very soft and shallow, and poor circulation makes him appear very pale. Often it will seem as if he is not breathing at all, which is why many new parents wake their tiny babies to check they are alive. Circulation and breathing matures as he grows, and you will get used to how a baby looks when asleep. Some babies continue for some months to be very pale and still when they sleep.

Is he all right?

'Is he OK?' is often the first question parents ask, even before 'Boy or girl?'. But, in most cases the question does not need to be asked. If something is wrong the medical staff caring for you quickly take over.

About 1 in 25 babies has a congenital abnormality. Half of these are minor – an extra finger, a loose hip, a couple of webbed toes. About 1 in 50 is more serious. Some of these are inherited, some due to damage at birth or soon after (often associated with prematurity). Many have no known cause.

Worries about newborn babies

Major problems are rare, but few babies are born without the odd bump, spot or waxy secretion. The most common are normal and will soon disappear.

The head

The skull of a baby is squeezed by labour and delivery. Because the bones of the skull have not fully fused together, they are free to move, which protects the brain but can leave the head looking a little odd. When the bones have returned to their normal position and swellings gone down, the head will look normal.

A bump on the back of the head is caused by the baby pressing on the cervix before it was fully dilated. Bumps on one or both sides are caused by the pressure of the cervix and vagina and/or by forceps. Bumps disappear within a few days. Dents or grooves caused by forceps also disappear in the first week.

The fontanelle

This is the pulsating soft spot on the top of the head. There is no need to be afraid of touching the fontanelle, nor does it need special care. If you notice that it is taut and bulging, or has shrunk away from the skull, contact your GP or take your baby to hospital.

Jaundice

Jaundice gives the skin a yellowish tinge and can make urine darker. Mild jaundice is common and treated by giving extra fluids and exposure to ultraviolet light; it disappears in a few days. It can make a baby rather sleepy and you may have to wake him for regular feeds. Serious jaundice is usually due to an infection or rhesus incompatibility.

If after returning home jaundice seems worse, give your baby boiled water and call the doctor at once.

The eyes

Most babies are born with puffy eyes, and many have bloodshot eyes. Both conditions soon disappear.

A newborn baby often does not have control of the muscles of his eyes and may have difficulty in focusing, which can make him look as if he is squinting. If it persists beyond three months, a squint should be checked (see pp. 165 and 370).

Watery eyes are common. Usually the cause is a blocked tear duct which will correct itself; it can be treated if it persists. A discharge from the eye may indicate infection and should receive attention straight away. Many infections can be avoided by cleaning your baby's eyes correctly each day (see p. 98).

The mouth

White spots which rub off are milk curds; those that cannot be rubbed off may be thrush (see p. 166).

Babies' tongues are small and they cannot stick them out very far, which often makes them appear to be tied by a membrane attached to the lower jaw. Most are not. A truly tied tongue does not affect feeding or speech.

Very occasionally a baby is born with one or two teeth. These should not affect breastfeeding.

Very pale face

The top of your baby's body may be pale, his trunk red and his limbs blue. This is due to immature circulation and poor temperature control. Keep him in an even temperature – heat the bedroom in winter to about 21° C (70° F) and take care he does not become overheated in summer. Undo or remove outer clothing if you spend time in heated shops or cars.

Spots on the skin

Urticaria neonatorum looks as if the baby has fallen in a bed of nettles. It only lasts a couple of days.

Milia are tiny white spots on the bridge of the nose and cheeks caused by a temporary blocking of sweat glands (see pp. 164–5).

White pearl spots on the body are caused by the mother's hormones and soon disappear.

See p. 341 for other birth marks.

Skin coverings

Lanugo is the downy hair which covers a baby's body in the uterus. An early baby may have some lanugo and premature babies have a significant covering. It disappears in the first few days after the birth.

Vernix caseosa is a waxy substance which covers all babies in the womb. How much is left at birth depends on your baby's maturity. It may seem unsightly but it is safer to leave the vernix in place as it may give the baby protection against infection.

Very occasionally a baby is born with some of the membranes still covering his head and body. So-called caul is traditionally thought to be a sign of good luck.

Other skin problems

Flaky skin is common in newborns, especially on the hands and feet. It is usually caused by the baby being overdue and rarely lasts more than a couple of days.

A wrinkled skin, caused by a long pregnancy, also disappears in the first few days.

Bat ears, or flattened ears

Ears are so soft at birth they can easily be squashed out of shape if your baby lies on them. They are no indication of later size and shape.

The genitals

Boys' and girls' genitals often seem out of proportion with their bodies. As soon as the mother's hormones have passed out of the baby's bloodstream the genitals look more normal. Girls may have milky vaginal secretions or a little vaginal blood, and boys spongy testicles for the same reasons. These also disappear.

Swollen breasts

This happens in both boy and girl babies. Sometimes the breasts have a little milk, also caused by maternal hormones. The milk and swelling soon disappear.

Dark green stools

A baby's first stools are dark green and sticky; this is meconium, digested mucus from the glands which lubricate the bowel. Most babies pass meconium gradually over the first three or four days.

Arms and legs

Extra fingers and toes are common, usually just tiny flaps of skin which are easily removed. Minor bends and twists of the arms and legs usually right themselves once the baby is active. All babies have bow legs.

Girls often have clicking hips, caused by an excess of hormones – it may affect other joints too. Clicks may need treatment (see Your Child's Health, p. 356).

Hernias

An umbilical hernia occurs when a loop of intestine pokes through a weak area of the abdominal muscle and lies under the skin. It usually rights itself in the first few years of life; there is rarely need for surgery.

A bulge above the scrotum in boys is also a hernia and can cause obstruction to the blood vessels; it can be corrected surgically.

YOUR CHANGING BABY

Newborn babies' looks can change quite dramatically in the first months.

Size
Small women have small babies – even if their partners are large – but some of these children grow as tall as their fathers. Early plumpness (or skinniness) can be deceptive. A baby born two weeks early will be thinner than one born a week late, but both may weigh the same at six months. Girls tend to be smaller than boys.

Skin colour
The skin colour of many babies darkens in the first months. Mixed race children are often fairer at birth than they will be later.

Eyes
Caucasian babies have blue eyes at birth. Many darken later. Brown-eyed parents may have blue-eyed children, but the children of two blue-eyed parents remain blue. Dark-skinned children are born with dark eyes.

Nose
A baby's nose looks quite prominent at birth. Sucking develops firm cheek muscles and within weeks he will have a more typical baby face.

Hair
The first hair is often different from later hair both in colour and texture. Early hair falls out gradually over the first months. It can take up to two years for the permanent hair to start to thicken; timing is no indication of later thickness.

Baby skills

At birth a baby will:
- Turn to a voice.
- Prefer high-pitched sounds.
- Move in time to his parents' speech (although the movement is too small to see).
- Recognize his mother's smell (within days).
- Recognize his mother's voice (within a week).
- Prefer salt to sweet (this quickly changes).
- Spend most of his day sleeping, and most of that sleep dreaming (he is dreaming when his eyes move).

At birth a baby will not know:
- That he can make things happen.
- Where his body stops and the rest of the world begins.
- That his mother exists when she has left the room.
- That his mother is not a different person every time he sees her.

At birth a baby cannot:
- Focus on very near or very distant things.
- See anything which is small.
- See colours very well.
- Move fingers independently.
- Remember anything for very long.
See The First Year, pp. 122–49.

Newborns have no muscle control, so heads 'flop'.

Within days, a baby mimics a repeated action.

BONDING

It is sometimes claimed that cuddling and holding a baby in the first few hours after birth is essential for parental bonding to occur. If this were true some fathers and grandparents would never bond to children, but they do. So do those who adopt children. There is no time limit to bonding: it happens when you love and care for a child. In fact up to 70 per cent of mothers say they were not really interested in their baby immediately after the birth, especially if labour was long and tiring.

The word 'bonding' implies something sudden and complete like an application of superglue which quickly sets. While this description will seem absolutely right to about 10 per cent of parents, it is not how most parents describe the growth of love. For them love develops gradually over the first weeks of the child's life.

The growth of love for a baby is no different from the growth of love for any other person. Few sensible people expect to fall instantly in love, nor fear that a relationship is doomed because it began with rather negative feelings about each other. Love for a baby is sometimes instant, at other times it grows.

Being with the baby helps the bonds to grow. Separation in the early days is certainly not good but it is not an insurmountable obstacle to love. A baby that is ill is rarely from your thoughts. Love can grow even though the baby is not with you. A photo of the child will help.

REFLEXES

A reflex is a response which is triggered automatically by a particular stimulus. Whenever the stimulus occurs, the baby makes the response. Adults also have reflexes – the knee jerk which doctors test by tapping just below the knee is one example and there are many more. Some, such as blinking when a puff of air is blown into the eye, are present at birth and remain throughout life. Others that exist at birth are less important as babies grow and disappear with age.

Certain reflexes are checked by your paediatrician or doctor soon after birth, and may be looked at again before you leave hospital, because abnormal or absent reflexes could be a sign of neurological damage.

Rooting, sucking and swallowing are probably the strongest reflexes at birth, since they are vital for your baby's survival.

Rooting reflex

If you touch a baby's cheek he will turn his head to the side touched. He also opens his mouth as he turns and searches for something to suck. If you have difficulty getting your baby latched on to the nipple, you can use this reflex.

Sucking reflex

When he gets his mouth around something – a nipple, teat, or even your finger – a baby lowers his tongue to create a vacuum and then automatically begins to suck.

Newborn reflexes

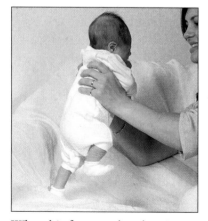

When his feet are placed against a firm surface, a newborn will bend his knees and 'step'.

The grasp of a tiny baby is strong and automatic, in both his fingers and toes.

If your baby is startled by a loud noise, he will throw out his arms and legs and open his hands.

Swallowing

Babies have a swallowing reflex from birth but it takes time to learn to co-ordinate this with breathing. Don't worry if your baby splutters and coughs when your breasts are very full (see p. 73).

The grasp

Babies automatically close their fingers when something touches their palms. Toes work in the same way. Stroke the sole of his foot and your baby will spread then curl his toes. This is called the Babinski reflex. The grip of the hand is strong enough to support the baby's weight at birth and even stronger in premature infants than full term. The grip weakens and is lost from the toes at about three months. It finally disappears from the hands at about seven months, when babies learn to poke and prod and use their fingers independently.

The step

If you hold a newborn baby in an upright position with his feet touching a firm surface he will 'walk'. If you hold him so his feet touch the edge of a solid surface – such as a table – he will lift his leg and step up. Most babies stop walking like this as their legs become plumper, since they do not have the strength to lift heavy legs. Such movements keep the joints from seizing up. Until the baby is mobile the joints are kept flexible by kicking – which is exactly the same movement.

The crawl

When placed on his stomach, a newborn baby will curl up with his knees tucked under his body. In this position he can sometimes creep along. Before it was realized that sleeping on the stomach increased the possibility of 'cot death' (see Your Child's Health, p. 371), many babies were put down to sleep in this position and over the course of a few hours often crept to the top of their cribs.

The Moro or startle reflex

A startled baby spreads his arms and legs with fingers outstretched and back arched. After the stretch he will curl, clenching fingers and toes and bringing arms and legs into his body. Your baby is likely to respond in this way if he is frightened by a sudden loud noise or jolt.

BABIES WITH PROBLEMS

Some babies are born with profound difficulties and will have special needs for the rest of their lives (see Children with special needs, pp. 173–5). Others, for a variety of reasons, may spend time in a special baby-care unit. Finding your baby taken to intensive care does not necessarily mean there is a permanent problem, but it may well be a precaution to make sure specialist staff are on hand at all times to monitor your baby's health.

Low birth-weight babies

A baby whose birth weight is less than 2.5 kg (5½ lb) is considered in need of special care. Some are small because they are born too soon, others because they have grown too slowly in the womb. About 8 per cent of all babies are premature, a smaller percentage are small for dates and many of these will be twins.

Premature babies

The skull of a premature baby is not hard enough to provide good protection for the brain during birth. The passage through the cervix may be so easy and rapid that the baby may arrive at the perineum before it has stretched so the fragile head comes up against the tight perineal muscles and skin. The impact can cause bleeding inside the skull, which damages the brain. Even if the baby escapes such problems it may be too immature to cope with the very different conditions outside the womb, with the result that some premature babies are doubly damaged. Technological advances in the care of such babies now give them the best possible start in life, particularly if they are cared for in one of the up-to-date neonatal intensive care units. Babies born before 24 weeks of gestation or weighing less than 1 kg (2¼ lb) are at greatest risk but many do come out of it unscathed – each case is different.

Small for dates

Some babies are small because they are underfed in the womb. The placenta may not have functioned well, one twin may not have received its fair share of nourishment or the mother may have smoked heavily.

Such babies are small and skinny with few fat reserves and wrinkled, dry and peeling skin.

Because small-for-dates babies have spent longer in the womb, their skull bones are harder and lungs more mature than those of premature babies, so they have fewer problems at the birth. However, the liver is often very small and jaundice is common. They can have quite low levels of blood sugar.

What happens in intensive care

There are many reasons why your baby may be taken to intensive care.

Resuscitation

At birth tiny babies often need resuscitating. All attention switches to them and you may be left without an explanation. It is difficult, but trust the staff – their major concern at this time is your baby.

If a baby does not breathe properly once the nose and mouth are cleared of mucus, he will be given oxygen through a mask. If this does not work a thin tube will be passed into the baby's lungs and oxygen blown in directly. This nearly always succeeds in inflating the lungs and the baby will soon begin to breathe by himself.

This is always an anxious period for new parents. The paediatrician or doctor will be too busy with the baby to explain what is going on, and you may be left in ignorance. Once the immediate crisis is over, it is a good idea for your partner or birth companion to ask for a reasoned explanation to reassure you, as you will be in a highly emotional and anxious state.

Hypothermia

A tiny baby cannot easily control his temperature. If he becomes cold, he cannot easily warm up because he cannot shiver or move about easily. To avoid hypothermia the baby is rapidly removed to a warm incubator. If he has become cold during resuscitation he may be wrapped in foil so that he can warm up gradually as rapid warming is dangerous.

Respiratory distress syndrome

Very small babies often have difficulty breathing because their lungs are immature, a condition known as respiratory distress syndrome. This is treated by increasing the concentration of oxygen in the incubator. Respiration is always monitored electronically with an electrode attached to the baby's chest. An alarm will sound if the baby fails to take a breath and he will be resuscitated. This can happen more than once but the staff in the intensive care unit are trained to act quickly in this situation.

Feeding

If a baby is not mature enough to suck, a tube must be inserted directly into his stomach and small amounts of milk passed down this tube. Sometimes you will be encouraged to express your own milk to feed the baby with, but if the baby is very small and premature, he will may well be given a special formula (see p. 75).

Exchange transfusion

Most premature babies suffer from jaundice because their livers are not mature enough to cope with breaking down the byproducts of foetal blood. These seldom rise high enough to cause concern, but very occasionally the baby may need an exchange

Hospital security

Most hospitals today are open places, with visiting hours – particularly in the postnatal wards – largely unrestricted. The majority of new parents want the freedom that this brings: fathers can be there when they want to be, and friends and relatives can drop in at convenient times. The downside of this, however, is that it is impossible to make hospitals secure.

Although cases always make headline news, baby snatching is very, very rare. But it does make sense to follow some simple guidelines.
- Don't allow anyone to take your baby anywhere without you. If you are told he needs a test, insist on you or your partner going too.
- Don't leave your baby in an empty room. If you are taking a bath or shower, ask one of the other mums to keep an eye on him, or wheel him into the bathroom with you.
- Every member of the hospital staff should have a security badge (not simply a name badge). If anyone approaches your bed without one, ask to see it.

transfusion during which his blood is completely replaced (see Your Child's Health, p. 359).

Getting to know a tiny baby

Getting to know a baby in an incubator is difficult. You will be encouraged to visit often and to stay with the baby but this may not be possible if you have young children or live some distance away. Beds in special-care units are not easy to find, and the one that can accept your baby may not be near your home. If you cannot see your baby every day have a photo (or better still a video) of him and look at it frequently. The staff of the unit will encourage you to touch, hold and feed him as soon as it is safe to do so (you may also be able to express milk for him, see p. 75).

If you find this time stressful (and you would be unusual not to) talking may help. Contact your health visitor, or one of the support organizations – they can almost certainly put you in touch with someone who has been through what you are going through now and come out the other side.

FIRST DAYS

In the days following birth, babies spend most of the time sleeping. This is obvious to all those who have a second baby but not perhaps to those with their first. Life with a first baby is one endless string of things started but never finished and at the end of each day it is hard to say if anything was accomplished or quite how the time was passed.

It is never possible to explain to prospective parents how it feels to be responsible for a baby or why it is so difficult to switch off. If the baby sleeps you check his breathing. If he is in his crib you go to the door and listen. If he sleeps more than four hours you pick him up to make sure he is alive. All of this is supremely tiring, achieves little and leaves no time to get on with the 101 things which must be done, but it is also a perfectly normal reaction of first-time parents. Even reading a book is difficult at first – you are simply too engrossed in the baby. It takes time to learn how to put the baby out of mind while you get on with other things but parents do eventually learn to switch off. Within months you will wonder how on earth a newborn baby could have taken up so much of your time.

First days for the father

Pregnancy and labour may be the mother's show but at the moment of birth it is the father who has the better view. In those first moments, first-time parents are on equal terms with each other as neither knows much about babies, but the equality is fleeting. He goes home to an empty house, you stay with the baby, holding and cuddling him. You soon learn how to pick him up, dress and change him. Your baby smells your smell, hears your voice and feels secure with them. The father is a stranger who has yet to learn any of these skills.

The demands made upon families today are inconsistent. Both parents are expected to work. Both parents are expected to share the care and responsibility of children. Yet there is little possibility of parents spending the night after the child's birth together, unless the birth is at home or discharge is after six hours, which rarely happens for first babies. However, while a mother may appear to have a head start in parenthood, it is important for both parents to accept this and find time at home to allow the father to get to know his baby. If your partner is returning to work after just a short break then this becomes even more important.

Mothers need to relinquish the baby's care to their partner to enable this to happen; fathers need to keep in mind how tiring as well as totally absorbing the care of a new baby can be and gently relieve you of that care when he is at home.

First days for the mother

After labour, mothers need rest but this is not always easy in a room full of other people's babies, or at home with older children or a stream of relations coming to visit. Hospitals used to confine mothers to their beds for two weeks and send babies to the nursery between feeds. In the night babies had bottles while mothers slept. Of course, it is essential to have your baby with you, but if you had a long and difficult labour you may regret that women campaigned so hard for change!

In most of the world tiny babies spend the night in their mothers' arms. When hungry they latch on to the breast and often neither wakes. If you breastfeed, you will find it much easier to combine feeding with a full night's sleep if the baby sleeps in the bed with you or his crib is next to your bed for the first couple of months. You need not be anxious about rolling on your baby while you are asleep – this does not happen, although it is important that you have not been drinking alcohol or taken a sleeping pill. Sleeping with your baby during the early weeks and months does not produce long-term problems providing you teach him to sleep in his cot at other times (see pp. 104–8).

Breast is best but not at the expense of your total exhaustion. A depressed mother can have far more serious implications for her child's development than the occasional bottle. If you are becoming overtired and overwrought the occasional bottle can actually help the establishment of breastfeeding: you will be less anxious if you have allowed your partner to feed the baby while you sleep (with earplugs) in a separate room. Expressing some milk before you go to bed and after the morning feed will ensure that your milk production does not drop. If sleep removes tension, this will also help your milk production. As long as you sterilize bottles, the baby is in no greater danger of illness. The immunity passed to the baby in breast milk does not miraculously stop because you give the occasional bottle (see Feeding Your Baby, pp. 70–83).

Older mothers

A late baby may mean a late conversion to motherhood. Some converts go a little overboard. You don't need to be a perfect mother – good enough will do.

There is no physical reason why women in their 30s or even early 40s should find labour or parenthood more tiring. Many women choose to start their families later so that their careers are properly established before they contemplate taking maternity leave. Most so-called older mothers are in fact more relaxed and better organized than younger mothers – they have already achieved something in their lives and can afford to take time out to enjoy parenthood. However, when problems arise it is often because mothers who have had a structured career expect to achieve something every day. At 20, most women (and men for that matter) are more laid back about the fact that days go by without anything being completed. At that age you are also less set in a method of working which encourages you to concentrate your undivided attention on one topic. (How many 30-year-olds can work with the TV on, as most teenagers do?) At 30-something, however, partners and friends are engrossed in careers. They, like you, find it hard to understand why you cannot even make time to read the newspaper. If you find yourself worrying about this, remember that a baby is a human being and not a machine that can be programmed to work to your preferred schedule. It does help to try to accept this and not to become too anxious about systems and routines.

Before you come home

A preliminary examination of your baby's current health and prospects for the future is carried out at birth (see p. 58). If any problems are suspected the baby will be taken into special care for observation. Babies who are premature, in distress during delivery or born by caesarean, normally spend the first hours in the special care unit where they can be observed more easily. If a baby is very small or if there are potential problems, he will remain in special care.

Before you take your baby home from hospital, the paediatrician will check that all bodily functions are in working order. If you had your baby at home, your family doctor will carry out the checks about five or six days after the birth, and your baby will be checked again at six weeks of age (see pp. 116–17).

Your baby's appearance

The doctor will check whether your baby has a very large or very small head, whether his backbone is normal and if there are signs of Down's syndrome. He or she will check muscle tone, the mouth and eyes. Common problems usually have recognizable signs. You will be told if an abnormality is suspected, and further tests will be given to confirm the diagnosis.

Listening to heart and chest

Some heart problems are evident at this stage; some are discovered later. If the baby remains blue, additional checks may be carried out.

Urine and faeces

The doctor will check that the baby has passed urine and had a bowel movement. Tests will be carried out to check that these are normal. If problems are suspected further tests will be given. Together these indicate that the digestive and urinary system are working well.

Feeding

You will be asked about how your baby is feeding so that the doctor can assess if everything is satisfactory.

Reflexes

His reflexes will be tested. Some problems associated with the nervous system can be detected this way.

Minor abnormalities

He will be checked for jaundice, loose hips, twisted limbs and hernia. If necessary, appointments will be made to recheck these in a week or so.

Infection

The doctor will check that the baby has no obvious signs of infection in the eyes, mouth or ears.

Testicles

The testicles of a baby boy should have descended into the scrotum.

Weight and size

Your baby's initial weight and size, including his body length and head circumference, will be measured.

Guthrie test

A blood sample from a heel prick taken between the third and sixth day after the birth will be tested for thyroid function and PKU (phenylketonuria). PKU is a rare but treatable disorder of the metabolism which, if unchecked, can produce severe mental handicap.

Vision and hearing

Visual and hearing tests are sometimes carried out at this stage. More normally they will be carried out when your baby is six to nine months old.

As well as these formal tests, the hospital staff will simply observe your baby. If they suspect abnormality they will carry out further checks. Similar checks will be carried out at six weeks (see pp. 116–7).

Growth in the first six weeks

At birth the average boy is 52 cm (20^1/$_2$ in) long and the average girl slightly less than that, 50 cm (19^3/$_4$ in). Both grow by about 2 cm(^{3}/$_4$ in) in the first six weeks.

Babies and children do not grow by a fixed amount every week. They grow fastest in the month after birth and slowest just before puberty. The rate of growth declines throughout childhood.

It takes six weeks to gain the first 2 cm (^{3}/$_4$ in), then 12 weeks to gain the second 2 cm (^{3}/$_4$ in), and 24 weeks to gain the next 2 cm (^{3}/$_4$ in). This doubling rule holds until puberty, although growth spurts (see p. 125), obviously, mean that the progression may not be smooth.

In the first week all babies lose weight. By the second week they have usually regained those losses and begun to increase in weight. By six weeks they have usually put on about 900 g (2 lb). As a very rough guide babies gain about 150 g (5 oz) per week. Girls take roughly five months to double their birth weight and about 13 months to triple it. Boys put on weight rather faster, doubling their weight in about four months and tripling it in about 11.

The good-enough parent

No one needs to be perfect. No one should even try. What child could cope with perfect parents? Good parenting is a compromise, a balancing of the needs of all family members – and that includes mothers. If you are a first-time parent, it may help to remember the following points:

- Babies do not need constant attention.
- Babies do not need endless stimulation.
- Babies do not need their nappies changing at night unless they are soiled or sopping wet.
- Babies do not need burping.
- Babies can sleep in your bed.
- Babies can have dummies.
- Bottlefeeding does not mean you have failed as a mother.
- Babies can be top and tailed two days in a row.
- Your partner can (and should) be left in charge.
- Some babies actually like wet nappies.
- Small babies do not miss their parents if they go out for the evening.
- Competent babysitters can look after babies.

CHAPTER THREE

Feeding Your Baby

Holding a tiny baby in your arms as you feed her is one
of the most emotionally fulfilling experiences of
parenting a young child. Watching her grow and
thrive is one of the most rewarding. How to feed
your baby, however, is one of the most loaded
issues. This chapter presents the facts
about breast- and bottlefeeding
so that you can decide
how you want to feed
your baby.

Breast or bottle?

The best way to feed your baby is the way that feels right for you. Breastfeeding is best for the health of your baby, but if you are uncomfortable about the whole idea, forcing yourself is going to help neither you nor her. So, how do you decide whether to breastfeed, or to give your baby formula milk in a bottle? For many mothers, there is no choice: they feel very strongly that they want to do one or the other, and cannot imagine even trying the other way. But if you are undecided, or genuinely wonder which method would suit you and your baby best, there are some points you need to know.

BIRTH TO SIX WEEKS

The first six weeks of your baby's life are when feeding becomes established. Most problems – if any – are usually resolved by the end of this time.

The facts about breastfeeding

It would be wrong of anyone to try to persuade you to breastfeed if you have deep feelings against it. But health professionals, and books such as this, do well to present the facts so that whatever your choice, you are making it on the basis of good information.

Breast milk has health advantages

This is unsurprising as breast milk, like all mammals' milk, is species specific – it has been 'designed' to offer optimum nutrition for baby humans. Formula milk is usually cow's milk, modified in the factory to make it more digestible for a new baby's system.

Breastfeeding offers significant protection against gastroenteritis, respiratory disease and ear infections in babyhood. In the longer term, it helps protect against the development of childhood diabetes and some childhood cancers. It may have a role in the prevention of allergy, and offer some protection against cot death. There are indications that it promotes intelligence, too.

It is not always understood why breast milk 'works' in these ways, but it is known to contain valuable antibodies which protect the baby in the first few weeks and help build up her immune system.

Breastfeeding is good for you

Mothers who breastfeed have less chance of pre-menopausal breast cancer. When breastfeeding is going well, it feels good. It promotes the secretion of hormones which help you relax while you feed – and many mothers derive great satisfaction from seeing how their babies thrive when fed on their breast milk.

Breastfeeding and medication

If your doctor advises you not to breastfeed because of your medical condition or because of medication prescribed for you, you may want to seek a second opinion. In very rare instances, breastfeeding may be ruled out. In other cases, your medication can be changed, or suspended or the dose may be altered to make breastfeeding possible. Some mothers with conditions such as epilepsy, for example, can learn to time their medication, and their feeds, so that the drug is not present in the milk when the baby feeds.

This, of course, takes organization and motivation, and plenty of support. If you know in advance that your medical history may be a problem to breastfeeding, discuss the whole issue with your health visitor or a breastfeeding counsellor, so that you can make an informed decision.

Breast milk is made independent of your nutritional status. Unless you are truly and consistently undereating, your breast milk will always be high quality, and suited to your baby's stage of development and growth. You will have enough breast milk, too – as few as 2 per cent of all women, according to World Health Organization estimates, have real underlying physiological difficulties in making enough milk for their babies.

Breast milk is, however, far more than a way of getting top-quality nutrition into a baby's stomach. Breastfeeding in modern Western society is not always easy, and understandably many women give up and turn to bottlefeeding. It is true to say that most problems are caused by avoidable factors and with help and support can be overcome.

Breastfeeding and your feelings

Your breasts may be linked in very powerful ways to your feelings about your body. You – or your partner – may be embarrassed by breastfeeding and may find the prospect of feeding in front of other people unwelcome – even though this can be done very discreetly (see box).

How breastfeeding works

You will make breast milk whether or not you intend to breastfeed. At first, the breasts produce colostrum, a highly concentrated fluid, rich in protective substances, that appears toward the end of pregnancy and for the first few days after the birth. This then changes to breast milk, under the influence of the hormone called prolactin which is secreted after delivery. This process is known by many as the milk 'coming in'.

You may feel this surge of milk production as a fullness, although it is possible you will not, especially if your baby has fed well from the start, in which case she will deal with the extra as it is made. Some mothers experience engorgement: when the breasts are so full of fluid – not just milk – they are truly uncomfortable (see p. 73). Your breasts may leak milk, in which case put breast pads or clean cotton handkerchiefs in your bra. If you do not want to wear a bra at night (you may be more comfortable if you do), you may find it helps to sleep on a towel. After the first few days, breast milk is made in direct

Discreet breastfeeding

It is worth thinking about your attitude to breastfeeding your baby in front of others before she is born, and to discuss them with your partner. If you find the idea unwelcome, there are ways around it.

- Choose clothes with care. Some tops have zips which enable you to undo one breast at a time in such a way that no one can see anything. Most loose tops and teeshirts enable you to feed your baby without your breasts being visible and a shawl or wrap hides everything.
- Go to a different part of the room, or a different room altogether. Alternatively, lie on the sofa with the baby in front of you.
- Find out which stores, restaurants, gyms and so on have parent and child rooms: local NCT branches and other organizations may have information. Some of the chain stores, especially those which specialize in baby clothes and equipment, have good facilities for breastfeeding mums.

Remember that a baby being discreetly fed is less noticeable than one who is crying because she is hungry. Once your baby is feeding well, breastfeeding her is likely to feel so natural that you will probably be able to feed her in almost any situation, regardless of how you thought you might react.

response to the baby feeding so this excess is less likely to be as great a problem. This process is twofold:

- the baby's suck stimulates the hormone oxytocin, which works on the storage areas inside the breast, and causes the 'let down reflex', pushing the milk down into the ducts and toward the nipples; and
- the removal of milk from the breast stimulates the hormone prolactin, which makes more milk to replace the milk taken away by the baby at that particular feed.

Prolactin levels remain high at first, which is why mothers continue to make milk for some time even if they are bottlefeeding. But the only way to ensure a good milk supply is to feed your baby as often as she wants, so that you pass on the right 'orders' to your body. Frequent feeding is normal initially.

What to expect

Feed your baby as soon as you can after delivery. If you are both well, there is no reason to delay it, and your baby can make use of that alert period straight after birth to come to your breast and to start learning about your taste and smell. Not all babies want to feed at this stage, but it is a good idea to give yours the opportunity to do so. In any case, the oxytocin produced as a response to your baby's suck stimulates the uterus to contract, which assists the delivery of the placenta.

For the first couple of days, babies vary. Some seem sleepy and uninterested in feeding, others feed very often – every two hours or more – and there are many other normal variations in between. When your milk comes in, however, your baby is likely to want to feed often. Between six and a dozen sessions at the breast in 24 hours are quite usual. This pattern may seem unpredictable, and time-consuming, and confusing – you may never be quite sure when your baby is likely to want to feed again, and may not always know when she has finished. But it tends not to last. If it did, no mothers of more than one child would manage to breastfeed their babies as well as getting breakfast for their older children and taking them to school – yet many do.

As long as your baby is showing signs of contentment and satisfaction some of the time, this feeding pattern simply indicates that she is establishing your milk supply, learning to feed and to adjust to the world outside. If she shows frustration, crying and she has frequent unsettled bouts of misery, it could mean that your feeding technique and management need some adjustment. Don't struggle on. Get help – see p. 74.

By three or four weeks of age, many babies are already a good deal more settled in their feeding behaviour, although there may still be occasions when they feed more often than the day before.

Night feeds

Your baby is likely to need feeding in the night for some time. One or two night feeds are normal for the first few weeks, and some babies need more. Very few babies sleep through the night before they are about 12 weeks (many take considerably longer). You can, however, expect your baby to have her longest sleep during the night. If she shows signs of having her

How to breastfeed

In order to breastfeed successfully, make sure that both you and your baby are comfortable before you begin. Choose a comfy chair that supports you well. If your baby is crying she may feed better if you soothe and calm her first.

If your baby is not well latched on, you can get sore or cracked nipples and it can be difficult for your baby to stimulate a good milk supply.

Make sure that she remains close in to your breast; if she is slipping off the breast, she is not properly latched on. Many babies take themselves off the breast after a good feed, tired and delightfully full: this is not the same as coming off in frustration because she cannot get at the milk waiting in your breast.

If your breasts are heavy and floppy, support them from underneath, but don't press on them from above.

Breast milk is food and drink in one. It even becomes more watery in very hot weather, so you do not need to give your baby any other fluids to satisfy her thirst. Giving other drinks, whatever they are, can interfere with the supply–demand production of breast milk. There is certainly no good reason to give anything else, nor is there any evidence that water, herbal drinks, or specially formulated baby fruit juices helps with wind or colic.

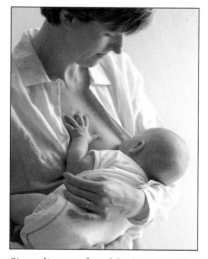

Sit or lie comfortably (see p. 74). Hold your baby on her side, so that she is chest to chest to you, with her mouth close to your nipple. She should not have to twist, turn or bend her head to feed and you should not have to slot your nipple into her mouth. You may need patience at first.

days and nights mixed up, and is awake more often at night than during the day, try changing her pattern by waking her up during the day.

Keep night feeds low key, to make them easier for yourself and to help your baby settle back to sleep as soon as she feels full. Do not change her nappy unless you have to: if it has leaked, for example, or if she has a sore bottom that could be irritated by a wet or dirty nappy. Keep the lights low, and try to rest yourself while you are feeding her.

You can feed your baby in your bed, and many mothers find this is the easiest way to doze off and conserve their energy. Lie down with your baby next to you. Make sure she does not get too hot under your bedclothes – it is safest to have a shawl or sheet over her, rather than slipping her under your own quilt.

Coping with problems

Although breastfeeding is the most natural and time-honoured way of feeding babies, at times it can feel anything but that.

Many mothers give up breastfeeding after a short time, and never reach the stage where they can really enjoy it, relishing the facts that it is quick, easy, convenient and cheap. Surveys show that mothers rarely give up because they feel they have breastfed long enough, or as long as they planned to. Far more common are reasons such as sore nipples, or anxiety about whether or not they have enough milk for the baby. Most problems can be overcome, often quite quickly, with the right information, encouragement and support.

Engorgement

This is most common in the first days, although it can happen at any time. Engorgement means that the breasts are uncomfortably, even painfully, swollen. If your baby is feeding well, the problem is likely to go by itself after a short time. If it does not, gentle expressing (see p. 77) to take off just enough milk to soften the breasts will help.

Sore and/or cracked nipples

A certain amount of tenderness as you and your baby learn about breastfeeding is normal. But soreness that gets worse rather than better, and that is painful rather than tingling or uncomfortable, needs dealing

When she opens her mouth wide, bring her on to your breast. If she is taking the breast correctly, her tongue will be forward and out, pushing her lower lip so that it rolls over. Her nose and chin will be touching, or almost touching, your breast. This is known as latching on.

If she is correctly positioned, there should be more of your areola showing above her top lip than below. Don't press on your breast – this could inhibit the free flow of milk through the ducts. Short, quick sucks at the start of the feed are normal with deeper glugs as the feed gets underway.

When she has finished one breast, offer the second. Some babies have one breast at each feed, others both; or one sometimes and two at others. If you need to take her off the breast for any reason, break the suction by inserting your finger into the corner of her mouth.

Help with breastfeeding

If you find it difficult, or if you are slightly concerned or puzzled about anything, seek help from someone who knows and understands about breastfeeding. If you are still in hospital, midwives there will help you. Some maternity units have a specialist adviser, usually a midwife with an interest in breastfeeding. At home, contact a community midwife, or your health visitor or one of the breastfeeding support groups. The National Childbirth Trust has a network of breastfeeding counsellors. You do not need to be a member to make use of this service. Look up local members in your phone book or contact the national headquarters (see Useful Contacts, pp. 248–51). La Lèche League also helps mothers who want to breastfeed (see pp. 248–51).

with straight away. Do not just grit your teeth, curl your toes and tell yourself to put up with it.

The most common cause of sore nipples is poor positioning of the baby at the breast (see pp. 72–3).

In fact, if you are sore and have never had any period of pain-free breastfeeding, you can be sure your baby's position needs changing. It is likely that she is sucking too close to the end of the nipple and does not have enough breast tissue in her mouth. The result is that the nipple rubs against your baby's hard palate as she sucks, or she pinches the nipple in order to keep it in her mouth.

Ask a breastfeeding counsellor or health professional to help you check the way your baby takes the breast into her mouth and how she sucks once she is there. If you need to break the suction for any reason once your baby is latched on, gently insert your finger into the corner of her mouth.

If you have had a period of pain-free feeding, then become sore, thrush may be the cause (see p. 166), although positional soreness can exist alongside thrush. You need medication for you and your baby from your GP.

Creams and lotions recommended for soreness do no good if the positioning of the baby at your breast is not corrected, although you may find that they soothe already-sore nipples, while the healing process takes place and the baby latches on in a different way.

Comfortable breastfeeding

In the early weeks you may spend a great deal of time breastfeeding; if you are not comfortable, not only will you find it more difficult to relax and enjoy feeding, but you also run the risk of backache and a stiff neck and shoulders.

Try out different positions and different chairs until you find the one that suits you best. If you prefer to sit, you may find an armchair or the sofa does not offer you enough support and, perhaps surprisingly, you will be more comfortable on something firmer. Make sure that both your feet reach the floor – put them on a box or a couple of thick books if they don't. A cushion in the small of your back may also help you feel more comfortable.

As your baby gets bigger and heavier, supporting her on a couple of cushions on your lap, may reduce strain on your back.

Finally remember that what works best at one stage or even one time of day may be less comfortable at others; be flexible.

Breastfeeding may be easier if you lie on your side with your head propped up comfortably. You may find a cushion helps. You can lie on the floor, bed or sofa, but if you choose the latter make sure it is wide enough – you cannot relax if you are worried about you or the baby being too close to the edge.

Nipple shields – used to protect a sore nipple – cut down on the milk available to the baby, and confuse her suck. Some babies become hooked on the shield and cannot then feed from a breast without them. If you use a shield, bear all this in mind and try to get rid of it as soon as you can.

Mastitis

Mastitis is an inflammation of the breast which can be, though it does not have to be, an infection. Mastitis usually begins when a duct (one of the pathways that take milk to the holes in the end of the nipple) becomes banked up with milk. A plug of milk blocks the duct, and starts to leak into the surrounding tissue, causing redness, and possibly swelling, tenderness and pain. It can be extremely uncomfortable to feed from the affected breast, but it is important that you do not just stop. If it is left, mastitis can become infected and a breast abscess – which may need hospital treatment to drain – can result.

Gentle massage, hot and cold compresses, feeding the baby first on the affected side can all help shift the plug. See your doctor or midwife if these measures do not begin to help straight away.

Not enough milk

While mothers almost always have the physiological ability to nourish their babies fully on breast milk alone for the first four to six months of life, not producing enough milk is a real phenomenon. If milk production is not stimulated well enough at the start, it is more difficult to build up a satisfying supply.

Giving bottles of formula in the early days and weeks fills the baby up, stops her being hungry for the breast and fools your body into thinking that breast milk does not need to be made. And if the bottle teat confuses her suck and makes it harder for her to get used to the breast again, there will be even less stimulation of the breast.

Poor positioning can also lead to a poor supply, as can trying to restrict the times and frequency of feeds.

If you think you may have a problem with your milk supply, check your positioning and let your baby feed as often and as long as she wants, staying on the first breast until she comes off by herself before offering the second. And try to fit in more feeds for a day or so.

It is also possible that your worries about not having enough milk are groundless. If your baby is

Feeding pre-term and special care babies

Babies who are born pre-term or who need special care after the birth can still be breastfed, although very tiny or sick babies may need tube feeding with expressed breast milk at first. It is a good idea to start expressing as soon as you can (see p. 77) to stimulate milk production. At first you may produce only a few millilitres, but this can still be used and is especially valuable to special care babies since they are more vulnerable to infection. As soon as your baby is well enough, hold her close to your breast so that she gets to know your smell and taste – even if she is not breastfeeding yet.

It is more and more common for special care babies to be given expressed breast milk from a little cup, once they move on from tube feeding, instead of a bottle and teat, which could teach them the wrong sucking action.

gaining weight well enough according to your clinic (even if the weight gain is erratic, as it often is in breastfed babies) and appears to be thriving, the chances are that there is nothing wrong with your supply. Seek support from other people who are confident about breastfeeding, and do not feel that every squeak from your baby is a sign that she might be hungry. A breastfeeding counsellor (see box opposite) will be able to help you decide about supply and what is and is not normal.

Baby fails to latch on/fights at the breast

Some babies just do not latch on easily at the start, and seem to get cross and frustrated; others seem to get ever more reluctant and even hostile to the breast. Often, the background of these babies indicates they have been handled roughly at the start of feeding, perhaps by someone who has tried to ram their head toward the breast. The situation can be compounded by the use of bottles and/or nipple shields (used to try to get the nipple into a shape the baby can grab or to draw out an inverted nipple).

If your baby feeds like this, and every feed seems to be a battle, you may need a lot of patience and skilled help. Your baby needs to learn that breastfeeding is easy, pleasant and rewarding, and the sooner you can get help and support, the more likely it is that you will overcome this hurdle. If it is a slow process, express your milk (see opposite) and give it to your baby by letting her sip it from a cup (this is better than giving a bottle of expressed milk, as a cup is less likely to condition her sucking wrongly).

Your baby is sleepy

Some babies are reluctant to feed, and sleep rather than make the effort to rouse themselves sufficiently. This may be only temporary, often the result of a long and tiring birth, or a side effect of drugs used during delivery. Be patient, and try not to resort to a bottle – which is easier to give, as the teat can be pushed into the half-open mouth of a drowsy baby – unless you are given a medical reason why your baby needs formula.

What you need

Looking after yourself, primarily by resting and eating well, is often considered crucial to the success of breastfeeding but, in fact, mothers all over the world breastfeed under adverse physical and dietary conditions. The breast milk produced is inevitably of high quality, and as long as the baby feeds unrestrictedly, the quantity is sufficient, too. It is, however, important to look after your health while you are breastfeeding, for your own sake. You will feel better, and have more energy to care for your baby, if you eat regularly, and listen to your body's needs when it comes to sleep and rest.

You do not need to eat anything special when breastfeeding, or to avoid any foods. Occasionally, mothers report that eating a certain food seems to

Breastfeeding twins

If you want to breastfeed twins, and these are your first babies, be prepared to spend a good deal of your day and night breastfeeding until it is well established. Once it is underway, however, you will produce milk in response to your babies' needs and there will be plenty for both. Ask your health visitor or a counsellor for help and advice in establishing feeding.

When your babies are very tiny, you may be able to cradle them both in your lap. Sit well supported, either crosslegged on the floor, or on the bed.

Sit well supported with each baby on a cushion in front of you. Tuck the babies' legs under your arms and cradle their heads with your hands as they feed.

A combination of the first two options may suit you best. Tuck one baby under your arm, supporting her head with your hand, while the other is cradled in your lap with her head supported on your arm.

Even when feeding is established, it may be still be easier to hold both babies in your lap. Use pillows and cushions to support yourself and them. Alternatively, you could lie back with them on top of you – this makes night feeds easier.

As long as one baby is prepared to wait, separate feeding may be easier. Sit on the sofa. Cradle the feeding baby in your lap and lie or prop the second one so that you can play with her. Try not to feed the same baby first each time.

Expressing milk

If you want to continue giving your baby breast milk but want the occasional few hours away from her, it is worth learning to express your milk. It can be difficult at first, but once your milk supply is established, it gets a great deal easier. Hand expressing is one way; the alternative is to buy a hand pump. (If your baby is pre-term or spends time in a special care baby unit, you will be asked if you want to express your milk using an electric pump.)

There are different pump designs on the market, but all work in a broadly similar way; simply follow the directions for use with the pump. Always sterilize it before use.

A breastfeeding counsellor or your health visitor can show you how to express by hand.

1 Wash your hands and sterilize a feeding bottle or large bowl. Support your breast in one hand and start to massage toward the nipple. Gently work your way all round the breast, at least half a dozen times to encourage the milk flow.
2 Stroke downward toward your nipple several times with your fingertips, but avoid pressing on your breast tissue. Press gently on the area behind the areola with your thumbs and fingers.
3 Press your breast tissue back while squeezing your thumbs and fingers together. Drops of milk should begin to flow through your nipple. Do this for a couple of minutes, then repeat the whole process with your other breast.
4 Keep massaging and squeezing alternate breasts until the flow slows down or until you want to stop.

Expressed breast milk keeps, covered and in a sterile container, for up to 24 hours in the fridge and for about three months in the freezer. It is quicker to defrost if you store it in ice cube trays – you can also match what you need to your baby's appetite.

---

result in a lot of crying or windiness in their baby and, although it is difficult to prove, it is possible that traces of some foods affect the breast milk. There is no case for deliberately cutting out fruit, fruit juice, sprouts, curry or anything else you may hear is bound to affect your breast milk, until you are sure it always causes a problem. There is some evidence that dairy products can cause colicky crying in babies, but the research is contradictory. If you have a baby who seems to cry a lot, consult your health visitor or doctor before cutting out anything major from your diet. If you do this permanently, you may have to adjust other parts of your diet to compensate.

It is normal to feel thirsty while you are breastfeeding, especially at first. Drink according to your thirst. Making efforts to increase your fluid intake – some books suggest litres a day – over and above what you want to drink, is pointless.

Limit your alcohol intake, do not take up smoking again and consult your doctor or pharmacist before taking any medicines while you are breastfeeding.

Bottlefeeding from the beginning

If you have made the choice to bottlefeed, either from the very start, or in the first few days before breastfeeding has really got underway, you do not need to wind down your breast milk supply. Although you may be uncomfortable for a few days – your body makes milk simply as a result of pregnancy and delivery, whether or not your baby uses it – this fullness should disappear as the supply is not stimulated by the baby coming to the breast (if you change your method of feeding at a later stage, you may need to introduce bottles more gradually, see pp. 84–5). Wear a well-supporting bra during this time.

The only non-human milk suitable for a young baby is a recognized infant formula, most of which are based on cow's milk. A few babies are unable to digest the protein in cow's milk, and milk based on soya is usually recommended for them. There are also formulas made from goat's milk, but what advantage these may have over cow's milk formula is not clear.

Formula manufacturers change the composition of their milks from time to time, in line with both research and the cost of raw ingredients. Your midwife should have up-to-date knowledge of the main differences between the various products on the market. However, there are two main types of formula – whey based and casein based. This refers to the major source of protein in the milk. Whey-based milks are sometimes branded as 'stage one' milk, and marketed as 'closer' to breast milk with the result that most babies start off on a whey-based formula. Mothers often make the change to a casein-based formula later on (see p. 86), although there is no nutritional reason for doing so.

You can expect your new baby to need several small feeds in a day at first – about six to eight is typical. Because formula milk takes longer to digest than breast milk, bottlefed babies tend to feed rather less frequently than breastfed ones. After the very first days, she may take up to 100 ml (3½ fl oz) of formula at a time, although it may well be more or less so be guided by her appetite. As she gets older, she is likely to have more milk, in five or six feeds, and take about 200 ml (7 fl oz) at a time.

In hospital, you will probably use ready-to-feed formula, in pre-sterilized bottles. These bottles are useful standbys and ideal if you are out and about, but they are expensive to use every day (you can also buy ready-to-feed formula in cartons). At home, powdered or granulated milk, which you mix with water and give in bottles you sterilize between each use, is more economical.

What you need

Modern bottles are made of plastic, marked to show fluid levels. You will need at least six 200 ml (7 fl oz) size bottles as a basic, and perhaps the same number of 100 ml (3½ fl oz) bottles to use at first. Teats are made of silicone or latex rubber. Silicone teats last longer; latex ones are softer. Most babies can use either, and there is no advantage in choosing one over the other. Generally speaking, small holes in the end of the teat are used for younger babies, who then progress to using teats with larger holes as they grow. (You can always enlarge existing holes with a razor blade. Do not make holes too large, however, or your baby may splutter and choke.)

'Orthodontic' or 'natural shape' teats are sold as being 'closer' to the shape of a mother's nipple. This may be so, but sucking on them does not imitate breastfeeding, as the baby's mouth and tongue are in a different position entirely. Some babies do, however, develop a preference for one shape over another, probably because they get used to it.

Crying and feeding

Crying is one way – and the major way – in which your baby can show you that she is hungry. This is not a problem in itself if she is feeding well, and the feed – whether breast or bottle – comforts and satisfies her. Frequent feeding is normal in the early weeks. However, if you feel she often cries with hunger because the feed does not fill her up, or leaves her happy for only a short period of time, speak to your health visitor or midwife. This may be no more than the erratic, unpredictable behaviour associated with newborn babies getting used to the world and a new way of feeding, but it may also indicate a problem that needs dealing with now.

A bottlefed baby may need more formula than the guidelines for weight and age normally suggested; a breastfed baby may simply need to be fed more frequently than you were expecting, perhaps only for a short time to build up your supply. Alternatively, she may be poorly positioned and not getting a good, satisfying feed. Poor positioning can lead to the baby crying with frustration and – possibly – hunger, after a breastfeed, yet refusing the breast if it is offered again, or taking it for only a few seconds before turning away.

Some breastfed babies take what they need in a comparatively short time, particularly as they get older. Your baby may cry simply because she does not want any more, and does not want you to keep trying to keep her on the breast.

Persistent crying is not a trivial problem, whatever causes it – seek help for you and your baby (see also Babies and crying, pp. 101–4).

Making a bottlefeed

When you buy a bottle, you will also usually get a cap (this fits inside the teat holder and allows you to cover the bottle for storage in the fridge without a teat) and a teat holder which screws on the neck of the bottle. Most bottles also come with a cover, which allows you to place the teat on top of the closed bottle for transportation without leakage or spillage.

You will also need tins or packets of dried formula (or – if you only give the occasional bottlefeed – cartons of ready-to-feed formula), plus sterilizing equipment. Always wash your hands before you start.

If you have used chemicals to sterilize the bottles, rinse them with cooled, previously boiled water to get rid of the taste.

All formula packs have instructions on them. You must be as accurate as possible when measuring out the milk; use the measuring scoop provided, rather than your own measure, and do not pack the milk down into it – you could dramatically increase the amount of milk that way.

You may find it easier to make up a whole day's feeds at a time. Made-up formula is safe to use for 24 hours as long as it is stored in the fridge, either in closed bottles with the caps on, or a lidded jug (but choose a jug with an accurate measure on the side and be sure to sterilize the jug too).

If you store a bottle in the fridge before giving it to your baby, you may find that she prefers it warmed. To do this, stand the bottle in a jug of hot water for a few minutes. Microwaving is not safe – the heat-through may not be even, and hot spots in the milk could scald your baby. Check the milk by shaking a few drops out on to your wrist. It should feel warm but not hot.

Sterilizer for use with chemicals

Formula

Bottle

Cap

Teat and teat holder

1 Boil the water you are going to mix with the milk powder. Pour the water into the bottle or jug up to the required level.

2 Add the right quantity of milk powder to it. Use the scoop provided, levelling off excess powder with a knife.

3 Shake or stir well so that the powder dissolves. If you are giving the bottle straight away, cool it under cold running water.

4 If you are storing it for later, cover with the top provided and keep in the fridge. Transport cold in a cool bag.

Keeping it all clean

Bottlefed babies do not have the protection against gastroenteritis that breast milk gives them, and warm milk, of any sort, is a great breeding ground for bacteria, so it is vital to be careful about cleanliness when you are bottlefeeding.

After each use, wash the bottle thoroughly in hot water with detergent. Make sure the inside and the thread of the screw neck are free of all traces of milk. Wash the teats inside and out, and wash the screw-on teat holders that fix on the neck of the bottle. Keep a bottle brush just for your baby's bottles to help you do all this properly (if you buy a complete feeding set, one should be included). Rinse everything in clean water, then sterilize using one of three methods – boiling, chemicals or steam.

The sterilizing routine is a chore until you are used to it, but you need to do it until your baby is at least nine months. It is easier to sterilize several bottles at a time, and keep them aside ready for the next feed.

Giving a bottle enables fathers to feel close to their small babies and play a real part in this basic aspect of their care.

- Boiling is useful if you only give the occasional bottle, but it is tedious to boil six bottles, teats and so on every day, as you may need more than one pan load. To sterilize in this way, boil a large pan of water and put everything you want to sterilize into it. Keep the water boiling and all items immersed (with no trapped air bubbles) for 10 minutes.
- Steaming is convenient and quick. Do it in a purpose-made electric steam sterilizer, which stands on your kitchen worktop and is designed to hold a day's worth of equipment. If you have a microwave oven, you can buy a steam sterilizer for use in this, for even quicker results.
- Chemical sterilizing uses cold water with sterilizing fluid or tablets made for baby feeding equipment. You immerse the items in a special tank, or other suitable container (such as a large plastic bowl) and leave them for the specified time. You need to use a fresh solution every 24 hours. Rinse off all traces of sterilizing solution with cooled, boiled water when you remove the items from the solution.

Once your feeding items are sterilized, you can keep them covered and away from any potential germs, and use them when you need to.

Giving the feed

Hold your baby close, and always tilt the bottle so the teat is full of milk to prevent your baby swallowing a teat full of air as she sucks (she is bound to swallow some air). Every so often you will have to remove the teat from her mouth so that the teat resumes its former shape: teats tend to collapse with sucking, and this stops the milk flowing through. Your baby will probably need to stop once or twice during the feed, and after it, to let any wind come up as a burp.

Do not insist that your baby finishes the feed if she has clearly had enough; let her appetite be your guide. And do not keep left-over milk from one feed to another. Throw it away.

Other needs

In hot weather, a bottlefed baby may need a drink of water to satisfy thirst. Boil the water first and then cool it before giving it to your baby. You need to boil the water, even if it is bottled mineral water, to make sure any bacteria are killed. Any mineral water you give your baby should be labelled as safe for babies – some types are very high in sodium or other salts.

SIX WEEKS TO FOUR MONTHS

After the first few weeks, both breast- and bottle-feeding tend to get easier and you and your baby get more used to a routine.

Breastfeeding

By the time your baby is about six weeks old, you are likely to be reaching a point where breastfeeding is easy, comfortable and enjoyable – even if you have had problems earlier on.

Your baby may still have times when she seems to need feeding more often – this is reflected in her growth, which will probably not be a smooth incline up the graph. This is normal; if you feed her as often as she asks, it is highly likely that your baby will revert to her previous pattern in a couple of days or so. It is usual for a baby of around three months to have six breastfeeds in 24 hours, with one of those feeds at night, and the others spread at fairly regular intervals through the day and evening.

Changes you will notice

Your baby may take less time – often dramatically less time – at the breast. This does not mean that she is 'going off' breastfeeding, so do not try to get her to stay on for longer than she wants. If she feeds when she wants, and comes off the breast happily by herself, the chances are that she is getting what she needs – even if she seems to you to be feeding for no more than a few minutes.

The major reason for this change is that you are producing more efficiently, and the let-down reflex is working beautifully, and your baby's skills in getting herself positioned correctly first time, and in sucking and swallowing have developed, too.

There is still likely to be at least the occasional feed which your baby likes to linger over – and times when she wants to be on and off the breast for an hour or two, especially in the evening when she is winding down to go to sleep. These are all normal variations, and unless your baby seems constantly or frequently unhappy, or shows signs of frustration, or appears to be unable to feed, these patterns do not indicate poor feeding or a feeding problem.

Coping with wind

Bottlefed babies, in particular, swallow a lot of air as they feed. This may make your baby uncomfortable; it could also make her feel full temporarily, but leave her hungry a short time later. When your baby – whether breast- or bottlefed – pauses, give her the chance to bring up any wind that may be trapped, without getting obsessive about waiting for a burp before you let her continue.

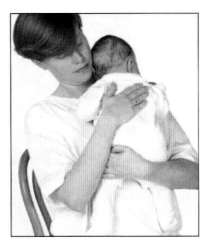

1 Place a cloth over your shoulder. Hold your baby so that her head is on your shoulder (support her head when she is tiny) and gently rub her back.

2 Alternatively, lie her across your knees and rub her back. You may need to put a cloth on your knees or on the floor since she will bring a little milk up too.

3 Once your baby is able to sit for short periods, cuddle her in your lap and rub her back gently so that any trapped air is released as a burp.

Changing your mind

It may be possible to build up your milk again after a period of bottlefeeding: this is known as relactation. Putting your baby to your breast often may be enough to start things up. A device called a nursing supplementer can give formula at the same time as the baby is on the nipple – a breastfeeding counsellor will help you to obtain one. Think carefully before you embark on relactation, though. It depends on having a baby who is happy to co-operate, and it takes time, energy and a lot of commitment. Remember: there is nothing to stop you putting your baby to the breast whenever she needs comfort and closeness, even if you have stopped feeding her in this way.

The other major change is one that may happen to you. At some stage, you may notice your breasts feel softer than they were when breastfeeding was just becoming established. You notice less of a dramatic change from the way your breasts feel full before your baby comes to you for a feed, and the much emptier feeling afterward. There may be times – for example, first thing in the morning if your baby has managed to sleep through the night – when your breasts do seem rather uncomfortable but, in the main, they now look and feel rather more like your breasts did before you became pregnant.

This does not mean you have run out of milk; quite the reverse. In the early weeks, the breasts are prone to overproduce. Now that feeding is well established, your breasts have replaced the fat that used to give them their fullness with milk-producing and storing tissue, which is not as bulky. And you are now making milk efficiently and in response to your baby's needs, without too much excess. Levels of prolactin (the milk-producing hormone) gradually fall during the first months after delivery, with the result that milk production becomes much more dependent on the baby's sucking action and the amount she takes at each feed.

You can still have problems breastfeeding a baby of this age, just as in the early days (see pp. 71–6), but as before, the right information and advice should sort them out.

Bottlefeeding

Bottlefed babies are likely to be more settled and predictable in their feeding habits by about six weeks, but it is still common for mothers to change formula in response to what they perceive as a lack of satisfaction in their babies. You may find that, although your baby is feeding more regularly than she did as a newborn, she still cries between feeds and perhaps after them. In such circumstances many mothers assume that their baby is not 'settled', and the maternal response is to change the feed, usually to a 'stage two' or 'follow-on' casein-based formula (see p. 86). Casein is thought to take longer to digest in the stomach than whey, and therefore fills a baby more effectively, but there is no real evidence that it makes a great difference. But if you are keen to see if a change of diet could make your baby happier, there is no nutritional reason why you should not switch. Ask your health visitor for her opinion before you make a final decision.

By the time they are four months old, most bottle-fed babies have gradually increased their intake to be taking 200 ml (7 fl oz) at each feed.

Changing to bottlefeeding

If you are changing to bottle feeding after a period of more than a couple of weeks of breastfeeding, the first thing to do is check that this is your only option. The right help with breastfeeding, plus encouragement from those close to you, may mean that you can continue to breastfeed if you want to. Nevertheless, if that help has come too late for you, or if you feel the whole thing is a struggle you would rather abandon, then a switch may well be the right thing.

Don't feel guilty

When you switch to bottles you may feel relief, or that it's a practical solution. But if you're doing so reluctantly, you may feel regret, disappointment, sadness and even anger. All are understandable; guilt, however, means you feel you are to blame that feeding has not worked out the way you wanted. You are not.

Cut down gradually

Top up each breastfeed with a small amount of formula, which you increase each day, as you take your baby off the breast before she falls asleep full. Alternatively, replace one breastfeed every couple of days with a bottle feed, so within 10 days to a couple of weeks you are fully bottlefeeding. If you have already been using bottles, you may find your supply decreases more quickly than this.

Do not make a sudden change

Your breasts will take a few days to learn not to produce milk, and if you suddenly stop breastfeeding you will feel extremely full – and possibly get engorged, blocked, and perhaps suffer a bout of mastitis as a result. If you feel your breasts are uncomfortable while you are trying to make the changeover, express very gently (not too much, as this will encourage more milk) to reduce your discomfort.

INTRODUCING SOLID FOOD

Solid food may be anything but solid. The term refers to foods other than milk, introduced to a baby who has until fairly recently been fed on a milk-only diet.

Babies do not need anything other than milk until they are about six months

old, the age at which they are assumed to require more iron than is available from either breast milk or formula. Since the first teeth are also starting to come through at about this age, it would seem nature is giving a clue as to when a baby can begin to cope with non-milk foods.

It is usual, however, to give solid foods rather earlier than six months. This is partly a cultural phenomenon, to do with the way parents feel they should be pushing their baby on to the next stage of growth and development, and reducing their baby's dependence on them. It is also done partly in the belief that solids will fill the baby up so that she will sleep through the night. (Studies have shown it makes no difference overall, although some babies may coincidentally start sleeping through at the time they begin on solids.)

It is advisable to introduce solid food no earlier than four months, which is still rather later than many families tend to do. The major reason for waiting is that younger babies are more susceptible to

Left: An interest in food and time for a 'chat' while he is eating help your baby appreciate the move on to solid foods.

Baby rice

Baby rice is a manufactured product and, as it is 'ready' almost instantly, it is very handy. It is an ideal first food. Mix it with water (boiled and cooled), expressed breast milk or formula, and serve it by itself or mixed with other foods such as fruit or vegetable purées.

A major advantage of baby rice is that it is gluten free. Coeliac disease, in particular, is an inability to digest the protein gluten, found in wheat. The incidence of coeliac disease has fallen, probably because babies are not introduced to wheat as early as they used to be.

given foods their digestive systems cannot cope with. In addition, solid foods inevitably take the place of at least some of the milk in the baby's diet, and young babies need a mainly milk diet for most of the first year.

Do not rush to begin solids. Once your baby is four months, these signs indicate that she may be ready.

- Does she show an interest in the food you are eating?
- Is she restless after milk feeds?
- Does she seem to enjoy the occasional bit of food off your plate, if you hold her while you are having a meal yourself?
- Is she starting to be able to grasp things?
- Is her weight levelling off?

Speak to staff at your baby clinic about introducing solid foods. They will help you to decide if now is the right time.

Take it slowly

Some babies are very keen on solids; others are reluctant at first. Let your baby set the pace. Begin by offering small tastes on the end of a spoon, and stick to bland food, one or two new tastes at a time, so that you can easily isolate any food to which your baby has an adverse reaction.

Give solids after or in the middle of the milk feed so that your baby has the chance to take the milk she needs, with solid food as an extra as far as possible. Offer solids once a day, building up to twice and then three times a day over a period of weeks. The later you start solids, the quicker your baby is likely to increase her appetite for them. A six-month-old baby is probably keen enough to move on to three meals a day in three or four weeks. A four-month-old may take five or six weeks. It does not matter how long your baby takes if you are going at her pace.

Try to arrange it so that your baby has her meals at the same time as you and the rest of the family. This makes eating a social occasion, and one she will enjoy for your company and the shared experience of it all. It is also more convenient, on the whole, for you.

Giving solids

A high chair is not essential, but even a small baby can sit propped up in one and it makes it easier and more sociable if she sits with the rest of the family for meals. Make sure she wears a harness.

Be prepared for mess. A good deal of the food your baby feeds herself is likely to miss her mouth and some will inevitably end up on the floor – you may find it helps to put a sheet of plastic on the floor under the chair.

Make sure the baby is wearing a bib, then help her feed herself.

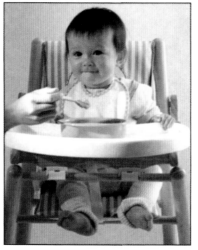

Begin by feeding the baby a couple of spoonfuls yourself, as long as she is happy to take it from a spoon.

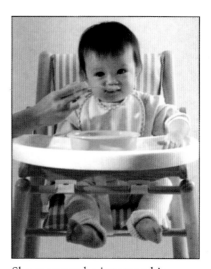

She may not be interested in feeding herself but if she is, give her a spoon. Keep one yourself so that some food goes in.

First foods

Suitable first foods include baby rice, puréed or mashed fruit, and puréed or mashed vegetables.

Keep foods smooth in texture and do not season.

Foods to avoid

Some foods are unsuitable for a young baby's digestive system and may cause adverse reactions. They should be avoided until she is about six months.

- eggs
- wheat and wheat products, including bread and breakfast cereals
- dairy products, including fromage frais, yogurt and cheese, unless their milk content has been modified
- citrus fruits
- fatty or fried foods; if you offer meat trim off all fat
- nuts
- strong or spicy vegetables, such as onions, peppers or okra

Second foods

When your baby is a little older, make her food rather lumpier and introduce different foods so that you increase her repertoire. By six to eight months, most babies can have most foods you have, apart from nuts (although ground ones are all right). Egg yolk should be hard-boiled until after her first birthday.

Solids and weight gain

If your baby does not appear to be gaining weight as she should, do not automatically assume that she needs solid food before the recommended age. It may be better to offer more breastfeeds, having checked that everything else concerned with breastfeeding (such as positioning) is going well, or to give more formula in some bottles if you are bottlefeeding.

Weight gain is only one indication of health in young babies – albeit an important one. If your baby is alert, responsive and contented, she may naturally be a 'slow gainer'. Some babies' weight levels out for a week or so without there being any problem, but talk to your health visitor if you are at all concerned.

Trim off all fat from meat and check fish for bones, then grill, bake or poach. Peel fruit and vegetables and remove pips. Mince or mash (and as she gets older chop) as appropriate.

What to drink

Breast milk is best throughout the first year and beyond. As a drink, formula is the next best thing up to a year, although your baby can have small amounts

Practice at using a spoon is important for your baby – the more she tries, the easier she will find it to reach her mouth.

Finger foods are ideal, since your baby is probably used to finding her mouth with toys and other objects (see p. 137).

A cup with a trainer spout, firm lid and two handles enables your baby to help herself to a drink when she wants one.

Food hygiene

You do not need to sterilize the serving dishes, utensils and preparation equipment you use for your baby's food. Washing in detergent and hot water and then rinsing (or washing in a dishwasher) is perfectly adequate. However, it makes sense to continue to sterilize your baby's bottles and teats and her spouted drinking cup for two reasons:

- traces of warm milk are excellent breeding grounds for bacteria; and
- it is more difficult to see just how clean these items are and to clean them effectively in the normal way.

Once your baby starts to put all manner of things in her mouth, it is usual to relax your cleanliness standards a little, but continue to sterilize bottles and cups until your baby is nine months to a year old.

of whole pasteurized milk mixed with other foods from the age of six months. Whole milk has the fat-soluble vitamins and calories that your baby needs; these are not present in skimmed or semi-skimmed milk.

Follow-on milk is marketed as suitable for babies from six months, as an alternative to whole pasteurized milk, mainly because it is higher in iron. There is no real reason to change to it, as it is no better for your baby than ordinary formula or breast milk. It is sold more as a 'marker' that your child is getting beyond the young baby stage: buying it is a consumer rather than a nutritional decision.

You can also give your baby plain water – there is no need to boil it after about six months – or well-diluted fruit juice. Avoid sweetened drinks or syrups, which can have a very bad effect on teeth, especially if they are drunk from a bottle.

Finger foods

Give your baby the opportunity to feed herself. She will enjoy it and feeling food with her hands before she eats it offers a valuable learning experience. She will make important judgements about colour, texture and taste far more easily than if you are spooning food into her.

Chop up food into bite-sized pieces and put it on her tray for her to pick up and handle. Bananas cut in half lengthways are good finger foods, though a bit sticky and messy, and you can give bread and bread sticks, carrot sticks and small chunks of peeled cucumber, slices of apple or pear, and anything else that is not naturally sloppy in this way. Most babies cannot manage a spoon themselves until well after their first birthday. Always stay with your baby when she is feeding herself, in case she chokes.

Baby food – bought or home-made?

Almost all babies have some pre-packaged foods in their first year. Most parents appreciate the convenience of giving their baby something suitable when they are not eating themselves, when there is something baby-unfriendly on the menu, such as an extra-spicy chilli, or when you are out and about and cannot be certain of finding anything suitable. Bought baby food is quick to serve, and liked by babies: each recipe is consumer-tested to make sure you will buy the product again and again, after all. The meals are consistent; all such foods today are prepared without artificial additives.

To give your baby nothing but jars, packets or tins is, however, very expensive, compared with home-cooked food. In addition, the fact that brand X cauliflower cheese always tastes the same may not necessarily be a good thing – home-made is always a little different in taste and texture, and as babies do need to start eating 'real food' at some stage, learning that things are not always smooth, lump-free and identical with the one before is important.

Your own home-cooked food is likely to be higher in quality than a lot of bought products. If you read the labels on baby food, you will see that many are bulked out with thickeners (these are responsible for that particular gloppy texture which makes them easy to spoon out of a jar or can). These ingredients are not harmful to babies, but they may mean that the food is poor value, both nutritionally and financially. It is not surprising that good baby foods with a high proportion of quality ingredients tend to cost more.

Remember that many of the foods you eat because they are 'instant', or almost-instant, are also suitable for babies: satsumas, bananas, raw vegetable sticks, bread and bread sticks, for example.

CONTINUING TO BREASTFEED

If you want to carry on breastfeeding your baby, do so. Worldwide, mothers continue to breastfeed well into toddlerhood and even beyond. The World Health Organization recommends breastfeeding for two years (though with a range of solid food as well).

In the West, breastfeeding for this long is not common and because it is not often seen, it is easy to assume that it does not happen at all. That, however, is not the case.

You may find that as breastfeeding becomes more established and easier and easier, you and your baby enjoy it. Stopping is just not an issue: why bother ceasing something that both of you find rewarding?

Meeting both your needs

Mothers who work (see p. 88) may find the feeds they enjoy at the beginning and end of the day and at weekends are a special way of staying close to their babies. It is not difficult, either, to get into a feeding pattern that suits you and your baby, as your baby grows – and as feeds for an older baby often last no more than a few minutes, they fit into even a busy day very well.

The exception to this 'few minutes a feed' is the evening or bedtime feed, which may well last longer. This may be a highly efficient way of winding your baby down for the evening, and it helps ensure smooth settling as your baby falls happily asleep. (The downside of this is that some babies can only easily get to sleep for the evening if you are there, which may be a problem if you are involved with even the occasional early evening activity.)

Do not believe the old story that your milk 'goes off' or becomes inferior the longer you feed. Breast milk is always a nutritious drink, and its infection-fighting properties remain (although as your baby gets older and can fight infection herself, these become less significant). Mothers of older babies are often thankful they have continued to breastfeed when their babies are ill: breast milk is often the only thing they are willing to take.

Once you have been breastfeeding for a few months, it is possible to keep the supply going with

Menstruation and ovulation

It is normal for your periods to cease while you are fully breastfeeding, because the breastfeeding hormones suppress ovulation, and therefore menstruation. Once your baby starts to take solid food, or to space her feeds out, or to reduce her number of feeds, your periods may return. On the other hand, they may not return until you have completely stopped breastfeeding.

Breastfeeding is the most commonly used contraceptive method in the world, but it is not considered reliable in the West, largely because so few women breastfeed as often as is necessary to prevent ovulation (at least every four hours; for some women, as often as every two hours). Also, since ovulation can happen before you have a period, it is hard to monitor accurately enough, so you can be fertile without knowing it.

very little stimulation. There is always some milk in the breasts, and as time goes by, breast milk is made more and more directly in response to the baby's sucking, almost immediately she feeds. The result is that mothers can keep breastfeeding on just one feed a day, without finding their supply dwindles to nothing. (This is not the case in the first days and weeks when the breast milk production system simply shuts down.)

Supply also becomes more flexible. It is possible to feed an older baby erratically, with more on one day than another, as you may do if you are away from your baby in the day from Monday to Friday. At first your breasts may feel uncomfortable as they adjust to this, and they may start to feel rather fuller after they have had some 'extra' demands placed on them, but this stage passes.

Coping with hostility

There are social reasons which make some women feel uncomfortable about breastfeeding; there are also some people who seem to disapprove of the whole notion of feeding babies this way. This attitude is even more prevalent with older babies. You may come across comments such as 'You're not still doing that, are you?', or 'She doesn't get any benefit from it now, you know'. Some people may even imply you are imposing breastfeeding on your baby because of some sort of selfish motives to do with wanting to be needed. The good thing is that having breastfed for some time, you are likely to be feeling a lot more confident about the whole process than you might have been in the beginning, and also about your abilities as a mother. You can see for yourself that your baby is thriving.

Biting and resistance

If your baby starts to bite at the breast (some do, once their teeth begin to come through), simply take her off, with a firm 'No'. This usually stops her. It is not a sign that your baby is starting to become vicious, or deciding she does not want to be breastfed any more.

A few babies under a year do voluntarily wean themselves, and show you by fighting, and refusing to suck, that they have had enough. Do not take this first sign of reluctance as a permanent refusal if you do not want to. Your baby may well come back to breastfeeding, given the chance, if you keep offering over a few days.

Working and feeding

If you are keen to continue breastfeeding when you go back to work, you have a number of options:
* arrange your hours and breaks so you can carry on giving your baby a breastfeed at her normal times
* combine breast- and bottlefeeding with formula
* combine breast- and bottlefeeding with expressed breast milk
* combine breastfeeding with cup feeding with expressed breast milk or formula

The one you choose may depend on the age of your baby. Babies under five months or so are just learning to take a cup, and are unlikely to be able to get all the fluids they need in this way. It is more difficult to combine breast and formula until your breast milk supply is well established, which can take as long as three months. Your choice may also depend on whether you can express breast milk and store it at work. Not expressing could leave you uncomfortable (though after a time this passes), and also means that you must spend a lot of time at home expressing your milk. If you want to express your breast milk (see p.

77) at work, you will need a private place and a clean fridge to store it. Transport it between your workplace and home or childminder's in a cool bag.

Don't feel you need to get your baby used to a bottle long before you have to leave her. A baby who is used to being breastfed may have a bit of a struggle learning to suck on a teat, but she will manage. If she finds the struggle too much, hold a cup of expressed breast milk or formula to her mouth and 'tip' it in (the vast majority of babies do not need this).

Using a cup

Babies can start using a cup from birth although this is normally only suggested if there is a problem with the way the baby sucks, or as a transition stage between tube-feeding a sick or pre-term baby and breastfeeding. It is also occasionally done as a supplement to breastfeeding, to avoid conditioning and confusing the baby's suck.

If you use a cup for a young baby, she will lap or slurp, rather than drink, but once she is about four or five months old, she may be able to start learning to drink 'properly' from a cup. This is a useful skill, as it means your baby can begin to have fluids other than breast milk or formula.

At first, think about choosing a spouted cup. Some babies are about seven or eight months before they can manage these well, and you may need to try a few different shapes and lengths of spout before you hit on one your baby can use easily. A double handle is useful at first, too.

You can of course use an ordinary cup from the start, but your baby will need help to hold it steady and to tip it up at just the right angle to avoid empty-ing the contents all over her face.

Offer a cup – whatever sort you use – with every meal, to encourage your baby to reach for it. Offer a drink of water, milk or diluted juice in a cup once or twice a day between meals, too.

It does not matter if your baby still prefers the breast or bottle for months, and even rejects the cup. Keep the cup on offer, and visible, and she will eventually come round. It is also not worth worrying about how much your baby drinks – she will not voluntarily stay thirsty. As long as the drink is there, and she has a breast- or bottlefeed when she 'asks' for one, she will take the fluid she needs.

WEANING

As your baby eats more solids, and at the same time as you do, you can expect her to join in family meals, and to have more or less the same food as you and the rest of the family. Do not add salt to your baby's food, and avoid heavily salted foods. She can have eggs, but make sure they are still hard-boiled until her first birthday. Whole nuts remain on the 'no' list until your child is five. Your baby will tolerate and chew lumpier food, and in fact it is a good idea not to concentrate on the smooth purées you may have started her on: babies can develop conservative food habits and start to dislike and refuse all food with any sort of texture. Make mealtimes fun, and sociable.

Once she is well established on solids, you may want to stop breast- and bottlefeeding.

Stopping breastfeeding

To make the changeover as smooth as possible, you may find some or all of these strategies useful.

Distraction
Start by distracting your baby about the time of, or just miss out, the feed(s) you feel she is least attached to. Offer a drink of something else, or simply take her out in the pram or buggy. Do not drop more than one or two feeds every few days, or your breasts could start to feel uncomfortable.

Keep the feeds your baby seems to enjoy the most until the other feeds have gone. You could drop your daytime feeds, for example, before you stop feeding at bedtime, or perhaps first thing in the morning.

Flexible babies
Babies under a year are more flexible – and can 'forget' about breastfeeding more easily – than older ones. Your baby may take quite happily to being put to bed without a breastfeed if your partner or a trusted babysitter puts her to bed, for example, or if you swap a story or a cuddle for the feed. If you leave it until she is older, you may have to think of more complicated strategies if your baby remains keen on the breast (you may end up feeding, as well as reading a story and having a cuddle), but she may also settle if someone else gives her milk in a cup.

Stopping bottlefeeding

The sound argument for phasing your baby's bottles out by the end of her first year is the risk of dental decay. Babies who suck anything other than plain water through a bottle teat are bathing their new teeth in potentially decay-causing fluid. This is less of a problem if bottles are restricted to mealtimes, as saliva can counteract the effect. However, older babies can hold their bottles themselves, and enjoy doing so. They can get very attached to them, to the extent that they have them for much of the day, with an all-day bottle of juice or milk for instant swigging.

Encourage a cup
A cup rarely gives the sucking comfort of a bottle, so offer that during the day. And try to prevent your baby from falling asleep with the bottle in her mouth, which might mean she needs to suck on a bottle in order to settle at all.

Comfort sucking
Older babies get a lot of comfort from sucking a bottle, especially at bedtime, and seem to need it to wind down after a busy day. If you find yourself relying on the bottle to help your baby go to sleep, try offering a dummy instead.

Weaning older children

You can breastfeed through a second pregnancy, but it is only fair to both children to wean the older off the breast well before the younger arrives. When you decide the time has come to wean your older child off the breast, you have a number of available strategies.
- Drop all feeds but the one to which your child is most attached (usually the bedtime one).
- At bedtime, settle your child down to sleep without offering your breast. Be prepared for several evenings of protest, but stay firm. If you give in, you are not being consistent or fair.
- Avoid situations or places where you know your child will want to feed: if you always fed her curled up on the sofa, sit somewhere else.
- Distract your child at times you think she may want to feed: offer her a drink or a snack instead.
- If your child is older, explain that big children do not have breastfeeds, they have cuddles instead.

CHAPTER FOUR

Your Baby at Home

Getting to know a newborn in the first few days and weeks at home is a thrilling experience, which reaches far beyond caring for his daily needs. In this time, he is learning about you and the rest of his family, and getting used to his surroundings. He is starting to learn about his home, in particular, and the rest of the world in general.

First days with a newborn

If you have had your baby in hospital, bringing him home when he is a few days old is an exciting milestone. But it can also be a bit unnerving. In hospital, there was always someone to turn to if you had a problem, and you did not have to worry about getting a meal, cleaning or any other domestic chores.

For the first few days, or even weeks, after you bring your baby home, life can seem to be an endless round of caring for his needs with little time for those of other members of the family, including the new mother. You will find that you spend entire days without achieving anything, and yet the baby may be sleeping up to 16 hours a day. The reason that you seem to do little else but attend to him is that his needs have to come first. If he cries, you have to pick him up because you are not sufficiently in tune with his cries to know whether he is genuinely miserable or simply a little grizzly (see Babies and crying, pp. 101–4). Nor is his feeding pattern likely to be so well established that you can judge when he is likely to need feeding again, particularly if you are breastfeeding (see chapter 3). And, you may be feeling tired, sore, weepy or simply very different now that the baby is finally here and your body is readjusting back to normal. All of these factors make it difficult to get any pattern to your days or nights – which is particularly frustrating if you were used to a job with a structure.

What you can do

In the first few weeks after your baby comes home, expect to spend 24 hours a day looking after him.

- Be flexible. Newborn babies do not run to a schedule, and you will only wear yourself out for no reason if you try to get yours to.
- Get as much rest as you can. It may seem alien to you to sleep in the middle of the day, but you probably did not get woken twice a night before the baby was born either.
- Forget about housework as far as possible. If you can get help here, try to do so, perhaps by getting someone to pick up a bag of ironing or clean for a couple of hours.
- This may be the time to buy a microwave, if you don't already have one, so that whatever time you manage to find for a meal, you can have something hot if you want. And if someone likes cooking, ask them to cook some dishes that can be frozen and reheated.
- Try to get some exercise, even if it's only pushing the baby round the park in the pram.

TAKING CARE OF YOUR BABY

In days when families were large and geographically close, older children took some of the responsibility for caring for younger siblings or cousins so that few children (and, especially, few girls) grew up unable to give a baby a bottle or change a wet nappy. Today, even these routine tasks can be daunting for many first-time mothers whose first experience of handling a tiny baby may be when the midwife puts him in her arms after the birth. Add to that, the lack of perhaps family or friends nearby to whom you can turn for advice and what should be a special time of nurturing and bonding can be worrying.

It helps to remember that this period does not last. Within weeks, feeding and nappy changing may take half the time they do to begin with and bathtime ceases to be an occasion to worry (will I drop the baby? will he slip out of my arms?) and starts to become a relaxing, sociable occasion.

Nappies

Changing a nappy is something you will do around 40 times a week in the first few weeks if you take sole charge of it, so try to share it out as much as possible (new parents spend seven hours a week on this task). It is important to change your baby's nappy every time it is wet or soiled to prevent soreness or nappy rash. The major causes of nappy rash (see pp. 96 and 163–4) are not changing your baby's nappy often enough so that urine and faeces remain in contact with his skin. Check your baby's nappy before and after a feed, unless you have just changed it.

Types of nappy

Today, you have more choice than ever before, but while you may be certain which type you want to use, it is worth considering the options.

Disposables

Used by about 70 per cent of new British parents, disposables are increasingly being made with the same type of technology as sanitary protection towels. This means disposable nappies have progressively more slimline and absorbent designs, and are often treated with a gel that draws fluid in to contain it within the nappy centre, away from the baby's skin.

PROS: Disposables are very convenient to use; simple to put on; are unlikely to leak; and are claimed to make nappy rash less likely. They also do not need washing or drying, which may be a bonus if you do not have a washing machine and/or tumble dryer, or anywhere to dry washing.

CONS: They are expensive – your baby is likely to get through 4,000 to 5,000 nappies before he is potty trained; there are also ecological concerns about their disposal. Disposables are not truly 'disposable': they go out with the domestic refuse into land fill sites that have to accommodate some 9 million soiled nappies every day. The plastic these nappies contain takes generations to biodegrade, especially if the nappies are wrapped in plastic sacks, and then in plastic bin liners as well. It is possible (although there is no proof) that viruses in the faeces many of these nappies contain may contaminate ground water supplies.

Disposables also contain wood pulp, which has caused a steep rise in the number of trees felled to cope with demand; also chlorine was used in the bleaching process (most manufacturers have stopped or switched to low chlorine bleaches). Chlorine produces dioxin, which damages wildlife and humans.

YOU WILL NEED: A packet of 36 a week and some nappy sacks to wrap up soiled ones (alternatively, keep supermarket plastic and paper bags).

Shaped cloth nappies (reusables)

They are shaped to look like disposables, but made from soft, padded, often patterned cotton. Usually available in three or four sizes, these are a compromise between terries and disposables.

PROS: They are quicker and easier to put on than terries, since they fasten at the sides with velcro; they are more environmentally friendly than disposables since they do not use wood pulp, bleach, gel or take up space in landfill sites; they are less bulky than terries (some makes even come with a waterproof shell so do not require plastic pants); they are cheaper than disposables over a couple of years although the initial outlay is high.

Choosing disposables

Manufacturers are continually developing nappies that are more absorbent, better fitting and generally more comfortable for your baby. Most produce several sizes from those for premature babies through newborn, up until your child weighs around 25 kg (55 lb). Buy the size that is most appropriate – a nappy that is too big may leak and one that is too small may be uncomfortably tight.

Apart from those for very tiny babies, there are different nappies for boys and girls: boys' have more padding at the front than girls'. Many manufacturers have also now introduced 'trainer nappies' for toddlers, which can be pulled up and down like pants so that children have the security of a nappy, but can start to register that they may need to use the toilet (see also Toilet training, pp. 189–90). For older children, too, special night-time nappies, which are thicker and more absorbent than those for use during the day, may be worth considering if your child cannot seem to rid himself of his night nappy.

Changing your baby's nappy

Always have everything you need ready to hand before you start. Wash your hands.

- changing mat
- clean nappy
- warm water or nappy wipes
- cottonwool
- barrier cream
- talcum powder (optional)

  Unless you are changing the baby on the floor, keep a hand on him at all times. Even tiny babies can twist off a changing table when your back is turned. If your baby is older and tends to wriggle, try putting a mobile above the changing mat.

1 Take off trousers or leggings and socks and open the legs of his sleepsuit or vest and roll it up to around chest height so that it is well out of the way. Undo the nappy.

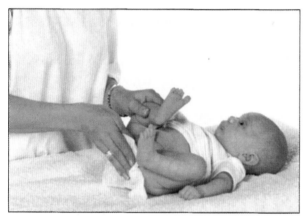

2 If the nappy is dirty, try to keep as much inside as possible. Fold it up and put it in a sack. Using cottonwool and warm water or a wipe, clean his bottom thoroughly. Clean girls from front to back. Dry the baby thoroughly with more cottonwool.

3 Let him kick for a while, then slip a new nappy under his bottom. If you want to use a barrier cream, do so, but wipe your hands thoroughly afterward: if you get cream on the tapes of a disposable, they won't stick.

4 Open the tapes and stick them down. Get the baby dressed again. Roll his vest or bodysuit down and fasten, then replace sleepsuit or leggings. Wash your hands.

5 If you are using a terry, slip a nappy and liner under the baby, then pin carefully through all layers. Put on waterproof pants, then dress the baby. Wash your hands.

CONS: Like terries, they require routine disinfecting, soaking, washing and drying; they may not be as absorbent as ultra disposables; you may need to try a few before you find the ones that suit your baby best; they are more expensive than terries.

YOU WILL NEED: About 15 reusables should be enough, disposable nappy liners, plastic pants, a lidded bucket, and nappy solution or vinegar for disinfecting soiled nappies. You will also need a washing machine and – possibly – a tumble dryer.

Terry cloth nappies

Traditional terry nappies are used with or without soft liners. (You can use muslin squares instead of terries for newborns, but use a liner with these.)

PROS: These are cheaper than disposables, even taking washing machine use and powder into account; one size fits all; they are also kinder to the environment (but obviously you use more energy in washing them and tumbling them dry).

CONS: They take longer to put on than disposables and also have to be folded and pinned (traditionally, midwives used to learn eight different ways to fold and pin, and even learning one can take a bit of practice); they are bulkier than both disposables and reusables, both for the baby to wear and for you to carry spares when you are out and about (and you must carry a soiled one home); they may also be less absorbent than the best disposables; and they need laundering (unless you use a nappy service).

YOU WILL NEED: About 24 nappies, nappy pins, disposable nappy liners, plastic pants, a lidded bucket, and nappy solution or vinegar for disinfecting soiled nappies. If you do not use a nappy service, you will also need a washing machine and – possibly – a tumble dryer.

Nappy services

If you are using terries, it is worth considering a nappy service, an idea imported from the United States. These companies supply you with clean nappies and a bin for dirty nappies, which they collect when they deliver fresh nappies to your doorstep, usually once a week. The costs are slightly lower than if you use disposables, but you do not have to do anything, even buy the nappies. Contact the Association of Nappy Services (see Useful Contacts, pp. 248–51) for your nearest one.

Folding a terry nappy

Lay the nappy flat, then fold in opposite corners at an oblique angle.

Bring the triangle at the top in to meet the other corners.

Fold the two layers at the bottom point in toward the middle.

Adjust this fold to make the nappy the right size for the baby.

The kite fold (above) is one of the simplest to master, suitable for both girls and boys, and enables you to lengthen or shorten the nappy to make it fit your baby. It is a good idea to fold a few nappies at a time so that there is always one ready for use.

Do terries cause nappy rash?

Reusables and terries are often said to cause more nappy rash than disposables. It seems likely, however, that both the waterproof plastic pants babies wear with reusable nappies and the plastic layer of disposables can create ideal damp, warm conditions for bacteria to produce ammonia, which is the substance that causes nappy rash. If nappies are changed often enough, this tends not to be a problem.

Reusables and terries are not as absorbent as disposables. You can, however, use additional nappy liners, change more frequently during the day and try double nappying at night.

Points to remember

- Whichever type you choose, it is worth having a few disposables for when you are out and about.
- Many hospitals no longer supply you with nappies while you are there. It is worth checking beforehand and taking some disposables with you when you go in.
- Shop around for the best and most effective buy and, as long as you have storage space, purchase disposables in bulk (some companies and large department stores deliver free).
- Do not buy too many 'newborn' nappies, as babies grow out of this size quickly.
- All babies are different. Help find out which type of nappy suits your baby best by taking advantage of free sample packs and swapping a few of your nappies with different brands from other mothers.
- Advice on reusables, from making washing easier to finding a stockist, is available from WEN (see Useful Contacts, pp. 248–51).

Points about changing

- Put the mat on a surface at upper chest height, so you do not bend your back (most changing tables are not made at back friendly heights). Raise yours up if necessary.
- If you are changing the baby on the floor, squat or sit so that your back remains straight, rather than hunched over.
- Beds, especially hospital beds unless you can manage to crank them up, are usually at a bad height for nappy changing.
- Keep cream well away from your baby's hands and feet. A wriggly baby can knock a pot over, which makes a terrible mess.

How to bath your baby

Have everything ready before you start. You will need:
- bath
- baby soap or bath-care liquid
- cottonwool
- bowl with boiled, cooled water
- baby lotion or wipes
- two towels
- apron and/or towel to keep yourself dry
- clean nappy
- barrier cream
- clean clothes

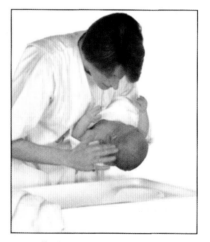

1 Fill the bath. Undress the baby and wrap him in a towel, then wash his face as if you were topping and tailing (see p. 98). Hold your baby's head over the bath and gently wash his hair, using water from the bath and babybath or baby shampoo.

2 Rinse his hair with water from the bath and towel dry it. Unwrap your baby and carefully lift him into the bath with both hands, supporting his head and shoulders with your arm and gripping his outer arm with one hand and leg with the other.

KEEPING YOUR BABY CLEAN

Cleanliness and good hygiene are essential throughout your child's early months and years because babies and young children are more vulnerable to vomiting and diarrhoea than older children or adults, and these illnesses can have much more serious consequences (see pp. 163, 167, and 375). Developing a habit of cleanliness is a good idea – you may feel you are already quite fastidious but it is surprising how many people do not always wash their hands before handling food, for instance.

Bathing your baby

The first bath is often an anxious occasion for first-time parents as they learn to handle their vulnerable new baby in water. Usually you will be given a chance to bath your baby under the supervision of a midwife at the hospital or at home when he is anything up to a week old to give you confidence.

It is not really necessary to bath a baby every single day, especially as some small babies don't enjoy the bath in their first few weeks. Others find it obviously enjoyable and bathtime can be a relaxing event for both baby and parent(s). Find a time that suits you and your baby best – it is a good idea to do it during a period of natural wakefulness before a feed, but not when he's really hungry, which may or may not be in the early evening. This often helps to settle a baby down for the evening, allowing parents a quiet time for themselves, and can be a relaxing part of a coming-home routine if one of you is working. If you have older children, however, you may find it easier to bath the baby in the morning perhaps when children are at school or nursery so that the bath can take place without distractions.

Bathing safety and hygiene

- Choose a warm room (it does not have to be the bathroom) without draughts.
- Make sure the bath is on a firm surface at the right height for you; you should not have to hunch over.
- Wash your hands thoroughly before you start and make sure the bath is clean.
- Assemble everything you need beforehand and make sure all is within easy reach.
- Pour the cold water in the bath first, then add hot. There is a risk of scalding your baby if you put the hot water in first. The water should feel warm to the touch on your wrist or elbow, not to fingers which can withstand much hotter temperatures.

3 Let him get used to the sensation of the water on his body for a few minutes while you continue to support his head and arm with one hand. With your free hand, start to gently wash his body, taking special care with all the creases.

4 If he enjoys it and the water and air temperature are still warm, let him kick for a while as you 'chat' to him. He may like having his tummy gently splashed with water, or prefer to have a toy to hold and play with. Be guided by him.

5 When you sense he has had enough, or runs the risk of getting cold, lift him out carefully with both hands. Remember that he will be slippery. Wrap him immediately in a towel and cuddle him close. Sit comfortably and dry him on your lap.

Topping and tailing

On days when you are not bathing your baby you can simply 'top and tail'. As with bathing, find a time when you and your baby can be fairly relaxed about it; it is sensible to do it after your baby has had a long period of sleep as this is likely to be the time when his nappy area will need thorough cleaning.

How to top and tail

Collect all the equipment together and wash your hands before you start.

- cottonwool
- boiled, cooled water in a bowl
- baby lotion
- soft facecloth or sponge – use for face only; keep a separate cloth for your baby's nappy area
- bowl of warm water with bath preparation
- small towel
- clean nappy
- clean clothes (as necessary)

You can 'top and tail' in a warm room on your lap or on a changing mat laid on a firm surface. Never leave your baby alone on a changing mat on a high surface – even when he is very tiny he is capable of rolling off it.

Protecting your back

Make sure that you bath, change and top and tail your baby at a comfortable height for your back. Baby-bath stands and changing tables are often not at the right level.

Stand at a changing table before you buy. If you are buying a bath, make sure it has a plug in the bottom, so you can stand it in your bath to use it, then easily let the water out, or place the baby bath next to the adult bath or sink for easy emptying. Heaving a full baby bath off its stand and carrying it across the room to empty it is one of the easiest ways to damage your back.

The umbilicus

After the umbilical cord is cut at birth, the remaining stump is clamped; it takes between a few days and a couple of weeks to dry up and come away completely, leaving a typical 'tummy button'. Your midwife will show you how to clean the area around the clamp in the first days after the birth. The hospital or midwife will also supply you with surgical spirit swabs and antiseptic powder with which to clean and dust the umbilicus to prevent infection. It is safe to bath your

Topping and tailing

1 Take off all clothes except his vest or bodysuit and wash his face using boiled, cooled water – there is no need to add soap or babybath to the water for his face – and cottonwool. Wipe the eyes gently from the inside corner to the outer edge, using a separate piece of cottonwool for each eye. If there is a lot of dried mucus, repeat. (Your baby may not like this process.)

2 Carefully wipe any dried mucus away from his nostrils with separate pieces of cottonwool. Do not poke inside your baby's nose with cottonbuds (or anything else) – this is unnecessary and may damage the delicate skin inside. There is no need to clean inside your baby's mouth until his teeth appear, but wipe the outside with a clean piece of cottonwool.

3 Clean the creases of his neck gently with warm, boiled water and cottonwool (do not use soap). Pat dry with the corner of a towel, making sure that the neck creases are not left damp. If there is any ear wax visible in the opening of the ear clear this away with a cottonbud. But don't push a bud right into the ear – this is unnecessary and dangerous as it could damage the ear drum.

Unhappy bathers

Some babies love baths from the start, others take longer to get used to them. Some like having a bath, but cry at hairwashing and vice versa. If your baby really does not like being bathed, top and tail him as far as possible, while you investigate ways to make bathtime more acceptable.

- If your baby does not seem to feel safe or comfortable in a baby bath, try lying him on a large, 'cut out' sponge (available from the baby departments of major stores, and specialist baby equipment shops). This also works well in a big bath.
- Consider taking him into the big bath with you and hold him close to your breast while you wash him gently. Make sure the water is much cooler than usual, have a nonslip mat in the bath and take extra care getting into and out of the bath while you are holding the baby. (The first couple of times you do this, try to have someone else in the room with you.)
- If your baby is not happy with any of these options, try taking his clothes and nappy off, wrapping him in a soft towel previously warmed on the radiator, then gently flannel bathing him with warm water bit by bit, cuddled on your lap. Use a different flannel (or wetted piece of cottonwool) for his bottom, and the rest of his body and use a separate piece of cottonwool for each eye.

baby before the umbilicus has healed or the stump has dropped off, provided you dry the area thoroughly afterward.

You may be a little nervous of cleaning behind the stump as it will look a little sore, but this is important. If any redness develops or the umbilicus area 'weeps' or any pus appears, contact your doctor at once as this is a sign of infection.

The foreskin

A baby boy's foreskin cannot be pulled back at birth, so do not try to do so or you could tear the skin,

4 Wipe his hands with a sponge, cloth or piece of cottonwool and dry them with a towel. If the room is warm and he seems happy, you can leave him in his vest while you clean his nappy area (see p. 94). If not, put the top half of a clean sleepsuit or a cardigan or jumper on him before you continue. If he is unhappy, play for a few minutes or give him a toy to hold and look at.

Cutting your baby's nails

A young baby's nails are very soft and flake off easily, but can still scratch – so keep an eye on the length of your baby's nails. Some parents find biting off 'hang nails' simpler than using scissors as it is easy to catch the skin on tiny fingers even with baby nail scissors.

Sit your baby in your lap. Using small, round-ended nail scissors, cut the nails straight across when they have grown beyond the fingertip.

Cut toenails in the same way. If you find it difficult to hold and cut, try cutting them when he is lying on his changing mat or while he is asleep.

causing later scarring. It could also introduce infection if the area becomes soiled with faeces. The foreskin separates from the glans of the penis during childhood; in the meantime it actually protects the tip of the penis from infection and from any irritation caused by wet nappies. Occasionally it may become sore and inflamed if nappy rash has already developed (see pp. 163–4); apply plenty of barrier cream in this case. However, if soreness or redness persists or you are worried, contact your doctor or health visitor who may recommend a suitable antibiotic cream to help the healing process.

Getting your baby dressed

Choosing clothes wisely for your baby in the first place makes dressing him easier than it might otherwise be.
- Make sure that anything that must go over his head has a broad, 'envelope' neck or buttons along the shoulder line. Otherwise, avoid over-the-head designs as far as possible.
- Nappy changing is easier if you choose suits that have poppers right down the legs.
- If you buy trousers, make sure that they are loose and have firm but stretchy elastic waists.
- Avoid anything with lots of tiny buttons.

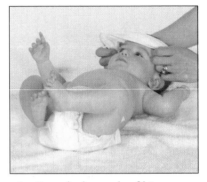

1 Stretch the neck of his vest and slip it over his head, supporting his head as you do so.

2 Holding one sleeve open, take your baby's hand and gently guide it through.

3 Ease the other hand through the armhole and pull the vest down. Do up the poppers.

1 Lie your baby on the stretch suit. Scrunch one sleeve up, and guide the baby's arm through.

2 Scrunch up the other sleeve in one hand; with your other hand, ease the baby's arm through.

3 Gently bend your baby's leg at the knee and ease it down into one of the legs of the suit.

4 Do the same with his other leg, then do up the suit. Put on a cardigan if necessary.

BABIES AND CRYING

Babies cry in all sorts of ways, from a small amount of grumbling (perhaps just before they go to sleep) to screaming loudly for several hours. Naturally, when your baby cries, you will be disturbed and distressed.

Babies also cry for all sorts of reasons. When they are very tiny, it is the only way they can communicate their needs. It can be something of a matter of trial and error when your baby is small to determine what he needs, but among the most common reasons for crying are:

He is bored or frustrated
Some babies seem to need more attention and activity than others and hate being left on their own. Try to keep your baby company as much as possible.

He is feeling lonely
He may want to be cuddled, talked to or carried, or propped up in a baby bouncer or pram where he can see you as you work around the house.

He is uncomfortable
Perhaps he is too hot or too cold (see pp. 106 and 128), his nappy may be too tight, or soiled, or the clothes next to his skin are irritating him.

He is tired
If he refuses to sleep in his cot but you sense that this is the problem, take him for a walk in the pram, or put him in a sling and go for a walk, or strap him in his car seat and go for a drive.

He is hungry or thirsty
Feed him or give him cooled, boiled water. The comfort of sucking may help, even if he is not hungry.

He is unwell
If the crying persists and/or you are at all worried, contact your GP. Doctors always take potential illness in small babies very seriously and prefer to see small babies sooner rather than later.

He is in pain
This may not be from anything major – colic and wind both cause real pain (see also pp. 104 and 162).

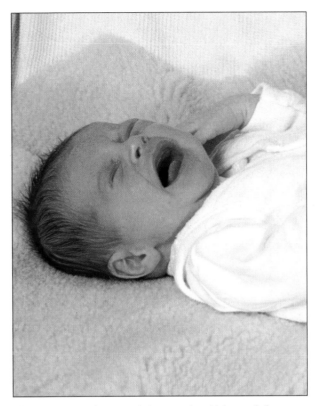

Above: Crying is the most obvious way in which your baby can let you know that all is not right with his world. In time, you will recognize the significance of his different types of crying.

He is alarmed
Many things might make him nervous or startle him, including such routine happenings as being bathed. There is also evidence that even the tiniest babies may experience bad dreams or relive their births for a while: if so, cuddling and your soothing voice are the best remedies.

He needs more peace than most
Some babies have a relatively low sensory threshold and do not enjoy a lot of handling and stimulation.

He had a difficult birth
A baby is likely to cry more than average for a couple of weeks after a birth that involved complications. If compression of his head was a problem – if he was a forceps delivery, or his head looks misshapen – some mothers have found a cranial osteopath helpful (see Useful Contacts, pp. 390–3). Some pain-relieving drugs given to mothers during labour seem to affect certain babies more than others, making them more irritable and generally harder to settle for the first few days or weeks.

He was premature

The nervous systems of premature babies may still be slightly immature, and after the bright lights and noise of a special care unit, many initially dislike the relative peace of home. Light and white noise in the background – say a radio tuned off station – can help, as can music played at a low volume, until he gets used to his new environment.

He has an allergy

This is unusual, and if your baby is allergic, there are usually additional symptoms such as diarrhoea or skin rashes. See pp. 160–1.

He is a high-need baby

Some babies are just high-need or extra-sensitive, crying a good deal not because there is anything especially wrong but because this is simply the way that they are. Such babies naturally need more attention and nurturing than other babies to keep them happy.

When all else fails

If your baby is inconsolable and you cannot bear his crying any longer, but you are sure there is nothing really wrong with him:

- Wrap him up and get out of the house with him in the pram.
- Get help: for immediate help, ring a telephone helpline. Then talk to your GP or health visitor. If you really seem to be getting nowhere, keep asking.
- When you really cannot bear any more, put your baby gently in his cot and go into another room for 10 minutes. Do not feel guilty about this. You have your needs too.
- The fact that your baby cries more than most does not mean you are not such a good parent as someone whose baby sleeps all day. Whether you have a calm or a high-need baby is a matter of luck.
- Experiment with the package of suggestions, talk to other parents about what helped them, and follow your instincts: you will almost certainly be right.
- Remember – it really does get better.

Your idea of excessive crying may differ from somebody else's, but you are not alone if your baby does seem to cry a great deal: about 1 in 10 does. Crying really is not due to any incompetence on your part (except in the most obvious cases – you have stuck the nappy tape to his tummy, for example, or put it on too tight).

If crying is caused by colic, your baby will have stopped by about three months; most other types of crying peak between about two and nine months, and decline fairly rapidly after that.

Crying is not something to feel alone with. Organizations which can help include CRY-SIS – which has trained telephone volunteer helpers who themselves were the parents of crying babies – and Parentline (their trained volunteers also are parents themselves). Both can offer a sympathetic ear at the moment you may need it most and practical advice (see Useful Contacts, pp. 248-51).

Remember, crying really does get better. And with a bit of help, you can either find the best coping strategies around – or see the situation improve faster than you had dared to hope.

What you can do

You know your baby best, so if he is not generally a crying baby and starts, or if he is often irritable but this is more than usual, check these factors first and take the appropriate action. If you are at all concerned, contact your health visitor or GP.

Is he hungry?

Breastfeed or bottlefeed.

Is he thirsty?

Breastfeed or offer previously boiled and cooled water in a bottle or on a spoon.

Is he in pain?

Try massaging his tummy (see Colic, pp. 104 and 162) or place a warm (not hot) hot-water bottle covered in a cloth on his tummy and hold it there, or cuddle him upright against your shoulder, so the bottle is gently sandwiched between his abdomen and your chest.

You could also try carrying him around in a sling, rocking him or cuddling.

What fathers can do

It is almost traditional for fathers to feel left out of the very close physical and emotional bond between a mother and her new baby. They may also have mixed feelings about breastfeeding. It can help to not only talk to each other about this as much as possible, but to share the tasks of caring for the baby.

Fathers who are allowed to build up their own strong, loving bond with their babies are less likely to feel jealous and left out of the mother–baby relationship.

Actively encourage him to feed (if the baby accepts a bottle), bath, change, burp, cuddle, sing to, walk around with and generally have the baby near him as much as possible. Babies of all ages like watching or just feeling their father's presence nearby while he is working, gardening, cooking or painting, reclining and reading or looking at the TV, while the baby lies on his chest, or is rocked to and fro in his pram by his foot.

Fathers do not always do things the way mothers do. But unless the baby is clearly

uncomfortable, a father's way is just as good as a mother's. Most fathers initially feel helpless and under-confident around small babies. If they do not become physically involved with them, these feelings remain, as do the resentments. Allow your baby the comfort of a loving father.

Breastfeeding or offering a bottle may help, although if he is in real pain, he may be uninterested; you could try gripe water or a dilute herbal remedy such as camomile tea.

Ear infections cause persistent, miserable crying, occasionally punctuated by silence as the baby falls asleep exhausted, which then starts again as he shifts position and wakes. If this pattern fits, suspect an ear infection and contact your GP immediately. On his or her advice you may be able to give Calpol (liquid paracetamol) until you can see the GP who will almost certainly prescribe antibiotics.

Always call your GP if your baby:
- seems to be getting no better
- actually appears worse
- has a temperature (sponge him with tepid water in the meantime)
- is crying in a different way than usual
- seems very lethargic
- does not seem to know you.

Is he uncomfortable?
Check his nappy is not wet, dirty or on too tight, or leave him to kick without a nappy for a while (put him on a towel to protect the carpet or bed). Check his temperature (see pp. 106 and 128). If he seems hot, remove some clothes or take him out in the pram; if he feels too cold, wrap him in a shawl or clean towel pre-warmed on the radiator and cuddle him close, or put on a hat, socks or mittens.

Check for clothing rashes and nappy rashes.

If your baby is lying down, see if he prefers to be propped up, or placed in a different position.

Is he extra sensitive?
Handle him quietly and talk to him gently and try to keep visitors to a minimum. Ask siblings to be gentle around him.

Do not overwhelm him with sights, sounds, movements and other stimulation, and try to get into a routine so that feeds, baths and outings happen at roughly the same time each day.

Is he tired but fighting sleep?

Offer breast, dummy or bottle; or rock him in your arms or in the pram. Try moving him to a quieter room or a noisier room, perhaps putting on a baby cassette with some gently soothing music or leave a clock with a regular tick in his room.

Walk up and down with him in a dimly lit room, at a pace of one step per second, patting him very gently on his back at the same speed.

Leave him to cry for a short time but if the crying does not diminish from loud to sniffling within five to ten minutes, cuddle again and rock.

As a last resort, wrap him up, strap him in his seat and take him for a car ride.

Is he generally irritable?

Carry him in a sling on your back or front, put him in a bouncy chair and rock it with your foot or take him out in the pram.

Rock him in your arms or the pram, gently talking or singing to him. Dance to gentle music, holding your baby in your arms or up against your shoulder. Try a change of scenery – a different room, the garden, balcony, having a warm bath, or gently massage his back, feet or head.

If he is irritable for more than a few hours and nothing seems to be working, consult your health visitor or GP, or a suitably qualified practitioner of complementary medicine.

Colic

Colic is characterized by regular attacks of piercing screaming, which tend to occur at the same time (or times) each day – usually early evening. While these attacks last, it is extremely difficult to comfort the baby for more than a few minutes at a time. Both the crying, and the difficulty of soothing the baby, can be exceptionally upsetting for you too.

Your baby is likely to have colic, rather than be crying for another reason, if:

- the crying is accompanied by your baby drawing up his legs as if in pain;
- there are loud rumblings from his abdomen, he is burping and/or passing plenty of wind;
- he is temporarily soothed by feeding, but this seems to make it worse in the long run. See p. 162 for advice on coping with colic.

SLEEPLESS BABIES, EXHAUSTED PARENTS

Definitions of what constitutes a 'sleep problem' vary, but basically if your baby's sleeping patterns are causing a definite problem for him – or you – then he has a sleep problem. Such problems cannot generally be said to exist until your baby is around six months old: before that age, most babies wake at least once in the night because they are hungry. After this time, however, problem sleepers usually fall into three categories:

- the won't go to sleepers
- the repeated night wakers
- the very early (4 am to 5 am) risers.

The effect on your baby

Whichever category fits your baby, the chances are that his lack of sleep will have few noticeable effects on him. He may suffer a little short-term irritability the next day, but if he is tired from his antics in the night (and some babies seem not to be), he will probably nap for a little longer than normal in the day to compensate.

As there is no specific research on the long-term effects of lack of deep sleep on babies and young children, it is difficult to know whether this may cause long-term problems. But it is believed to be better for them to sleep properly; if they do not, they may be missing out on the deep sleep that fosters optimum growth and physical or mental development.

How much are babies meant to sleep?

Babies' needs vary enormously, but as a rough guide (including naps) your baby may sleep in the region of:

Week 1	16½ hours
1 month	15½ hours
3 months	15 hours
6 months	14½ hours
9 months	14 hours
12 months	13¾ hours
18 months	13½ hours

The effect on you

If your baby falls into one of these categories, the effects on you may be profound. They include:

- continual tiredness, with the result that you become obsessional about sleep
- your parenting skills may be affected
- you may feel inadequate as a parent
- your relationship with your partner may suffer
- your other children may suffer from your lack of energy for parenting
- clinical depression is strongly linked to long-term exhaustion and sleep deprivation
- you may develop negative feelings for your baby, and the guilt associated with them.

Babies' sleep problems can turn a loving, rational parent into an exhausted wreck. Human beings cannot function properly on insufficient sleep. It can put terrific strain on relationships within families and has even been cited as a cause of marital breakdown and child abuse.

Some sleepless nights are inevitable with young babies, and bearable. But continual interruptions two, three or four times a night, leading to deprivation of sleep for months (even years) are not. People whose children did not behave in this way naturally have no idea of the distress and potential damage it causes.

Below: Cradling a tiny baby in your arms as you talk quietly to him may make him sufficiently relaxed to fall asleep.

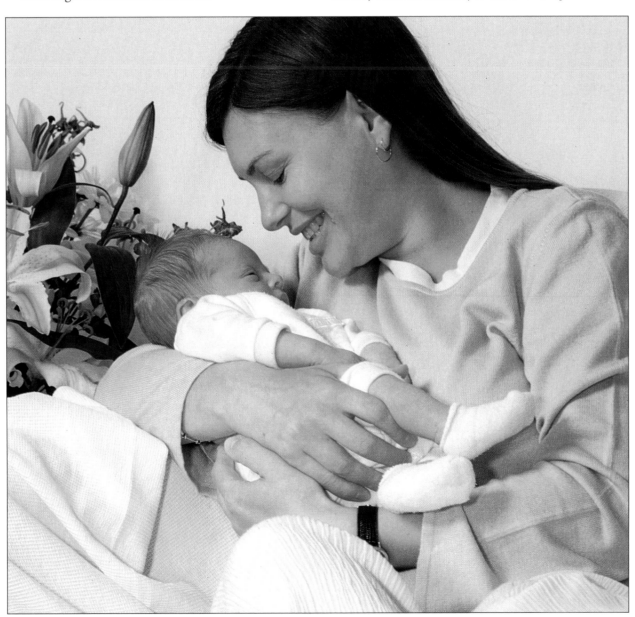

They tend to dismiss it as an exaggeration on the part of the sufferers or even an indication that they are not doing a very good job, which can be almost as upsetting as the lack of sleep itself.

Parents used to be told simply to wait until their child grew out of sleep problems. Now a greater understanding of this type of problem has produced a broad range of potential solutions and coping mechanisms, ranging from baby behavioural training and drugs to support networks involving other parents.

The good news is that, today, it is almost always possible to find the combination of factors – or the one thing – that works for you and your baby. Do not despair, and do not try and struggle through on your own. Get help.

The facts about sleep

Babies should be sleeping through the night (at least six hours) more nights than not by the time they are around six months. If yours is not, something in his routine, or response to his night waking, needs adjustment. If he wakes and wants to be fed, it is now likely to be more of a comfortable habit than a necessity. (Specific sleep disorders, such as sleep apnoea, can also be solved with the help of a specialist doctor, see Useful Contacts, pp. 390–3.)

Babies have more potential for waking up at night than adults. This is because people sleep in a series of cycles. At the end of each cycle, most people stir slightly, stretch, wake briefly then fall asleep again. The brief waking happens every 90 minutes to adults – but every 60 minutes in babies. Not only that, but adults have developed the ability to put themselves back to sleep when they wake. Babies and infants need to learn this skill. If, however, babies are automatically picked up or fed each time they wake, it is arguable that they may be slower to learn how to put themselves back to sleep and remain reliant on you for (repeated) help at night, for longer.

Physical problems

It is worth checking that your baby is not waking repeatedly because of a physical problem which needs treatment, or an environmental one which can be easily resolved. Check:

- Is his room too hot or cold?
- Is he too hot or cold: check blankets, sleepsuit and so on.
- Is he kicking off his bedclothes at night and waking up cold? Try a warm sleepsuit with only light bedclothes.
- Is his night-time nappy – and undersheet – repeatedly sopping? Perhaps cut back a bit on late night drinks, or consider double nappying or putting an absorbent pad inside the nappy.
- Might the washing powder you use for his night-clothes and bedding irritate his skin? Try a very gentle brand, and double rinse in the machine each time.
- Is he nervous of the dark? Try leaving a dim night light on by his bed.
- Is the room too light at night, and disturbing him? Try it darker.
- Is he bored or lonely in his cot at night? Try adding a musical toy or two that he can operate by pressing, or pulling a string on the side of the cot, cuddly toys, an interesting mobile, pictures stuck to the inside of the cot.
- Has there been an emotional upset in the family recently, has either you or your partner had to go away for a while, have you moved to a new home? Is there some trouble at home?

Your baby could also have an underlying medical problem that is preventing him sleeping well. These can include:

- Mild eczema, which can be sufficiently uncomfortable as to keep him awake at night. If so contact your GP and National Eczema Society (see Useful Contacts, pp. 390–3) for prompt help and advice.
- A mild recurring ear or bladder infection.
- Recurrent nappy rash. This may begin to sting in the small hours as a nappy becomes soggy with urine. See Nappy rash (pp. 163–4) and put on a great deal of cream at night as both prevention and treatment.

If none of these seems to be causing a problem, ask your GP to give your child a full physical check up.

What you can do to help yourself

- Ignore parents whose babies sleep right through the night.
- Cat nap whenever your baby sleeps, and go to bed when he does, even if it is 7.30 pm – anything to get a full, uninterrupted three- or four-hour sleep.
- Take turns to be on night duty with your partner – again so you can both get an uninterrupted few hours at least once a night. Sleep in separate parts of the house if necessary. If you are breastfeeding, express some milk so that someone else can give one feed. After the first few weeks, this will not affect your milk production (see p. 77).
- Do the same with any friends or relatives prepared to help, rather than just offer advice.
- Ask for and accept help of all types (baby minding for a couple of hours, shopping, cleaning) to conserve what energy you have.

What you can do to help the baby

Although you cannot expect him to sleep through the night until he is six months old, there are things you can do from the start to promote good sleep habits later.

- Try not to feed, rock or cuddle your baby until he is sound asleep, and then lay him in his cot. This may make him develop the habit of only being able to go back to sleep if he has been suckled, rocked or otherwise had attention from you.
- Make a clear distinction between night and day.
- Have a set bedtime routine as soon as possible, so that your baby has plenty of cues to recognize that bed is coming. These may include: a warm bath, dim lights, a feed, a cuddle, a particular comfort blanket or soft toy, and/or a special song or tune from you or played by a tape or mechanical toy. Round off with 'goodnight' and a kiss. (This is seldom practical for the first few weeks as very new babies tend initially to show no pattern or routine, but it becomes easier after about two months.)
- Avoid anything noisy, or exciting in the hour before bedtime. This includes boisterous play, loud music, or evening visitors who want to hold and play with the baby. If siblings want to play with him, it has to be low key.
- If you need to feed the baby at night, keep the lights dim, or do not switch them on at all; talk in a calm, low voice or do not talk at all. Do not change his nappy unless it is very wet (rather than slightly damp) or soiled. Keep the baby warm and comfortable – perhaps feed him cuddled inside your dressing gown. Wind him gently. Alternatively take him into your bed and feed him there.

Many parents find that sharing their bed with their baby, or with the cot placed flush next to their bed, perhaps with the side adjacent to you down, works well. There is no danger of you rolling over and squashing your baby, as long as you have taken no sleeping or recreational drugs or any alcohol. (If your baby shares your bed, he will receive the warmth from your bodies so only needs to be dressed lightly. A fluffy sleepsuit would make him far too hot.)

Changes in sleeping patterns

If your baby was a good sleeper and suddenly starts to wake up again at night, there may be an obvious cause. A bad cold or earache, or other minor health problem may make him sufficiently irritable to disturb his usual pattern. Holidays, too, upset normal routines with perhaps later nights and later starts in the morning, and can throw babies out of gear.

Some babies have problems when their first teeth start to come through, then when the molars make their appearance between 12 and 18 months. Preparations such as Bonjela and Teejel, and homeopathic teething powders (available from your pharmacist or homeopath) may help, as does Calpol (liquid paracetamol).

Once you have tackled all the obvious causes of sleeplessness, you may find gentle behaviour modification works. Do not try to use this technique until your baby is at least six months. Babies are increasingly receptive to such techniques from six months onward.

The checking routine

This technique is used by many parents who contact CRY-SIS for help, with largely positive results. If you are thinking of trying it with your baby, consult an experienced health visitor, your GP or speak to CRY-SIS first for fuller details and support (see Useful contacts pp. 248–51).

Before you start:

- Make sure that both you and your baby are well.
- Choose a time when you have no major commitments or pressures.
- Try and clear four or five days – or begin the routine on a Friday night, with, if possible, the following Monday off.
- Discuss what you are doing in detail with your partner, your health visitor, GP and any relevant help organization.
- If you have not already done so, establish a clear bedtime routine first.

How checking works

If your baby cries after being put to bed, allow him to do so undisturbed for a set time – between 3 and 10 minutes. Return to his room and 'check' on him. Avoid eye contact, but tuck him in gently, say goodnight and leave within 30 seconds. Do not pick him up, cuddle or feed. Do this as many times as it takes before he falls back to sleep. Remain gentle, but firm.

Your baby may cry for some time (anything between half an hour and several hours) but continue to return, check and leave. This will reassure your baby that he has not been forgotten or abandoned, but that nothing enjoyable like a cuddle or a drink is forthcoming. He will conclude that it is not worth the effort. However, be prepared for a battle of wills.

You may find a noticeable improvement in a couple of days; it may take longer. The success rate of the approach (in that it brings at least a substantial improvement, or sleeping through the night properly) is about 90 per cent.

Making it work

Checking does not work if you (or your partner) cannot stay firm. Keep a sleep chart of how long your baby is awake and how long he cries: improvements may give you the impetus to carry on.

It is upsetting to listen to your baby cry. Consider ear plugs, going to another room and watching TV or playing music for the time between checks. And, think positive. Go through all the things you will be able to do again if you can get some more sleep. Try not to feel guilty. Interrupted sleep is preventing you from functioning properly, and it is not especially good for your baby either. The whole family will benefit when you can sleep through the night.

WHAT ABOUT YOU?

While you are busy getting used to caring for your baby's everyday needs, in the six weeks immediately after your baby's delivery (often referred to as the puerperium), your body gradually starts to return to its pre-pregnant state. Although a woman's body is never exactly the same as it was before the birth of a baby, the changes you can expect in this period include the following:

- You will be losing blood through your vagina. Known as lochia, this is coming from the raw site on the wall of your womb to which the placenta was formerly attached. It helps to wear soft, thick, comfortable sanitary towels (rather than the harder very slimline ones) and wash the area regularly with cool water, then pat it dry with toilet paper to prevent it remaining constantly moist and sticky. For the first 24–48 hours, this bleeding is normally quite heavy, but if it seems to you to be excessive, ask advice from your midwife or doctor. After a couple of days, the blood loss slows, gradually becoming reddish-brown, then brown. It should fade completely within four to six weeks. If it starts to become red again after fading away, consult your doctor as this may be an indication that there is still a piece of placenta remaining. If so, it will have to be removed.
- Your breasts begin to swell considerably with fluids, including colostrum and blood, between the second and fourth days after delivery, as you begin to produce milk.
- Between two and six days after the birth, you may develop some measure of temporary postnatal 'blues' (see box on p. 120). The symptoms include weepiness, anxiety and irritability. This feeling is partly due to the profound changes in hormonal levels your body is undergoing – those hormones which maintained your pregnancy and fuelled your labour plummet, while those that produce breast milk rise rapidly. Nine out of 10 women who experience the blues find they pass within a couple of days. If they do not, let your GP, midwife or health visitor know.
- Your uterus gradually shrinks back to its normal compact size. Immediately after birth, it weighs some 1.2 kg (2¾ lb), a week later 500 g (1 lb),

and after six weeks have elapsed, it has returned to its non-pregnant weight of around 70 g (2½ oz).

- Your cervix, which during delivery opened up so that the small hole in its centre – the os – measured 10 cm (4 in) across, closes up again. It may now be a slightly irregular shape, and the os is a slit rather than a dimple in the middle.
- Your blood volume returns to normal after about three weeks; during pregnancy this increased by around 50 per cent.
- One in eight women is ovulating and able to become pregnant again as early as six weeks after the birth; this proportion rises to one in three after three months.

Temporary discomforts

It may be a relief to no longer be pregnant, but you may suffer discomfort during this postnatal period. Some problems, such as those caused by stitches from tearing or episiotomy, do not affect everyone; others such as vaginal bleeding are common to all newly delivered mothers. The good news, however, is that most discomforts can be significantly reduced quite easily and all are temporary.

Afterpains

You may feel pain as your womb slowly contracts back to its former size. So-called afterpains last for up to a week and range from being uncomfortable (like a mild period pain), to almost as bad as labour pains. You may not be conscious of them at all with your first child, but they tend to become progressively sharper after the birth of subsequent babies.

Afterpains are especially noticeable if you are breastfeeding because the hormone stimulated by your baby's sucking helps your womb muscles contract. They may be particularly uncomfortable if you had your baby by caesarean.

WHAT YOU CAN DO Strong painkillers may be the only effective treatment. If you are in hospital, ask for them; if you are at home, ring the doctor and ask for a prescription. Do not exceed the recommended dose.

You could also try placing a warm hot-water bottle against your lower abdomen, as the heat can have a comforting, muscle-relaxing and mildly analgesic effect. And any breathing or relaxation techniques you learned to use in labour may help.

Blood clots

You may pass blood clots after the birth, usually when you urinate, although they can sometimes be left on your sanitary towel. If they are substantial or you have passed two or three, tell your midwife or doctor. If possible, show them one as it may be a piece of retained placenta. If it is, you may need minor surgery to remove it before it causes an infection.

A raised temperature, pale skin, rapid pulse and very tender abdomen can all be signs of such an infection. Report them to your doctor immediately as you may need antibiotics in addition to minor surgery to remedy the problem.

Bruising and soreness

You may feel sore and bruised just about everywhere, as labour is usually a hard physical effort and demands the full co-operation of muscles you may not have known you had.

WHAT YOU CAN DO Try soaking in a warm or hot bath for at least 20 minutes. And persuade someone to massage you afterward, when your muscles will be more relaxed and easier to work on.

Soreness around the coccyx (which moved back out of the way during delivery) and sore swelling around the perineum and vulva can all be soothed with ice packs. Use a small packet of frozen peas or sweetcorn (which can be endlessly re-frozen) on the area for 10 minutes at a time. Wrap a thin tea towel or scarf around the pack so the frozen surface does not come into direct contact with your skin as it could give you ice burns.

Pain on urinating or emptying your bowels

If it hurts passing urine, the measures suggested under stitches (see p. 110) are all helpful.

Avoiding constipation is one of the best self-help measures. Drink as much plain water as you can (avoid tea and coffee, which are both diuretic and may make matters worse) and eat plenty of fresh fruit (ask a visitor to bring a bowl full). Grapes are especially good as they are easy to graze on throughout the day, and are ideal in the hot, dry hospital environment. Try also to move around as much as is possible, even a short careful walk several times a day will help.

Straining to open your bowels will not burst your stitches, but if you are worried, hold a soft sanitary pad against the stitches. A glycerine suppository can gently help get any waste matter in the rectum moving, and lubricate the passage to make things easier and less painful. An enema may be suggested if by the fourth or fifth day after delivery you are still unable to open your bowels: if you do not want one, you should say so.

Stitches

Perineal stitches may be the result of a tear, or of an episiotomy. They usually heal quite quickly as the blood supply to this area is very rich. A tear or episiotomy should be noticeably better after a week and may give little trouble after 10 to 14 days or so (the stitches will dissolve after about a week). If yours still trouble you months after your baby's birth, mention the matter, forcibly if necessary, to your GP and request that you be referred to a gynaecologist to find out what the problem is.

WHAT YOU CAN DO Keep the area very clean and dry. Change your sanitary towel regularly, wash the area in warm water and pat it dry with toilet paper after urinating or opening your bowels. Stitches heal better when they are dry, and the drier they are, the less likely they are to become infected.

Ice packs (as for general bruising) may help, as do Epifoam – a mildly anaesthetizing foam containing a steroid to reduce inflammation, which is sprayed on – or lignocaine, a gel which also contains a local anaesthetic. Both of these are only available from the hospital or on prescription from your GP.

Ultrasound may help heal this type of soft tissue damage: ask whether this is available from the hospital's physiotherapy department.

You could also try bathing in warm water with antiseptic liquid added, although this can make the bath rather slippery. Salt baths – add enough salt to be able to taste it in the water – or lavender baths – add 10 drops of good-quality lavender essential oil – may also help.

A herbal infusion of one handful of uva ursi, one of shepherd's purse and one of comfrey, boiled together and left to steep for 30 minutes, then added to the bath may ease discomfort, or put a few drops of Hyper Cal, a homeopathic tincture, on to a soft sanitary pad.

If you find it uncomfortable to sit, use a child's inflatable swimming ring as a cushion and carry it about with you. If your stitches sting when you

Stitches that persist in hurting

If the stitched area is still hurting months after it has technically healed, it may be that:
- the edges of the tear or cut were unevenly sewn together, in which case an operation is needed to make a clean incision over the same place and re-sew it very carefully;
- an excess of scar tissue has developed into a sensitive lumpy area; this is known as keloid scarring and it can often be treated with injections of cortisone, or (failing this) another incision and additional careful stitching;
- there may even be a small nerve trapped in the area – an experienced gynaecologist should be able to diagnose this.

Do not put up with pain that lingers. Talk to your GP and get help.

urinate, pour water over them as you do so. Or pass water at the end of your bath or shower, and clean (or get someone else to clean) the bath or shower stall thoroughly with disinfectant afterward.

Piles and haematoma

Piles (haemorrhoids) are enlarged varicose veins in the spongy walls of the anus. They can appear during pregnancy for the same reason as varicose veins in the legs – because of the rise in progesterone which relaxes all muscle tissue, including that of the vessels of your circulatory system. They can be tender, especially during a bowel movement, itchy and may bleed after a bowel movement too. You may also find they prolapse – push out of their surrounding tissue – after a bowel movement and need to be tucked back in with your fingers each time.

Haematoma are small sacs filled with clotted blood. They feel like tender lumps under the perineal skin and tend to appear after the strenuous pushing of labour. If they persist, fibrous tissue may develop around them, this in turn can form scar tissue and they may become infected. These can be treated by your doctor.

WHAT YOU CAN DO Haemorrhoids can be soothed by holding an ice pack (as for general bruising) against the skin, or ask your GP for a prescription for a haemorrhoid shrinking and soothing cream. It also helps to avoid constipation, as straining to empty your bowels makes piles worse (see Pain on urinating or emptying your bowels, p. 109). Minor surgery may be advised if piles persist.

Haematoma need professional treatment under anaesthetic, usually only considered once six months have elapsed since the birth. Talk to your GP or ask to be referred to a gynaecologist.

Sore breasts

Your breasts swell considerably during this time because hormonal changes are preparing them to feed your baby – whether you actually wish to do so or not. The result is an influx of fluid (including blood) to the area which makes your breasts very full and taut. The stretching of the breast skin can become uncomfortable, the breasts tend to become hard, hot and tender to touch.

WHAT YOU CAN DO Wear a comfortable, supporting maternity bra day and night. You can also try warm baths deep enough to soak your breasts in, and either warm or cool flannels over each breast (try both to see which you find more comfortable). A traditional remedy – reputed to be very soothing – is to place a leaf of washed, dark green Savoy cabbage inside each bra cup so it curves around the breast.

If you do not wish to breastfeed, your breasts should go down to their usual size within about a week. If you wish to discourage milk production, you could bind your breasts gently but firmly with a soft, wide crêpe bandage (you may need to insert a breast pad over each nipple as they will tend to leak a little colostrum). Bromocriptine, available on prescription only, also inhibits milk production but it can have unwanted side-effects such as nausea.

See pp. 73–6 for advice on dealing with discomforts related to breastfeeding.

The blues

The blues often coincide with the milk coming in to your breasts, the initial euphoria induced by the hormones released during and after labour wearing off, and your becoming aware of the full impact of any physical discomforts – everything seems to be either leaking or hurting.

These feelings usually disappear within two or three days. See Postnatal illness, p. 120.

WHAT YOU CAN DO No treatment is usually necessary for the blues since they disappear on their own. But it helps to have peace and quiet to bond with your baby, and support to get feeding well established.

Practical help with domestic chores and caring for other children can help, as does the emotional support of your partner, friends and relatives.

Getting back into shape

Along with the pleasure at looking down to see your feet for the first time in months, you may feel some alarm at the flabby tummy, perhaps complete with stretch marks, that greets you after your baby's birth. Internally, too, your body is far from normal. Among other changes, the muscles of your abdomen, which are usually aligned and close to one another, stretched to accommodate the growing baby, and may well have parted company with each other. And those of the pelvic floor have been stretched to the limit during the birth. Fortunately there is plenty you can do – almost from birth – to help the changes which are naturally occurring to restore your body to normal.

Apart from eating sensibly and getting as much rest as you can, the most important factor in getting back to normal is exercise. Postnatal exercises are at least as important as antenatal exercises: they result in strong abdominal muscles to protect your back from the demands of lifting a baby, good pelvic floor muscles (see p. 26) to prevent stress incontinence (see p. 35) and good thigh muscles to keep your knee joints flexible. The better you feel, the fewer problems you will have with the everyday demands of caring for a new baby.

The earlier you begin to exercise after your baby's birth, the easier you will find it to get into a routine, and the faster you will notice the effects on your body, which in itself can be a good boost to keeping the exercises going. But remember that immediately after the birth your ligaments will still be softer than normal due to the effect of the pregnancy hormones, so you must take it easy. An obstetric physiotherapist will almost certainly visit you on the postnatal ward – if you are in hospital for all but the briefest of stays – and give you advice on what is suitable for you. It is particularly important to get advice on exercise if you have had a caesarean.

Remember, too, that it is never too late to start. If the first couple of weeks after your baby's birth seem

POSTNATAL EXERCISES

In all the excitement of giving birth and having your baby at home with you, it can be difficult to remember that mothers, too, have been through a demanding experience. In caring for your baby, it can be easy to overlook that your body is not going to return to its pre-pregnant state in terms of muscle control and tone, unless you actively take steps to ensure that it does. Postnatal exercises are vital and the more you can do, the better.

Curl ups

These help to draw your parted abdominal muscles together and generally firm and tone them.

1 Lie on your back with your knees bent and feet flat on the floor. Place your hands on your thighs. Pull your abdominal muscles in and tighten your buttocks.

2 Breathe out as you slowly tuck your chin in to your chest and lift your head, then your shoulders, off the floor. As you do so, slide your hands along your thighs toward your knees.
  When your head, shoulders and upper back are off the floor and your hands have reached your knees, hold for a count of three, then slowly lower yourself back to the floor. Repeat the whole sequence.

Leg slides

This exercise strengthens your abdominal muscles and closes the gap that the growing baby caused to open between them.

1 Lie on your back on the floor with your elbows bent and hands under your head. Bend your left knee so that your foot is on a level with your right knee. Keep your foot flat on the floor.

2 Breathe out, pull your abdominal muscles in firmly and raise your head, tucking your chin in to your chest.

3 Keeping your head into your chest, change legs: slide your left leg so that it is flat on the floor and bend your right knee. Now lower your head. Repeat the whole sequence.

Waist twists

The skin around your middle and your abdominal muscles stretched enormously to accommodate your growing baby. If you could see your vertical abdominal muscles, before the birth they resemble parallel lines of muscle; afterward, they can be an ox-bow shape. This exercise helps to pull your waist back to its 'normal' state and improves the range of movement in your upper body.

1 Sit on a chair with your back straight, knees apart and feet flat on the floor. Fold your arms at about chest height. Keeping your buttocks on the chair and your abdominal muscles pulled in tight, twist slowly to the right. Hold for a count of three.

2 Twist back to centre and without relaxing your abdominal muscles, twist as far to the left as you can. Hold for a count of three, then return to the centre. Only then should you relax your abdominal muscles. Repeat the whole sequence.

Outer thigh lifts

This exercise works on your abdominal muscles, but also increases the strength and tone in your thighs.

1 Lie on your left side, with your head on your left hand. Place your right hand on the floor in front of you for balance. Pull your abdominal muscles in and keep them tight throughout the exercise.

2 Raise your right leg as high as you can, while keeping it as straight as you can. Hold for a count of three, then lower back down. Repeat six times then turn on to your right side and do an equal number, raising your left leg. Repeat, working both sides equally.

to pass in a blur, start exercising when you can. It helps to try to do a set of exercises at the same time each day, simply so they become part of your routine, but if you do not have a routine to begin with – and most new parents do not – do them when you can. If you are too exhausted one day to do them at your normal time, do them later, after you have had a rest. If you feel full of energy one day do an extra set, but take it easy and do not overdo it.

All these exercises work on the muscles that have been most affected by your pregnancy. In each case, start by repeating the sequence six times and gradually increase as your muscles return to their former strength and flexibility.

Where to go
You may find it easy to exercise at home. The exercises given here, together with many antenatal exercises (see pp. 26–7) will give you a good basis on which to work. Alternatively, consult a book on post-natal exercise – the hospital obstetric physiotherapist will be able to recommend one.

Some hospitals run postnatal exercise classes, and if you attend antenatal classes there it is worth asking what they can offer. Or, try your local leisure centre which may run classes for new mums, or your nearest NCT branch which may be able to give you advice on what is on offer locally. Your health visitor or GP's surgery should also be aware of what is available in your area.

CARE AFTER A CAESAREAN

One in every seven babies in Britain is born by caesarean. Although this is a safe, common operation, it is still (rightly) classed as major surgery since both the abdominal wall and womb are opened. Additional aftercare and help are therefore necessary after a caesarean birth.

Depending on how much help there is at home, how you are feeling and on the hospital's policy, you may spend up to ten days in hospital.

Immediately after a caesarean

- The incision area – usually a bikini cut from side to side just above the pubis – is covered by a light dressing. This will be painful at first, and you will probably need strong, effective pain relief for at least 48 hours afterward.
- A drain, which draws off any excess blood and fluid from the incision site, stays in place for the first few hours only. (It may not be necessary to have a drain at all.)

After the first few days

By the time you go home from hospital, you should be feeling far more mobile and no longer need strong painkillers. But you should still take care, limiting the amount you do to ensure that your body heals as quickly as possible.

Energy
Many people lack energy for several weeks or even months after major surgery of any type. Take it easy.

- Avoid heavy lifting during the first six to eight weeks. This is easier said than done if you have a toddler as well as a new baby to care for. Try to get as much help as you possibly can, and also try: crouching down without bending to cuddle a toddler instead of lifting him; using a step-up (pillows, a cushion, a cardboard box) to help him on to the sofa next to you, or on to your bed. To feed a toddler, sit on the floor on a cushion and put his meal either on a low table or in the low version of a convertible high chair so that you do not have to lift him in and out.
- Avoid any housework that means you need to stretch, pull or push for six weeks – this includes hoovering, ironing, changing beds and carrying shopping or laundry.
- You should not drive for two to six weeks after a caesarean. Ask the hospital for advice.

Exercise

Many of your pelvic floor exercises are similar to the ordinary postnatal exercises done after a vaginal birth (see pp. 112–113) but you should do them slowly and gently, at your own pace. Others, because you have had major abdominal surgery, are rather different. The hospital physiotherapist should see you before you go home, and will give you full details and a sheet of exercises. If you do not get to see her, ask to do so.

Alternatively, contact the Association of Chartered Physiotherapists in Obstetrics and Gynaecology (see Useful Contacts, pp. 248-51).

Feeding

Your incision site will stay sore for a while, so whether you are bottle- or breastfeeding, it helps to keep the baby's weight off the area.

If you have a vertical scar (which is uncommon these days), feed sitting up with pillows across your stomach to absorb the baby's weight. Alternatively, lie on your side with the baby next to you. It may take a bit of practice at first to get the baby at the right 'height' to breastfeed in this way, but once you get the hang of it, this is very comfortable, especially if you are feeling tired, or have taken the baby into bed with you to feed him at night.

If you have a bikini scar, lie the baby on a pillow 'tucked' underneath your arm, so that his head is facing your breast or a bottle and his body is under your arm (see Feeding twins box on p. 76). Or, sit up with a cushion or pillow supporting you on either side, and put the baby's head on one pillow and his feet on your thighs.

Infected incision

This is the most common problem following a caesarean. Signs that the wound may be infected include a raised temperature, a red, inflamed and weepy wound, hard lumps developing behind the scar, increased pain in the whole area and the wound opening slightly.

Such infections can be quickly and easily treated with antibiotics.

Pain and soreness

If pain persists, ask the hospital for milder but effective pain relief tablets to take home with you in case you need them. Make sure they know if you are breastfeeding so that any drugs they give you do not harm the baby. If you hired a TENS machine for the birth, know how to use it, felt that it helped, and do not yet need to send it back, this can be very useful for relieving pain (see p. 53).

Warm baths can also have a very soothing, slightly analgesic effect, although you may still need some help getting in and out of them. Don't bath when you are alone in the house, or lock the bathroom door.

Scar pain

The initial pain should wear off within a couple of weeks. After that you will probably feel some discomfort in your scar area, especially when you bend, lift or push – or at night when lying in a particular position may pull on it. If you experience more than the occasional twinge months later, or if the pain is worsening rather than diminishing, go and see your doctor.

Scar appearance

Over time your scar will change from red to pink, and finally to silvery white. In most cases, the scar from a bikini cut will be hidden when your pubic hair regrows. You may, however, find that the area is itchy for months afterward, or that the flesh on either side feels numb for some time.

Tiredness

You have had a major operation, so although you may feel fine within a few weeks, you may well continue to feel tired for several months more than a new mother who has given birth vaginally. If getting as much rest as possible means letting any household chores go for a while, then do so.

Get as much help as possible, from your partner, a parent, friends, neighbours. If there are no volunteers and you can afford it, spend money on cleaning and cooking help, or help with any other children you may have. Ask your health visitor too what sources of state help may be available to you, especially if you are a single parent.

What to wear

Soreness from the incision site will fade away to itchiness and tenderness before it disappears altogether. Try to wear waist-high cotton pants if you have a bikini scar, and loose clothes – either dresses or baggy cotton leggings with teeshirts or sweatshirts over the top – while you are healing. Flattish shoes or trainers will help your posture and prevent you from tipping forward or off balance.

Making love

Unless you had a caesarean after a trial labour involving episiotomy, you may be ready to make love a couple of weeks after the birth, as long as you use positions that keep any pressure off your scar site. Equally you may not feel like having any sexual contact for several months. Both reactions are perfectly normal. You may feel less attractive than before the caesarean, although your pubic hair will hide the scar almost completely. If you feel this way, buy the most attractive new nightdress you can find and wear it to make love in until you feel confident enough to take it off.

If lovemaking is still physically uncomfortable for you two or three months later, tell your GP, since this could indicate a lingering infection around the incision site which needs treating.

If you or your partner do not feel emotionally comfortable with the idea of lovemaking because of the caesarean, try to talk it over together; if this is difficult, contact Relate or the Caesarean Support Network (see Useful Contacts, pp. 390–3), which may be able to put you in touch with other couples who experienced similar feelings.

Emotional recovery

Caesarean birth can be a very positive, fulfilling experience, especially if it was planned in advance, properly discussed with you, you were kept well informed throughout, and the operation was handled sensitively by the hospital staff. In many cases, emotional recovery can be very rapid. But some women who give birth by caesarean do feel very distressed indeed by the experience (especially if it was an emergency procedure), and for them, emotional recovery may take far longer. In general, it can be described as a four-stage process:
- physical and emotional shock
- denial (there is nothing for me to get upset about)
- sadness, and anger
- acceptance of what happened and coming to terms with it.

However just as every woman's reaction to vaginal birth is different, there is a huge variation in the reactions of individual mothers to caesarean birth. It is not unusual for some sadness and anger to appear after many months of positive feelings about the birth. If you feel there are any issues about your caesarean which remain unresolved, discuss them

fully with your doctor at your six-week postnatal check-up (see below). Particularly if it was an emergency procedure, you may want to discuss the reasons why it happened more fully, and the chances of your needing a similar operation if you have another baby (there is often no reason why you cannot give birth vaginally after a caesarean). It can also help to talk to one of the help and support organizations (see Useful Contacts, pp. 390–3).

THE SIX-WEEK CHECK

Whether you had your baby at home or in hospital, you will be given a date on which to see your GP, or return to the hospital, for a postnatal check-up. This usually takes place around six weeks after the baby's birth. There is nothing especially magical about six weeks, but after this time, most new mothers have recovered from the immediate after-effects of the birth and most babies – who are also looked at – are settled into some sort of feeding and sleeping routine, and smiling with delight at the sight of their parents.

Voicing any concerns

The six-week check is an ideal opportunity to discuss anything that is worrying, concerning or has simply crossed your mind about your baby's health and development and your new role as a mother. It is a good time to talk about contraception (see p. 119), diet and exercise (pp. 111–14) and anything else that may be troubling you (lack of sleep, for example).

You can also ask about the changes you can expect to see in your baby, and when (see also Chapter 5). The range of 'normal' behaviour for babies is enormous, so do not worry that anything is going to be too trivial. No one is going to think you silly, no matter what you ask. It is far better to be told that there is nothing to worry about, than to fret at home later, when you should be resting or enjoying your baby. Worrying is a natural, positive and necessary part of being a parent: you would not be a 'normal' mother or father if you did not worry.

The six-week check does, however, have considerable psychological significance. It marks your final signing off from the usual obstetric services (at least as far as this pregnancy is concerned – another pregnancy is classed as a separate patient 'episode') and completes your health record for this pregnancy and delivery. It also provides a good opportunity to talk to the doctor about anything that might be worrying you (either from your own point of view, or about the baby) and to have a general health check.

Checks for the mother

- Urine test, blood pressure, examination of the site of any stitches.
- Breast check to ensure that there are no problems, such as blocked ducts or any infection, and – if you are not breastfeeding – that you are not still producing milk.
- The doctor will feel and palpate your abdomen and will do an internal examination to check that your uterus has contracted back to its normal, non-pregnant size and that all is well with your cervix and vagina.
- You may be offered a blood test for postnatal anaemia. It is worth accepting, if it is offered, since if you are suffering from it, you may have no symptoms other than tiredness, which you may be putting down to the unavoidable fatigue of new mothers. Undetected anaemia can persist for months and leave you drained of energy. If you are not offered a test, but do feel exceptionally tired, ask for one. If you are still exhausted after three months, go back and ask for a test to be done.
- You may be offered a smear test, if this was not done at your booking-in appointment (see p. 22–3) and you have not had one in the last four years.

Checks on the baby

Some of these checks are repeats of those done at birth or shortly afterward. They include:
- He will be measured
- He will be weighed (naked, which he may not like)
- His skin colour will be looked at
- His or her genitalia will be examined
- His hips will be checked for 'clicky hip' (see Your Child's Health, pp. 356–7).

Registering your baby's birth

It is the law in England, Wales and Northern Ireland that you must register your baby's birth before he is six weeks old (this must be done before he is three weeks old in Scotland). The address of the local registry office will be in the phone book. If you live in a different district from the one in which the baby was born, you can register at your local office, but the registrar will then send the details on to the 'birth district' and the birth certificate will be sent to you by mail.

If you are married, either parent can register the birth, with both mother's and father's names on the certificate. If you are not married, the mother can register the birth alone, but if the father's name is to appear on the certificate, he must go along in person.

At the same time as you are given your baby's birth certificate, you will be given his National Health Service number. This will enable you to register him with a GP (see p. 153).

In addition, the doctor or health visitor will check your baby's skills in the following areas.
- **Motor development**
  The measure of control a young baby has over his body, even at this age, will be looked at, perhaps by holding him up to see his degree of head control, or by lying him down on his stomach and noting whether he lifts his head and tries to turn it from side to side.
- **Hearing**
  The doctor will ring a bell or shake a rattle out of his range of vision to see if and how he reacts.
- **Sight**
  A bell or rattle will be moved across your baby's line of sight to see if he follows it with his eyes.

Don't worry if your baby cries during these checks, and/or refuses to look or listen to the rattle. These are not tests which a baby passes or fails, but general indicators of his well-being. It is undoubtedly true that doctors prefer a baby that screams healthily to one who lies back placidly and is unresponsive to everything around him. You can always ask for these checks to be redone at any time at the baby clinic if you are worried.

SEX AND CONTRACEPTION

Traditionally, women wait until after the six-week postnatal check-up (see pp. 116–17) before starting to make love again. But apart from the risk of sexual intercourse introducing infection into the vagina, there is no reason why you cannot have sex as soon – or wait as long – as you both feel is right.

Why sex may be difficult

There are scores of reasons, some specific (continued soreness after stitches, for example), some more general (overall fatigue), why you may not wish to make love after the birth of your baby.

But many couples do acknowledge that their sex lives improved after the birth: some women say they have a better body image, are less inhibited and have more powerful orgasms than before. Many couples feel that because they make love less frequently, both partners made more effort to make it special.

Nonetheless, the physical demands of being a new parent often mean that given the choice between an hour of peace for making love or an hour's un-interrupted sleep, you tend to choose the latter. You may find yourself caring for your new baby 24 hours a day for many months, unless he rapidly learns to sleep through the night. Fortunately this phase does not last, and there are many different strategies you can adopt to make sex begin to seem like a pleasurable option once more rather than something you feel you ought to be doing but for which you cannot quite summon the energy. These include both physical problem solving, and practical arrangements.

Body image

Feeling that you are unattractive because your body is not as it was before you became pregnant can inhibit your sexual response or your desire to have any sexual contact at all.

WHAT YOU CAN DO Talk to your partner, honestly, about how you feel and try to accept his reassurances at face value. And carry on, as long as possible, with your postnatal exercises (see pp. 112–14), both for your pelvic floor (see p. 26) and for the rest of your body. The easiest time to lose the extra weight you

put on during pregnancy is the eight weeks after childbirth. If you can, take up gentle all-over toning exercise, such as swimming once or twice a week. And even if you cannot lose all the extra weight – white women are on average 4.5 kg (10 lb) heavier after childbirth, Afro-Caribbean women up to 8 kg (18 lb) – remember that bigger, toned bodies are more sexually attractive than slim, flabby ones.

Stretch marks fade, but if you are unhappy, buy a beautiful new nightdress. This also helps to obscure your larger postnatal contours while you reduce them.

Have a professional massage – several if you can afford it. When you feel ready, try some massage with your partner, taking turns.

Breastfeeding

Breastfeeding can cause vaginal dryness; it can also make you feel differently about your sexuality. The sensual and emotional aspects of breastfeeding can be so satisfying that you have little desire for sex. You may also feel that your breasts temporarily 'belong' to your baby and that it is inappropriate for them to be erotic zones as well.

Because breastfeeding affects your oestrogen levels, it can also reduce your sex drive. Your libido fully returns when you stop breastfeeding – providing you are not still very tired, or sore.

Sexual stimulation often also stimulates milk flow, which can be disconcerting.

WHAT YOU CAN DO Try to make love soon after feeding your baby so that your breasts are empty, or press the heels of your hand firmly against your breasts for half a minute if milk begins to flow from them during lovemaking.

Soreness

Sex after childbirth can often be uncomfortable at first, and it may take time, an understanding partner and many gentle attempts before you feel completely happy about making love again. Give yourselves time to become sexual beings again, after a period of being affectionate, rather than erotic, with each other.

WHAT YOU CAN DO You may feel happier with non-penetrative sex, including sensual massage and gentle oral or manual stimulation, for a while.

If you have had stitches, the area may remain sensitive to pressure or friction for a few weeks, even months. If it continues to be a problem, see your GP and if necessary ask for a referral to a consultant gynaecologist, or go to a well-woman clinic at your nearest family planning centre. You may not have healed well, which can be treated by injections.

Experiment with different positions for lovemaking, to find those which put the least pressure on any area which is still sore.

If your vagina feels sore and tight, try KY gel or contraceptive cream smoothed around your vagina, labia and your partner's penis, before penetration. This may be a problem if you are breastfeeding since breastfeeding causes a temporary reduction in your levels of oestrogen, which affects vaginal lubrication. Also ask your GP about oestrogen cream (available only on prescription), which can help to rehydrate and lubricate the vaginal tissues more effectively.

Your vagina

Although the vagina stretches to allow your baby to be born, it returns to its former size afterward. As long as your pelvic muscles are toned, it is virtually impossible for a partner to tell the difference.

WHAT YOU CAN DO Keep up your pelvic floor exercises (see p. 26). These have three important effects: they strengthen the sling of your pelvic floor to keep it strong for any future pregnancies; they help in treating or avoiding postnatal incontinence or prolapse of the womb later in life; they strengthen the vaginal wall muscles themselves, so they can grip a partner's penis firmly. If you did not bother to work on your pelvic floor muscles before you were pregnant, you may well find that they are better toned after birth than they were before.

Postnatal contraception

Contraception is usually the last thing on a woman's mind when she has just had a baby. But if you resume lovemaking fairly soon after the birth and are bottle-feeding, a combination of breast- and bottlefeeding, or simply not breastfeeding sufficiently often (see box on p. 87) you can be fertile and therefore pregnant again as early as three weeks after your baby's birth.

Try to sort out contraception as soon as possible after your baby's birth. Do not wait until you have had your first period because you will be fertile before that. You may want to wait until your six-week postnatal check-up, which gives you the opportunity of being in

your GP's surgery, to discuss contraception. But if you want to make love before then, make an appointment with your GP or family planning clinic; your midwife or health visitor can also advise you on which method(s) you may find most suitable.

Which method to choose?

You have the same basic choices in method of contraception after the birth as you did before you became pregnant and it is a good idea to discuss your options with your GP or at the family planning clinic. There are, however, a few factors which you should take into account after the birth of a baby.

- The combined pill is not suitable if you are breastfeeding, as it reduces the amount of milk your body produces.
- The progestogen-only pill (or minipill) does not affect the amount of milk you produce, although some traces of progestogen will enter your milk. What effect this has on your baby is uncertain. This pill is also less effective if you weigh more than 70 kg (11 stone).
- If you start taking either pill more than 21 days after the baby's birth, it will not be reliable for the first seven days, so you should use something else too (such as a condom).
- The female condom (or Femidom) may be uncomfortable if your cervix and vagina are still bruised or sore.
- If you used a diaphragm before you became pregnant, it will not fit any longer. It is vital to get a new one fitted and to change again each time you lose or gain 3 kg (7 lb) in weight.
- An IUCD (coil) cannot be fitted until after your postnatal check-up, when your womb has returned to its normal size.

A time and a place for partners

The combination of tiredness and little or no free time may put considerable strain on your relationship with your partner, leaving little opportunity for enjoying much time together.

However, it is important for you both as parents and lovers to get at least a little regular time on your own together, if only for a couple of hours a week. Many new parents try to make this an unbreakable weekly date, no matter how tired they are and say that

Postnatal illness

Feelings of sadness and depression after childbirth can vary widely from the baby blues, which last only a few days (see p. 111), to postnatal depression which without treatment might last for many months. Postnatal psychosis requires admission to hospital. Postnatal illness of any type is not common; half of all mother experience no problems at all. Of the rest, between 50 and 80 per cent feel some degree of the blues and between 10 and 15 per cent experience some degree of postnatal depression. As few as 1 in every 1,000 recently delivered mothers develop postnatal psychosis.

If it happens to you, don't panic. Do not feel you will never get better – because you will. Call the Association for Post Natal Illness (APNI, see Useful Contacts, pp. 248–51) and talk to some of their helpers, all of whom have experienced postnatal illness and recovered fully. You are not unbalanced or weak in some way. It can, and does, happen to any woman. It is not your fault if it happens to you. (If you are the partner of someone who you believe to be suffering from PNI, you may have to call on her behalf. Be very persistent with your GP or your partner's gynaecologist to get yourself heard.)

it was this 'time out' together, with as much mutual support as possible, which kept their relationship strong – even when one was surviving on three hours' sleep a night and the other was doing the housework and cooking each night after a day out at work.

You have needs too, both for each other's company and (especially if one of you is at home all day with the baby) for that of adults in child-free surroundings. You also need a little time and space to nurture your own physical relationship. Although it can seem to require so much organizational effort as to be off-putting, you will find that you have more emotional and physical energy to spend on being a parent if you allow yourselves some private time (see also Taking a break, pp. 231–3).

But if your new baby is temporarily sharing a room or a bed with you, you may find his presence simply too inhibiting.

What you can do
- Try making love somewhere other than your bedroom for a while.
- Arrange one night or afternoon every week when a trusted babysitter, friend or relative has your baby in their home for a while.
- Ask the sitter to come over to your house to babysit. If you feel embarrassed about both retiring to your bedroom, say you are having broken nights and badly need some sleep.
- Ask the sitter to take your baby for a long walk.
- Opt for frequent cuddling rather than sex. The most important thing is that you are comfortable with your relationship.

If you feel the quality of your sexual relationship – or lack of it all together – is a problem or that it could quite easily turn into one, now is a good time to tackle it. Contact Relate or a psychosexual counsellor at a large family planning clinic or a well-woman organization (see Useful Contacts, pp. 248–51) before unwanted patterns become well established.

GOING IT ALONE

In Britain, there are currently 1.3 million single parents bringing up 2 million children. One in five British families is headed by a lone parent, 90 per cent of whom are women. And there is no doubt about it, it is much harder work to bring up a baby on your own than if you have a helpful partner.

Single mothers are placed under a good deal of stress. Single parents of both sexes suffer far more ill health than those with partners. Whether you chose to have your baby alone, or whether the situation was thrust upon you, and regardless of your feelings during your pregnancy, the effect is about the same.

The most common pressures include:
- Being the one person who has to try to carry out all the parental roles in your baby's life for most of the time.
- Shortage of money: only one in three absent fathers pays any maintenance; you may find child care takes a large proportion of your pay, if you have paid work outside the home. Research suggests that 9 out of every 10 lone mothers without jobs would return to work if suitable, affordable child care was available.

- Housing problems are far more common for single parents than for those with partners.
- Keeping in contact with the baby's father, if both sides are willing, can bring difficulties of its own, as well as benefits.

You may need extra support in certain areas either at specific times during your baby's or child's life, or on an on-going basis or both. Among the organizations which can help you are Gingerbread, The National Council for One-Parent Families, The Maternity Alliance, Parentlink, Homestart, MAMA and Parents At Work (see Useful Contacts, pp. 248-51).

Coming home with your baby

If at all possible, try and arrange beforehand for someone to be there when you return with your new baby, perhaps your mother, sister, a friend or neighbour who can either come and stay or pop in regularly. Emotional support and practical help in the form of cooking, shopping, cleaning and even short periods of babysitting take the pressure off you so you can concentrate on your baby.

Money

You may be entitled to one or more different kinds of financial benefit. To find out, phone the local DSS (see the phone book, or your local Post Office can give you the number). If you need further advice or find the often complex DSS forms hard to work out, try the Citizen's Advice Bureau or any of the organizations mentioned above.

If you have a room in your house that might be rented out to a lodger to provide you with an income, seek advice from the help organizations – and other single parents – before you do so. It can work out well, but a parent – especially a woman – alone with a child is also quite vulnerable.

Housing

If you are homeless with a young baby, currently the local council is obliged to offer you one potential place of accommodation. This does not have to be what you – or any other parent – might consider 'suitable' and the council only has to offer you one, which could be a hard-to-let flat in a high-risk area. If you turn an offer down, the council is not by law obliged to offer you anywhere else.

Financial aid is often available to help with payment for existing rented accommodation. If you already have your own place with a mortgage, a contribution toward payments should be made for you by the council if you are on Income Support.

Back to work

A major hurdle in trying to earn a living can be finding good, affordable child care. Single parents – and even today, single mothers more than single fathers – may find they are little better off financially if they do go out to work. However, as a single parent who wishes to work, you should be given priority for any assisted or free creche and community nursery places available.

You may need to be persistent about this, so begin asking about it and going to see nurseries concerned very early on. Again, local Gingerbread groups will have information on what is available in your area, and perhaps know which the best ones are. Your local authority Social Services department will also have a list of nursery addresses, though they cannot make specific comments on their suitability.

Back up

All parents need extra back up, single parents doubly so. Networks of other single parents in your area can be exceptionally supportive and helpful; also, try to collect people who offer to help with anything whatsoever, from the odd bit of shopping when they do their own to giving you a couple of hours off once a week. Sort out which ones really mean it, and take them up on their offers.

Try to cultivate at least two people (apart from any childminder you may have, although a good childminder will almost certainly know other local minders who may be able help in times of need) whom you and your baby like and trust. There will definitely be times when you need them. Even if you do not call on them, knowing they are there helps to reduce the pressure on you. See also Chapter 9: Help with Your child, pp. 228–47.

CHAPTER FIVE

The First Year

Being the parent of a small baby is about far more than looking after her physical needs, although they can seem overwhelming. It is also about watching a tiny person make sense of the world around her, learning to move through that world and interact with it. The first year of a baby's life is an unforgettable time for the whole family.

Your baby's development

At birth an average baby weighs about the same as three bags of sugar and is about as long as the distance from your elbow to your fingertip. By one she will stand about as high as the kitchen table and by two she will be half her eventual adult height. As she grows up, she also grows out. In the first six months your baby will probably put on 550–800 g (20–28 oz) in weight and grow about 25 mm (1 in) every month.

Babies do not just grow: they grow up. If you pick up your one-year-old the fact that she now weighs as much as a dozen bags of sugar is of minor significance compared to the other changes that have taken place. Between six weeks and one year almost everything about a baby changes. At birth her muscles are weak and literally watery. Her bones are bendy and the brain in her tiny head is small. She is not very good at controlling her temperature, blood pressure or breathing. She can do almost nothing and understand even less.

By her first birthday her bones and muscles have changed in structure, her heart beats strongly, she can control her breathing, and her brain has grown considerably. What you see is the effect of all these changes. She now walks around the furniture, draws

in a breath before she shouts long and loud, says 'pss-pss' when she sees the cat, plays pat-a-cake and almost always stops when you say 'No'.

This chapter traces the changes you can expect between six weeks and the end of an average baby's first year, and when you can expect them. Development is not a race, however, and being a month ahead is of no significance. Girls develop a little faster than boys, and Afro-Caribbean babies a little faster than European. There is no correlation between how soon a baby walks or talks and later sporting prowess or intelligence. If your one-year-old is still sitting on her bottom saying nothing it is reassuring to know that Albert Einstein did not say a word until he was two (he also had early learning difficulties, but his name is still synonymous with prodigious intelligence).

Average means in the middle. Half of all babies are ahead of the average and half behind. Most (some 60–70 per cent) are close. It is those babies at the very bottom (or sometimes the very top) of the scale who give cause for concern. Not those who walk late, but those who walk last. Not those above average weight, but those in the top 5 per cent. If your child was

One year of growth

Height: Adds 25–30 cm (10–12 in) by her first birthday.

Weight: Doubles birth weight by four to five months; trebles birth weight by 12–14 months.

Brain: Fastest growing organ in the baby's body.

Skeleton: Bones are quite flexible at birth, but flexibility declines with age.

Muscles: Muscles start off weak and watery, but change in size and composition with use.

Circulation: The heart becomes much stronger and more efficient and blood pressure decreases.

Digestion: Food is only partly digested, with possetting (bringing back a small amount) common; this should decline by six months.

Immune system: The baby slowly produces her own antibodies to replace those passed to her by her mother while in the womb; her mother's antibodies are also passed in breast milk.

Lung capacity: Increases and the lungs become sensitive to irritation; the baby gradually becomes able to combine breathing and moving.

Teeth: Erupt between six months and three years.

premature, she will take a long time to catch up; when you are looking at her development, start from her 'due date' and add a bit to that. If she was a very premature baby, do not expect her to reach the usual developmental milestones at around the same time as her peers until she is about three. It really does take a long time.

Babies who are damaged at birth will also be very slow to begin. Their rate of progress gives a better indication of future potential than their age. Specific disabilities can have quite wide ramifications in the first years: a blind baby, for example, will be slow to walk and to communicate.

YOUR BABY'S GROWTH

For years doctors assumed that children grew at a uniform rate, with babies considered to grow about 0.5 mm (⅕ in) a day. When a group of babies was measured, however, it was found that often they did not grow at all for several weeks, then suddenly there was a spurt, with some growing as much as 12 mm (½ in) in 24 hours. Growth charts, by their very nature, only give averages. This unevenness in her rate of growth will be particularly apparent to you when your child starts wearing shoes. One size might last for six months and the next for only six weeks. Nor are these stops and spurts confined to measurable growth. Children do not learn to do one new thing every day. They learn eight things in two days and then nothing at all for a couple of weeks. If you keep a diary of your child's achievements in the first year you will find that some weeks are full and others quite empty.

Measurable and developmental growth both take energy, which is one of the reasons why babies have such plump bodies. They need to stock up on fuel for the spurts in increased height or weight, and in achievements. Both sorts of growth spurt will probably make your baby tired, hungry, fussy and 'out of sorts'. Being out of sorts or even regressing to more babyish behaviour generally precedes a physical and mental 'milestone' like starting to walk. This fussiness is often attributed to the frustration of not quite being able to do what she wants to do.

Before a 'leap' your baby may be particularly easy. As the leap begins, she becomes difficult and demanding. She then 'grows up', and gradually settles back to her old self. You will find her baby- and childhood peppered with these settled and more difficult times, which can last for weeks, or even months. Fortunately the good times in between are usually longer.

Is she ready?

Babies can only do things if their bodies are ready. No amount of practice will make your baby walk unless the parts of her brain which control her posture and balance are working, and the parts of her brain which allow her to decide which muscles of her legs and trunk she wants to move have developed. Even then she will not walk unless the structure of her muscles has changed so that they can now support the weight of her body, and her bones have hardened and become less flexible so that they can support the movement of strong muscles. In short she walks because her body and brain have grown up. The practice you give her at walking into your arms is the icing on a cake she has already baked.

There is nothing you can do to speed up this development. Early walking runs in families, as does late walking. It is more or less true to say that your baby will walk on the 'appointed day' whatever you do to encourage her.

Your baby's brain

The reason babies are born so helpless and grow to be able to do so much is that their brains grow. The brain controls everything from talking to breathing, from reading books to running races. Because a baby's head needs to pass though her mother's pelvis, it has to be small. Inside the small head is a small brain, only 25 per cent of which is functioning. Since brain cells do not get bigger, as hands or leg bones do, this means that at birth 75 per cent of the brain's functions are missing. During the first three years of life the brain grows faster than any other part of a baby's body.

Present at birth The bottom or lower part of the brain grows and matures first (while the baby is still in the womb). Those parts next to her neck and above the roof of her mouth are all functioning at birth. The lower part of the brain is concerned with automatic actions such as breathing and circulating the blood. At birth your baby can control breathing, heart rate, blood pressure, digestion, arousal, waking, sleeping and elimination. She can also attend to things and recognize that something is familiar. In fact your newborn baby can do all the things she needs to do.

Still to grow The upper parts of the brain are concerned with organizing movement, deciding to move, and all manner of skills from writing to carving statues. They govern making plans, interpreting what is seen, heard and felt, thinking, speaking, reasoning, and committing things to memory.

This area also deals with finding your way around and locating where things are in space, understanding other people, communicating with them and predicting what they might do next. In short, the upper parts of the brain are concerned with everything that tends to be labelled 'human' and all those things that adults, unsurprisingly, do considerably better than babies.

Below: Toward the end of his first year, your baby is almost unrecognizable as the tiny newborn you brought home.

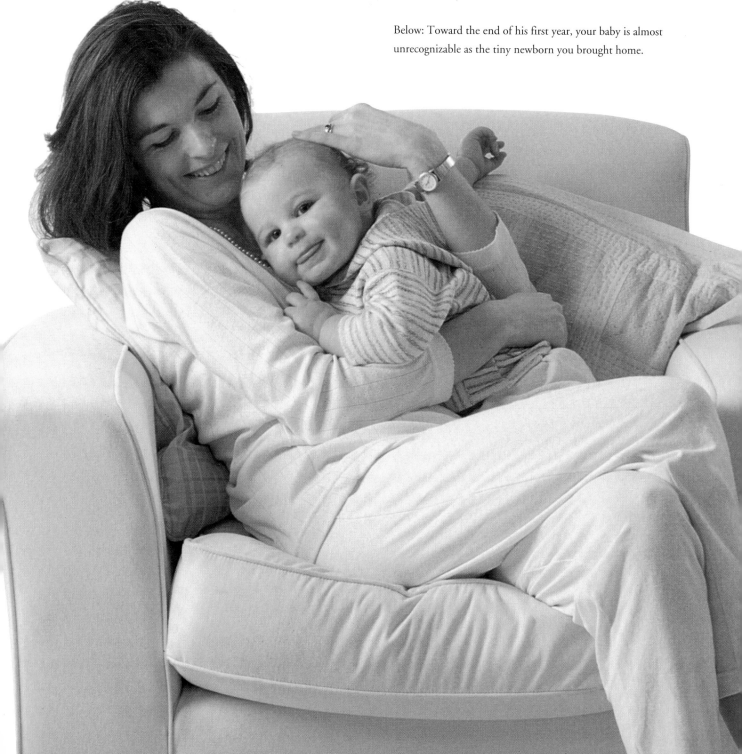

Although many of the higher centres of the brain are in place at birth most other systems have a lot of growing to do. It is because the brain grows so fast that your baby's abilities improve at such a phenomenal rate. Compare how a baby changes in the first two years with how a teenager changes, for example.

The brain matures in a certain order, with the result that the body does so too. Inputs into the brain are better developed than the outputs from it, so your baby finds it easier to see the rattle you are holding out to her than to organize a hand to reach out and touch it. Control of the upper body also develops before the lower body, so that your baby will sit before she stands and be able to reach for a ball before she can kick one.

The higher centres of the brain start to grow and expand between three and six months. As this happens your baby will become better able to control what she is doing now, will begin to remember what she did before, and develop the ability to organize what she will do next.

Boys and girls There are differences between boys and girls in the rate of brain growth. The connections between the left and right segments of the brain grow more quickly in girls, so they tend to reach developmental milestones faster. The connections in boys' brains develop more slowly and boy babies may need more stimulation to help them catch up.

What you can do

Love your baby. Nothing grows unless it is fed and watered, but after birth (in contrast to before birth when it is vital) good nutrition is probably less important for the growth of your baby's brain than loving care and the stimulation such care brings. Babies learn because they are happy and they learn best when helped by people who love and care for them.

Because you love to see her laugh you show her things and play games that make her smile. You also know when she has had enough, so you stop. Then she likes to 'cuddle in' while you hold her close and talk to her. Your baby is programmed to know what she likes and what she needs: you are programmed to love her. The things your baby needs to see, feel and touch are the same things that make her happy. She needs them for as long as she remains interested.

YOUR BABY'S BODY

The changes in your baby's body in her first year are phenomenal; almost everything about her changes in size, and composition.

Bones

At birth babies have soft bones made mostly of cartilage, which makes them very flexible. After birth minerals are deposited in the bones which cause them to harden, a process called ossification. It begins before birth and continues to the end of adolescence, happens faster in girls than boys, and in black babies than white ones. This is one of the reasons why girls walk a little sooner than boys, and why black babies are physically more advanced than white.

Muscles

Babies are born with a complete set of muscles, but like everything else these have to mature. They do so in the same order as the nerves which control them: starting at the neck, working down the body and out toward the fingers. As they mature their structure changes. Mature muscles contain less water and more protein and minerals than immature ones, which gives them added strength and stamina.

Digestion

If babies were fed as nature intended, they would probably be breastfed more or less exclusively for at least two years. Until then their digestive systems are immature. This is demonstrated through examination of babies' stools: in the first year many things pass through undigested. Some do not even pass through, since most newborn babies bring back part of their feed. So-called possetting declines with age and normally stops by about six months. Digestion is helped by 'friendly' bacteria which take up residence in the gut in the first few weeks.

Temperature

If you get too hot you sweat and blood moves into the small blood vessels below the skin (making you turn red). The evaporation of sweat from the skin

Hot or cold?

Since babies have such poor control over their temperature, it is important that you do what you can to help her.

She may be too hot if:
- she is red in the face
- she appears to be sweating
- she feel too hot to your touch

She may be too cold if:
- she seems unusually pale
- she looks blue
- her breathing has slowed dramatically.

As a rule of thumb, when you go out wrap her as if you knew you had to stand at a bus stop for a good while. Remember she is not moving to keep herself warm as you do. Indoors, if the central heating is on, take off her outdoor clothes (even if she is asleep). At night, heat her room, or dress her more warmly than you dress when you sleep alone in an unheated room.

then cools you down. You can also help matters by moving into the shade or reducing your level of activity. If you are cold you do not sweat, and your blood moves away from the surface to the centre of your body which is warmer. You shiver, become active and do things which conserve heat like huddling close to others or putting on extra clothes.

Babies are not very good at any of these things, which is why they cannot exert control over their temperature until they are 12–18 months old. The smaller your baby, the poorer her control.

Breathing

If you compare how a very young baby breathes with how you breathe you will see two differences. The first is obvious: the baby uses her stomach muscles, you use your chest and diaphragm. The second is more subtle. Adults have two breathing systems, one automatic and controlled by the nature of the gases (oxygen and carbon dioxide) in the lungs. This is what prevents you from holding your breath until you are dead. When the oxygen falls below a certain level, you have to take a breath. Everyone has this system. The second system is voluntary and can to some

extent override the automatic. This is what enables you to breathe in before you speak or take a deep breath before you dive into a swimming pool. It enables you to eat without things 'going down the wrong way' and to speak without running out of breath in the middle of a sentence.

Newborn babies do not have this system. They cannot co-ordinate breathing with eating, so they splutter when feeding and if they cry may gasp for breath. In general they breathe in slowly and breathe out quickly. By 6–12 weeks of age they begin to take some control over their breathing and the pattern changes, so that they take in a breath quickly and let it out slowly. You will notice how this alters the way she cries, with her crying becoming more melodic. As she begins to mesh breathing and action she will begin to kick for longer periods. (If you remember how difficult it was to swim a width before you learned how to combine breathing with swimming you will sympathize with babies who have not learned to breathe in before an activity and pace the activity with their breathing pattern.)

This may seem simple, but it underlies your ability to speak and move. Babies are believed to learn the 'in quick out slow' pattern by following your pattern as they cuddle in to your chest. Later they practise breathing and moving as they kick in their cots.

Teething

There are 32 adult teeth but only 20 baby teeth. One baby in 1,500 is born with a tooth, rather more do not have any teeth until after their first birthday. Early or late teething runs in families, but most babies cut their first tooth between five and seven months. The others follow in fairly rapid succession. For some time before they erupt you will see the baby's teeth as little white patches underneath her gums. Just before they break through, they form pale bumps on the gums.

Whenever a baby is 'out of sorts' teething tends to take the blame but since there are only 20 teeth it is not usually at fault. Apart from the short period when the tooth breaks through the gum, there is no reason to suppose that a tooth growing is any more or less painful than a bone growing. Since, at puberty, teenagers often feel 'growing pains' – and are equally out of sorts – it is much more likely that babies are out of sorts because they are growing rather than teething.

Being miserable is one thing, but being ill another. Illness in babies can get out of hand very quickly and should never be ignored. Teething *does not* cause fever, diarrhoea, sickness or convulsions. Such symptoms should not be dismissed as 'teething' (see A–Z of Baby Health, pp. 165–6).

The dos and don'ts of tooth care

It is never too soon to begin to look after teeth – you do only get two sets, after all. Instilling good cleaning and care habits from the start with milk teeth is far easier than trying to establish them when your child is older. If your child loses a first tooth too early, the adjoining teeth may fill the gap, so that when the permanent tooth is ready to emerge, there is nowhere for it to go. This can cause the second teeth to come through irregularly and badly positioned, and lead to problems such as overcrowding, or crooked teeth.

Tooth decay is caused by plaque, which covers the teeth with a sticky bacterial substance. When the bacteria comes into contact with sugar it produces an acid which attacks the teeth. As soon as your baby's first teeth appear, they are at risk from decay, so start cleaning them as soon as they erupt.

- Keep to a good diet during pregnancy.
- Tell your doctor you may be pregnant if medicine is being prescribed, and avoid tetracyclines.
- Make sure that your baby has plenty of calcium (milk, cheese and yogurt are good sources, after six months, see p. 85).
- Make sure she gets vitamin D (egg yolk, oily fish, dairy products, vitamin supplements).
- Limit sweets, cola and ice cream to special times and clean teeth afterward.
- Do not add sugar to drinks or cereals.
- Do not dip dummies in anything sweet.
- Do not let your baby go to sleep sucking a bottle of milk or juice; give her a dummy or bottle of water.
- Give chocolate, cake or biscuits in preference to chewy sweets or sweet drinks because they do not stay on the teeth quite so long.
- Dilute juice is better than squash.
- An apple is better than apple juice.
- Watch for hidden sugars – glucose, sucrose and honey are all sugars.
- Wipe gums (and later teeth) with a soft cloth and a small amount of fluoride toothpaste; ask your dentist's advice on fluoride tablets (see p. 166).
- It does not matter how children clean their teeth as long as they do!

Soothing your teething baby

See pp. 165–6.

Gumming

Babies 'gum' everything, which does not necessarily mean they are teething. The mouth is used for exploring objects. All four- to six-month-olds 'gum', even those who do not get teeth until after their first birthday. See From hand to mouth, p. 137.

The teeth

Typically a baby cuts her first tooth between five and seven months, the rest follow in the order indicated. Your baby should have cut all her teeth by the age of around two and a half.

1 lower incisors; **2** upper incisors; **3** upper side teeth; **4** lower side teeth;

5 first upper back teeth (molars); **6** first lower back teeth;

7 upper 'eye' teeth (canines); **8** lower 'eye' teeth;

9 lower second molars; **10** upper second molars.

YOUR BABY'S PHYSICAL DEVELOPMENT

When babies are tiny, it is easy to wish their lives away. A baby, especially a first baby, always seems to be about to reach the next milestone. It can sometimes be a race with the baby next door. Naturally you want yours to win, but motor control is largely genetically programmed. Whether she walks at 10 months and 4 days or 16 months and 10 days depends on the programme she inherited. Some families walk earlier than others. It signifies nothing at all about your child. All the evidence suggests that early walkers are no more likely to be athletes or dancers than late ones. Nor is a child who walks at nine months likely to do better at school or preschool than one who does not walk until she is 16 months.

The only thing that early walking tells you about your baby is that she is likely to reach other milestones early too.

Practice seems to have very little effect on the timing of any motor-control skills. At best a baby walker can advance when your baby walks by a day or two. Researchers watching more than 100 pairs of identical twins noticed than in almost all cases the motor skills of one twin matured at the same time as the other. But weight makes a difference. A child with heavy arms and legs needs more strength to get going.

'Tables' can only give indications of the order in which skills develop. Some children never crawl, some crawl as soon as they can sit and others sit for a long time before they try to crawl. Most children can stand before they are able to walk and walk before they can run. A few run on tiptoe before they can stand still or walk slowly – they need the speed to keep balance!

Your baby's progress in one area is a better guide to her physical skills than her age. A walking baby should be able to pick up a pea between her fingers and thumb; a crawling baby should be able to pass things from hand to hand.

Milestones in head control

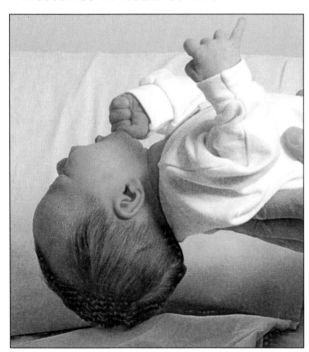

Weeks 1–4: No head control at all

1–4 weeks If you pull your baby by her arms from a lying to a sitting position, her head lags completely behind her body.

8–10 weeks If you pull your baby by her arms from a lying to a sitting position, her head still lags a little behind – but not completely.

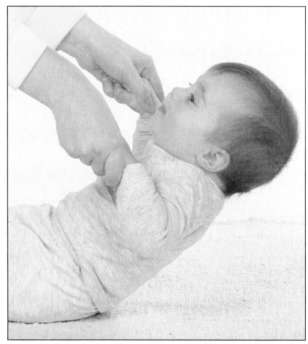

Weeks 16–20: Head only slightly lags behind rest of body

16–20 weeks By now, her head lags only slightly behind; if you hold her upright, she can turn her head in all directions.

24–28 weeks Your baby lifts her head spontaneously when you pull her into a sitting position, tucking her head into her chest.

Learning to sit

Sitting gives your baby a better view of the world, and gives you a better view of her. The major advantage a sitting baby has over one who is still lying down is the level of interaction sitting makes possible. People tend to ignore a baby lying on her back and she is confined to looking at the sky and the occasional tree when you are out walking. Once she can sit, she can see everything you can, and 'talk' to and smile at people.

For this reason, sit your baby in a bouncy chair or a car seat indoors, and choose a buggy that allows her to sit propped up if she is not tired.

Milestones in becoming upright
1–14 weeks Your baby is quite passive if you pull her up past a sitting position.

16–24 weeks She begins to push up by raising her buttocks but cannot sustain this position.
36–44 weeks If you raise her up, she will lower her legs and begin to push down; she becomes somewhat more erect.
48–52 weeks She stands erect, but movement is still an effort.

Learning to move

Being able to move changes your child's interaction with the world and with other people because she can find new things to explore and new things to do. Babies who can crawl can also follow their parents and siblings around the house. In cultures in

Milestones in sitting

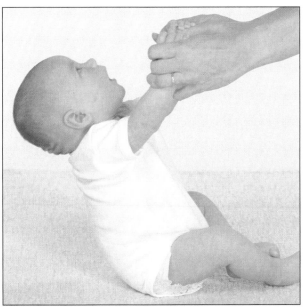

Weeks 8–12 She cannot sit until she has head control

1–4 weeks If you support your baby in a sitting position, her back is uniformly rounded and she has no head control.
4–6 weeks If you support her in a sitting position, her back is rounded but she holds her head up intermittently.
8–12 weeks Supported in a sitting position, her back is still rounded, but she now can raise her head and flex her knees; she can sit for as long as 10–15 minutes if her back and sides are wedged or propped with cushions.

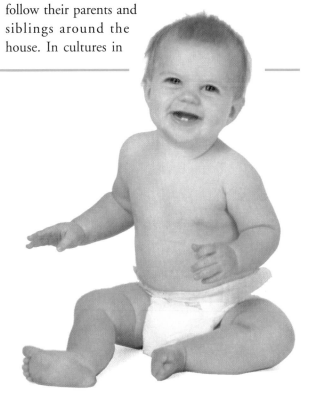

Week 36: She can sit alone for long periods

16–20 weeks Her back is now straighter and she can hold her head erect without any sign of wobble; she can sit for 30 minutes if she is well supported.
20–24 weeks She sits with slight support and can pull herself up to sit; she sits well balanced on a chair.
28 weeks She sits alone steadily if briefly; can push herself into a sitting position.
32 weeks She sits alone, can move and bounce while sitting.
36 weeks She can sit for long periods of time.
40 weeks She can lower herself to sit from standing.

which babies are put on the floor to play, crawling increases the amount of time the child spends with her prime carer. No one leaves a crawling baby alone in a room: you take her with you when you leave. A mobile child cannot be trusted to sit and play quietly.

Not only can a moving baby find more to see and more to do, but this movement and activity are accompanied by chatter. Because you must watch a mobile baby, you look at her and catch her eye more often. You will comment on what you are doing, and are likely to name the objects she touches. 'What have you got there?' you may say, 'Have you got a sock?' with emphasis on 'there' and 'sock'. If she touches something she should not you say 'No' and move her away. You start to use phrases like 'Down you come' or 'That's naughty' in consistent ways.

When you talk to your mobile baby, you make the meanings of words clear. The words you use to comment on something your baby is doing make the association between the sound and the object or action increasingly obvious. And this, of course, is how your baby will learn to talk.

What you can do to encourage crawling

Your baby will not crawl until she is ready, although you can encourage her to creep forward by putting her on her tummy to play and by calling to her when she is on her hands and knees. A nice soft surface also

Milestones in crawling

Weeks 1–14: Makes crawling movements

Weeks 26–28: Rolls over, and can turn head to side

1–14 weeks When lying on her front, your baby makes crawling movements, moving the arm and leg on the same side of her body; she is unable to turn from her front to her back and vice versa; turning her head has no effect on the rest of her body.
16–20 weeks She rolls from stomach to back; lying on stomach, can push her hands and flex her knees.
26–28 weeks She turns her head to the side and toward the back, raising her shoulder and curving her spine; her legs and arms move to the side; she manages to roll from her back to her stomach; she lies on her stomach and pulls herself ahead with her arms; if she is placed on her hands and knees, she rocks.

From creeping to crawling

28–30 weeks She creeps forward rather unsteadily on her hands and knees; pivots from side to side on her stomach.
34–38 weeks She starts to roll intentionally (but – beware – she has no realization that she can roll off the bed); she may move by a combination of rolling and stomach pivoting; creeping and crawling become better coordinated.
48–52 weeks She begins to roll intentionally to get into a sitting or crawling position; she shows some sign that she can adjust to her whereabouts; she is less likely to fall off the edge of the bed or attempt to crawl downstairs.

helps – the fact that today's babies crawl much sooner than babies used to probably has a lot to do with the fact that they have warm carpeted floors, while 100 years ago they had to contend with cold rough slabs.

Crawling babies love to play hide and seek games. Try chasing her behind the settee or round and round an armchair. Drape a cloth over the kitchen table and let her crawl underneath. Keep peeping or crawl under yourself. Such games increase the level of activity and encourage boisterousness and teach her to expect, anticipate and plan (skills which are the basis of so much later learning). Most of all they are good, loving, social fun.

Once your baby starts to crawl, if you have not done so before, you must 'baby proof' the house (see Is your child safe?, pp. 168–72).

Milestones in walking

Weeks 18–24: Supports her weight in your lap

Weeks 26–30: Cruises around the furniture

1– 14 weeks If you support your baby under the arms, her posture is limp; she steps with high knees when her feet touch a sloping surface; she kicks using the same movements when she is excited or upset.
18–24 weeks If you support her under the arms, she holds her head in line with her body; she supports most of her weight when standing on your lap; she may stamp or push down with her foot; she will begin to hold a posture as she moves; if she steps, she holds out her arms or turns to adjust her balance.
26–30 weeks Her postural adjustment improves; she can now support her weight when she holds on to the furniture; may pull herself up, and be able to move her feet when standing; begins to 'cruise' around the furniture holding on and adjusting her balance with each step. At first she clings with both hands, then uses one to hold and the other to explore. Barefoot walking promotes strong feet, ankle and leg muscles; using walkers for too long can damage hip sockets.
40–48 weeks Stepping and postural adjustment are more obvious; she can lean out to reach something while she is standing; she pulls herself up and sits down again with confidence; she can walk if you hold both her hands; she can lift one foot when standing.
50–58 weeks She can stand by herself and walks if you hold one of her hands; she may soon begin to walk alone, but she loses balance if she stops suddenly and falls often.
18 months She can walk forward, sideways and backward; she is able to pull a toy behind her or push one in front; she can use a sit-and-ride bike; she may be able to run but still falls easily.

Choosing a walker

There are two basic types of baby walker: those that babies sit inside and those that they push. The first are for immobile babies, the second – which are often like little carts or convert into sit-and-ride bikes – are for babies who are already beginning to walk around the furniture.

Many health professionals advise against using the sit-in type of baby walker. There have been innumerable accidents associated with their use and over-use may actually delay the development of walking. If you do buy a walker:

- Ensure it cannot tip, especially if your child can push a sit-in walker against the furniture. Ordinary push-alongs are not safe to use as walkers and should be only be used by children who can stand up without help.

- Fence off stairs: walking aids give babies speed before they have sense. Remember they can (and do) push themselves down steps and stairs (including the slightest change in floor level) and into radiators, glass cupboards and other dangers. The walker may also tip over causing head or leg injuries. Before putting a young baby in a sit-in walker, baby-proof the room (see pp. 170–1) and make sure that sharp edges and doors have protective corners (babies do not always look where they are going at speed).
- Never leave your baby in a walker unattended, and don't leave her in it for too long. A walking baby sits down when her ankles are tired. Babies left in sit-in walkers for long periods can damage their ankles.

What you can do to encourage walking

For some while before they walk, children pull themselves up and walk around the furniture. Make this more fun by arranging the furniture for her. Once she can walk the length of the settee put a chair near enough for her to cross to it. Once she can manage this, move it a little further away. Remove all unstable furniture such as rocking chairs (once she starts to pull herself up, she will try to do so on anything which is the right height). Tablecloths can also be dangerous – she may pull both cloth and anything on top of the cloth down on to her head.

Although there is no evidence that baby walkers speed up learning to walk, there is evidence that they can bring babies some of the advantages of mobility by allowing them closer contact with their parents and more language training. It is not clear, however, whether this has any long-term advantage. Such babies may be quicker with their initial understanding of language but they may not maintain this advantage. Those left to sit and play soon catch up.

Push-along baby walkers can help a baby gain confidence once she can stand up by herself. However, sit-in walkers are not considered safe (see above) – in the long run it is probably better to leave your baby playing safely on the floor and to take the trouble to spend time talking and playing with her rather than leaving her to scurry after you in a baby-walker. A crawling baby has far greater opportunities to explore with her hands than one imprisoned by a baby walker. She'll also have more incentive to learn to pull herself up to stand and it's always better to encourage her yourself than leaving her to her own devices in a baby-walker.

Once she can walk intermittently a push-along walker can give her more freedom to explore, which many children enjoy, but choose models for stability (see box above).

Left: Some time between her first birthday and 18 months, your child will walk confidently.

HOW YOUR BABY'S SENSES DEVELOP

The overwhelming majority of babies can see and hear at birth, of course, but in the first year of your baby's life, her reactions to what she sees and hears, and the way she builds on these primary senses to shape her understanding of the world around her develop and change.

Learning to see

Your newborn baby spends about 5 per cent of her waking time scanning the environment for something special to look at; by the time she is two, this will have increased to 35 per cent. And, of course, her waking time has considerably increased.

Milestones in seeing

Birth The pupil of the eye adjusts to light; baby blinks; she can focus for a moment on an object held about 20–25 cm (8–10 in) away; if her head is moved to the side, her eyes follow slowly.

4 weeks She is very interested in faces; recognizes her mother's face; can cry tears.

6–12 weeks Can see 'out of the corner' of her eyes; her eyes work together and move to focus; she looks at edges and corners.

12–20 weeks She knows when things are familiar; she looks at her hands; and focuses on her reflection in a mirror.

20–28 weeks She develops hand–eye co-ordination; she prefers looking at complex things; she pats her image in a mirror and adjusts her posture to get a better look; she can see 800 times better than she did at birth.

28–44 weeks She can focus on very small objects; she likes to look at new things; and she registers depth.

45–52 weeks She can follow a rapidly moving object; her vision is almost as good as yours.

What do babies look at?

If you show a month-old baby a square she will look at the edges and the corners, and hardly bother about the pieces in between. When she looks at your face she does not meet your eye but concentrates on your chin and hairline – the bits that she 'recognizes' when she sees you. At first, babies tend to focus on one characteristic of an object at a time. They probably do not notice the differences between a red circle and a red square.

By two months, your baby shows more interest in the features of a face and the relationship between them. She likes your eyes to be open; she prefers you to turn so she can look into both your eyes at the same time. As you meet her eyes she shows interest and excitement and her gaze moves between your eyes and from your eyes to your mouth and back. She probably only glances at your hairline. By five months, she can differentiate those faces she has seen before from those she has not.

What you can do

Show her things with clear lines and choose dark or brightly coloured objects (babies generally prefer red and blue) or things that glitter and sparkle and catch the light. Until about three months babies seem to prefer movement and find it easier to 'latch on' to things that both move and make a noise.

- Mobiles – especially musical mobiles – are an obvious choice, but buy one that gives your baby the best view. Cardboard shapes look very pretty as you enter the room but may be unimpressive for a baby lying flat on her back. If the mobile does not make a sound, add a few tinkling bells (available from pet shops).
- Babies are especially interested in pattern, texture and depth, which are the factors that enable them to learn to recognize objects and understand what certain things have in common. A cup, for example, can be all sorts of colours and quite a few shapes and vary in brightness depending on the light, but it always has the same arrangement of handle and container (pattern), the same glossy surface (texture), and an open top and closed base (depth). Until she knows what cups have in common she cannot begin to fit a name to them.
- Until she is old enough to grab, attach all manner of things to your baby's cot. Very young babies enjoy familiar things and variations on a theme. Watch while she looks at the shapes. If she likes some better than others look for things which are similar. If she likes a mitten she may love a glove. Fix a pole across the cot and hang things from short pieces of wool.

● The stage beyond looking is swiping. Once she starts to kick and wave her arms, tie some toys where she can accidentally hit them. The movement of the toy will excite her further and she will kick and flail even more. If she hits the toy again it will move again, and so on. It is in these simple games that your baby comes to realize that she can actually make things happen and starts to gain the motivation to learn how to do these things for herself.

Milestones in hand control

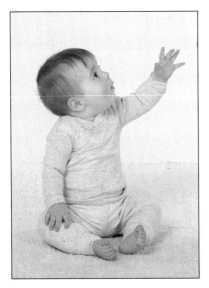

Weeks 22–30:
Keeps eyes on hand when reaching

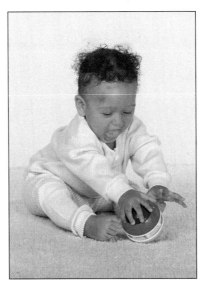

Weeks 32–36:
Catches a ball rolled toward her

Weeks 36 onward:
Palmar grip develops

0–8 weeks Hands predominantly closed.

8–12 weeks Hands still usually closed, but can be held open; holding objects is a reflex action; her grasp is haphazard. By three months her hands are usually open; she grips objects but does not look for one she drops; dropping is not deliberate. Nor is reaching deliberate, but if she accidentally swipes an object tied to the bars of a cot and it excites her, she may repeat the action.

12–16 weeks Clasps her hand round an object; watches her hand; is distracted if it comes into view.

16–20 weeks Her hands are usually open and she may begin to reach out and touch, bringing her hands together deliberately. Cannot grasp an object until it touches the palm of her hand and grasping involves only closing her fingers. If you offer her a toy, she will look back and forth from hand to toy, focusing attention on one then the other.

22–30 weeks She uses her eyes to help her reach an object, keeping her eyes on it while she reaches for it. She begins to grasp objects by cupping her whole hand around them and using her thumb. By seven months she can move her hand to reach for a noisy object in the dark; she uses her thumb to oppose all her fingers; and she can use both hands together.

32–36 weeks She can catch a suspended object or ball rolled to her; she uses her hands separately; passes an object from one hand to store in the other. One hand becomes the active hand, the other the passive. Toward the end of this period the 'palmar' grasp is clearly developed: when grasping, your baby uses the palm of her hand and her fingers together, rather than simply closing her fingers over anything that happens to be in her hand.

36 weeks–15 months The palmar grip develops and matures; she moves her thumb to oppose her fingers. Begins to anticipate; her hand moves into a grasping position before touching the object she intends to grab and will be 'lined up' correctly; moves her hand down and reaches from the top; she begins to use a pincer grip, picking things up between her thumb and forefinger.

By 9–10 months she begins to drop things deliberately and to poke and prod with her fingers; she may also point. She can hold a crayon and feed herself little sandwiches or peas.

Tests

Vision, hearing and movement tests are all part of regular developmental checks (see Chapter 6). Always tell someone if you are worried that your baby is not developing as you think she should and make sure that your concern is taken seriously. The sooner a possible defect is noticed, the better it is for your baby.

Seeing her hands

In her first weeks your baby does not see her hand or know that it belongs to her. One day she might reach out with one hand and find the other. The touch probably interests her, so this new hand becomes something to play with. She does not realize that it is part of her body. If her hands make a noise (because they contain a rattle) she will like them even better. At this stage a wrist rattle or a wrist band with a little bell attached will encourage her to watch her hands. The noise helps her to 'connect' what she sees, what she hears and the movements her body makes.

By 12 weeks, she will sit or lie and watch her hands waving in front of her eyes. By now she has probably also learned how to hit out and make something move and to put out her hand to touch a noisy toy. She does not watch how she does these things: they are reflex responses. Babies are born with a capacity to reach for the place noise comes from or where they see movement. When she first begins to reach for objects rather than respond automatically to a noise she is totally distracted by her hand coming into view. She sees the object, moves her hand toward it, sees her hand and then forgets what she intended to do. Slowly she learns to ignore her hand.

It is tempting to keep putting the toy she reaches for into her hand, but if you do she does not learn to reach. If she is having a lot of difficulty move the toy nearer but let her do the last bit.

Rattles with a narrow stem are easiest to grab, and those which are well balanced easiest to hold. A dumb-bell-shaped rattle or a light ring is ideal.

Reaching is a complex skill

You prepare your hands before reaching, taking into account the object you are reaching for. You judge if you need one hand or two to clasp. You turn your hand to line it up with the object. You open your hand wide enough to grasp the object and extend your arm to the correct place. You decide whether to use your hand like a cup or your fingers like crab claws. You are not aware of doing any of these things. Babies have to learn how to do them all.

From hand to mouth

By five months your baby is likely to be ready to reach out fairly directly to take objects from you without making intermediate adjustments. When she has something in her grasp she will begin to take it to her mouth. She can hold a teething ring with shapes on it, lollipop-shaped rattles, soft bricks and chewing shapes and the interest an object has for her tongue is as important as its shape or colour. Rough and smooth surfaces, things that crackle when chewed or feel both warm and cold to the touch are all stimulating for her.

Babies are not teething when they put things in their mouths: they are exploring. Until she can use her hands to explore or move her fingers at will to poke and prod, stroke and feel, she uses her lips and tongue. These also magnify how things feel (this is why a tooth feels so big in your mouth). Babies explore with their lips, gums and tongues until their hands have matured enough for their fingers to take over. After this they put things into their mouths less often.

The gape test

When your baby takes things to her mouth, she is aiming to get her fist to her lips. In doing so, she can push anything she is holding into the back of her throat or poke herself in the eye. All toy manufacturers have to ensure that their products pass a 'gape' test so that they cannot be poked deep into the throat, and that they do not have sharp edges or corners that could cut or harm the eyes.

To make a gape tester for yourself, cut an oval hole in a piece of card the size of your baby's mouth at its most open. Any object, or part of an object, that goes through the hole is potentially dangerous.

You may think that you will not take your eyes off her, but you will: the phone rings, you smell the potatoes burning, you hear a commotion outside. It only takes a couple of seconds.

Making sense of the world

The human eye is often likened to a camera, but what you see is infinitely more interesting than a photograph. The camera transfers a world which has depth to a flat surface; a photograph is and looks flat. Things nearer the lens seem bigger than those further away because they take up more of the picture.

The world you see with your eyes is not like a photograph: you see that some things are close to you and others further away and take this into consideration when you are judging their relative sizes. This 'interpretation' applies to shapes too. Square table-tops always look square and round plates always look round whatever angle you view them from, but if you are trying to draw the table and can see the legs you do not draw a square top, nor do you draw the plate round, you make it oval. Scientists call this phenomenon 'constancy' because you perceive objects as having the same constant size and same constant shape (and constant colour and brightness).

Babies do not have too many problems in interpreting the world because they move (or are carried) about. When you stand up, all the world below eye level changes shape. When you sit down again it goes back to the way it was. When you walk toward the bus stop, everything gets bigger but the relationship between objects stays the same: children are still smaller than adults, and adults are still shorter than the bus stop sign.

Perceiving depth

By the time they can crawl and walk, most babies are able to perceive depth. In experiments in which a glass barrier was placed over a hole, babies did not crawl out on to it. Some very early crawlers ventured on to the glass, although they were uneasy once they had done so. This suggests that babies both see and respond to depth by about eight months.

Constancy

They respond to constancy a little sooner, at about five months. Babies who are very interested in something suck hard on their dummies. When they are bored they stop sucking. The way constancy is tested is to show a baby one object and then move it so that she looks at it from a different angle. If she starts sucking the dummy after the object is moved,

she thinks that she is looking at a new object; if she does not, she realizes it is the same one. At three months most babies suck, at five most do not.

Understanding that things exist

A baby needs to know that her mother is the same person every time she sees her and she needs to know that she continues to exist even if she cannot see her. Psychologists call the first skill object identity and the second object permanence. Babies develop object identity at about five months: your baby knows there is only one mother. Before five months there is a new mother every morning.

Learning that people and things continue to exist even when they cannot be seen takes longer to absorb. Babies play with this idea for about a year, which is why they love games in which things are seen and then disappear. Most toys aimed at children between 9 and 18 months have something that can be used to play hide and seek – Jack-in-the-box, shape sorters, stacking cups and toys with little doors and hidey-holes are obvious examples – and she will also love 'peek-a-boo' and collecting things in little bags.

At about nine or ten months babies begin to behave as if their parents exist even when they cannot see them. Your baby will cry and fuss if you leave the room and remain miserable for some time after you have gone. (Previously she would have stopped crying once you were out of sight as if she had forgotten all about you.) About the time she gets this sorted out, your baby will probably become fearful of strangers. Once she knows that people continue to exist when she cannot see them she becomes perturbed by those she has not seen before, including close relatives who visit infrequently. She may have beamed and gurgled at Grandma last time she visited, but now she screams and cannot be induced to go to her.

In the early months you could take toys away from her quite easily and if she dropped something she never looked for it. At about the same time she becomes clingy and fretful if you try to leave her, you will notice that she begins to look for the things she has dropped and to lift a cover you place over a teddy to hide it from view. This is a precursor to throwing something from her cot or high chair deliberately so she can look at it on the floor. (Because it gets a response from you, this soon becomes a highly social game as beloved – by the baby – as 'peek-a-boo'.)

Regardless of all the practice and all the games she plays it will be months before your baby works out the complexities of inside, outside, under and over. Until then she will play endlessly: putting one thing inside another, looking at it inside and then taking it out; gathering things in a bag, emptying the bag and then putting everything back; looking for dogs under flaps in books and pictures under puzzle shapes; and taking the car keys to hide in her trolley.

Milestones in perception

0–20 weeks Does not look for an object she drops; soon settles if you leave her; if something is hidden behind a screen she will look surprised if the screen is lifted and there is nothing there, but is not surprised by a change of object.

20 weeks Watches an object go behind a screen and looks for it emerging on the far side; does not look surprised if a new object emerges (if you cover a teddy with a cloth and remove the cloth to reveal a toy train she does not seem surprised).

26 weeks Watches if she drops an object; looks for a partially hidden object.

32–40 weeks Moves one object to reach another hidden from view; looks for objects dropped from cot (and plays the game incessantly); looks for an object where it usually is – not necessarily where she saw it last; clings when you leave; is afraid of strangers.

12–14 months Looks for object where she last saw it; plays lots of hide-and-seek games; enjoys shape sorters, hidey-holes, and 'swag' bags (see p. 211).

Learning to hear

All babies are different. Some sleep through almost anything, some wake at the slightest sound. The same baby may be interested in a rattle when she is happy and distressed by it when fretful. There are, however, some general guidelines:

- When they are alert and awake babies are more interested in gentler sounds. Your baby will become more alert when she hears approaching footsteps, a rousing signature tune or water running from the tap.

- Slow rhythmic sound calms babies, especially when they are ready to sleep. It changes the baby's breathing and heartbeat from a pattern typical of waking babies to one associated with sleep. A steady hum such as a fan, the vacuum cleaner, or the engine of a car can have the same effect. A fretful baby can often be soothed by strapping her to your back and vacuuming the house.

- Babies like female voices most of all. Most people take this preference into account when they talk to babies – children as young as four raise the pitch of their voices.

Babies are born with the ability to hear low- and high-pitched sounds, and to locate them approximately in space. From a very early age they link hearing with seeing and look to see what is making a sound. They also reach out and grab for the sound-making object. At first they are not good at locating a sound that comes from above, behind or to one side, particularly when they are lying down, but if a baby is propped up she can look around and turn her head to explore the world; she will also look up when you call. If you are off to one side she may turn but may not be able to find you.

By eight weeks she will look in the right general area, by 12–16 weeks she will look in exactly the right place. Within another month she will be able to locate something above her head or behind her back.

Milestones in hearing

Birth Startled at a noise; turns toward a voice; moves very slightly in time to speech (this is called the language dance); quietened by low-pitched sounds.

4 weeks Can distinguish sounds such as 'p' from 'b' and 'dah' from 'tah'; prefers complex sounds; likes to be told stories even though she cannot understand them.

8–12 weeks Turns her head to right or left in response to a sound from that direction.

12–16 weeks Can locate where a sound is coming from; looks to see.

16–24 weeks Can find a sound made above or below head level; can distinguish more complex sounds like 'baba' from 'bagay' and recognize a sound hidden in a string (in other words, she can recognize the 'ba' in 'kobabo'); she can tell tunes apart; and distinguish individual voices.

24–32 weeks Responds to her own name.

32–52 weeks Responds to simple commands such as 'give me', 'show me', and 'no' and to the names of familiar objects such as 'dummy' or the names of familiar people.

When to worry

About 85 per cent of deaf babies are born to hearing parents. Early detection of deafness is important. Although all babies occasionally fail to respond to sounds, one who consistently fails to respond, or turns only to certain sounds, or in the direction of one ear should have a hearing test.

You can carry out some simple tests if you are worried about her hearing. Call from different areas of the room. Shake a rattle from left, right, top and bottom and see if she responds. Can she also do it if you ring a bell? If you are not reassured by such tests ask the clinic to check her hearing (see p. 155). Even if she does seem to respond you should remain vigilant and continue to report your concerns. She may have some hearing loss.

What you can do

It is natural to call your baby's name and wait until she catches your eye, or walk into her line of vision, or show her a rattle, shake it to attract her attention, wait until she turns to find it and then shake it again. In all these things, you are helping her to improve her ability to locate where sounds are coming from.

Expectation

By about three months a baby will begin to expect certain sounds to accompany certain activities. A toy duck is expected to squeak so if it barks she may cry. By four months she will cry if she hears a recording of your voice coming from one side of the room while you stand on the other. By six months she can match voices and faces, and remember sounds. This is essential before she can begin to understand language.

LEARNING TO TALK

There is a lot more to language than speaking the words. Although babies do not begin to understand what is being said until the end of the first year, they make preparations long before this by engaging those around them in conversation. Babies are especially tuned to speech. Within hours of birth they are dancing in time to language and turning to the sound of voices. You will not see this first phase of the dance because the movements are very small (researchers record them on film).

From soon after birth you can look directly at a baby and pull a face, perhaps poke out your tongue or raise your eyebrows. If you keep doing this and smile and talk as you do so, your baby will probably make the same face (see p. 61). You do it, she copies, you do it back. This is the turn-taking of a conversation.

By the time she is 4–6 weeks your baby will probably be moving her mouth in answer to your questions. These movements look exactly like speech, and they may or may not be accompanied by sounds or bubble blowing, but she certainly breathes as she would if she were speaking, drawing a breath in quickly and letting it out slowly. As she does this, you will automatically stop and wait. When she has finished and you take your turn, she stops all activity to listen to you. She may raise her eyebrows in answer to your questions. You may see her hands joining in this conversation from as early as three weeks; certainly by eight weeks she will be clearly waving and moving her hands when it is her turn to 'speak'.

Milestones in language

4 weeks Responds to the human voice.

8 weeks Moves mouth as if talking; makes noises and 'talks' back.

12 weeks Babbles and coos when spoken to.

16 weeks Cooing changes pitch and volume; talks to objects and faces; talks more when happy; makes sounds h, n, f, p, b.

20 weeks Babbles become more elaborate and sound more like speech.

26 weeks Combines sounds; says something like 'kibee'; varies pitch and rate of speech; talks to toys or her mirror image; calls to you.

30 weeks Repeats syllable, such as 'numnumnum', 'dadada'; tone of her babbling rises and falls like adult speech.

34 weeks Shouts for attention; shows emotion through sounds; responds to 'no' and 'bye bye'; may say 'pss, pss' when she sees the cat.

38 weeks Says one meaningful 'word' or has one meaningful sign; it could be 'dog' or something of her own like 'num, num' for food, or lifting her arms for 'pick me up'; babble now sounds like speech (as if she is speaking a language of her own).

44 weeks Says 'No!' or 'Hi!' and begins to understand more words.

48 weeks Says two or three words or has two or three meaningful signs; uses 'babble' as if she knows it means something.

52 weeks Says three words or has three meaningful signs; points; jabbers; understands more complex requests such as 'bring your shoes here'; may have one word for a whole class of objects, so, for example, all animals are 'pss, pss', all men are Dada.

Taking turns

Turn-taking is the basis of all social interaction. You speak, she listens. She smiles, you watch and listen, and then answer her with a smile and a compliment or question. When you talk to your baby, use sounds, smiles, gestures and words. She will reply with sounds, smiles, facial expressions, kicks and arm waving. What is said is unimportant, but the way it is said is vital. You must both take turns, since the art of conversation has as much to do with being a good listener as it does with being an interesting talker.

Not all parents are good conversationalists. If you go on speaking without offering your baby a turn, or smile without breaking off for her to smile back she will look away. She will also look away if you start again before she has finished. If you continue to smile she will cry. Repeated time and again, poor conversations can teach babies to withdraw or to become over-demanding. In both cases they develop poor conversational skills.

When you talk to a baby exaggerate what you would do when talking to an adult. Make your voice particularly high pitched, and your eyebrows disappear into your hairline and leave your mouth open wide as you wait for her response. Once you have drawn her into the conversation, let her take control. She will decide when she has had enough.

Babies like imitation: initially at least your baby will respond best when you return the noises, facial expressions, smiles and hand movements she makes to you. Toward her fourth month this will begin to change, as she takes charge. If you ask her how she is, she may look away to find something to watch. You will notice and comment on it. Then and only then does your baby respond. Having learned how to have a conversation, your baby is now looking for something to talk about.

Understanding you

By nine or ten months your baby will begin to read your intentions and seek your approval by observing your face and listening to the tone of your voice. Before going to the cupboard she will look at you, make sure you have understood what she is going to do, then crawl over. She will not necessarily obey spoken or unspoken commands.

Your crawling baby may wait for you to say 'No' before starting on some task and recognize some ambiguity in your response. She crawls toward the cupboard. You know this is fun. She knows this is fun. You say 'No', lift her away and you both laugh. Yet when you say 'No' as she crawls toward the fire, she stops. By the end of her first year your baby takes your response into consideration. Naturally she can do something 'just to annoy you' and will. But this development gives a reason for language, something to talk about and share. The look on her face as she crawls to the cupboard says 'What do you think?'

From 'coo' to 'dada'

Speaking involves moving the mouth, lips and tongue in quite precise ways and also controlling breathing.

At birth your baby is poorly equipped to do either of these things. She breathes by taking air in slowly and letting it out in a rush and the muscles of her tongue are not formed for speaking. At about the time that the vocal muscles are developing for speech, your baby will begin to coo and babble. In the early months she makes all the sounds used in all the languages in the world, not only those she

Right: Babies chat to beloved toys, as well as people – getting a reply is less important than practice in making sounds.

hears. In fact hearing sounds has nothing to do with the sounds she makes because deaf babies produce the same sounds.

By four months these cooing sounds change pitch and volume to sound more like the language(s) she hears around her. She concentrates on the sounds h, n, k, f, p, b, babbling repeatedly whenever she is on her own.

Within a month she will have added vowel sounds to say a, aa, e, ee, i, aye, o, oo, u, and will incorporate these sounds into 'conversations' with you. Within another month she will begin to combine vowels and consonants, to say ka or pa and repeat sounds to say 'papapa pa' or 'numnumnum num' and later 'papanumga' and other combinations. By six months she will be more selective, concentrating on the sounds she hears around her and putting them into long speech-like sequences. As she gets older these sound more and more like real speech. It sounds so real that you may find yourself asking 'What did you say?' or assume that she understands what she is trying to communicate. Sometimes she may. Most families have stories about a child asking something like 'Gumga, pi cacifna?' and when she received the answer 'Yes' going to find her coat.

At around seven months your baby will start to copy the sounds you make. You may find that she answers you with an echo. These sounds will not be complicated – the favourites are naturally 'Dada' and 'Mama'. She will not attach any meaning to these sounds; at this stage she is simply perfecting her sound production. Meaning is, however, not far away.

Words and sentences

In the beginning babbling is simply vocal play, only later do the sounds begin to have meaning. They may not be generally accepted words but you, your child and the rest of the family will understand them. She will babble less once she can produce real words, but children as old as two may revert to babbling when they are excited or when playing. Baby talk is positively good for your child: do not discourage or be afraid to let her know you understand – she will use the 'proper' word when she is ready.

Once children know the sounds and patterns of their native language they begin to attach meaning.

The language of signs

By the time she is seven or eight months old your baby will have one or two meaningful signs. Some are obvious (right), others more subtle. A child who has watched her older sister sing 'The wheels on the bus' may wave her hands every time she sees a bus. Often she accompanies signs with sounds, to draw your attention to the fact she is making them. The best response is to tell her in words what she is telling you in signs: 'It's a bus', 'You want more'.

A child who can make signs may not yet understand spoken words but she has begun to understand why and how language is used. Telling her you understand reinforces this. She may put out her hand for more, or turn her head away, for 'no'.

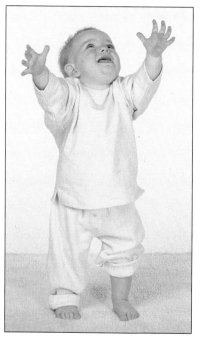

Your baby lifting his arms imploringly skyward is the clearest way he has to tell you that he wants you to pick him up.

When he sits on your lap, his persistent raising of his bottom tells you his intention: 'Jog me up and down.'

Seven per cent of children say one word at about eight months and about two per cent do not attempt to say a word before they are two. The rest fall in the middle. Again this is not an indicator of intelligence. Late talkers probably have problems in producing, rather than understanding, language. Children who speak later often have a detailed understanding although they say nothing. Those who start early sometimes do not understand anything they cannot yet say. If your child understands and follows instructions there is probably nothing to worry about – but do ask the doctor or clinic to check, just in case.

What you can do

- Talk even though she does not understand.
- Give her a turn; wait for her response.
- Create opportunities for conversations.
- Comment on things when she does them.
- Name the things she picks up.
- Show her books, give names to the things you look at together.
- Encourage sign language: stroke the picture of the cat, kiss one of the baby, smack the big bad wolf.

Language in deaf babies

Deaf babies cry, coo and babble and initially sound exactly like hearing babies. They also communicate with smiles, gestures and sounds. At some point though they seem to lose interest in babbling – perhaps because they cannot hear themselves doing it, or because they cannot perfect their sounds. At this age it is difficult to teach a deaf child to communicate by making noises. It is, however, quite easy to teach deaf babies sign language. Those who have done so say that deaf babies progress to becoming skilled language users just as quickly (and in some cases more quickly) than hearing children.

- Say things simply.
- Reinforce her efforts: if she lifts her arms say 'You want to be picked up'; if she says 'num num' say 'You want numnum. You want dinner?'
- Sing to her, read nursery rhymes, play games like 'This little piggy'.

Helping with language

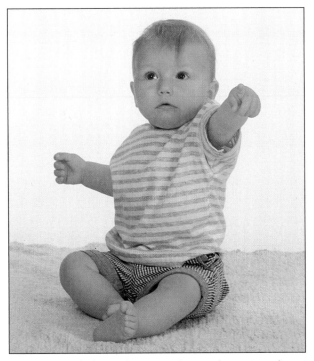

Asking your baby to point to objects shows you that he has understood what you asked and 'knows' the word for an object, even if he cannot say it yet.

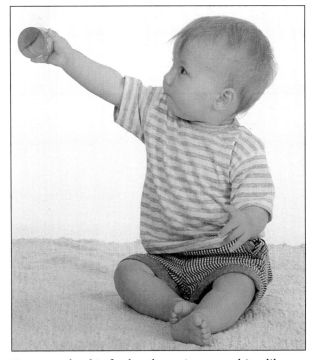

You can take this further, by saying something like 'Where is the ball? Can you give it to me?', to encourage language skills and interaction.

LEARNING ABOUT RELATIONSHIPS

Whatever happens between you and your child now or in the future, she has the power to break your heart. This bond between you is generally known by the rather bland word 'attachment'. Attachment can happen suddenly in the first moments after your baby's birth or more slowly over the first weeks of her life. Her attachment to you happens more slowly and many believe it forms a model for all the close relationships of her life.

Love and consistency are vital for 'good' attachment. Firmness or indulgence are probably less important than the fact that if you love your child and treat her consistently she will know what is expected of her and know that her love and security will not suddenly be undermined.

How attachment develops

When your baby is less than six weeks old, everyone is her friend. Although she prefers the smell, voice and sight of her mother, this is a small preference. Over the next months people become less equal in her eyes and it is soon clear that she prefers her main carer. She smiles more, laughs longer and watches more carefully when he or she is around. The warmer, more caring and responsive the carer, the more firmly does the baby become attached. By six to eight months her preference is pronounced: her face lights up, her arms go up for a cuddle and she calls out in delight.

Fear of strangers

Once your child can recognize you, she can recognize that other people are not you and will scream when she sees them. The only way to deal with this is to approach strangers very gradually. Hold your child firmly, cuddle her in your arms and do not make her look at the stranger (even if it is Grandpa). Sit together without placing any stress on your child and she may come round, but do not assume too much. Looking from the safety of your arms is not the same as sitting on Grandpa's knee.

Babies form attachments to all of their family and those who regularly care for them. They love those who give them time, love, care, comfort and consideration. They also love teddies, bottles and blankets. Since they frequently spend time alone in bed, it is not surprising that babies find security in the things that surround them as they sleep. A love object can comfort a child who is upset, hurt or afraid.

About half of all Western children form these attachments and keeping the blanket clean, or finding it when it is lost can challenge even the most resourceful parent. You will not be the first who has had to scour the shops for an identical teddy – only to be told it does not smell right – or searched the garden with a torch at midnight.

Attachment to objects is a good thing. It gives a child confidence and helps her to deal with difficult situations. Even adults need to 'psych' themselves up to face potentially difficult situations. Children use comfort objects to give themselves courage and often cope better with new situations for doing so. This can hold true for children as old as ten (although they will change the object to which they are attached for something more suitable for their age).

Separation

As early as four months some babies like to have something familiar nearby. Anything that 'puts you in mind' such as an old jumper will help. Most children spend some time separated from their loved ones. How well they adjust depends on how long the separation lasts and how old the child is at the time. Children under six months, for example, adjust quite well to their mothers' returning to work because out of sight is out of mind. At eight months they may scream persistently because they miss *you*. At this age, and later, long-term separation – if your child has to go into hospital, for example, and you cannot go too – is almost always difficult and disturbing.

This obviously can cause problems if you return to work at this time. When a parent who has always been there disappears a child assumes that he or she has gone for good, and cries or screams and clings to those she knows. But, be reassured: as long as you have handed her care over to someone who is going to love her in an environment that is going to offer the sort of stimulation she knows, she will settle.

Milestones in relating to others

0–4 weeks Watches your face intently as you talk to her; settles better when with someone familiar; imitates facial expressions.

8 weeks Smiles; takes turn in a 'conversation'.

12 weeks Very interested in surroundings; stops crying when you enter the room; recognizes familiar people; aware of strangers and strange situations.

16 weeks Demands attention by fussing; bored if left alone; enjoys people; anticipates feeding when she sees bottle; shows excitement by squirming, squealing and laughing; shows interest in strange people and places.

20 weeks Smiles at herself in the mirror; pats bottle or breast with both hands; subject to rapid mood changes; people make her laugh and kick with excitement; makes noises to show her pleasure; can tell strangers from those she knows.

26 weeks Begins to fear strangers; holds out arms to be picked up; laughs when you play 'peek-a-boo'; excited on hearing footsteps, door opening, and so on; imitates more complex behaviour; has definite likes and dislikes.

30 weeks Begins to look for things she drops; fear of strangers increases; frets when prime carer disappears; imitates simple actions; plays 'peek-a-boo'; expects certain things to happen. Bites aggressively; keeps mouth closed if she does not like food. Tries to attract your attention; may have a few simple signs.

34 weeks Increasing anxiety when prime carer leaves; fear of strangers and strange places; may dislike being dressed; may become quite disturbed when you are away from home.

38 weeks More dependent on prime carer; increased interest in pleasing prime carer; afraid of being left alone even in familiar places; puts up hand to avoid

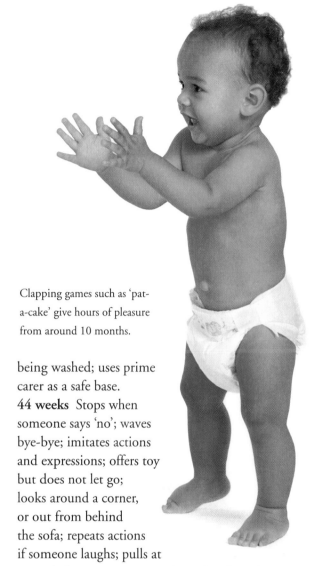

Clapping games such as 'pat-a-cake' give hours of pleasure from around 10 months.

being washed; uses prime carer as a safe base.

44 weeks Stops when someone says 'no'; waves bye-bye; imitates actions and expressions; offers toy but does not let go; looks around a corner, or out from behind the sofa; repeats actions if someone laughs; pulls at your clothes to attract attention; plays 'pat-a-cake'; reacts to your moods; cries if scolded; becomes independent; wants to put on shoes; tests your patience; looks at books; looks at you to check your expression before doing anything.

48 weeks Experiences joy when she achieves something; shows her frustration especially if stopped from doing things she wants to do.

52 weeks Understands simple requests; anticipates – she is, for example, ready to be tickled when you play 'This little piggy'; shakes head for 'no'; covers her face to play 'peek-a-boo'; may also show jealousy, affection, anger and fear; explores away from you; clings; needs her dummy, teddy or security blanket; points to show you things.

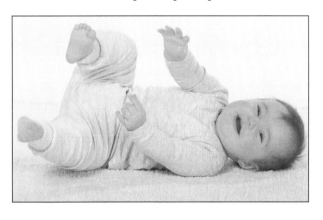

Left: At 20 weeks, she laughs and kicks for the sheer pleasure of doing so.

Being a warm family

The first thing a child recognizes is what psychologists call the emotional tone of her family. It is hard to say exactly what warmth is because different people express it in different ways, but a warm parent cares, responding sensitively and with understanding. He or she can put herself in the child's shoes, often puts the child's interest first, expresses affection and shows enthusiasm for the child's activities. A hostile parent does none of these things. The message he or she gives is one of rejection. Children from warm families:

- have higher IQs in preschool;
- are more secure;
- have higher self-esteem;
- show more understanding of others;
- are nicer to others, helpful and responsive to their distress.

What you can do

You may know you love your baby, but to a baby love that does not show might as well not exist. Even if you are not the sort of adult who touches and hugs other adults you should cuddle and hug your baby as much as you can.

If you give your baby lots of love she will know how to demonstrate love later on. Be guided by her: some babies squirm to be put down, some cuddle in as if by keeping still you might forget they are there. If you enjoy cuddling her, and she enjoys your cuddles, do it, but do not force yourself when you do not feel like it. Pretending does not fool a baby who is tuned to your emotions.

Nobody can give all the time nor do all the things they would like to. Life with a baby or small child is always a compromise between her needs and those of the rest of her family – and that includes her parents. If your baby knows she is valued whether laughing or crying, sweet or sour she will return the compliment. A child who knows that love is always the bottom line does not need you to be constantly happy or constantly attentive to her wants, needs and games. She will know instinctively that your current distraction or preoccupation does not mean she has lost you for ever.

LEARNING ABOUT FEELINGS

Some babies are easy-going, adaptable and sunny. Some are easy-going when you get to know them but cautious about accepting new people or new things. Others are difficult.

In the same way that grown-ups do not fall into neat categories, babies vary enormously, but some differences seem to be there from birth. 'Easy' babies have regular habits from the start. They quickly settle into a feeding schedule, a sleep pattern and even have bowel movements at the same time each day. They take new places, foods and people in their stride. If things go wrong they do not over-react. An easy child whimpers if food is delayed: she does not scream. Most of all she is sunny, smiling and easy-going.

All this may sound great news for you, but because an easy baby is so good and makes so few demands she may receive less attention from her parents. A study in America showed that the middle-class parents of easy infants tended to leave them to fend for themselves more often than did the parents of more difficult babies. Easy babies tended to fall behind the achievements of more difficult children.

Children who are slow to warm up are less regular, show more caution, need persuading to take new food or enjoy new places and are slower to smile. Difficult children are irregular. Even at ten years of age she may not have a regular sleeping pattern and when she has not had enough sleep she is likely to be bad tempered and weepy. She is difficult to wean and will remain picky about food. Disasters are always around the corner. A line wrong, a word misspelt and she flies off the handle. She gets homesick.

Difficult babies make demands. They face more stress (much of it of their own making); life is never straightforward. In certain situations they fare better, surviving times of stress; they also however make up the majority of individuals who need counselling as adults.

Milestones in expressing emotion

Birth Has a 'windy' smile, shows that she is startled, distressed or disgusted.

4 weeks Develops a social smile.

12–16 weeks Laughs; shows anger, surprise, sadness.

20–28 weeks Shows fear.

24–32 weeks Shows shame and shyness.

Smiling and laughing

Babies smile in a 'windy' way almost as soon as they are born, but the smiles have nothing to do with wind. A young baby's smile is not a big broad beam but rather a pulling back of the lips, sometimes on only one side of the face. These first smiles only occur when babies are falling into a deeper sleep or coming from a deeper to a lighter sleep. Later she will smile in her sleep if she hears certain high-pitched noises.

You will see (and be able to recognize) her first real smiles when she is four to six weeks old, depending on her maturity at birth. Those born before the due date are likely to be older when they first smile. Blind babies smile quite readily at this stage but by six months most have stopped smiling. If you want your baby to smile you need a high-pitched sound and a nodding head; later she will want to look at your moving smiling face; finally she will smile directly at your still face. By the time they are five or six months old, babies smile most frequently at the faces of people they recognize.

Laughter is a more intense emotion than smiling, but just as infectious. Babies begin to laugh at about three to four months. At first laughter is produced by a combination of speech and physical activity, such as tickling, and is deep and hearty. Laughter is entirely social and is about anticipating and sharing. The more you laugh with her, the more she laughs back, although you will not be as successful at making her laugh as her older siblings.

What makes her laugh?
0–2 weeks Falling asleep or beginning to wake.
2–3 weeks A high-pitched sound while she is asleep.
4–8 weeks Smiles when awake; a high-pitched sound; a nodding head; things that move and make sounds; your moving talking face.
10 weeks Your still face.
20–24 weeks Familiar faces; laughter.
4–6 months Someone laughing or talking.
6–12 months Social games like 'peek-a-boo'; being jogged on your knee; games involving anticipation such as 'This little piggy'.
12 months Unexpected things like you wearing her hat; as a response to things she has done such as knocking over bricks, or making the Jack-in-the-box jump; anticipation of events.

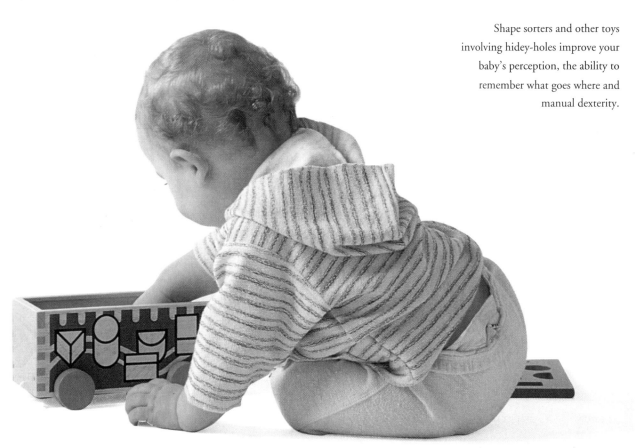

Shape sorters and other toys involving hidey-holes improve your baby's perception, the ability to remember what goes where and manual dexterity.

LEARNING TO REMEMBER

A child cries because she is hurt; because something has caused her to be afraid; and because she wants attention. The first sort of crying is unlearned. The second two are learned.

Young children quickly learn that one thing leads to another, so uncoupling your bra precedes a feed, the sound of running water precedes a bath. They can also learn that being in their bed precedes sleep and nappy changing precedes a game. The learning process is simple – event A usually precedes event B.

Babies learn by trial and error that they can make things happen. Your baby would like the mobile to move but does not know how to make it happen. She looks at it ... she waves her arms ... nothing. Then one day when she is kicking at the side of the cot the mobile moves. When she stops kicking it stops. She has learned that if she kicks the bars of her cot, the mobile moves. By the same process she learns that she can make you come when she cries, and that people will play with her if she smiles and laughs.

Your baby does not only learn what you want to teach her. She learns about emotions, beliefs, attitudes and roles. Coming home precedes relaxation; getting into the car precedes tension. If you always draw her away from dogs, she will learn to be wary of dogs. She can also learn that being good makes her loved, or that when she is good, she is ignored.

Try occasionally to stand back and look at the messages you are giving your children. If you are giving the wrong messages, remember that what has been learned can be unlearned. The child who has learned that A is followed by B can also learn that A is no longer followed by B. And a child who has learned that crying always brings her mother to her side can learn that in some instances it will not.

What babies know

In the first weeks of life, most of the things babies can do are 'built in', or reflexes (see chapter 2). Your baby automatically turns her head and opens her mouth when her cheek is touched; she cannot choose to keep her mouth shut. Nor can she open and close her mouth to see how it feels, since such voluntary actions are beyond her capability. By two months, she is beginning to replace reflexes by voluntary actions. She can choose to reach for the teddy tied to her cot. Until she is about three months she can only control one voluntary action at a time. She can choose to cry or to reach but cannot reach and cry at the same time. She can kick and cry because kicking automatically goes with crying. If she does two things only one of them can be of her choosing.

By about six months she can do two things at once, suck her thumb while she plays and bang a drum while she shouts. She can also use one of these actions to produce another, so she can press a button to make the Jack-in-the-box jump and repeat such activities. One of the two 'things' she does can be to have an intention, the other to act, so that she realizes she needs her mother and knows how to summon her.

In the first months babies hold all toys in their hand and bang them on the table or put them in their mouth and gum them. As she begins to be able to do two things at once, she can push something because she remembers that pushing makes it move, and can hit something to knock it over.

By the time your baby is about 10 months old, she begins to co-ordinate and plan more complex actions. Now instead of being limited to two 'thoughts' or actions, she can integrate several: remember that a toy is in the cupboard, go to the cupboard to get it and take it to the sofa to play, for example. She can look, shout and crawl while grasping a spoon in her hand.

In the early months babies live in the moment, reacting as if nothing went before and nothing is coming after (this is why your baby drops a toy but does not look for it, see pp. 138–9). At around 10 months they begin to act as if they can remember what went before and can predict what might come after. When you take off her sock to play 'This little piggy', she is already prepared to laugh. When you show her a book she waits for the picture of the dog (and knows if you have missed out the page with the dog, and gone to the picture of the cat).

Paying attention

Grown-ups can do more than one thing at a time. As you read, you can hear the clock ticking, the traffic moving, someone in the room may be watching TV. You are aware of all of these things, but they are not the focus of your attention: you focus on the words you are reading. If you are asked a question you can switch your attention, answer and then go back to reading. Babies cannot do this. They can only concentrate on one thing at a time. They are easily distracted and once distracted cannot return.

If your child sees a toy car on the far side of the room she will crawl rapidly to it. It is the centre of her attention. But if she notices a half-eaten biscuit on the floor as she is passing, she stops and starts eating, and forgets that she was heading for the car. She can only hold one thought at a time. Only if she happens to notice the car again will she return to the first activity. As children grow up they become better able to focus their attention, and can look away and then return to an activity.

How memory develops

Your baby's ability to remember changes as the first year progresses. Tiny babies do not consciously remember the past. They only know that something is familiar.

If you change something your baby has just looked at (take a car from the table and put it in the drawer), she notices. If you show her something she has seen before (the car in the drawer), she remembers; she cannot, however, do both things at once. By seven months she can. If a car was in the drawer the last time she looked, that is where she will search for it first on the next occasion that it is missing.

Intelligence

Measuring infant intelligence has always been controversial, not least because it is unreliable. It is possible to say how old the average child will be when she can sit without aid or when you can expect her to say her first word. This really does not predict how well she will do when she starts school. Children who seem a little slow at one stage may be top of their class later on. What the scales and charts can do is identify children with potential problems. A child who is consistently late at reaching milestones may have an unrecognized problem.

In infancy play and cognitive development are always closely related. When a baby plays she is both practising and learning. Watching her gives a very clear view of what she can do and how she understands the world.

Avoiding superbaby syndrome

- Remember that she has a right to her childhood.
- Be realistic and reasonable.
- Make any learning fun.
- Play down the competition; most children cannot and do not win – the child in line for 13th best might as well try something else.
- Guide but do not push. Recognize what she wants and what you want and do not confuse them: if you want to play the violin take lessons yourself.
- Do not insist.
- Take your cue from your baby: pushing when she is not interested is pressure not stimulation.
- Do not be afraid to let your child have fun: 'All work and no play makes Jack a dull and stressed superbaby.'
- Give her a choice: jumping on the beds is just as good an exercise as learning to swim.
- Babies only need loose timetables and free time is at least as important as 'quality time'.
- A child who is entirely organized may never learn to organize herself.
- It is the effort that counts, not the end result.

Too far too fast

Obviously you want the best for your child, but the line between encouraging and pressurizing is very fine. Some American parents worry that their two-year-olds will not pass the entrance exams for the 'best' preschool and there are reports that some spend 50–60 hours a week cramming two- and three-year-olds to help them get ahead, to ensure their child's place in the competitive market.

Researchers have watched hurried babies become bored toddlers and unmotivated and stressed schoolchildren. Doctors have seen more and more overstimulated children develop headaches, stomach upsets and sleep disturbances. Psychologists have monitored the development of behavioural problems. The situation has become sufficiently serious in the USA for the American Academy of Pediatrics to issue guidelines to help pediatricians recognize what has been dubbed the 'superbaby syndrome'. Do not push too hard: your child deserves the luxury of a childhood.

CHAPTER SIX

Your Baby's Health

Parents worry, often unnecessarily, about their babies' health and safety. For most of the time, babies are well, and commonsense precautions and careful choice of what you buy for your baby will keep him safe. There is, however, a network of health professionals to consult about your baby's well-being; these people will also ensure that he is developing as he should.

Your baby's well-being

As well as the joy and pleasure that a new baby brings, you may – like many other parents – also experience feelings of panic or apprehension about caring for him.

These days, many people do not live near their immediate family, and you may be the first of your friends to have a child. It is easy in these circumstances to feel alone in caring for your baby. And, even if you do have family and friends with children close by, you may well receive conflicting advice about what to do if your baby does not want to feed, sleep or stop crying.

As you get to know your baby you will gain more confidence as parents, and will be able to spot more easily when something is wrong. You will begin to recognize your baby's cries and know when he is hungry, sick, or just needs a cuddle. But there is also a team of professionals there to help and advise you on the care of your baby, and to keep a check on his health and development.

WHO CAN HELP?

All parents of young children can call upon the services of an individual, named health visitor, your GP and the child-health or well-baby clinic.

Your health visitor

Health visitors are part of the National Health Service community health services. All are registered general nurses who have undergone further training, and have experience in child health and development, preventive health and health promotion. Health visitors work closely with GPs, and may be based at your GP's surgery or at a health centre or child-health clinic. The overwhelming majority are women.

Every family with a child under five has a named health visitor. You may have met yours when you were pregnant, but if you did not, she will be notified of your baby's birth, and should visit you at home when your baby is around 11 days old – get in touch with your GP's surgery if she does not. At this visit, in addition to talking to you about your own health and that of your baby, your health visitor will explain the health care system in your area to you. This information may include, for example, the days and times of your nearest baby clinic, and the immunization programme. She will usually then visit you at intervals throughout your child's first five years, more frequently in the first year and if you have any special problems. In addition you can see your health visitor at the child health clinic, you can telephone her for advice, or you can ask her to visit you at home.

Your health visitor is there to listen to you and to help and advise you in all sorts of situations. She is not there to check that you are bringing your baby up correctly, or to impose her own views on you. She is, however, the person you can turn to for advice on any aspect of your baby's health such as feeding, colic, crying, teething, rashes or immunizations. She can also advise you on minor illnesses and their treatment. Together, you and your health visitor can monitor your baby's developmental progress, and if there is any concern she can arrange for your baby to be seen by a doctor or paediatrician. She may also carry out some of your child's developmental reviews either in your home or at the clinic.

What else can she do?

Your health visitor is not just there for your baby. She is also there for you and your whole family.

- She can advise you on other matters which affect your health and well-being such as child-care facilities, local support groups and networks, caring for elderly relatives, relationships, relaxation and healthy lifestyles.

- She can let you know what welfare benefits you may be entitled to claim and can put you in touch with other agencies such as social services, if that is what you wish.

Try to treat your health visitor as a family friend and do not be afraid to talk to her if you are feeling depressed, unable to cope with the baby or are having other difficulties. Sometimes just talking about a problem can help you to put it into perspective. She will not be shocked by anything you say or be in the least censorious.

Your family doctor

Your GP is a second key person who can help you to look after your family's health. If your baby is not well he or she will make a diagnosis and reassure you or prescribe any necessary treatment. Your GP will also refer your baby to a hospital specialist if necessary. GPs are increasingly doing developmental checks too.

If you think that your baby is ill or suspect that something is wrong, phone your doctor or take your baby to the surgery. Do not be anxious about bothering the doctor with what may be something trivial: most doctors prefer to see a sick child early, and are pleased to reassure you if all is well. If you are really not sure about seeing the doctor, phone the practice nurse or your health visitor and ask for her opinion first.

Most doctors now immunize those babies who are on their lists, although vaccinations can also be done at your local NHS trust or health authority clinic. Your GP may also run a well-baby clinic, and do some of your child's developmental reviews.

Except in an emergency, you must be registered with a GP before he or she can treat you. When your baby is born, register him with your own GP and if you move house, register with a GP as soon as possible. It helps to choose a doctor within easy reach, but ask neighbours with children whom they recommend — some are infinitely better with small children than others. Alternatively, visit one or two practices before you decide to register, ask for the practice leaflet describing the services on offer, talk to

the doctors and look around you. Are there toys in the waiting room, for example, and is there an easy-access toilet?

The child-health clinic

The well-baby or child-health clinic is a free service, provided by your local health authority or NHS trust, or by your GP, for children under the age of five. You can attend a well-baby clinic whenever it is open – an appointment is not necessary.

At the clinic you can discuss any worries you may have about your baby with your health visitor, and have your baby weighed. Always take your child health record book with you so that information about your baby and any advice given can be noted. The clinic is also a good place to make contact with other mothers. Go as often as you want to: most parents of new babies attend weekly for the first few weeks, then fortnightly, then monthly for the first year. But, initially at least, if it is a hassle to get there, do not force yourself (remember you can ask your health visitor to see you at home). Developmental reviews or checks and immunizations will also usually be done at the clinic, although probably at a different time from the well-baby sessions, and you will be sent an appointment for these (if an appointment is not convenient, ring and change it).

The other services that these clinics offer vary according to where you live. Some also run postnatal groups or mother and toddler groups and offer other facilities such as dental sessions. The physical location

Your child's health record book

You will normally be given a personal child health record book, also known as a parent-held record, either when your health visitor makes her first visit to you, or at your first clinic appointment. This is for use by yourself and health professionals, and helps you to keep track of your child's progress, immunizations, and any illnesses he may have had, until he leaves school. Try to remember to take it with you whenever you take your baby to the clinic, to see your doctor or to the dentist. Remember, this is for your use and can be filled in by you as well as professionals.

of such clinics also varies enormously: in some areas you will find the clinic in a purpose-built health centre, in others a church hall, your doctor's surgery or even a mobile caravan. In theory, you can choose to go to the clinic which is most convenient for you, but changes in the NHS may make the choice more limited in some areas. If you are unhappy with facilities in your area, it is worth getting together with other parents and approaching your CHC (Community Health Council) and FHSA (Family Health Services Authority) – the numbers are in the phone book.

Health is a partnership

Caring for your baby's health and monitoring his progress should be a partnership between parents and professionals, so make any decision about your baby's health in consultation with the health professionals. Professionals do not have all the answers and you undoubtedly know your own baby best. Ask questions if you feel you are being kept in the dark about any aspect of your child's health or development, and do not be afraid to disagree if you think a doctor or health visitor is mistaken. Ask for a second opinion if necessary.

If you are not happy
It sometimes happens that for some reason you and your health visitor or doctor do not hit it off. Or misunderstandings arise which need to be talked through. If these differences cannot be resolved, try visiting the clinic on another day when there is a different health visitor or doctor there. If there is more than one health visitor in your doctor's practice, ask to change to one with whom you feel more comfortable. If you wish to change your doctor, go to a new GP and ask to be taken on to his or her list.

What the law says
You are entitled to refuse entry to a health professional who has no legal right to enter your home. Taking your baby to the clinic, having developmental checks and having your child immunized are all voluntary. However, if for any reason the health or social services have grounds for serious concern about your child's health, development or well-being, you may be asked to allow your child to be assessed by a health professional. This could be done by your family doctor or by an independent professional.

If you refuse to co-operate with a proposed voluntary assessment, the social services department can apply to the court for a child assessment order, so that an assessment can be made.

REGULAR HEALTH CHECKS

In addition to attending the well-baby clinic for general advice on your baby's health and progress, you will also be invited to take him for routine health and developmental reviews or checks at certain ages, under the child health surveillance programme (these may also be called developmental assessments, or screening tests).

Although not compulsory, these reviews are important. Their purpose is to detect any problems such as developmental delay, or hearing or vision impairment as soon as possible so that any necessary treatment can be started early. They also give you the opportunity to sit down with the health visitor or doctor and discuss any concerns you may have about your child's health or behaviour or simply to be reassured that everything is 'normal'.

Even if you have no worries about your child, the review is still worth having – some problems such as a hearing impairment or a congenital dislocation of the hip are not always apparent. The developmental review also gives you a record of your child's progress at certain ages, so if problems do develop later, you have a useful reference to look back on.

The age at which your baby has a developmental review and even the content of the review, varies slightly in each area. Most areas, however, tend to follow the recommendations made by a Department of Health backed team of experts, including paediatricians, GPs and health visitors. In most parts of the country, therefore, you will asked to take your child for a developmental review between the following ages:

- Six and eight weeks
- Six and nine months
- 18 months and two years
- Three and four years
- Four and a half and five and a half years (often referred to as the preschool check)

These reviews are carried out by your GP, health visitor or both, and may take place at your doctor's surgery, at the child-health clinic or in your home.

There are wide variations in the rate at which babies and children develop (see Chapters 5 and 7), and each child develops at his own pace. So the developmental reviews are not 'tests' that your child passes or fails, but an indication of his overall progress. If he was premature, he should be assessed from his expected date of delivery, rather than his actual date of birth. So a baby who was eight weeks premature, for example, will be assessed at eight months as a six-month-old baby.

See Chapter 4, pp. 116–17 for the six-week check.

Six to nine months

This is the age when most babies are learning to communicate, sit and have increasing visual alertness. It is also the best age to check your baby's hearing.

The examination is usually carried out by the health visitor on her own, or by the health visitor and doctor together. The review includes:

- A general look at your baby's progress; whether you have any concerns about his health or growth, teething, feeding and sleeping problems and so on.

- An assessment of his motor development; whether your baby is starting to sit, roll or perhaps beginning to crawl.
- A check for congenital dislocation of the hips; even though your baby will have been tested earlier for this, it can sometimes be missed.
- Observation of his learning and communication skills: whether your baby is alert and responsive, is making a variety of sounds and is able to grasp objects.
- His head circumference, length and weight may be measured (this is not always done).
- A check for a squint and any vision defects; you will also be asked if you have noticed a squint or whether there is any family history of squints or vision defects; the examiner will also check that your baby is visually alert and able to focus on objects.
- (For boys only) A check that the testes are descended into the scrotum.
- A hearing test will be done by two people, one to distract your baby, the other to make various sounds behind your baby to see if he can hear them; if your baby fails to respond to this test, you will be asked to return in three to four weeks so that it can be repeated.

Six to nine months

This is a good age to test many of your baby's reactions and skills. Remember that some babies reach milestones earlier than others; this review simply gives a general impression of his progress.

Your baby's movement will be observed. It will be noted if he can crawl, or if he is showing signs of doing so soon, by rocking on all fours, for example.

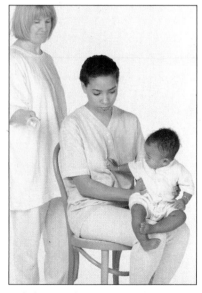

While you distract your baby, a rattle will be shaken outside his field of vision to see whether he reacts to it, and whether he turns in the direction of the sound.

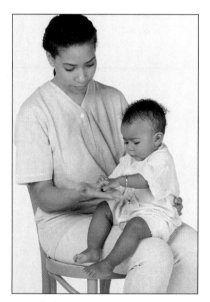

Your baby's manual dexterity will be checked, to see whether he can pick up a building block, and how well his palmar grip is developed (see p. 136).

If your baby still fails to respond, you will be referred to an audiology clinic where more sophisticated tests can be carried out. Do not be alarmed if your baby does not respond to all the sounds first time. He may be tired or bored, or might have had an ear infection.

18 months to two years

Children of this age can be difficult to evaluate in a clinic and this review may be carried out by the health visitor in the more relaxed atmosphere of your home. Again, your health visitor will review your child's progress with you and discuss any problems you may have. Management problems such as food refusal, sleep disturbance and temper tantrums are common at this age. You may also want to discuss potty training. Other important parts of this review are your child's walking and language skills.

Specifically, your health visitor will:

When to worry

Before your child reaches the age of five, any major developmental or health problems should have been picked up. But you know your child best. Draw to your health visitor's attention any concerns you have over:

- Speech: if your child stutters or lisps badly, or has difficulty with certain sounds, for example
- Vision: if he cannot see his friend at the other side of the play area, or consistently misses a ball rolled to him
- Hearing: if he seems not to hear when you are to one side, or directly behind him
- Social behaviour: if he is unduly anxious about starting school, and is shy
- Understanding: if he does not seem to understand what you are saying, even when you rephrase a question.

You are not wasting anybody's time in asking for any aspect of your child's development to be checked, more than once, if necessary. The sooner a problem is identified the better.

If you have any concerns about your child when he is at school, raise them with the school nurse or doctor (see p. 268), or your GP.

- Check that your child is walking normally: by the age of 18 months, 97 per cent of children are walking, but those who 'bottom shuffle' may not be, especially if late walking runs in your family.
- Ask if your child is saying several words and understands simple commands such as 'shut the door' or 'give it to me'.
- Monitor his hand–eye co-ordination, seeing whether, for example, he can pick up tiny objects such as crumbs from the carpet using his finger and thumb, or build a tower of about three bricks.
- Measure his weight and height (not all health professionals do this at this review, and not all children are co-operative).

If she is concerned about any aspect of your child's development, your health visitor may ask you to return for a further check, or refer you to your doctor or another health professional such as a speech therapist for a second opinion. In some parts of the country, children at this age may also have a blood test for anaemia.

Three to four years

This review may be carried out by your health visitor or doctor or both, and in some areas is regarded as the preschool examination. The aims are to ensure that your child is physically fit and there are no medical disorders or problems with development, language or behaviour which may have educational implications. The doctor will carry out a physical examination, such as a general check of your child's heart and (for boys) testes. (If in your area the preschool examination is carried out between the ages of four and a half and five and a half, a physical examination may not be done at this review.)

The health visitor may do a formal assessment of your child's developmental progress by, for example, asking him to build a tower of bricks or do a simple jigsaw. Or she may assess him informally by watching him play and run around. However the review is done, the health visitor or doctor will discuss your child's progress and any concerns you may have about his health or behaviour. In addition, your doctor or health visitor will usually:

- Check for vision or hearing problems (in some areas, the doctor or health visitor may do a formal vision or hearing test).

- Check your child's thinking skills, for example, his ability to understand and reason.
- Check his language and ability to communicate: does he know a nursery rhyme? can you understand him clearly when he speaks?
- Check his motor skills: can he ride a bicycle? can he jump up and down?
- Check his social maturity, his ability to cope with unfamiliar situations, for example, and whether he is shy.
- Check his weight and height.

Four and a half to five and a half

This may be called the preschool entry review, or it may take place once he has started school. This may include a physical and vision and hearing test, his immunization status will be checked, and he will be given his preschool booster injection (see p. 159).

IMMUNIZATION

When your baby is in the womb, and while he is breastfed, antibodies (substances which attack bacteria and viruses) are passed to him by his mother, with the result that new babies have some immunity to infection (although not whooping cough). After a few months, protection against diphtheria, tetanus and polio wears off, and by the time your baby is about a year old, he will also have lost his immunity to measles, mumps and rubella. Because these antibodies are not replaced, it is necessary to protect children against these infectious diseases, by immunization.

What is immunization?

Vaccination or immunization means introducing a substance into the body to stimulate immunity to a particular disease. The vaccine works by giving the child a tiny amount of the particular bacteria or virus which causes the disease. The body reacts by producing its own defence against the disease, so that it can fight the infection if it encounters it again. For maximum protection the full course of immunizations is necessary. If enough children are immunized (at least 90 per cent), the level of disease in the community is reduced, leading to so-called herd immunity.

Immunizations given

Your child should receive five sets of vaccines. Some come in three doses and others in one, but each vaccine protects against a specific disease (see table, p. 159). Most immunizations are given by injection, usually in the upper arm or outer thigh. Polio vaccine is given by drops placed on the baby's tongue.

Diphtheria, Tetanus and Pertussis (Whooping cough)

Known as DTP for short, this is a triple vaccine that gives protection against all three diseases.

Diphtheria is now rare, but outbreaks still occur in some countries. It is a serious disease which starts with a sore throat and a low fever. A 'membrane' develops which blocks the nose and throat, causing choking and breathing difficulties. A severe attack can kill.

Whooping cough (*Pertussis*) is a dangerous and distressing disease, particularly in the first year of life. It starts with a runny nose, fever and cough, which are followed by bouts of coughing in succession in the same breath, ending with a 'whoop' as the child gasps for breath. During such fits, the baby may turn blue from lack of oxygen.

Is immunization necessary?

Although many of these diseases for which your child will be immunized are now – because of widespread immunization – rare, they still exist, and outbreaks can occur both in Britain and in other countries you may visit. They can all make your child seriously ill, can have severe complications and may even cause death.

Serious side effects from immunization are very rare, and research has shown that the risks of harmful effects from the diseases are far greater than that from the immunizations. In the years between 1978 and 1989, 118 anaphylactic reactions (where the child has a severe and sudden reaction to the injection, see Allergy, pp. 160–1) were reported out of approximately 25 million childhood immunizations.

If the figures do nothing to allay your fears of possible side effects, discuss immunization with your doctor or health visitor before making the decision to have your child immunized or not.

These coughing bouts can occur up to 50 times a day for several weeks, with vomiting common after coughing; this may lead to dehydration or weight loss. Complications from whooping cough can include convulsions (fits), pneumonia, bronchitis, hernias, ear infection, brain damage and even death.

Tetanus is not an infectious disease, but it is still dangerous. It is caused by germs from soil or dirt getting into an open wound (especially if this is a deep 'puncture' wound) or a burn. It then attacks the nervous system causing muscle spasms which can affect breathing, and may be fatal. Although tetanus is quite rare because of immunization, the germ spores which cause the disease are always present in the soil.

Hib (Haemophilus influenzae type b)

These bacteria can cause a serious form of bacterial meningitis in under-fours; a severe form of croup known as epiglottitis; pneumonia; blood poisoning and infections of the bones and joints. Before Hib immunization was introduced, one in 600 children under five developed some form of Hib-induced meningitis, which resulted in 65 deaths and 150 cases of brain damage every year. Hib immunization only protects against one form of meningitis; a vaccine to protect against another type is being tested.

Polio

Polio attacks the nervous system and paralyzes the muscles in any part of the body. Permanent paralysis can result if it attacks the legs; if it attacks the respiratory muscles, artificial help in breathing may be needed and the child may even die. Polio has technically been eradicated in Britain because of immunization, but it can still be caught abroad, and may

Alternatives to immunization

Some parents choose to have their children 'immunized' homeopathically. There are, however, no proven effective alternatives to immunization and, in fact, the Council of the Faculty of Homeopathy strongly supports the immunization programme. The Council recommends that immunization be carried out using the conventional tested vaccines as long as there are no medical reasons not to do so.

then be re-introduced. Also, the virus can be excreted in a baby's faeces for up to six weeks after immunization, so adults who have not been immunized may catch the disease from changing a newly immunized baby's nappy. If you have not been immunized against polio, ask your doctor about having it done, and wash your hands after changing your baby's nappy. Because there are three types of polio virus, the vaccine is given three times to ensure full protection.

Measles, mumps and rubella (MMR)

This immunization is given as a triple vaccine. However, in certain circumstances your child may receive the vaccines separately. Check with your GP.

Measles is often seen as a mild childhood disease, but it can be dangerous. It starts like a bad cold with a cough, runny nose, watery eyes and rising temperature. A blotchy red rash then appears on the face and body. Complications from measles can include encephalitis (inflammation of the brain, which may cause brain damage), convulsions, ear and eye infections, croup, pneumonia, bronchitis or death.

Mumps causes headaches, fever, dry mouth and difficulty in swallowing, with swelling below the ears and/or in front of the jaw. Although it is usually a mild disease, it can have serious consequences. Mumps can cause deafness and encephalitis and it is the most common cause of viral meningitis in under-15s. It can also cause inflammation of the testes in boys, and a painful infection of the ovaries in girls.

Rubella (*German measles*) usually starts with a cough, sore throat and runny nose before a bright pink rash appears. Although it is normally a mild disease, if a woman who is not immune catches it in the first four months of pregnancy, there is a risk that her child may be born deaf, blind, or with heart or brain damage. Rubella immunization is important for all children to avoid passing the disease on to pregnant women.

Tuberculosis (TB)

TB can affect the lungs and other parts of the body. Not so long ago, it was a serious disease that required months of treatment; it was also a major killer. Good public health measures and prevention by vaccination meant that TB was virtually wiped out in Britain, but as routine immunization was stopped, it has recently started to make a comeback. At present, the policy on giving protection against TB varies in each area. If giving protection against TB varies in each area. If your baby is thought to be at risk from the disease, or you live in a high-risk area, he may be offered BCG protection at birth. Elsewhere, schoolchildren may be tested for immunity against TB (the mantoux test) and if necessary, immunized. If you are travelling to a country where TB is common (check with your GP), your baby should be immunized.

Side effects of immunization

After an injection your baby may be a little irritable or have a slight fever, or he may have side effects such as pain, redness and swelling. These effects are normally only temporary and you will usually be advised to give your baby a dose of liquid paracetamol to relieve any pain and bring down a temperature. If your baby screams briefly after an injection, this is probably due to pain or fright; if, however, his screaming is high-pitched or prolonged, it is likely to be due to a reaction. If this happens, or your child has a high temperature, or seems very unwell, contact your GP for further advice.

Reports of permanent brain damage after the whooping cough part of the DTP vaccine have probably been the single most important factor in dissuading parents from having their children immunized against any diseases at all. However, neurological illnesses which can cause this type of damage can develop from a variety of causes in the first year of life in both immunized and unimmunized children. There has been a lot of research into the whooping cough vaccine, but no conclusive evidence has been found to show that this causes permanent brain damage. Whooping cough, however, can cause brain damage, and the risk of being damaged by the disease is infinitely greater than that of being damaged by the vaccine injection.

When not to immunize

If your child is unwell, immunization may be postponed. Your health visitor will discuss any contraindications with you, but these may include:
- A severe reaction to a previous injection
- A severe allergic reaction to eggs (MMR injection only)
- If your child has a malignant disease such as cancer.

The immunization timetable (0–5 years)

Vaccine	How given	Age
Diphtheria **Tetanus** **Whooping cough**	One injection (DTP)	2 months
Hib	One injection	
Polio	By mouth	
Diphtheria **Tetanus** **Whooping cough**	One injection (DTP)	3 months
Hib	One injection	
Polio	By mouth	
Diphtheria **Tetanus** **Whooping cough**	One injection (DTP)	4 months
Hib	One injection	
Polio	By mouth	
Measles **Mumps** **Rubella**	One injection (MMR)	12–15 months
Diphtheria **Tetanus**	Booster injection (around school entry)	3-5 years
Polio	By mouth	

There is usually no reason to delay immunization if:
- Your baby has the 'snuffles'
- There is a family history of convulsions
- Your baby has epilepsy
- There is a family history of adverse reactions following immunization
- Your baby is premature, or has a disability
- Your baby is being breastfed
- Your baby has asthma, eczema or allergies
- Your baby has had one of the infectious diseases
- Your baby is on antibiotics or steroids (unless he is ill that day)

A–Z OF BABY HEALTH

The overwhelming majority of health problems experienced by babies in the first year of life are minor, shortlived and easily treated, although some – such as allergy – can continue to be a problem into adulthood. The most common problems experienced by babies are listed here in alphabetical order.

Allergy

An allergy is an abnormal response by the body to a substance or 'allergen' which does not affect non-allergic people. Allergies can affect even very young babies, and in the first year of life children are particularly susceptible. The proportion of young children affected by allergies appears to be increasing. There may be several reasons for this. Firstly, allergies are more often diagnosed than they were in the past. Secondly, potential sources of allergens such as the house dust mite, pollution, food additives and chemicals have become more widespread in recent years. In addition, breastfeeding, which may have protected some babies from allergens in the past, has declined.

The term 'atopy' is sometimes used in place of allergy. Technically, atopy is an inherited tendency to develop allergy. Atopic may also be used as an adjective to describe an allergic condition

Is allergy inherited?

A general tendency to allergy or atopy does run in families, although children may not necessarily inherit it (if you have identical twins, both will be atopic but only one may develop an allergy). If your child is atopic, this may appear in a variety of ways, for example, as eczema, asthma or food allergy. The risks of your child developing an allergy are:

Both parents have the same allergy	60–80 per cent
Both parents have a different allergy	40–60 per cent
One parent has an allergy	20–40 per cent
Neither parent has an allergy	10 per cent

Common allergens

Almost any food or substance can produce an allergic reaction, but the most common are:

- Non-food: house dust mite; pollens (grass, trees, flowers); moulds; animal fur and feathers; chemicals; medicines
- Food: milk; eggs; wheat; fish; oranges; nuts; pork/bacon; food additives, colourings and preservatives (discuss the matter with your health visitor).

Types of reactions

Reactions to allergens may be immediate, such as an asthma attack or (rarely) a severe reaction such as swelling and difficulty in breathing, the first time a child is exposed to an allergen (this is known as an anaphylactic reaction). Alternatively, the reaction may be delayed and occur 12–48 hours after exposure to the allergen, as in the case of a food. A delayed reaction, usually vomiting or a rash, can make it difficult to pinpoint the cause of your child's allergy.

Food allergies

Intolerance of or allergy to a food is controversial, but there is no doubt that certain foods can cause adverse reactions in young children. Food allergy can cause or contribute to many conditions such as eczema, rashes, hay fever, bronchial asthma and gastrointestinal problems. Coeliac disease is caused by an allergy to the gluten in wheat, rye, oats and barley (see pp. 83–4). To reduce the risks of food allergy:

- **Try to breastfeed**
  It is best to breastfeed your baby for four to six months, longer if you can.
- **Do not wean too early**
  Weaning foods should not be introduced before four months of age. Potentially allergenic foods such as wheat or eggs should not be included in your baby's diet until he is at least six months old.
- **Give one new food at a time**
  Where there is a strong family history of allergy, introduce one new food at a time so that you can pinpoint any food that causes a problem.

Cow's milk intolerance

Intolerance to cow's milk can be due to an inability to digest the lactose (sugar) in milk, or a reaction to the protein in milk (see p. 77). About 2 per cent of children under one year are thought to suffer an adverse reaction to cow's milk protein. This is usually shortlived, and your child may well grow out of it by the time he is around three or four years old.

Symptoms of this type of allergy are:

- Gastrointestinal, such as vomiting, diarrhoea, colic, abdominal pain, abdominal distension
- Dermatological, such as atopic eczema, or rashes
- Respiratory, such as asthma or runny nose
- Behavioural, such as excessive crying and general irritability

Not all these symptoms are due to cow's milk allergy, however, and it is important that you seek professional medical advice. If cow's milk allergy is confirmed, special infant formula will be prescribed. This may be a milk based on hydrolysed milk protein or on soya. Soya itself can cause an allergic reaction in some babies so it is important that you talk to your health visitor or doctor before introducing this into your baby's diet. Goat's milk and sheep's milk are low in vitamins and minerals and should not be given to babies under the age of one (you can give it once your baby reaches this age, but you must use pasteurized milk and boil it first).

Asthma

Although asthma attacks in children under one are often set off by viruses, they can also be triggered by allergies. Symptoms include wheezing and coughing (attacks vary in severity). As it is difficult to treat asthma in young children, precipitating or trigger factors should be avoided as far as possible.

- Cigarette smoke is especially harmful. Do not smoke anywhere near your child – preferably not in the house at all – and insist that others do not. Try to avoid smoky atmospheres completely.
- Pets (both animals and birds) can cause allergic asthma in babies. Exposure to cats in the first year of life can cause hypersensitivity to cat fur in later life.
- House dust mites are responsible in some cases; try to reduce the number in your home.
- Food allergies can trigger asthma; if you think that food is a trigger, ask to be referred to a specialist before cutting anything from your baby's diet.
- Polluted air, particularly at pushchair level – the level of car exhausts – may trigger asthma; do your best not to stand near cars emitting fumes when you are waiting to cross the street.

Preventing allergies

If allergies or atopy runs in your family, it makes sense to try to minimize your child's chances of developing them, by taking preventive measures in his first year of life. This is not always easy, but the following measures may help:

- Try to breastfeed for four to six months or longer.
- Avoid weaning before the age of four months.
- Do not smoke, or let anyone else smoke, near your child.
- Keep pets such as cats, dogs and birds out of the house for his first year.
- Keep your house well ventilated and try to avoid damp.
- Do not use irritants such as spray polishes, perfumed cleaners or air fresheners.
- Try to keep your baby away from high traffic areas, particularly when he is in a pushchair.
- Try to keep house dust to a minimum. It is difficult to eradicate the house dust mite completely, however thoroughly you clean your house. In particular it thrives in places such as carpets, bedding and soft toys. Your child will, however, probably have a washable cover on his mattress and will not be using a pillow, so the problem will not be so severe in his first year.
- Consider replacing the carpet with cork tiles or linoleum.
- Wash bedding at 55–60°C to kill the mite.
- Wash soft toys regularly, or put in a plastic bag in the freezer for 24 hours once a week.

Colic

Infant colic, also known as evening colic or three-month colic, is thought to affect between 15 and 40 per cent of young babies between the ages of two weeks and three months. Although a baby with colic is not ill, colic will distress him and you.

Symptoms

In a typical attack of colic, a baby who has been his normal self during the day, will suddenly start emitting shrill, piercing screams at around 5 or 6 pm. His face may become red and congested and he will draw his legs up and down. His tummy may be hard and distended and you may hear it rumbling.

The crying bouts can last from about two to 20 minutes and occur at regular intervals throughout the evening. Your baby will finally fall asleep, exhausted, by which time you will be exhausted too. A baby with colic will not have diarrhoea or vomiting, and will have normal stools, a normal temperature and continue to gain weight normally.

Causes

Many theories have been put forward to explain colic, but the cause remains unknown. Rest assured, however, that it is not your fault. The most likely cause is thought to be gas trapped in loops of the bowel. This then builds up into bubbles and causes spasms in the bowels, resulting in abdominal pain. Continual crying, during which your baby swallows air, compounds the problem.

What you can do

If your baby has colic, he will continue to thrive, and the condition will eventually get better. Picking him up and cuddling him can help, and you are not 'spoiling' him by doing so. For temporary relief, try:
- Giving him a dummy to suck.
- Massaging his abdomen.

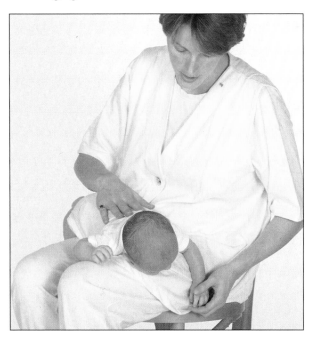

Above: Lying your baby with his tummy against the warmth of your body while you gently and rhythmically stroke his back may help relieve the misery of colic.

- Rocking him.
- Placing him on your knee and rhythmically massaging his back.
- Driving him around in the car.
- Giving him infant colic drops before a feed (these have a progressive effect and may take up to five days to start making a difference). Or try gripe water.
- Giving small amounts of camomile or fennel tea (make a weak solution using a herbal tea bag) or try camomile colic drops.

Do not automatically put your baby's crying during the evening down to colic. Always check other causes (see pp. 101–4). If he seems to be ill or has vomiting and diarrhoea with abdominal pain, this is not colic and you should consult your doctor.

Constipation

Since babies tend to open their bowels infrequently, and go red in the face and grunt when they are filling a nappy, parents worry that their baby is suffering from constipation. The number of times a baby opens his bowels varies enormously, however, and grunting is normal for babies. Only if your baby's stools are hard and compacted and he passes them with difficulty or appears to be in pain, should you suspect constipation.

Causes

Babies may become constipated when changing from breast- to bottlefeeding – breast milk is more watery in hot weather than formula, which is the same consistency all the time – or if they are simply not having enough fluid. Occasionally constipation may be due to a congenital disorder.

What you can do

If your baby is constipated, check that you are making up his feeds correctly, and try giving extra boiled water or well-diluted fruit juice between feeds. If your baby is more than four months, try giving him puréed fruit and vegetables once or twice a day, in addition to extra fluids. If the constipation is severe or these measures do not work, consult your doctor.

Coughs and sneezes

Sneezing is very common in newborn babies and does not mean that your baby has a cold. The lining of a baby's nose is sensitive to substances such as dust and sneezing is your baby's way of clearing out his nasal passages. Frequent sneezing can also occur if your baby has a cold as he cannot blow his nose to clear any congestion. If your baby's nose seems blocked, tickling his nose with a teased cottonbud to make him sneeze will help him clear it. Coughing in babies may have several causes, including a cold, measles, bronchitis, or whooping cough (see pp. 157–8).

What you can do

If your baby develops a cough or wheeze and seems unwell, or vomits after coughing, consult your doctor. Never give 'cough mixture' unless it is prescribed by your doctor. To ease a cough, give your baby extra fluids, such as boiled water. During the day sit him up in a baby chair. At night raise him up slightly by putting a book or pillow under his mattress.

Cradle cap

Thick, greasy yellow or brown scales on the baby's scalp are known as cradle cap. This can occur soon after birth and is not usually seen after the first year. Although cradle cap looks unsightly, it does not cause your baby any distress. Do not pick the scales off.

What you can do

Gently shampoo your baby's scalp daily with a mild baby shampoo, using tepid water. If the scales are not easily removed, massage some warmed olive oil or arachis (peanut) oil into the scalp. Leave the oil on for an hour or overnight before shampooing it off.

If the scalp still remains scaly, massage aqueous cream (from your pharmacist) into your baby's scalp and leave it for several hours, then wash it off. (Aqueous cream can also be used instead of soap for dry skin and as a moisturizing cream.) Repeat this treatment until your baby's scalp is clear.

Diarrhoea

Most babies have occasional loose stools and it is important to distinguish between these and true diarrhoea which can be dangerous in young babies. Diarrhoea is the passing of loose, watery, foul-smelling stools which may contain mucus and which may be brown, yellow or green.

Causes

Acute diarrhoea is usually caused by an infection. Chronic diarrhoea in babies could be a symptom of a problem such as cow's milk intolerance (see p. 161).

What you can do

How soon you should consult your doctor depends on your child's age (if your baby is only a few weeks old, the risk of dehydration is greater than in older babies), whether he is continuing to take fluids, and the severity of the symptoms.

You should continue to breastfeed, and may be advised to give cooled, boiled water or an oral rehydration solution after feeds. Bottlefed babies should continue to be given normal feeds and an oral rehydration mixture. You can also continue to give solid food. Do not give any anti-diarrhoea mixture.

Eczema

This is a common condition in which the outer layer of skin becomes inflamed, itchy and rough. Eczema usually starts in the first year and children often grow out of it (see Allergy p. 160). In the meantime, it can be treated with creams from your GP.

Meningitis

Meningitis occurs when the meninges – the layers of tissue that surround the brain and spinal cord – become infected and inflamed. Meningitis may be caused by a virus or a bacteria; viral meningitis is the most common cause, but bacterial meningitis is much more severe.

Symptoms vary with the age of the child. Children and adults usually experience neck stiffness, vomiting, fever, severe headache and intolerance to bright lights. A baby with meningitis is more likely to be very irritable and to have a bulging fontanelle, the "soft spot" at the top of the skull. The most serious type – meningococcal meningitis – may be accompanied by a characteristic purple rash, which does not disappear when pressed. You can check this by pressing the rash with a glass and looking through it.

What you can do

If you suspect your child may have meningitis call your doctor at once for an urgent home visit. If your doctor suspects meningitis, he will refer you immediately to hospital. If your doctor cannot make a visit immediately, take your child to the nearest accident and emergency department. The hospital will confirm the diagnosis with a lumbar puncture, or in the case of a baby, a needle will be passed through the anterior fontanelle. If your child has bacterial meningitis, he will be given antibiotics. Some types of viral meningitis can be treated with anti-viral drugs.

Members of the family and others close to the child, such as playgroup or school contacts, will be offered vaccination, and in the case of meningococcal meningitis, may also be treated with antibiotics to prevent any spread of the infection.

Nappy rash

Nappy rash is common in young babies and can range from a slightly red bottom to an angry inflamed rash with broken skin and blisters.

Causes

Contact with ammonia in the urine and bacteria in the baby's stools can irritate the skin and cause nappy rash, as can reactions to irritants such as washing powder, or some bath products.

Nappy rash may also be caused by thrush (*Candida albicans*, see p. 166) or seborrhoeic eczema. Suspect thrush if the rash does not clear up after treatment and if the skin is a shiny, brick red colour, with white or yellow pustules around the edges. In this case your baby will need to be treated with an antifungal cream.

What you can do

Change your baby's nappy as frequently as possible, and clean the skin each time with a gentle non-soap cleansing product which does not irritate (do not use wipes – which contain alcohol – or harsh soaps). Then apply a cream to protect your baby's bottom and heal the rash; there are a number of these on the market and you may need to experiment to see which one

Giving your baby medicine

The two most common forms of medication for small babies are medicine (such as antibiotics and liquid paracetamol) and drops, for conditions such as earache, blocked up nose (which can make feeding difficult), or sticky or infected eyes.

Medicine

Sit your baby in your lap with his head back and hold his free hand with yours. Place the spoon on his lower lip and when he opens his mouth, gently tip the medicine in. Try to get it as far back in his mouth as you can.

Eye drops
Gently pull down your baby's lower lid and squeeze the drops into the gap between the white of the eye and the lid.

Nose drops
Lie the baby on a flat surface and tip his head back a little. Squeeze the drops into each nostril in turn, trying to get them high inside.

Ear drops
Lie the baby with his head on one side with the infected ear toward you. Squeeze in the drops and try to keep him still for a minute.

suits your baby best. Whenever you can, let your baby spend as much time as possible without a nappy.

Regurgitation

Also known as possetting, regurgitation is the spontaneous bringing back of some of the contents of the stomach. Milk regurgitation is very common in babies immediately after feeding, and can occur as the baby brings up wind. This is not the same as vomiting (see p. 167) and is not projectile.

Spots and rashes

Skin does not fully mature until adolescence so a baby's skin is affected more by the environment and is more prone to dryness and irritation than an adult's. It is, therefore, a rare baby who does not have some type of spot or rash in the first few months of his life. These can include atopic eczema, seborrhoeic eczema and nappy rash (see p. 163–4). If you are concerned about your baby's rash or it appears infected, consult your doctor or health visitor.

Miliaria

This is a red rash with raised bumps, caused by inflammation of the sweat glands due to the baby getting too hot. Miliaria is also known as a heat rash or prickly heat. Keep your baby dry and cool.

Milia

Also known as 'milk spots' (for their appearance), milia are tiny white or yellow spots usually on the cheeks, the nose and creases at the side of the nose and the forehead. They are caused by blocked glands on the skin and no treatment is necessary – they disappear within three to four weeks.

Squint

A squint is a condition in which the two eyes do not look in the same direction at the same time, because the eyeball muscles are not balanced correctly. It is the most common eye problem in young children.

There are several types of squints and their cause is not always known, although they can run in families. A baby may be born with a squint (congenital squint) or one may develop later.

What you can do

If you think your baby has a squint, always mention it to your doctor or health visitor. Squints can lead to poor vision and even very young babies are treated early these days. Treatments include surgery, glasses, eye drops or patches.

Sticky eyes

Sticky eyes usually refers to yellow–green discharge from a young baby's eyes which gums the lids together, especially after sleep. It is common, and usually due to a mild infection. If this is the case, your doctor will give you drops or cream to clear it up.

What you can do

To clean sticky eyes wipe each eye separately with a clean cotton wool ball, soaked in cooled boiled water, starting from the inner corner and working outward (see Topping and tailing, pp. 98–9).

Sudden Infant Death Syndrome

This syndrome is commonly known as 'cot death' and is the situation where a baby is tragically found dead in her cot for no apparent reason. If this misfortune happens to your baby, seek help. The Foundation for Sudden Infant Death provides practical and sympathetic support, especially with the care of a subsequent baby (see Useful Contacts, pp. 248-51).

What you can do

Obviously this is a situation where prevention is the key. The following steps are recommended as a result of research into the causes of cot death:

- Always put your baby to sleep on her back.
- Do not let your baby become too hot; use blankets and sheets, not a quilt, so that you can remove layers if necessary. Room temperature should be around 16–20°C (61–68°F).
- Don't use cot bumpers as they can impede circulation of air.
- If you put a baby in a big cot, make sure her feet are in line with the foot of the cot so that she cannot wriggle underneath her bedding.
- A relationship has been found between smoking and cot death, so never expose your baby to cigarette smoke.

Fluoride supplements

Fluoride is a mineral which makes tooth enamel more resistant to acid attacks from plaque, and so helps to prevent dental decay. It is found in water in various amounts, and is added to most toothpastes. Fluoride supplements can be given to babies from the age of six months if the level of fluoride in the water in your area is low.

Many children, however, tend to 'eat' toothpaste and giving fluoride supplements can result in overdosing, which causes brown stains, a condition known as fluorosis. For this reason, current dental thinking is that fluoride supplements should not be given as a matter of course, unless there is a high risk of dental decay (for example, if childhood dental decay runs in your family, or if your child has special needs). Instead, take the preventive measures outlined on p. 129 and clean your child's teeth with a children's formula fluoride toothpaste. (The level of fluoride in adult formula fluoride toothpaste is too high for children, and these toothpastes in any case taste too strong for small children.) If you think your child needs fluoride supplements, consult your dentist before giving them.

Teething

Some babies cut their teeth without any problems at all. Others may be a little irritable or fretful, dribble, gnaw hard objects or chew their fingers. Some babies also have flushed cheeks, and red or sore gums where the tooth is coming through. Some babies have problems with some teeth, but not with others.

If your baby seems to be suffering when teething, extra cuddles and plenty of drinks of cool boiled water will help, as may one or more of the following.

- Try giving him something hard to chew on, such as a piece of crust or carrot or a chilled (not frozen) teething ring. *Never* leave your baby alone while he is chewing food, in case he chokes.
- If your baby's gums are red and sore, gently massage them with your fingers or a tiny piece of ice (but be careful – babies can get frost bite). Try applying a little sugar-free teething gel.
- If he seems to be in pain from teething, liquid

paracetamol may help. Always use sparingly and in the correct amount for your baby's age. Never give a child under 12 aspirin.
- Dribbling may cause a rash (sometimes called a 'teething rash') or sore patches on or under your baby's chin. Protecting the skin with petroleum jelly or a barrier baby cream can help.
- Cuddle and comfort. Put him in a sling and walk about. Go for a ride in the car.

Going to the dentist

It is never too soon to start looking after your baby's teeth (see p. 129). You can register your baby with a dentist soon after birth. Dental treatment and preventive care are still covered by the NHS and are free for children. Your dentist can also give you further advice on caring for your baby's teeth.

It is also a good idea to take your baby to the dentist as soon as his first teeth come through and when you yourself go for a check-up. In this way your baby will get used to going to the dentist as a normal part of his life, and learn that there are plenty of occasions when he goes to the dentist and does not need to have treatment.

Thrush

The yeast-like fungus *Candida albicans*, which causes thrush, is naturally present in most people's bodies and does not usually cause any harm. Babies are particularly susceptible to a thrush infection as their immune system is not fully developed, and some can catch it from their mothers at birth. Thrush can occur in both breast- and bottlefed babies.

Always check his mouth for thrush if your baby cries when he is feeding. (Thrush looks rather like milk curds but cannot be wiped off.)

What you can do

Your baby will be prescribed an antifungal cream or drops. If you are breastfeeding and your baby has thrush, you will also need to treat your breasts. If you are bottlefeeding, take extra care to sterilize your baby's feeding bottles and teats, and his dummy if you use one. Never put your baby's dummy in your mouth in case you are carrying the infection which you can pass on to your baby. Thrush can also appear as a nappy rash (see pp. 163–4).

Umbilical problems

Babies' umbilicuses or navels vary greatly in shape and size. Umbilical hernias are also common and usually heal spontaneously by the time the child reaches the age of two.

The stump that is left after the umbilicus is cut usually shrivels and drops off in about a week to 10 days. Your midwife will clean this for you, and advise you on keeping it clean and dry. Once the stump has fallen off, your baby's navel should only need cleaning as part of your general routine when you bath or top and tail him (see pp. 97–9). Slight bleeding is usually nothing to worry about, but if the bleeding is heavy or the umbilicus looks red, swollen or inflamed, contact your doctor or community midwife.

Vomiting

There are several causes of vomiting in young babies, including infection, overfeeding, food intolerance or a sign of a disorder such as pyloric stenosis.

What you can do
Consult your doctor if:
- Your baby vomits two consecutive feeds.
- He cannot keep any fluids down.
- He has diarrhoea with vomiting.
- He is ill or feverish.
- He appears to be in pain.
- The vomit contains blood or is brown.
- The vomiting is violent or is 'thrown' across the room (so-called projectile vomiting). Projectile vomiting is immediately obvious – if it is not thrown a good distance, it is not projectile.

Vomiting accompanied by diarrhoea (see p. 163) is called gastroenteritis (see p. 353). The treatment of vomiting depends on the cause and the age of your baby. In general, you need to replace the lost fluid by giving sips of an oral rehydration mixture to prevent dehydration. Oral rehydration mixtures, which can be bought from the pharmacist, contain a balanced mixture of salt and sugar to be mixed with water. You should also continue to breastfeed.

Teeth and teething

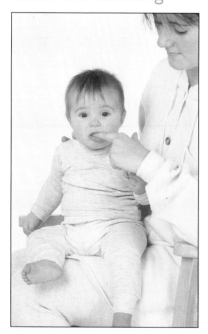

Teething gel
Sugar-free gels can soothe sore gums. Their effect is not very long lasting, so this remedy may work best just before bed, giving relief until the baby falls asleep.

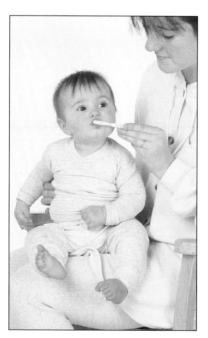

Brushing first teeth
It is never too soon to start cleaning your baby's teeth. As soon as the first one is through, use a soft brush and baby toothpaste to gently clean.

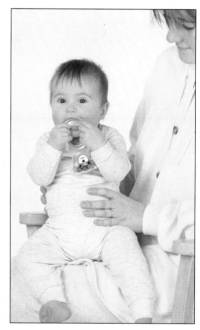

Teething ring
A cooled teething ring can soothe aching gums temporarily and give the baby something hard to gnaw. Put the ring in the sterilizer when it is not in use.

IS YOUR CHILD SAFE?

Children under the age of five run the greatest risk of having an accident of any age group. Every year some 600,000 children have to go to hospital because of an accident in the home. Accidents are also the most common cause of death among children between the age of one and five.

But exploring his environment is an essential part of your child's development, and he is naturally curious. With the best will in the world you cannot keep your eyes on your child for 24 hours a day. Taking adequate safety precautions around your home to prevent accidents is, therefore, vital.

Accidents can happen even to the youngest child. So right from your baby's birth you will need to think about how to protect him from various dangers in and around the home. There are five major sources of potential danger in the home: keep these in mind as your child grows.

Unsafe equipment

When you buy anything for your child's room, any electrical appliance and any toy, check to see whether it carries a British Standards (BS) number, Lion mark, Kitemark or CE symbol (see box). All toys should carry the BS 5665 or BS 3443 and should be appropriate for the age of your child.

If you buy secondhand equipment, make sure that it complies with safety standards. Check that safety harnesses and straps are firmly attached and not worn, and that toys do not have sharp edges or small, loose pieces that your child could swallow.

Choking and suffocation

Choking and suffocation are the third most common cause of accidental death in preschool children.

Feeding
- Don't leave a young baby alone with a propped-up bottle. Not only does your baby need the security of your arms, but he could inhale milk and choke.
- When your child starts on solid foods, do not leave him alone with finger foods such as bread, carrot or apple – if a lump breaks off, he could choke.

What to look for

The kitemark indicates that an item conforms to British Standards for safety and quality. It should be accompanied by a BS number.

The new 0–3 sign replaces written warnings that a toy may be unsuitable for children under 36 months because of small parts.

The Lionmark can only be used by accredited toy manufacturers and is an indication of quality and safety.

The CE mark is used on toys and indicates that a to conforms to European Union safety standards for such products.

- As he gets older, do not give him large, hard sweets or let him run around with food in his mouth.
- Do not give whole nuts to under-fives; peanuts are especially dangerous as they contain an oil which can damage the lungs if inhaled.

Dummies
- Do not tie a dummy around your baby's neck with ribbon – this could strangle him.
- Only buy a dummy made to BS5239, and check it regularly for wear and tear.

Bedding
- Cot bumpers are not recommended; they impede air circulation with young babies, and may be used as a step to help an older baby climb out of his cot.
- Remove the polythene cover from a new mattress to avoid the risk of suffocation.
- Do not use a pillow until your baby is at least a year old. Pillow should conform to BS 1877.
- Make sure your that baby's cot and mattress conform to BS 1753 and that the mattress fits the cot properly. A gap of more than 40 mm ($1^1/_2$ in)

anywhere round the mattress could trap your baby's head – a smaller gap could trap his fingers. Carrycots should conform to BS 3881; buy a safety mattress if your baby is sleeping in the carrycot.
- A baby nest should meet BS 6595; do not use a nest as somewhere for your baby to sleep. Always wash the nest in detergent powder, as soap can clog the fabric and stop air passing through.

Clothing
- Do not let your child wear clothes with ribbons or cords that can be pulled tight around the neck.
- Avoid open-weave clothes or blankets in which tiny fingers can be caught and trapped.

Other items
- Keep polythene bags and plastic away from babies and small children, and teach children never to put these over their heads.
- Check that there are no small parts on toys which a child could swallow and take care that your child does not pick up tiny items such as beads, buttons and coins. Button batteries are especially dangerous as they may contain mercury that can leak if swallowed. If your child swallows one, take him to the nearest accident and emergency department at once. Call an ambulance if necessary.

Scalds, burns and drowning

These can happen at any age, but young children are vulnerable as they learn to crawl, climb and walk.
- Never carry a hot drink when you are carrying your child. Hot water can scald for half an hour after it has boiled.
- Do not leave a hot-water bottle in your baby's cot as this could cause burns, and do not leave an electric blanket on when your baby is in the cot.
- Put cold water into the bath before adding hot, and test the water with your elbow – your fingers can stand much greater temperatures – or a bath thermometer before you bath your baby.
- Do not leave your baby or small child alone in the bath even for a moment. A baby can drown in just a few centimetres of water. If the telephone or doorbell rings, ignore it or get the baby out.
- Do not leave buckets or bowls of water where a baby or young child could fall into them.

Falls

Falling over is common when children are learning to walk and run, and one or two bumps are almost inevitable. Injuries sustained from a fall from a height or on to a hard surface can be much more serious.
- Babies learn to roll at a surprisingly early stage. If you change your baby on a high surface, keep a hand on him. Don't leave your young baby asleep on the sofa or bed, unless he is firmly tucked in.
- Sit-in baby walkers (see p. 134) have tipped babies into fires and down stairs.
- Babies usually love bouncing chairs and they can be a great help in rocking a fretful baby, but never put one on a high surface or a vibrating machine. Even a small baby can make them move, and if the chair falls, your baby may fracture his skull.
- Fit a harness conforming to BS 6684 to your pram, pushchair and highchair and use it every time you put your child in the pram or highchair.
- Make sure that the bath and shower have slip-resistant surfaces or a slip-resistant mat. The bath should have a safety grip handle.

Upwardly mobile

Before your baby starts crawling and walking – which will be sooner than you think – go around your house with this checklist looking for the danger zones.
- Glass in and around doors and low cupboards can break or splinter if your child bumps into it, and may cause serious injuries; replace it with safety glass or plywood if possible, if not cover it with safety film.
- Fires, whether open, gas or electric, should be shielded by a fireguard fixed to the wall; guards should conform to BS 6539.
- Fit locks to windows; make sure that your child cannot open them more than 10 cm (4 in), but that you can open them easily in case of fire.
- Move furniture away from in front of the window so that your child cannot use them as stepping stones in order to get up on to the windowsill.
- Floors should be non-slippery; avoid scatter rugs on polished floors.
- Furniture must be stable and not tip over easily. Sofas and chairs should be made of fire-resistant material; anything purchased since 1988 should

have been treated with a fire-retardant material, but if you are buying secondhand be extra vigilant since there are no guarantees.

- Fit protectors on sharp table corners and put small objects and ornaments away out of reach.
- Fit safety gates at the top and bottom of the stairs once your child starts crawling.
- Check that your child cannot fall through, crawl under, climb over, or get his head, hands or legs stuck in, banisters or landing rails (block them in with hardboard if necessary).
- Bunk beds are generally not recommended for children under six.
- Wires that could trip your child, or entangle and strangle your baby should be secured.
- Fit proper locks to the washing machine, fridge, freezer and video. A clip-on video cover will not put off a determined child for long.
- Fit finger protectors to doors that are heavy or that slam shut easily.

Smoke alarms

Despite intensive government campaigns promoting the fitting of smoke alarms, not every home has one. Fit one before your child is born in a place where you will be able to hear it all over the house. Follow the manufacturer's recommendations on siting and installation.

Test it by holding a recently snuffed out candle beneath it. Every six months, check the battery in the same manner.

Once a year, remove the cover and vacuum clean the alarm and change the battery.

- Sockets should have safety shutters or covers.
- Cupboards and drawers should have locks fitted. Childproof catches do not stay childproof – every tug weakens them further. If you really want to keep him out, fit a proper lock.

In the living room

Hidden wiring

Window locks

Safety film

Flame-retardant fabric

Safety covers

Safety film

Ornaments out of reach

Door wedged ajar

All-round fireguard fixed to wall

Corner protectors

The kitchen

The kitchen is one of the most dangerous places for your baby. Not only is there a risk of accidents such as scalds, or poisoning from cleaning products, but babies can easily get under your feet when they are crawling or walking about.

- If your baby is in a chair, put it where you cannot trip over it and your baby cannot grab anything.
- Keep trailing iron and kettle flexes well out of your baby's reach; use curly flexes or cordless appliances wherever possible.
- Make sure that saucepan handles do not stick out ; use the back burners or fit a cooker guard.
- Put tablecloths away until your child is older; keep hot drinks and dishes out of pulling distance.

Poisoning

A crawling baby will be into every cupboard and treat everything he finds as a potential toy.

- Lock chemicals, medicines and cleaning materials away or place them where your child cannot climb to reach them – children are excellent climbers!
- Buy products with child-resistant tops, but remember they are only child-resistant, not child-proof.
- Do not transfer chemicals to other containers.

Out and about

When you visit other people's homes (especially those without children), look for cupboards containing chemicals or tablets lying about. When you take your toddler out on the streets, use reins or a wristband to keep him securely by your side.

Electronic devices, which can help you locate your child if he wanders off and strays out of transmitter range, are now available. These are, however, no substitute for keeping hold of your child and as he grows up teaching him about safety.

In the kitchen

In the garden

Like the house, this can be a potential danger zone.

- Make sure that gates can be locked and that fences are secure, so that your child cannot wander off.
- Fit electric lawnmowers, strimmers and so on with circuit breakers.
- Keep sheds or garages which contain chemicals or equipment locked and the keys well out of reach.
- Some plants can cause unpleasant symptoms in children. Teach your child never to eat anything from the garden. If you suspect plant poisoning, go to the nearest accident and emergency department.
- Fence off ponds and pools.

In the car

No car journey is safe. Making sure that your baby is securely strapped into the appropriate and correctly fitted car seat for his age and weight, however, reduces the likelihood of injury in an accident by two-thirds.

The law says

- Children under the age of three travelling in the front seat of a car must be in an approved child restraint appropriate to their weight. In the back seat, a child restraint must be used if available.
- Children aged 3–11 years (and under 1.5 m/5 ft tall) must use an appropriate child restraint if one is available; otherwise, an adult belt must be worn.

Buying a car seat

Purpose-built child restraints to suit children of all ages and sizes are now widely available and the new EC44 regulations are designed to make car seats easier to fit and use. When buying make sure that:

- The seat carries the Kitemark or CE mark and is correctly fitted by a professional if in doubt.
- It is appropriate to your child's weight and size.

Stage 1 *Birth to 9 months old or 10 kg/22 lb*
These fit, rearward-facing, in the front or the back of the car although they must not be used in the front of a car fitted with air bags. They are safer than carrycots.

Stage 2 *9 months to four years or 9–18 kg/20–40 lb*
These seats are larger and heavier than stage 1 seats, and may be combined with stage 3 seats.

Stage 3 *Four to 11 years or 15–36 kg/33–80 lb*
These bring your child up to the level where he can be secured safely with an adult seat belt.

If you need a seat for a child with special needs, ask your local road safety officer for advice. If you are carrying three children in the back, get a shoulder harness fitted in the centre of the back seat. Check your baby regularly to make sure he is not too hot or cold. Never leave your child alone in a car.

Stage 1 seat held in place with adult seat belt – baby secured with harness

Stage 2 seat held in place with adult seat belt – child secured with harness

Stage 3 seat used with adult seat belt

CHILDREN WITH SPECIAL NEEDS

Every parent wants his or her child to be physically and developmentally perfect. 'Is everything all right?' is usually the first question a mother asks when her baby is born, ahead of even 'Is it a boy or a girl?' Sometimes, however, everything is not 'all right'. Some children have a temporary or permanent physical or mental disability. In the past, children who had a disability such as a developmental delay or cerebral palsy were labelled 'mentally' or 'physically handicapped'. This kind of labelling, which only focused on the child's disability and not on him as an individual, is no longer used. Children who have a mental or physical disability are now described as 'children with special needs'.

It is estimated that one in five children has special needs at some time in his childhood. These can range from a severe developmental problem or a rare congenital syndrome, which are permanent and lifelong conditions, to a minor speech difficulty which will respond to help within a few months or years. Problems such as a cleft lip and palate can cause considerable distress and require treatment, including surgery and speech therapy, over a number of years, but the outcome is usually good.

Identifying special needs

The discovery that a child has special needs may occur immediately at birth, or soon after (you may even have discovered while you were pregnant and chosen to go ahead and have your baby). A neural tube defect such as spina bifida, for example, or a cleft palate or Down's syndrome are obvious from the start. On the other hand, a learning difficulty or hearing impairment may not be detected until your child is a few months or even a few years old. Sometimes the disability may be discovered during a routine developmental check, or you, your GP or health visitor may suspect that all is not well with the baby after observing his progress over a period of time.

Depending on your child's problem, he will be referred to the appropriate specialist. If he has a hearing impairment, for example, he will be referred to an audiologist. If you or a health professional suspect that your child is not progressing as well as he should be, then he is likely to be referred for assessment to a paediatrician. After assessing your child, the paediatrician may – depending on the problem – then refer him to another specialist.

In some areas, your child may be referred to a child development centre. Here a multi-agency team of professionals including doctors, therapists, psychologists, health visitors and social workers work together to identify the specific needs of your child, and to offer the appropriate treatment, advice and support. As your child gets older, educational, psychological and psychiatric assessments may be made if necessary. If you do not understand anything, ask for it to be explained again; if you are still not happy with anything, make a fuss and ask for a second opinion.

Coping with your feelings

Parents' reactions to the realization that their child has a mental or physical disability depend on several factors: the seriousness of the problem; the way in which they are told of the diagnosis; and, often, their own personalities. If you have strong religious beliefs, you may feel you have been given a special child to care for. If you know someone with a child with a similar problem, you may feel more able to cope than if you are totally ignorant of its implications. If you have been worried about your child, having an actual diagnosis may give you a sense of relief. Most parents, however, experience shock, disbelief and guilt and, if their child has a severe or permanent disability, an overwhelming sense of loss.

When you suspect all is not well

You may well be the first people to suspect that all is not well with your baby. So if you are worried, ask your doctor or health visitor to check. If you are not satisfied, ask for a second opinion from a specialist such as a paediatrician or audiologist. Remember, you know your own child best, so follow your instincts, and do not be afraid to make a fuss if you have to. The earlier a diagnosis is made, the earlier treatment can be started and the more likely treatment is to be successful.

Your feelings may resemble those of the bereaved, including all or some of the stages of grief such as denial, anger, blame, despair, bargaining and acceptance. Having all, or any of these reactions, is perfectly normal. You are, after all, grieving for the loss of your 'normal' child, and need time to come to terms with your feelings.

You may also experience a mixture of feelings toward your child – protectiveness, resentment, love and dislike. Again, these feelings are perfectly normal. You need time to work through them, before you can start to accept your child as he really is.

Getting help

It is important that you and your partner talk to each other and share your feelings, and that you do not bottle everything up. You may also find it beneficial to talk about how you feel to an outside person such as a health professional or a member of a voluntary organization or support group, or to go to a counselling service.

Services are also available to support you in caring for your child, and to help your child reach his full potential. These are provided by health and social services and by voluntary organizations. Unfortunately, accessibility to and availability of some of these services are not uniform, and depend to some extend on where you live.

What the law says
Under the Children Act, local authorities have a duty to provide services designed:
- to minimize the effect on disabled children in the area of their disabilities; and
- to give such children the chance to lead lives which are as normal as possible.

By law, children with disabilities must be treated first and foremost as children with particular needs, and are entitled to the same general level of social services as other children in need, to enable them to live as normally as possible.

Professional and statutory services

Your GP, health visitor, paediatrician and social worker can all give you general advice and support in caring for your child. In some areas, specialist health

visitors are available to give extra help and to act as a liaison between hospital and home. You may also have a paediatric community nursing service in your area which can provide a nurse to visit you at home and help in managing your child if he has a severe handicap, chronic illness or was born prematurely. Your health visitor, GP or local hospital can tell you more about this service.

Depending on your child's needs and age, other specialist help includes: physiotherapists, occupational therapists, speech and language therapists, psychologists, nurseries and family centres. Always ask what is available in your area and make a fuss if you have to in order to make sure that you and your child get the help to which you are entitled.

Home learning service
If your preschool child shows signs of developmental delay, you can be helped to teach him new skills through home-visiting schemes such as Portage, which is run by the local education authority. Through this scheme, a home visitor will visit you on a equal basis and together with you decide what new skills to teach your child. These may include simple skills such as holding a rattle for a young baby or showing him how to play with bricks, to toilet training and early reading as your child gets older. Voluntary organizations such as Kids may also provide home learning teachers (see Useful Contacts, pp. 248–51).

Voluntary organizations
Whatever condition or syndrome your child has, there is likely to be a voluntary organization or a parents' group to offer you help and support. Often too, the best person to talk to is another parent whose child has the same difficulties as yours, and who has been through similar experiences.

Some organizations are familiar. They include Scope (formerly the Spastics Society) for people with cerebral palsy, the Down's Syndrome Association and the National Deaf Children's Association. If your child has a rare condition or syndrome which no one else seems to have heard of, try Contact a Family. This organization not only supports a large network of self-help groups covering all disabilities, but also maintains a network of national groups specializing in rare syndromes (see Useful Contacts, pp. 248–51).

What you can do

Once your child's condition has been diagnosed, try to learn as much as possible about it. This will help you to feel more in control about the management of your baby, so do not be afraid to pester people if necessary. If you do not understand anything a professional tells you, ask him or her to explain again. It is difficult to take everything in at first. If your partner is unable to be with you when you see a specialist or your child has an assessment, ask a friend or relative to go with you to help you remember what is said. Write down any questions you want to ask before you go, so that you do not forget to ask anything important. Remember too, that even if your baby has a disability, he will also have similar needs to other babies. So he will still need cuddling, talking to, playing with and to be treated as an individual. As he grows up, he will also need the discipline you give to your other children.

- Encourage ability – praise, stretch, present him with things he can do and things you think he may be able to do.
- Be sure to praise progress even if it is only a very small advance.
- Encourage independence. It is so easy to teach a child that he 'cannot', but he can learn and should be encouraged to try.
- Treat him normally and do not be afraid to discipline him or sometimes to put yourself, your partner and your other children first.
- Try to look beyond his special needs to a child who must grow up to face a real world which will not always make allowances for his disabilities, and try to fit him for that world.
- Accept his frustration. Things are not easy and he should feel free to say so.
- Do not deprive his siblings in a misguided attempt to treat your children equally: they should be allowed to do things he cannot do and deserve as much of your time as you can give.
- Explain as much as you can as honestly as possible to his siblings; remember that they too need time to adjust to the fact that their new brother or sister is not 'normal'.
- Encourage his siblings to take some responsibility, but do not be unreasonable in what you ask them to do.

Play

Even if your baby does not seem to respond to you, it is important that you play with him. Play is important for all children, and can enhance the learning skills of children with special needs. Depending on your child's condition, he may need extra encouragement to play, and may take longer to acquire new skills. Toys should match your child's mental age and ability (but if an older child is using a toy made for a younger one, make sure that it is strong enough). All toys should be bright and colourful, and offer action and stimulation. Again, a charity or support group will have members who can tell you how to adapt a toy for your child and where to find toys suitable for children whose bodies are older than their minds, and vice versa.

There are a number of excellent books aimed at encouraging play in children with various different needs and which offer solutions to problems such as keeping toys within reach. These should also help you to understand how to stimulate your child and how to play to his abilities, rather than concentrating on what might be seen as his problems.

A child who is blind or partially sighted will need toys with an interesting texture to offer some tactile variety, and with sound or music. If your child has a hearing impairment, the toys should vibrate when they are shaken. Further advice on suitable toys for your child can be obtained from the National Association of Toy and Leisure Libraries, which can also tell you where to find your nearest toy library (see Useful Contacts, pp. 248–51).

Educational provision

Local education authorities have a statutory duty to ensure that special educational provision is made for pupils with special educational needs. This includes making an assessment of your child's needs if he is over two (or under two if you request it).

Financial help

If your child with special needs takes a lot of looking after, you may be entitled to financial help, such as the Disability Living Allowance. For further information about this, ring the Benefit Enquiry Line, or ask at your local Benefits Agency. You may also be entitled to help from the Family Fund (see Useful Contacts, pp. 248–51).

CHAPTER SEVEN

Toddlerhood and Beyond

The years between one and five are often those that parents remember with most affection. Between these ages life itself is an adventure, and it seems that hardly a day goes by without your child mastering a new skill, speaking a new word, understanding a new concept, or playing a new game.

The preschool years

It is hard to say exactly when a baby becomes a toddler, but you will find the transition quite sudden. At some point between about 9 and 18 months you will realize that your child is not really a baby any more. Yet in many ways her progress is gradual. She pulls herself up and cruises around the furniture, so you expect her to walk. But she does not. It may be six or eight more weeks before she walks alone. It is because she progresses on so many fronts at the same time that the movement from baby to toddler seems like a sudden leap, but lots of little things have added up to that big step out of babyhood.

Walking is one, obviously, but in spite of calling them 'toddlers' this is not the most obvious difference. The main thing which distinguishes a baby from a toddler is that your toddler shares her experiences with you. She communicates her excitement and her fears. And, more subtly, she looks up to you and smiles as she plays. She understands. She lifts her arms when you ask and stops when you say 'No!' Her movements are more fluid and she gives the impression she has a clear intention. She knows what she wants, although cannot necessarily work out how to get it.

The whole is still, somehow, more than the sum of all these parts. Each new skill you write in her baby record emphasizes that she is not a baby. In some small sense she is now your companion. What you do together is partly on her terms: and from now on this will always be the case.

GROWING UP

Your baby's development in her first year (see chapter 5) was almost certainly characterized by periods of transition in which she learned a new skill, followed by periods of consolidation in which she practised and perfected it. There are three major periods of change in the first year: the first is birth, the second happens at about six to eight weeks when she begins to interact with the world and the third happens at about nine months. There is another major transition between 18 months and two years as she begins to exert her will more strongly and enters 'the terrible twos'. There is a smaller one between about three and a half and four when she becomes able to understand other people's points of view, and another major change at six years when she begins to think more logically. Finally there is the major transition of puberty between about 12 and 15 years.

At each transition children become more difficult. At six weeks there is an increase in the level of crying.

Letting go

Babies are wonderful. Every smile, movement, gesture is guaranteed to overwhelm you, make you feel amazed at your ability to produce such a miracle. And a baby's vulnerability brings out the protectiveness many parents did not even know they possessed and adds an unimagined dimension to their feelings for each other.

It can be difficult to accept that your baby is growing, that with each day that goes by, she needs you just a bit less, can do just one more thing herself. This is often made worse by the fact that as she takes each step on the road to independence, she may pass through a phase of being particularly difficult.

Don't be afraid to let go. Your children need you in different ways throughout childhood and even adult life. Each stage of their development brings its own charms and rewards, in addition to its own problems.

At nine months children start to cling, moan and/or wake at night. At 18 months children become more wilful and may have temper tantrums. At three and a half they are often disobedient and quarrelsome. At six they bicker with you and their siblings and at 13 all hell may break loose. But during the periods of consolidation – which last much longer – children are easier and happier.

How well your child weathers each transition depends partly on her underlying temperament and partly on her relationship with her main carers. An easy child may sail through despite indifferent caring. A difficult temperamental child needs sensitive parenting to see her through. 'Growing up' may reflect changes in the way she thinks or in what she can do, but whichever it is, you will find that, afterward, the old patterns of parenting do not work. Something new must evolve.

Getting it right

There are no simple formulae which ensure that you get parenting 'right'. In this century alone, advice to parents has wavered from the extreme indulgence of the flower power era to the 'spare the rod spoil the child' mentality that was a throwback to Victorian times, and every shade in between. The reason for this variation is that applied consistently most systems work. You can beat children into compliance (though few would now advocate this), but between the firm and free it is clear that no one has all the right answers. Nor can one set of principles be applied to all behaviours or at all ages. To live in society your child needs to acquire self-discipline and the best way to teach discipline is to apply it consistently. But, so that she is not down trodden by the stronger members of society she must also learn to be assertive of her own needs. Allowing her to unfold, to know she has her say, is the best way to teach this. Getting the balance between these two is one of the most difficult tasks you face as a parent.

- All children need opportunities to unfold, and sometimes their needs should come first. They should be able to put their point of view and you should listen even if you overrule the request.
- Although complete freedom is unrealistic, allow your children to do things for themselves even if they make mistakes.

- Your family is your child's first model of society. If you want her to grow up to consider other people (and have a society which does this), you have to teach her that her parents and siblings also have those rights. Sometimes she must do the washing up while you are having a few minutes' peace.

There is probably a series of things – bad behaviour, rudeness, running into the road, expecting to be waited on, refusing to settle down to sleep – that you (and every other reasonable parent) want to stamp out. Sometimes you can change things by discussion and understanding; at other times you have to insist. How you balance the two is a matter of taste. There is no right and wrong way. There are no rules that are suitable for all children or for the same child at every age. Decide on your family message, your way of doing things, and do it consistently.

What kind of parent are you?

There are shades in every parent and probably no one fits a category exactly, but there are general trends in the way all parents behave.

Accepting permissive

You are warm and loving to your children and create a democratic environment. Your children's needs are considered and their views treated with respect. You are permissive about most things and your children are free to try new things.

RESULTS: Children tend to be independent, outgoing, active, assertive, popular and democratic.

DANGERS: You can be so permissive that your children grow up unable to control impulses and since they lack self-control, they lack maturity. You may raise an individual who expects everyone to fit in with her: self-indulgent, self-centred, selfish, rebellious and disobedient.

Being permissive about the wrong things, such as aggression, can lead to increased aggression and a lack of care for the feelings and property of others.

Accepting demanding

You accept your children and are warm and loving toward them but nevertheless exert a great deal of control over them. You know your children and are not afraid to confront them.

RESULTS: Well-behaved, but often submissive, children who are polite and obedient. They may, none the less, have high self-esteem and outperform children from more permissive homes (this is particularly true of children with learning difficulties and other special needs).

DANGERS: Overprotected children can become too dependent on others. They may not be able to stand up for themselves and may be insecure without the controls you exert.

Rejecting permissive

You do not show love and concern, nor do you control your child's behaviour.

RESULTS: Disobedient, and sometimes delinquent, children who show little concern for other people. They can be quarrelsome and aggressive and may become bullies.

Rejecting demanding

You are demanding and at the same time hostile toward your children. You put forward a strict set of rules and require unquestioning obedience and punish if it is not forthcoming.

RESULTS: Socially withdrawn and often sullen children who may be quarrelsome and shy. Such children often turn the aggression they feel toward others inward upon themselves and may become the victims of bullies.

FROM BABY TO CHILD

These are the changes you can expect to see in your child and the ages at which you can expect to see them, all of which contribute to her transformation from baby to toddler to child. But remember all children are different and develop at different rates: yours may be earlier or later in one or more of these areas.

If you are concerned that your child is continually below the average in several of these skills, consult your doctor or health visitor.

9–12 months

Physical skills

Mobile: most children crawl or walk around the furniture, some walk independently. Becomes increasingly confident when upright.

Uses her hands to manipulate and explore; passes an object from hand to hand; holds an object with one hand, explores with the other; she pokes, prods, strokes and twists to unscrew.

Thinking

Knows that an object continues to exist even when she cannot see it; can solve simple problems.

Shows persistence in doing things and makes connections (pressing the button will make the Jack-in-the box pop up); she can pay attention quickly to anything that interests her.

Can look away from what she was doing and return to it; she can put two ideas together to make a plan (like wanting a biscuit and crawling to the cupboard to get one). This gives the impression that behaviour flows, since she does not simply react to the moment.

Language

Understands simple commands like 'No!'

Understands and may produce one or two words; communicates with sounds and actions.

Can imitate sounds.

Matches a face to a voice, looking for someone she knows when she hears them speak.

Can discriminate between different facial expressions.

Social skills

Has formed a central attachment to one person and is dependent on him or her.

Looks for approval and disapproval.

Clings and cries if left with strangers; likes to be near you or carers at all times; may have a comfort object.

Communicates her intentions.

Follows your gaze, looking where you look or point.

Initiates and plays games with you; understands social signals and imitates what you do.

Self-awareness

Knows her own name; touches her image in a mirror but does not recognize herself.

Emotions

Delighted to see you; calls to you in the morning and needs to be told when you are going to leave; less promiscuous in her affections; afraid of strangers and attached to her immediate family and carers – parents, siblings, grandparents, childminder and babysitters.

12–18 months

Physical skills

Stands (on one foot with support), walks, sits.

Can throw a ball.

By about 14 months, she may be able to place one brick on top of another.

Can twist her hand and feed herself; she can use a sit-and-ride, push a trolley and carry an object.

Can scramble up and down stairs.

Self-awareness

Knows her own abilities.

Can show you her shoes if you ask her to.

'Into' everything.

Teases.

Wants her own way; protests when she does not get it.

Does not forget immediately.

Less clinging, moving further away from you.

Likes to watch herself in the mirror.

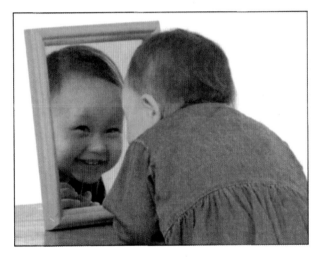

Thinking

Unwraps parcels; takes the lid from a box.

Can put simple shapes in a puzzle board.

Names some objects and understand names of others.

She explores and is generally more purposeful and persistent.

Emotions

Shows preferences.

Expresses emotions: affection, anxiety, fear.

Likes to be with other children.

Language

Jabbers and uses between five and 20 words.

She makes lots of signs and generally tries to communicate.

She understands more than she can say.

Social skills

Plays pat-a-cake.

Responds to requests and stops when told to.

Focused on main carers: parents, nanny, childminder.

Likes other children; may offer a toy but does not play (although she will play with an older sibling).

18 months to two years

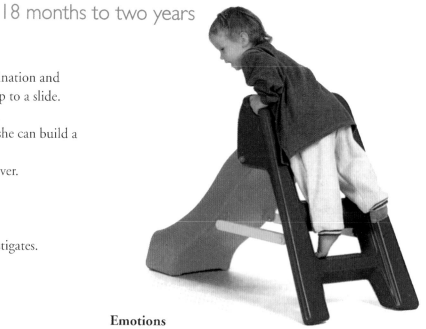

Physical skills
Climbs on to a chair; runs with co-ordination and
climbs stairs; climbs on to a frame or up to a slide.
Pushes toys and pulls them behind her.
Hand co-ordination improves, so that she can build a
tower of many blocks.
Stops to pick up a toy without falling over.

Thinking
Names familiar objects.
Plans activities; explores, watches, investigates.

Language
Says 50–200 words.
Starts using two-word sentences.
Uses 'me' or 'I' and 'you'.
Follows verbal instructions.
Listens to simple songs and stories.

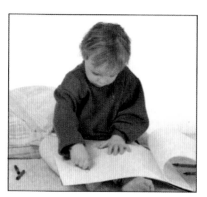

Social skills
Scribbles.
Likes to play
with your
possessions and
mimics what you
do; likes 'adult'
toys such as
kitchens and
lawn mowers.
Follows simple directions and orders people about.
Tests, fights, has tantrums and says 'No!' often.
At 18 months plays in parallel with other children but
by two years may begin to interact with children she
knows well.
Begins to imitate your intentions rather than simply
your actions.

Self-awareness
Recognizes body parts of teddy or doll.
Recognizes herself in a mirror.
Challenges your wishes.
Wants to 'do it myself' and make her
own choices.
High sense of self-importance.

Emotions
Wants independence and may react forcefully if she
does not get her own way. Laughs and gets very
excited.
Has tantrums and screaming bouts.
Likes to please and may be very loving but also quite
aggressive; she may bite, kick and hit parents, siblings
and other children.
May hurt herself on purpose to gain attention.
Likes to solve problems but is easily frustrated.
Delighted by own achievements.

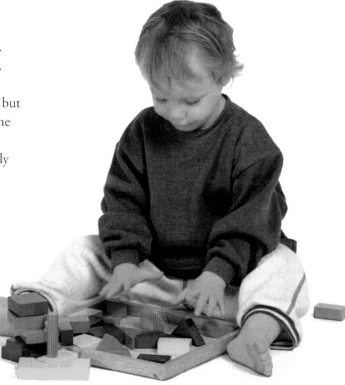

From two to three years

Physical skills
Jumps and hops.
Walks up and down stairs.
Knows what is safe and dangerous.
Begins to dress and undress himself.

Thinking
Names many objects.
Begins to understand the concepts of 'one' and 'lots'.
Memory span grows.
Begins to give reasons and solve problems.
Makes comparisons ('that cake is bigger than mine').
Knows some colours.
Respects rules.
Interested in 'why' and asks often to keep you talking.

Language
Communicates thoughts and ideas.
Uses language to express social and affectionate relations.
Enjoys talking.
Understands 'up', 'down', 'later', 'now'.

Social skills
Tests limits, saying 'no' but doing it anyway.
Enjoys being with people and plays with other children.
Likes to 'be like' an adult.
Likes to race about but also to play simple pretend games such as cooking dinner for teddies.

Self-awareness
Contrasts himself with others.
Expresses preferences.
Expresses pride.
Possessive about his things.

Emotions
Strives to master skills and tolerates more frustration.
Accepts substitutes.
Independent; seeks to do things for himself.
Less aggressive.
Uses language to express wishes and feelings.
Shows beginnings of a sense of humour.

From three to five years

Physical skills

Runs, starts and stops suddenly and dodges; gallops, skips, hops and jumps, raising feet high and taking strain as he lands.

Walks up and down stairs with alternate feet. Uses his hands to manipulate small objects. Throws and can catch a large ball. Dresses himself, but may still have some difficulty with laces, small buttons and zips.

Thinking

Talks fluently and questions frequently.
Begins to understand what numbers mean.
Can give and discuss reasons and solve more complex problems.
Makes frequent comparisons and can put some things in order.
Names many colours.
Begins to show sympathy and empathy for others; cries at sad stories.
Understands that you do not see what he sees and will explain things to you. Pretends to be someone else, talking for his toys and instructing himself as he plays.

Language

Communicates thoughts and ideas fluently using the past tense as well as the present. Uses language to express feelings; enjoys talking.

Distinguishes between reality and the pretend world; says 'Pretend that you are the Mummy and I'll be the Daddy'.

Social skills

More obedient and less testing with you, but more likely to quarrel with both siblings and other children.
Most children have stopped having tantrums.
Enjoys being with other children, but can sit quietly by himself.
Likes to race about, especially with other children.
Gets bored and tells you so.
Shows glee.
Begins to tell jokes but does not understand what makes something a joke.
Acts out roles based on TV or films; imitates other children.

Self-awareness

Concerned about what others will think, so may refuse to wear shorts or insist on wearing pink.
Contrasts himself with other children and what they have and are allowed to do. Says who and what he likes.
Likes to do 'grown up things' such as choosing and paying for things in the shop.

Emotions

Independent, may insist on trying things for himself.
More dependent on other children.
More aware of how he should act and influenced by the culture of other children in ways you may not approve (for example, boys should not cry and girls should be good) and may start to conform to that culture.
Does not always tell you his thoughts and feelings as he used to.

Influences on development

A child's development is influenced by biological factors – her heredity, the fact that she may have been damaged at birth, and by sickness and/or health. But environmental factors also play a part – the love and stimulation she receives; what happens to her; where she grows up; and how her family and others relate to her. The sort of child she is also influences her development: her temperament, security, confidence and how easy or difficult she is to love.

An attractive lovable child may draw attention and stimulation in ways a more difficult or less attractive child might not.

Heredity

Some aspects of development are more strongly influenced by inheritance than others. Physical development generally happens to a set timetable. As long as the environment and nutrition are within the normal range, it progresses along its pre-ordained road. Identical twins, who have exactly the same genetic inheritance, usually sit and walk within days of each other.

Language also emerges more or less regardless of what you do. The amount you talk to your child influences how many words she will say and how rapidly she learns, but most children learn how to communicate by the time they start school. Unless a child is severely neglected or has some specific language disability, she will know how to ask questions or speak about things in the past tense by the time she is four or five.

Becoming an intelligent adult, however, does need parental input. No child can reach her true intellectual potential without the love of her carers and a stimulating environment.

Your child's personality

Although babies seem pretty much alike, as children grow up they become more different from each other, their individuality and personality go with them into every situation. Some children always look before they leap: others invariably leap before they look. When faced with something new one child looks carefully before she reaches out to touch; another rushes in. The way a child interacts with the world tends to remain fairly stable. Impulsive toddlers were probably impulsive babies and may well in turn grow up to be impulsive adults, although this tendency may be overstated.

Being reflective is more likely to endear your child to her teachers and, initially, at least, your reflective child may do slightly better at school, but it is not as big an advantage as it might seem at first sight. Impulsive children are used to getting it wrong. They are more willing to 'have a go' and less likely to have their confidence undermined by what people think.

Your child's temperament

Sunny babies tend to be sunny children, and miserable babies tend to grow into miserable children (although if the cause of their misery is discovered and remedied, they will not). Extreme children make their parents fit in with them: you tiptoe around your child if you know that she might otherwise scream for an hour and a half. She then learns to use the threat of her temper to manipulate you. At the other extreme a sunny baby probably learns how to manipulate with her charm.

How children who are less extreme turn out is less predictable. 'In between' children probably learn more than one 'trick'. Sometimes they charm, sometimes they demand. One may realize that charm works best, while another finds confrontation far more successful.

HOW CHILDREN GROW

Throughout her preschool years, your child will grow about 50–75 mm (2–3 in) taller and put on around 2.6 kg (6 lb) each year. Fat peaks at about nine months, after which she should start slimming down, although many children remain more 'stocky' than they will be as adults.

Bones

Your child's bones will continue to grow and since her limb bones grow faster than those in her trunk, her proportions change. The small bones of her wrist increase in number (there are nine bones in an adult wrist, but only three in a baby's). By the time she is two her fontanelle (the membranous space between the bones of her skull) will have closed.

The brain

The power of the brain comes from the thousands of interconnections between the different brain cells. The word 'cell' gives the wrong impression of brain cells which are in fact more like trees, with branches that reach out to communicate with other cells. If you imagine all the large branches, small branches and twigs of a large tree, and then all the veins of each leaf you will get an idea of how much each cell reaches out to influence other cells. Each little vein finds a connection. If you then consider all the roots and root hairs you will get an idea of how many other cells reach out to interact with the brain cells.

Although most brain cells are present at birth they are not well connected. Nor are they all in the right place. First they move to the right place and then they start to make connections. In forming the connections, the brain increases in weight from 350 g (12 oz) to 1.35 kg (3 lb), most of it in the first two to three years of life. As well as making connections, the brain also starts to break some of those it no longer needs. When your child is about two, her brain will start pruning out these connections.

Myelination also occurs. Myelin is a fatty sheath which covers the nerves, in much the same way that electric cables are covered with a plastic sheath, insulating them so that impulses can pass along them more quickly. (Appreciating that multiple sclerosis is a disease in which myelin breaks down gives some idea of its importance.)

Milestones in physical skills
13–14 MONTHS Walks without help
18 MONTHS Goes up and down stairs without help
TWO YEARS Runs, walks backward, picks things up without overbalancing.
TWO AND A HALF Balances on tip-toe, jumps with both feet.
THREE YEARS Balances on one foot; goes up and down stairs by stepping and then bringing both feet together on one step; hops; and runs with a flat-footed action. She cannot change direction when running, shuffles if asked to skip and is unlikely to crouch or bend her knees when jumping.
FOUR YEARS Walks up and down stairs by placing one foot on each step; runs in a controlled way; can start, stop and turn suddenly, but may not be able to change speed without stopping first. She can hop about eight hops, climb up and down on the climbing frame and take alternate steps when walking on a wall. She skips with a flat-footed step if at all. Most children can now do hurdle jumps.
FIVE YEARS She can skip with both feet alternating; gallops starting with either left or right foot; runs, dodges, changes speed and direction without stopping first. Hops ten or more hops. About seven out of ten children can climb a rope ladder or a 'firefighter's pole'. She jumps smoothly using an arm thrust and crouch to take off and absorbing the impact by bending her knees.

What you can do

Everything your preschooler learns she learns by watching somebody else and then by doing. She keeps on trying until she succeeds. Once she has the basic skill, she practises. Most physical play is practice for the things she has already learned to do. There will come a stage where she loves to jump off the stairs on to a pile of cushions or walk along a wall while you hold her hand.

- **Encourage walking**
  Go for walks without the pushchair – you do not have to go far (remember her stride length when planning walks). Walking after dark when the street lights are on is a great treat.
- **Encourage running**
  Most children need little encouragement to chase and run around to music. Games like 'statues' enable children to practise running and standing still; chasing games encourage dodging, starting and stopping.
- **Walk backward**
  Can she weave backward through a maze of cushions? She can certainly walk to them and then fall over. Can she walk backward with her coat on backward?
- **Help her balance**
  How fast can she pick up her toys? Can she get them all before the music stops? Can she run around the garden filling a small bucket with leaves? Make stepping stones across shark-infested water (paper plates across the carpet), or let her 'walk the plank'. Balance two shelves across two piles of books.

- **Jumping**
  Play horses galloping over the 'jumps' (piles of cushions are probably the best choice for these). Most children enjoy skipping or running as fast as they can.
- **Hopping**
  Hopscotch is an obvious game, but you could also try 'Simon says "Stand on one leg". He also says "Hop around the room".'
- **Climbing**
  The sooner a child learns to go up and down stairs by herself the sooner she learns caution, but do not assume she has sense – she may try to carry something big like a bicycle up or down stairs. Climbing frames and slides offer practice. Check that they are sited on a safe surface and watch children as they play.
- **Make obstacle courses**
  Even small children can climb and crawl around an obstacle course. Make a tunnel behind the sofa, stepping stones with cushions, climb on to the coffee table. Obstacle courses for bike riders encourage spatial skills and teach them to weave and stop and start.

Using her hands

By her first birthday your child could probably move her thumb at will and curl her hand up so that she could wrap it around an object. Once she can twist her wrist, she places objects by holding them from above, and turns her hand to line objects up before she places them.

What you can do

Providing opportunities for skilled hand movements is the best way to develop your child's skills in this area. This does not need elaborate toys. Turning pages; finger painting; feeding dollies; spreading jam on bread; ripping paper into long strips, rolling it into balls and throwing it; posting shapes in shape sorters; building with bricks – the list is endless. You may also want to try some of the following ideas.

Construction kits

Fit the kit to your child's ability rather than the age on the box. A toy is useless unless she plays with it. The easiest kits, such as Stickle Bricks, fix together without a great deal of precise wrist movement. Once she has mastered these, offer something chunky such as Duplo which requires a little more precision. If your child enjoys building, she can be drawn forward if you gradually increase the difficulty of the task you set her.

Jigsaws

Some children love jigsaws; others hate them. When you buy a puzzle look carefully at the pieces. In a well-made puzzle it should be possible to see what is depicted on each piece.

Encouraging movement

Exercise need not be formal. Watch children coming out of the classroom into the playground: they explode into activity. All children need to let off steam. They need a time to race about, jump on their beds, roll down grassy banks, turn windmills or dance wildly to music. If they have other children to do it with, so much the better. Silly games are not as silly as they seem. Through them children make friends. They also practise spatial skills: those they absorb through playing with building bricks are as nothing compared with those they learn by riding a small bicycle through an obstacle course. Chasing and catching a child who is ducking and dodging requires even greater skill.

You cannot teach your baby to swim, ride a bike or dance, but you can provide the atmosphere in which she can learn, by taking away her fears and showing her the pleasures. Dancing involves using a physical skill to interpret music and express feelings and since toddlers are not much good at either of these, formal lessons are out of the question. But toddlers do enjoy moving to music. Since they particularly enjoy doing this with other children, early 'dance' classes can be great fun. Similarly children who are much too young to start formal training in gymnastics get a great deal of pleasure jumping and climbing their way around a baby gym.

Painting and drawing

At first children just scribble. Give your child one short fat crayon. Try this variation. Mix two or three tablespoons of cornflour with a little water to make paste that flows. Add a drop of food colouring. Put it into a cake tin and let her 'draw' in it with a blunt pencil. The lines will be clear for a moment and then close over so she can start again.

Dressing dolls

Putting on dolls' clothes – and taking them off – requires good hand–eye co-ordination.

Cutting

Trying to cut out pictures is difficult, but you can make long thin strips of paper and let her snip across them to make confetti.

Unskilled hands

Providing games is one thing: getting your child to use her hands is quite another. Some children love jigsaws, dressing dolls, construction kits and drawing. Others would far rather race about on bikes or sit and watch videos. The problem with many children is getting them to sit still long enough, so the obvious solution is for you or her carer to organize your preschooler's day – much as a nursery school would. Make a timetable. Morning and evening is the time to let off steam. In the afternoon there is a time for silly, noisy or messy games. Between times find slots for her to do some housework, baking, drawing, go for a walk, read, play quietly with toys and watch TV. Not only will such organization help her to fit into the structured environment of school and nursery, it will make her feel secure.

If you need to add a little bribery to that organization, get her to do the things she does not like as a condition for doing the things she prefers. Washing down the table before playing at the sink. Make things more fun. Pick up all the toys and put them away before the music stops. Then make an attempt on last week's record.

Getting dressed

Girls tend to be a little more competent than boys at dressing themselves. Whether this is motivation or practice is not really known: girls after all do need partly to undress every time they go to the toilet. Easy dressing is rarely compatible with children's fashions. Doing up fly buttons and zips, dealing with dungarees, shirts with buttons, or shoes with laces, is quite beyond the scope of a two-year-old. Many five-year-olds still find these difficult.

Vests, teeshirts and dresses

If your child looks at the front of a teeshirt or dress before she puts it on, it is then the wrong way around when she picks it up, so she puts it on back to front. Select clothing with pictures or buttons on the front and show her that these have to 'hide' before she picks them up.

Manual dexterity

Initially your child will simply cut pieces from paper; the ability to cut out a shape comes later.

Finger painting is messy, but all children love making pictures in this way.

Jigsaws can be great fun for children who take to them. Start with a few pieces and build on that.

Dressing dolls and teddies is excellent practice at manipulating small objects.

Getting clothes over her head can be problem, so choose those with wide necks. Show her how to burrow in from the bottom. Again, it helps to put the vest down with the neck furthest away from her. Teach her to put her arms through the sleeves before putting her head in.

Pants and trousers

Avoid buttons and bibs until your child is skilled at dressing herself: they are too difficult for two-year-olds. Elasticated waistbands enable a two-year-old to pull trousers and knickers on quite easily, but tights remain a difficulty throughout the second year, and often beyond.

To get trousers the right way round, the front has to be facing upward before she starts, so lay them out with the front up and waist closest or – better still – select trousers which do not have a specific back and front. Try to select pants in which the leg holes are clearly different from the waist hole.

Coats

Place the coat on the floor button side up and tell your child to walk around to the head end and put her arms into the sleeves. She can then raise her arms up high, sweeping the body of the coat over her head.

Socks and shoes

When you put out your child's socks, place them with the heels touching each other to reduce the possibility of the heel ending up on top of your child's foot. Or, better still, buy socks without heels.

The easiest way to get shoes (and wellington boots) on the right feet is to step into them from the stairs.

Toilet training

Most parents can predict when their one-year-olds are likely to move their bowels: they may be quite regular in their habits, and may strain or go red as they pass stools. If you always sat your one-year-old on the potty at the right time, you could probably go for several days without a soiled nappy, but that would not mean that your child could control her bowels. Children can only do this when they have developed the necessary muscle and sphincter control, which for most is some time between the ages of 18 months and two and a half. However hard you try to train her,

your child is unlikely to be dry day and night until she is around two and a half and many children are considerably older than this.

In these days of disposable nappies, washing machines and dryers, and plastic mattress covers, it is easy to be relaxed about potty training. Leave it until your child is ready, and it will happen quickly.

Before you start

- Are you free from family stress?
- Are things normal – no holidays, illness, visitors and so on?
- Can you make light of accidents?
- Does your child have quick release clothes? If in doubt, wait.

Is your child ready?

You cannot train a child who is not physically ready to cope. She must be able to stand and walk; to sit on a low chair and get up again without toppling over; and pull her pants up and down easily (a child with jeans with zips or buttons, or dungarees is not going to learn).

Showing signs that she knows she is about to go or telling you afterward indicate that she may be ready to learn, as does going for a couple of hours between wet nappies. Finally, make sure that she knows the words your family uses ('wee', 'pee', 'pooh' and so on).

What to do

- Draw attention to any signs she makes that she may be about to go; ask 'Did you do a wee then?'
- In summer let her spend time without a nappy on, so that she feels what it is like to wee without one.
- Buy some quick-release pants.
- If she shows signs of needing to go, sit her on the potty for a couple of minutes; if nothing happens, get her off.
- Suggest she sits on the potty at 'likely' times: before her bath, before bed, when she wakes up.
- Let her know when you want to go and take her with you.

Making it work

- Praise her when she gets it right; tell her she is grown up.
- If she does not seem willing or able, put it all off for a week and try again.

- If she manages to use the potty, let her help you empty it, wipe her bottom from front to back, flush the toilet and wash her hands.
- If she asks to use the potty, praise her even if it is too late. Be ready to move quickly – at first she will give little warning.

What not to do

- Don't force the pace or compare her with other children – girls usually manage sooner than boys.
- Don't scold, punish, get emotionally involved or make a fuss.
- Don't be surprised if she wants to look at or play with the contents of the potty. Let her look.
- She may also want to play with the water in the toilet or dip toothbrushes in it: don't leave cleaner in the bowl overnight.
- Don't show frustration or expect her never to make a mistake again.
- Never hold her on the potty.

Night times

Some children 'crack' potty training in one go, others take a year or more before they are dry at night. Some children continue to make mistakes well into their school years. If you or your partner had problems with bed wetting, your child is also likely to.

There is no rush. Leave off a night nappy when your child is often dry in the morning; take off the plastic sheet when she always is (see also p. 93).

THE DEVELOPING SENSES

At one year children see almost as well as adults. Their hearing is also acute and in the higher ranges they hear better than adults do. Your child will use her hands to feel, screw up her face at unpleasant smells and delight in those she enjoys. She may still, however, blow down her nose to smell rather than sucking air into it. She is also ready to explore a range of tastes.

Learning to see

If you had puzzle books as a child you may remember pictures in which you were asked to find objects hidden in a landscape. From such puzzles, psychologists identify two types of people: field dependent, who find it difficult to ignore the background; and field independent, who find it much easier. Generally speaking children become more field independent as they get older. But individual differences remain.

Children who are able to ignore the background tend to be good at manipulating and building things. Those who are more distracted by (or appear to take greater notice of) the background tend to be more socially skilled.

Drawing

Your child's first pictures are likely to be round scribbles which she makes without taking the crayon off the page. With practice she progresses to lines and dots and perhaps a small squiggle. The broad sweeps become her drawings and the little squiggles her writing. At first she does not intend to draw. She draws first and looks to see what it is later. One day her round swirls and dots look like a person, so she draws like this again. When she draws a person she basically draws a head. Even when she later adds arms and legs the head remains the focus of her picture, bigger and more detailed than the body. When children start to add fingers and eyes their first concern is to add, the second to add the correct number and only then to get them in the right place. Even at seven she may be unconcerned about relative size: the proportions of the various elements in her pictures will be wrong.

When children add eyes or fingers to a person or windows to a house they do not necessarily count how many there should be. The important thing is that people have fingers and because they are important they are also very big, perhaps as big as an arm. The way she draws reflects the way she looks at the world. Children rarely notice a change in size or position but do notice whether things have disappeared. They focus on one thing at a time, not the relationship between them. When they are thinking about fingers they are not comparing the size with the head, arms or body. They are drawing something new and important.

Children's drawings improve because they practise, which is why elderly people who have not drawn since childhood may produce the naive drawings of young children.

Milestones in drawing

18 MONTHS TO TWO YEARS A picture may look like scribble but the lines are not aimless and the pattern is well balanced: something on the left is usually balanced by something on the right. Drawings are not meant to be anything, simply patterns.

TWO TO TWO AND A HALF YEARS Your child will still not set out to draw anything in particular, but because you ask her what it is, she tells you what she has drawn. This is the stage when children make good circles which can and do stand for anything: ask two days running and the answer may well be different.

TWO AND A HALF TO THREE YEARS It becomes more obvious that children see their drawings as representing something and your child may well tell you what she intends to draw before she starts (although she will depart from the original plan if she thinks it is looking like something else).

THREE TO THREE AND A HALF YEARS Gradually you will notice circles, squares, crosses and combinations of these elements. Children start to enclose things within some circles. You may see a cross within a circle, or dots and lines. Lines radiate out from the circle too, as your child draws a sun. It is probably in these shapes that she notices she has drawn a person and thereby makes her first representational drawings. She sets out to draw a person and she does. Sometimes she puts things in the wrong place. The eyes may be in one corner of the face or even in the stomach. It is more important to get the parts in the picture than to get them in the right place.

THREE AND A HALF TO FOUR YEARS Positioning becomes more important; she places the eyes in the face. The body may still be missing but the legs come out of the bottom. She may use circles for the head, the eyes, the nose and the mouth.

FOUR TO FIVE YEARS Children are more skilled. They add more details, so that people have arms as well as legs and little details such as buttons and hair. Pictures become 'busier': there may be a plane in the sky or a tree by the house.

From now until your child is about eight years old, her drawings are symbols of the objects drawn not pictures of reality. 'My house' has a chimney, four windows – two upstairs and two down – and a central door, even if you live in a flat. Drawings include what should be there, so if she draws a dog side on, it will still have four legs, lining up underneath. Faces of animals turn to grin full face; cats have whiskers, cars four wheels.

Drawings also include things that are not normally seen, a baby inside a mother's stomach, for example, while a picture of a man sitting in a chair will include all the man and all the chair.

Learning to listen

Although preschool children can only sing a few notes, they like to dance, sing and clap along to music. It soothes and it excites them. A love of music is best fostered by encouraging your child to listen and join in. Because music is made up of lots of little sounds, listening for small background noises can improve a child's 'ear' and helps her to develop musical skills. Stop and listen to the silence, birds, ticking clocks or distant traffic. As she gets older, try listening out for one particular instrument or repeated theme in a recording.

Learning about taste

Children know what they like to eat and it is usually sweet and bland because most of the food they are given (including breast milk) is bland and sweet. Baby food – especially pre-packaged baby food – tends to be very bland indeed. Like all young animals, children are naturally conservative about foods. This is sensible: sorting out good from harmful foods is not something to do by trial and error, so children rightly treat all new foods with caution. They accept what they know and slight variations on that theme but will not take more than a mouthful or two of a new food.

Different cultures have different basic foods but the principle in expanding the number of foods your child will accept is the same. To go from carrots to spinach add gravy to the carrots and then a little spinach to the carrots and gravy. Once she accepts this, gradually reduce the carrots and then the gravy. Once accepted, spinach can then be paired with a little cheese. And so on.

LEARNING TO TALK

Most children say their first word between 10 and 17 months. The average is about 14 months. The first word is usually a noun like 'dog' or a simple verb like 'go' or 'eat'. By 20 months, most children can say about 50 words. Like Goldilocks, children go for nouns that are 'just right'. When they see a poodle they don't say animal (that is too big a category) nor poodle (that is too small) they say dog because dog is just about the right compromise between too broad and too precise.

How children learn

Your child's first word may well be 'Dada', but that does not necessarily mean her father. It means man. In the same way that 'woawoa' means all small animals. By the time they are 16 years old most young people have a vocabulary of 40,000 words; if you include names and idiomatic expressions the number doubles to 80,000. That means they have learned about 100 new words in every week of their childhood. Children with large vocabularies may acquire words at twice this rate. The only workable learning strategy is to grab the word, and to work out the precise meaning later. You can help by correcting mistakes and telling her when she is right: 'No, that's not a horse. It's a zebra' or 'Yes. That is yellow.'

Whatever language they learn to speak, most children do things in the same way. They refer to the things they see and can point to. They learn lots of nouns and then a few verbs. (Of the first 50 words about 40 are nouns and about 7 verbs.) However there are always a few children who do it differently. Instead of pointing and saying 'bus' their first words are things like 'you', 'me' and 'please', and words they run together like 'do-it' or 'go-way' and 'love-you'. Rather than commenting on objects, they comment on social relationships, needs and feelings.

Children learn to speak by listening for the emphasis in a word. This is why they call an elephant an 'efant' but can say 'helicopter' – where the emphasis is more evenly placed – clearly. Help her by talking about what you are doing, by pointing and naming, and by looking at the things you are talking about. Your child will also begin to follow your gaze at about the time she begins to understand language.

Her pronunciation may remain immature because vocal apparatus does not fully mature until a child is about six years old. But although children often mispronounce words, they know how words should be said. She may say 'bo' for bottle but will expect you to say 'bottle'. You may not because you find her words endearing: there is nothing wrong with this. Children who hear two languages learn to speak both. Calling a bottle a 'bo' will not slow her development.

What you can do
- Talk to her frequently.
- Listen to what she says.
- Pronounce things clearly for her. You do not need to correct what she says: just let her hear the correct word.
- Speak clearly, emphasizing the words she understands. 'That is DADDY's SHOE.'
- Look at books together (choose those with simple clear pictures of familiar everyday objects).
- Put pictures on the wall and look at them and talk about them together – murals of familiar animals or household objects are good.
- Sit down together for a game of point and name: Where is her foot? Her nose? The cup? Mummy's nose?
- Talk as you shop. 'Here are the beans'; 'Let's get some apples.'
- Let her know you understand what she says; the best way is to expand for her. If she says 'Shoe' answer, 'It is a shoe.' If pointing at the shoe she says 'Daddy' say, 'That is Daddy's shoe.'
- Songs and rhymes are good sources for early words, since the tunes often help her make longer sentences than she might otherwise **manage** (see Fun with music and song, pp. 218–20).

Making sentences

Putting words together to make a meaningful sentence happens at around 21 months. Sentences are more than strings of words: they have structure, and a meaning that comes from the way the words are arranged. Her first real sentence will be preceded by word-gesture sentences. 'Biki' she says, putting her hand up to the tin. She is asking with her hand outstretched, 'Can I have a biscuit?' When she points to the coat and says 'Mummy' her hand is in a different position. It is a different sign. She cannot yet say 'That's mummy's coat' but between her hand and her one word she can express the meaning.

Most children know about 200 words before they begin to speak in two-word sentences. The sentences they use are rather like the gesture-words that went before, short, simple and telegraphic: 'Want biki' and 'Mummy coat'.

In her early sentences, your child will:

- Make statements: 'That house', 'It ball'.
- Note possession: 'Daddy book', 'Mummy shoe'.
- Note location: 'Teddy bed', 'Cat table'.
- Describe action: 'Car go', 'Eat dinner'.
- Make demands: 'Come here', ''nother book'.
- Describe: 'Big dog', 'Red ball'.
- Ask questions: 'Where ball?', 'That hat?'.

Rhymes with simple, repeated words and a good rhythm to clap along with are an excellent way to help your child learn to talk.

Children use words in the same order each time they make a sentence because in English word order expresses meaning. 'Teddy is in bed' means something different from 'Bed is in Teddy'. If you say 'I can see a bed with Teddy in it', your child will say 'Teddy bed'. She is selecting the part of the sentence you emphasize as you speak, not simply copying what you say or putting two words together at random. She is arranging words to convey a specific meaning.

Language is creative. She may take her cue from you but she can create sentences she has never heard before. If you tell her a puppy is a 'baby dog' she may create a new sentence by calling a lamb a 'baby sheep'. Even when she has started to say two-word sentences, she will continue to use gesture to clarify meaning.

What you can do

- Expand sentences so that it is clear to your child that you have understood what she said.
- Use short simple sentences.
- Repeat what you have to say in a number of ways: 'It is a dog'; 'It is a small dog.'
- Talk about things she can see and hear.
- Talk about what she is doing.
- Talk about what you both see in her books.
- Ask her to fetch things for you.
- Talk as you feed, change, dress and bath her: early sentences are often about familiar activities.
- Talk about possessions.
- Sit down every day for a cup of tea and a chat.
- Speak in a higher pitched voice and at a slower pace than you do normally.
- Pause for longer at the end of sentences.
- Use short grammatical sentences (adult speech contains long and unfinished sentences and is frequently ungrammatical).
- Use very simple and basic grammar ('Where is Teddy? Can you see Teddy? Teddy is there. Look, there is Teddy').
- Repeat your child's sentences, recasting what was said, so 'Mummy shoe' becomes 'Yes that is Mummy's shoe'.
- Talk about what you can see and point to and select the word you think your child will understand.
- Stay in touch with your child's language; know what she is saying and keep one or two steps in front so that you draw her forward.

Absorbing grammar

From two-word sentences, your child will move on to grammar – such as adding 's' to make a plural, and 'ed' to indicate the past tense – and prepositions (such as 'on') and articles (such as 'the'). The earliest example you will probably hear is 'I playing' or 'I crying'. Soon after, you will hear prepositions in sentences like 'Cup on floor' and plurals like 'cats'. She starts putting 'a' and 'the' into her sentences. So she will say 'This a pig', or 'Where the cat'.

Children do not just learn the words they hear. They learn how to express things by working out the rules which underpin language. So they do not just learn to say cars and bikes, they learn that in English the plural is made by adding 's'. She starts by learning a few examples, such as 'sweeties' and 'cars', then once she uses the rule will apply it to everything. She may previously have said 'feet' and 'sheep', but now will say 'foots' or 'feets', and 'sheeps'. Similarly, with verbs, she may say 'goed' for 'went' and 'comed' for 'came'. By the time she starts school, she will know all the common tenses and know when to add words like 'to' (as in 'going to bed'). She may even be able to say things like 'We went to the circus, didn't we?'

Children also use language to monitor their own behaviour. As she tries to put the wrong shape into her shape sorter, she may say 'No, not there'. Using language in this way is common in two- to three-year-olds, peaks at about five or six years of age, then goes 'underground'. Some children practise what they want to say: a string of loosely related ideas such as 'Teddy here. Teddy in cot. What colour Teddy? What colour blanket? Blanket here … ' is typical.

LEARNING TO THINK

Before their first birthday babies often repeat those things they discover by chance, but rarely take them further. As your child approaches her first birthday, she begins to experiment, testing and trying to see how various actions affect outcome. In her high chair she takes a spoonful of potato and drops it. She spills her juice on to the floor. She drops her cup. She watches as things go splat, splosh or bounce and roll away. She dips her hand in water and then she dips her sleeve and examines the difference.

When to worry

The fact that a neighbour's child chatters away and yours says almost nothing may be of no significance whatever. But, if you are worried, tell your doctor or health visitor and ask for a hearing and developmental test. Telltale signs that she is experiencing difficulties include:

- If a hearing test suggests that she may be having problems.
- If you suspect she is having hearing problems.
- If she is saying nothing at all at 21 months.
- If she does not seem to understand one word at 14 months or any language at 18 months.
- If what she says is very unclear, even at three.
- If she starts to stutter.

If your child needs speech therapy, the sooner she starts the better.

As she experiments she learns that the harder she throws, the bigger the splat and that some things get wet and stay wet, and other things get wet and can be dried. By 18 months she can think of things she cannot see, and imitate things she has seen in the past.

Seeing is believing

By the time she is 8–12 months old your child will search for something where she expects it to be (see pp. 138–9). By 12–18 months, she watches to see where you put a toy and searches for it in the last place she saw it. She only looks for something where she has seen you putting it. She only believes her eyes.

As she approaches her second birthday your child can ignore what she sees and imagine where an object might be. Once she is able to imagine things which are not in front of her, her thoughts do not have to be the same as her actions. She can think about one thing and do something else.

If the door to the kitchen is closed and she wants to carry a cup of juice to the lounge, she puts the cup down to open the door. She may put it in the path of the door but then realizes the door will knock the cup over. Before she tries to open the door, she moves the cup out of the way. A younger child cannot imagine how the door will move. She will only realize she has to move the cup when the door bumps into it.

Concept-forming

A three-year-old may have strange ideas about the world around her. If you give her a pile of objects and tell her to pick out all the ones that go together she might pick two cars, three blocks and a scarf, and explain that 'The cars go together because they are cars. The blocks go with the blocks because they are the same. The blocks go with the cars because you can build a bridge with the blocks for the car to drive under. The scarf goes with the blocks because they are all red.' Small children put one and one together and do not think beyond those two. Tomorrow, her choices – and the reasons for them – could be different.

Working one step at a time leads children to jump to conclusions. If mummy came out of hospital with a baby, Grandad must get a baby if he goes into hospital. If she flew to Spain on holiday and her friend flew to Greece, Spain and Greece must be in the sky.

What you can do

- Buy model cars, farm animals and coloured bricks which can be arranged in various ways. Can she pick out all the baby pigs? All the red bricks?
- In the kitchen can she separate the onions from the carrots? The tins of beans from the tins of tomatoes? Her socks from Daddy's socks?
- Look for puzzles which show a progression of pictures from small to large. Arrange tins of food, toy cars or plastic animals in the same way.
- Read books which emphasize big and small, in and out, thick and thin, under and over.
- Play lotto or picture dominoes which match pictures and numbers or colours. When she is a little older, try work books which ask her to put objects into groups and to match things which look alike.

Theory of mind

One of the nicest things about toddlers is that they believe you can perform miracles: you can make the blanket tuck in, the sock go on straight and stop the bricks falling over. Children believe that a teddy can miss them when they are at playschool and that a statue by the hotel door can look after their bucket and spade. Nor are things simply alive: they also know everything that she knows.

Three-year-olds do not allow that your experience is different from theirs, but around three and a half, they are able to understand that you have thoughts and feelings that are separate and hidden from them, and they have thoughts and feelings which are separate and hidden from you. Psychologists call this 'theory of mind' and it marks an important stage in your child's development. Until she has a theory of mind she cannot fully understand why hitting her brother should be so naughty. She knows her brother cries, but because she does not feel the pain herself she cannot empathize. If she is upset it is because you will be cross with her. Because she does not know you see and think differently from her it is difficult for her to deceive you or lie convincingly.

Make believe

The best way in which a child learns to understand that other people have thoughts and feelings which are unlike her own is by being someone else.

The preschool years are the time of make believe. As children pretend they manipulate ideas, thoughts and emotions in games. They pretend to be other people, and that the things they are playing with are not what they seem to be. A teddy is in hospital. An empty cup is full of tea. Playing pretend games becomes more and more important as your child approaches three and for some years afterward.

What you can do

You play a pivotal role in encouraging pretence in your child, from buying the right toys and reading the right stories to joining in her games. Throw a blanket over the table then ask her if she wants her tea in her house. Refer to her dolls as babies.

- **Books and stories**
  Young children are introduced to the idea that other people have feelings and experiences when they sit on your lap with a book. The words tell them something is happening, but the pictures do not fully support the story. The story tells more than she can see. She knows that the fox is dressed up as Grandma, but she also knows that Red Riding Hood does not know.
- **TV and videos**
  When young children pretend, all the players need to know the story. They need to hang role-play games on a well-understood story line. So they play

house, Mummys and Daddys, shopping and driving cars. To step outside the domestic story, they use the shared experience of TV or video.
- **Little worlds**
  At home children do not always have friends to take part in pretend games, so they need props. Tea can be made for the soft toys; little people can be taken to the shop in a car. They learn the rules and the story by playing the game with you.
- **Soft toys**
  Small families can never provide all the players for an elaborate game and even if they could there would be some dull parts nobody would want to take. Here soft toys come into their own. They can be the sick children in the hospital, the naughty schoolchildren who cannot go out to play and the extra passengers who have to stand on the bus.
- **Friends and family**
  Familiar friends are good partners for pretence and siblings are better still. A good family pretend game can be taken out like a favourite toy. Children with shared experience understand. If both children go to hospital to visit their grandmother, they know about the lift, they both saw the flowers, the charts and the beds. A schoolfriend would not understand 'those papers hanging on the bed' because she did not see the nurse looking at them and your child does not understand enough to explain.

Attention and memory

By the end of their first year children begin deliberately to focus their attention, but they do not do it well. If several things compete for a child's attention, she concentrates on how something looks. So she quite literally watches TV and may ignore the words or music.

Because her store is so limited a preschooler often has to 'clear her mind' by doing what she is thinking about first. When playing 'Pairs', she finds it impossible to think where two cards might be hidden at the same time. Holding the thoughts about one card displaces thoughts about the other from her memory. Most of the time this store is filled with more important things than card pairs, so adults resort to making notes. A small child cannot do this, which is one of the reasons she finds it so hard to think logically. It is also the reason why small children talk in short sentences. To think logically, or construct a long and complex sentence you have to be able to 'hold on' to more than one idea at a time.

What you can do

Children do not begin to think logically until they are about six or seven, when they begin to rehearse things they want to hold in their 'working' memory and can remember enough to be able to sort out simple ideas. But long before then, you can help your child by laying the groundwork.

- Explain things simply and answer her questions.
- Encourage her to determine how things work by letting her explore sand, water and building materials (see pp. 217–18 and 210–11).
- Listen to her explanations of how the world is.
- Play board and card games.
- The age when children begin to think logically is also the age of 'collectables'. Between four and seven most children have a collection of some sort. Collections help them to think about things in more than one way. A card is a football player, a goalie and a member of Manchester United. It is also a 'swap' because she already has two.
- Know your child's likes and dislikes and tailor activities, toys and speech appropriately.
- Encourage her to talk and listen.
- Provide something to see and do. Label the world for her by telling and showing her what things do.
- Talk often but when she is engrossed let her concentrate on what she is doing. Remember that she has difficulty listening to you and getting on with the task in hand.
- Encourage her to try.

LEARNING WHO SHE IS

Self-awareness is the sense of being you, the knowledge that when you wake tomorrow you will still be you. Children are not born with an idea of self. If you put a small smudge of lipstick on to a six-month-old baby's nose and then sit her in front of the mirror, she looks at the reflection but does not show any interest in her red nose. By 12 months she would reach out and touch the mirror and may even touch the reflection of her red nose. Sometimes she may even look for the little girl behind the mirror. But she does not know that the baby with the red nose is her. At 21 months a child with a smudge on her nose will look at her reflection and rub her own nose.

Somewhere between one and two years children become aware of themselves, but this awareness is not the same as your awareness of yourself. Your child knows herself by contrasting herself with others, by what she can do and what she possesses. She is the girl with the red coat and the girl who can jump off the second step. It is only when they reach about eight that children start to talk about themselves in terms of their personal history, hopes, feelings, personality, experience and belonging to a family or culture group (although they have memories of the past before this).

Girl or boy?

From a very early age children are interested in the sex of other children. By the time they can say the words 'boy' and 'girl', children know which sex they belong to, although they do not necessarily understand that they always were and always will be the same sex.

At three your child may insist she is a girl now, but assume (if all the babies she knows are boys) that she was a boy when she was a baby. Boys may talk of being 'a mummy'. By four children usually know that they started off as a girl, are now a girl and will grow up to be a woman. But it still might not be entirely clear. By six they have sorted this out and know that dressing up changes nothing.

Almost as soon as they can say the words, children tell us Daddys drive tractors, Mummys do the washing, boys are naughty and girls are good. By two they know about sex roles and their views are always traditional in the extreme. Toys, too, have become more rather than less sexist. And yet children see both parents working, fathers doing the washing and pushing prams and women driving fast cars and joining the army and the police. Children ignore the evidence of their own eyes because they need sex roles to define what it is to be a man or a woman. For a girl to understand that she will grow up to be a woman she has to know what being a woman means, which is more difficult than it was in the past. And it is equally difficult for your son to know what being a man means.

As the 'real world' roles of men and women have become less distinct, children have turned more and more to fantasy worlds to define things.

LEARNING TO FEEL

Infants cannot say how they feel: you imply your baby's emotions from her reactions and expressions. As children enter their second year, they begin to be capable of angry moods and petulance, although such moods rarely last long. By 21 months, their growing sense of themselves as individuals means they are able to think about what they want, and contrast this with the rules you set for them and your expectations of their behaviour. They are capable of defiance, start to feel shame and to feel pleased and proud of themselves.

By two your child can make people cry intentionally, by two and a half she may be afraid of things she imagines. She begins to offer simple explanations of why other people feel certain emotions, so she will say, 'Daddy cross. I broke cup.' She knows which actions should go with which feelings, so she might say, 'I not cry now. I happy.' She also knows how her actions can affect others. She might say 'I cry. Mummy pick me up.'

Between about two and a half and four children begin to understand how emotions work. They know that facial expressions 'match' certain emotions. They know that people calm down and that the initial intensity of emotion always subsides. They begin to realize how their thoughts and feelings can be related to certain consequences and that their emotions can be used to manipulate others. Your three-year-old might say, 'If you go out, I will cry.' She knows that you and others use emotions to manipulate her. She will say, 'He cried 'cause he wanted me to give him the car.'

This understanding of their own feelings and the experience of other people's emotions and actions gives children the capacity to feel social emotions such as guilt, concern, responsibility, jealousy, hostility, in addition to feeling miserable, resentful and horrified.

Being helpful

As babies become toddlers and toddlers preschoolers, they become more and more co-operative and helpful. This is partly because they copy you and others who are helpful toward them, but they also like and enjoy being helpful. They are pleased with themselves when they have watered the plants or washed the table.

Problems arise because Western society values competition, so children are praised for winning. By the time they are in junior school competitiveness has

Life and death

Children worry about things that they do not understand. As she begins to realize that she always was the same person, and always will be, she begins to think about ideas of life and death. She is aware of the fact of death but too young to understand what it means.

Preschoolers worry about death without really understanding what it means. It is not real. They cannot understand that death is not transitory and reversible. At the same time they think that all sorts of things will make them die – from stepping on the road without holding your hand to eating a worm. After the cat dies they may expect it to come home as usual in the morning. After Grandad's funeral they expect him back again.

Children are equally worried by the beginnings of life. 'What was I before I was born?' is a difficult question for you to answer and a worrying concept for a child. Even though you explain about the baby growing 'in your tummy' she does not really understand. 'What was I before I was thought of?' she asks.

A child faced with death is forced to come to terms with the reality of its permanence. The loss of a loved one is often reflected in withdrawal. Talking about death helps understanding. Children have long used a favourite psychological technique for dealing with their fears. They think about worrying things when they feel most happy and relaxed. This is why they play monsters, ghosts and games in which people die in endless crashes or hospital beds. A child who has nightmares about monsters can come to terms with her fears by fishing for monsters, or escaping from them in gleeful screams when chased by her pals at playschool. She can laugh as she imagines the monster chasing her. If she does it often enough, the fear will go away.

driven out some of children's natural helpful tendencies. Seven-year-olds are less co-operative than they were before they started school and find it quite hard to work together. The obvious reason for this change is that they see competition all around them and are praised when they do better than others.

What you can do

Some cultures are far more competitive than others. City children are on the whole more competitive than those brought up in rural areas; boys tend to be more competitive than girls. Competition leads to quarrels and fights; try to tone the competition down.

- Encourage co-operation, but set an example: children will not co-operate if what they see all around them is competition. Competitive parents have competitive children.
- Create a 'we' environment. Encourage your children to help you and each other not as a favour but as a matter of course. Do things together.
- Love your children uniquely for who and what they are. Never say 'I love you both the same' instead say 'You are the best Lauren in the world' and 'You are the best Paul there could ever be'.
- Selecting two toys of exactly the same value and worth for two children is impossible. Buy Lauren the book when you see one you know she will love. Buy Paul a treat next time you go shopping. If you are always 'even handed', children spend their time looking for which one got the bonus. Everything they do, all the time you spend with them gets embroiled in life's great competition.

LEARNING RIGHT FROM WRONG

Preschool children know right from wrong. They can say something is naughty and something is good, but they tend to think that rules are fixed by nature rather than by communal decisions. It is only after she starts to play with other children and finds that the rules of a game can be agreed among her friends, and varied sometimes, that your child begins to understand what rules mean. A five-year-old tends to think that the deed rather than the intention is important. Accidentally breaking six glasses is much naughtier than deliberately breaking one glass.

Tantrums

Most children have tantrums. In any population of two-year-olds, rather more than half are having tantrums on a more or less daily basis. A few start earlier, a few later. Some have tantrums for years, most have them for a couple of years, some children never have a tantrum. The average child who has tantrums has one a day and the average tantrum lasts about five minutes. But some children have more than five a day, and some tantrums last more than an hour.

Tantrums start with shouting or crying. There is usually a note of protest ('No!'; 'Won't!'), and a demonstration of anger (slamming the door, hitting, kicking, stamping the floor or screaming). When the tantrum gets underway children wave arms, kick legs, stamp feet, arch their backs and fall to the floor. They go red in the face and cry and scream. They may deliberately kick you or the furniture. They throw things and may hurt themselves. Your child may bite her arm until it bleeds, or bang her head until it is bruised. Such behaviour is alarming but common.

Most children grow out of self-mutilation just as they grow out of tantrums. Not all children show all of these behaviours. Not all tantrums are severe.

Tantrums have definite phases. Before the crying or screaming starts, children seem to be 'spoiling for a fight'. They are contrary, and easily frustrated. Sometimes they seem to provoke the tantrum on purpose, by asking for something they know they cannot have, or asking in a way that you will not be able to understand. They then have a tantrum because whatever it was they wanted is not forthcoming.

Once the tantrum is underway, the early part is invariably intense. Your child will shout, scream, kick and flail. This phase may be followed, particularly in older children, by a quieter phase when she is sad and sorry. Sobbing replaces screaming and she may come and sit or stand beside you. This sadness then gives way to a period of forgiveness when she may need to be cuddled, in spite of which she may still be angry and in a bad mood afterward. The older the child, the more likely that the anger and bad moods persist.

Very young children blow their tops quickly. The tantrum comes from nowhere and disappears as rapidly, almost as if nothing at all had happened. The older the child the more complex the tantrum and the more sorry and upset she is afterward.

Why do they happen?

Tantrums almost always occur when your child is with you or another major carer, rarely when you are not there. About half of all the children who have tantrums when alone with their mothers also have them when alone with their fathers. Very few have them with nursery school teachers or playgroup leaders. Children who spend most of the day with a childminder may only have tantrums when at home.

Most tantrums occur at home, usually when you are trying to do something from which your child is excluded. Children have more tantrums when you are upset, down or ill. They also have them when they are ill, tired, frustrated or fastened into a chair. And for no obvious reason at all.

Tantrums are nevertheless about relationships: love, attachment, security and anger. Just as you lose your temper with those you love most, so your child loses hers with you. Just as you shout and cry more easily in the safety and security of your home or car, so does she.

What you can do

There are no easy answers and what works one time may not work again, but some people have found one or more of the following to work.

Head it off

It is sometimes possible to head off an impending tantrum by simply distracting your child. Read a story, engage in a boisterous activity or play a very silly game. If she is spoiling for a fight, try to find something out of the ordinary to do.

Left: Hugging a child in a tantrum may make the tantrum less severe, or last for less time.

Ignore

Once the tantrum is underway, walk out of the room and leave her to it. Tantrums do not occur in a vacuum: they occur within a relationship. If you are not there to witness it, she will stop.

Be consistent

If your child knows your 'bottom line', she is less likely to fight against it, and will be less frustrated by your 'no'.

Hug

Hugging tightly by gathering her up and trapping her in your arms, 'squeezing' the tantrum out more quickly. Opinions differ as to whether to look her in the eye as you hug, or look away. It is worth trying both.

Cuddle

Children who are cuddled when they become sad and sorry have fewer tantrums than ones who are left to fend for themselves.

Talk

Talking about the causes of the tantrum, and how to avoid them in the future seems to reduce their frequency, especially in older children.

What not to do

Try hard to avoid:

- Slapping, which seems to increase the frequency and duration of tantrums. It is also associated with more violent tantrums.
- Giving in, which enables your child to manipulate you through her temper. If she gets what she wants by having a tantrum, she will have more tantrums because it is worth it.

SPREADING HER WINGS

One-year-old children are almost always self-absorbed. They may like to look at other children or be with their siblings, but it is always a case of the older child playing with the baby. Babies are invariably more social in the months after their first birthday when they begin to extend those skills they learned with you and other members of the family to a wider circle.

The importance of play

Play launches a child in the wider social world and toys lure children to play side by side. Learning how to play on an equal footing is an ability perfected over many years and can only happen when she spends time with other children. It is easier for children with siblings. If she is dependent on playgroups, personality will ease the task, out-going children develop social skills sooner than shy children, as do attractive children. A conventional name helps too!

Relationships with adults or older children are no substitute for play with children of the same age. Adults make allowances for immaturity and clarify their intentions in a way that peers cannot do. When talking to another two-year-old she has to learn to make herself understood. She must also understand the imperfect communication of her friend.

Broadly speaking, children do not play together until they are two to three years old. They usually talk to the assembled company rather than an individual and what they say is likely to be a comment on their own behaviour – 'Me make castle' rather than 'You make castle'. Nor do they comment on what others might have said.

This does not mean that they do not react with others. One child may shout and another then laugh and the sequence may be repeated to the great delight of both children. Or one child may pass something to another, but they do not share games or take turns with toys or have discussions. If there are older children in the circle a two-year-old may watch to see how they interact. She will not try to join in and may turn away or cry if you try to make her do so. She is happy to watch from a distance.

The role of language

When she starts to try and play with other children, she often eases her way into the social group with a few words. She might go up to the children in the sand pit and say 'I've got a kitty' and if one of them then answers 'I've got a ginger cat' or 'My Daddy's got a new car' she has her invitation. When children first start playing together, the conversation and the game are often quite separate. They may exchange statements about their pets or garden toys while sharing the cups and teapots at the water table. Once they have mastered the basics, toddlers begin to play interactive games, like throwing and catching balls, chasing and being chased, follow my leader and so on.

As language blossoms between the ages of two and a half and three, social interactions take on a new richness. What children actually say to each other may make little sense to you – conversations follow the 'Red bike' 'Red bike' 'Yep' 'Go there' 'Red bike' 'Yes' pattern – but the children are communicating. Good friends share activities, they look at each other, smile, laugh and shout together. If such a game starts in the nursery, other children may join in. By three most children are taking turns, sharing toys and games. Popular children tend to be leaders because they have the social skills necessary to manage other children without dominating.

By the time they have passed their third birthdays the majority of children's talk while they are playing is likely to be about the game they are sharing.

Making friends

Friendship is fuelled by familiarity, but you cannot make children be friends. It is not easy to pinpoint what turns two toddlers into bosom pals: similarity of temperament, developmental stage and behavioural style are almost certainly factors. Friends meet because they gravitate to the bikes, the library or the house corner. They start to talk together because they are the ones who often sit at the top of the climbing frame. There is a special joy in being with friends for which time with her parents and other grown-ups is no substitute. Nothing makes a child laugh quite so much as jumping off the step or running in and out of the sprinkler with her best friend. Happiness and laughter are shared with the family but to be really full of glee she needs a sibling or a friend.

From babyhood, children direct distinct kinds of behaviour toward you and other children. By your child's third year, you are there to talk to and provide security: her peers are her partners. Opportunities for playing with other children are important for her social development. These days, most preschool children only make friends if you make the opportunities for them to do so (see pp. 244–7). While other children practise their social skills, your child will lag behind if you do not make an effort now, and you may hamper her ability to settle into nursery and school quickly.

Getting ready for school

You can prepare your child for school intellectually, through the skills she develops and learns through her play (see Chapter 8, pp. 204–27) that lay the groundwork for later reading, writing and number work. You can also prepare her socially, by providing her with opportunities to be with other children (see pp. 244–7). And you can help her emotionally, by making sure she can manage without you.

If you do not want to send your child to playgroup or nursery, make sure that you take time to instil some of the skills she will need at school.
- Encourage her to sit still.
- Encourage her to work through a problem (or finish a painting) without constant reassurance.
- Encourage her to plan.
- Have friends around to play and encourage her to mix with other children – and try not to interfere if one of them tries to take over.
- Make sure she understands what coming second or third feels like.
- Do not let her first day at school be her first day without you.
- Let her have a really big hug of her comfort object before she sets off.
- Make sure she understands what all day means.
- Make sure she understands that she cannot stop going to school; even if she hates it (don't suggest she might), she has to go tomorrow.

HAVING A SECOND CHILD

Obviously, it is up to you whether you have a second child. Only children can have clear advantages in later life, so long as they grow up in an environment in which they are encouraged to make friends. If you do not want a second child, don't have one and don't feel pressurized by talk of the 'an only child is a lonely child' variety.

But a child growing up with other children gains a great deal of social knowledge and usually finds it easier to get on with other children. A young child can be drawn into games much earlier than she could construct activities for herself. An older child has a better playmate than a teddy bear. They have more to love and a wider base for security.

There is no ideal age gap between children. Those born close together may be good friends, but they can equally be good enemies. If you have them further apart, you may find it easier to treat each child uniquely. The best gap tends to depend on the personalities of the children: they can be close in age without feeling they have anything in common; they may be four or five years apart and very close. How well children get on together is a matter of luck.

Coping with jealousy

Jealousy is natural: you will not be the first parent to feel a pang of jealousy and resentment when your child runs to her childminder or says she wants Grandma to put her to bed. A child's jealousy of a new baby is inevitable and you should probably worry more if it does not happen, than when it does.

- **Let her voice her feelings**
  Don't dismiss negative feelings about a sibling. If she regresses into more babyish behaviour, understand that at the moment life may well look more rosy for a baby than a two-year-old.
- **Be on her side**
  Let her know you understand; don't be afraid to say, 'I know sometimes you wish she would go back into my tummy'.
- **Accept that she is unsure**
  Don't tell her how nice it will be once the baby is big enough to play with her: she cannot think that far ahead and in any case it may not be true.
- **Love her**
  Love her differently from the baby. Make sure she knows that she is the very best Claire in the world.
- **Allow her aggression**
  Aggression arises from frustration and jealousy, so find ways for her to vent and express her feelings. Invent a bad-tempered child she can 'play' at being, and let her be that child, throwing a teddy on the floor or stamping and shouting. If she shows aggression toward the baby, stop her.
- **Make time for her**
  Find times to put her first. If the baby wakes in 'her time', then the baby may have to cry. Listen to her when she talks to you. Even when physically dealing with the baby, you do not need to shut her out. If you say 'just a minute', make sure that you do then come back to her after the minute is up.

Sibling rivalry and love

It should be easy to anticipate how your children will behave toward one another. If you have siblings you may remember the mean and nasty things you did to each other at various times. Why then are all parents shocked at their children's capacity for meanness?

Siblings quarrel because they know each other so well. A child who has lived all her life with another knows exactly how to needle, exactly how to get you on her side in any argument, how to put her sibling in a bad light. Rivalry for your affections, for the larger piece of cake, for your attention, rivalry about anything and everything fuels feuding.

If you can understand negative feelings you will make life easier for yourself. Show you understand. Say, 'I can see why that would make you cross' when you are trying to handle disputes.

- Encourage children to talk and listen by showing them how to express anger to each other. Get your children together and let one tell the other, 'I get angry when you use my toys without asking.'
- Try to avoid labels. Whatever the reason for the initial quarrel, children can both revel in the after-effects. If you shout at the aggressor, she gets your attention (and a sure means of claiming it in the future). Her brother learns that she will get into trouble if he can needle her into hitting him. Next time he wants to be one up on her he knows exactly what to do. Labels have a way of sticking. If children are fighting physically it is better to ignore the aggressor and give your attention to the injured party, but try not to blame or take sides.

How to handle disputes

- The best way to handle bickering is to ignore it. Leave the room.
- If the bickering is serious, acknowledge the anger and describe what you see from each child's point of view. Express confidence in finding a solution: 'I think you could sort it out if you tried.'
- Handle fighting by trying to describe it: 'I see two children who are going to hurt each other.' Then separate the children, send them to different rooms to calm down.

CHAPTER EIGHT

Learning Through Play

Children love playing. To your preschooler, anything can be a game, as long as he has the tools and materials he wants, or the company and props he needs. You have only to be there, encouraging and ready to get involved if he asks you to, for your child to start to learn about the world around him through his games and other activities.

The importance of play

All children want to play. From the early months parents do not have to persuade their babies to learn through their playful actions; the babies are poised and ready to go. Babies and children are fired up with enthusiasm to discover, to find out and explore. Long before your child will be asking the questions in actual words, his behaviour will show you that he is keen to find out answers to a whole host of questions: 'What's that?', 'What does that do?', 'What going to happen if … ?', 'Can I get there?', 'Can I do what he's just done?', 'Can I poke this … drop that … climb into that?'

Very young children are avid watchers of what is going on around them. They are keen to copy the actions of the adults' world and older children they meet. You will see your toddler copy your actions when he goes round the garden with his own watering can, because he wants to do the flowers like you. You will hear your voice and your words as your children put their dolls and teddies to bed or organize a pretend tea party. And through all this imitation you will also see your child's own individuality flowering and realize that your child, as much as he is learning from you, is nevertheless also developing a very personal way of going about his play.

Younger children want to be able to do what adults and older children are managing. They are highly motivated to start the long road of learning everyday skills that will make them independent. Their play is the vehicle for practice and trying out skills in many different ways. But although you do not have to push children into playing, it is possible to discourage them and prevent their learning as much as would otherwise be possible.

The essence of children's play is that they are enthusiastic about it and satisfied with the outcome – whether they have made something in particular or have simply had a good time and not been bored.

Children sometimes take their play very seriously, yet, if you watch them, you will see how some kinds of play are also for the sheer pleasure in using physical skills – watch your toddler in the garden when he first learns to pedal his own tricycle or do a forward roll – or the power of their voices. Listen to the interminable imaginary dialogue between teddy and dolly, or the words of a favourite song sung over and over again.

Play can be the way children learn to concentrate and see a task through, even when it gets difficult. They often need the help and support of an adult to get them over the more difficult patches. Children can also put a great deal of mental effort into their play through planning, thinking out how to do something, remembering what they have seen or heard before and puzzling out why something is not working, or on occasions why it is working.

As a result children's play does not always go smoothly and it sometimes ends in tears of frustration or fury, which need your helping hand or calming approach. But overall children's play will be a great source of emotional, as well as intellectual, satisfaction to them.

HOW CHILDREN LEARN THROUGH PLAY

You can help your children to learn through the play of their early years when you understand how children learn.

Learning is a continuous process

Babies and young children have a breathtakingly large amount to learn. All their skills and their growing understanding of how the world works, including people's reactions, are built up from many different experiences. You may notice that your child reproduces your ways and phrases. Often you will not even have been aware that your child was watching or listening. So no single playtime and no one toy, however well designed, is going to ensure that a child learns all he needs to know about a physical skill, how to engage someone in conversation or the meaning of abstract ideas like number, colour or shape.

Understanding through doing

Children learn a certain amount through quietly watching and listening but they cannot learn how to do things properly unless they have a chance to try them for themselves.

The most effective learning for children involves activity – trying something out, making sounds, exploring something that has caught their interest. Young children have a particularly pressing need to do it for themselves and some find great difficulty in staying still for long. So their particular kind of doing is often being on the move between places and objects of interest. They will also vocalize constantly – play is accompanied by a running commentary, much of it imaginative and fanciful. Here play is helping them develop their use of language.

If you need special help

If your child has special needs, all the ideas in this chapter still apply. However, depending on the pattern of his disabilities, you may find that some specialized play materials will help. Sometimes, children's disabilities mean that they are progressing at a slower rate of development, so that it becomes important to have a wide range of materials and possible activities suitable for their current interests and skills – if you do not, children get bored (see also Children with special needs, pp. 173–5). It is worth getting advice from specialist professionals in your area (see also Useful Contacts, pp. 248–51). They will also know of toy libraries and other resources you may find useful in helping your child with his play.

Play is a good guide to a child's development so if your child does not play, plays in a strange way or has difficulty in physically manoeuvring a range of toys and games, ask your health visitor or GP to investigate.

Children need plenty of practice which gives them the opportunity to use similar skills in different ways. They need to make links between different skills and what they have learned.

What you can do

It is not enough to give your child a range of play materials and expect him to 'get on with it'. Some children are happy to play alone for short periods, but that does not mean that you should not be involved. There are many ways in which you can help your child get the most from his play.

Look through your child's eyes

Children cannot always work out why they cannot do something or understand an idea. This is where you can use your broader perspective to try to grasp what your child has understood so far and what is confusing him at the moment. Adults can offer hints and suggestions, useful short-cuts and guidance, without taking over completely.

If you relax and are responsive to your child's stage of development, without trying to hurry him in to the next, you can enjoy the freshness of discovery with him. One of the delights of playing and talking with your children is that they can surprise you with their questions and their discoveries.

Make allowances

Your child has a lot to learn. You have lived with a wide range of skills and chunks of knowledge for so long that it is easy to forget that all this was learned. Nobody is born knowing that eggs dropped on the floor smash, and stay smashed. Your toddler may have safely dropped all sorts of other things, and some even bounce back up again, so the smashed egg has to be chalked up to everyone's experience.

Be physically close

You cannot support your child in his play from a distance – if you are in different rooms (this just leads to, 'shouting' and 'interfering'!) or across a large room or the length of the garden. If you are not actually involved already in what your child is doing, then you need to be close enough to move easily to look at something and to hear and reply to his conversation or questions. This is equally true of your carer, if you are at work. If you are a working parent, try to be with your child as much as is natural, without upsetting his normal routine.

Help when help is wanted

As an adult you have a much broader base of knowledge than your child. However, in order to be truly helpful, you need to make the effort to recapture the feelings and perspectives of a child who is still finding out about life. Adults who stand on a pedestal of superior years and supposed wisdom come across as impatient and critical know-it-alls, and children learn to avoid them.

It is fun to find out, so children do not want some adult spoiling the surprise of discovery. But on the other hand they do not want to be left struggling when you, another adult, or even an older brother or sister, could give them a clue or show them a more reliable technique.

If you tune in to your child, you can offer guidance and suggestions that go with the flow of what is interesting him today, though it is important not to take over your child's play. You can communicate through actions as well as words.

Be close enough to offer help when help is wanted, and join in your child's games sometimes.

What you can do

- Show him how to turn around a shape so that it fits through the hole in his posting box. What you mean will be much clearer through action than just explanatory words.
- Start a little tower of bricks for your toddler and offer him a brick to add on top.
- Play alongside your child in a way that he can copy, for instance in putting teddies to bed.
- Demonstrate to your child another way of holding his paintbrush that may work better. Showing and offering can be very effective and works especially well with very young children. Of course, you do not have to be silent – use words as well.

WORD PLAY

It is a good idea to say something simple as you show your baby how the rattle works or your toddler how to put together the simple pull-apart car. Naturally, it is not helpful to talk so much that it comes out like verbal wallpaper, and it is very important to leave a pause for your child to reply.

Talking about play

You can describe in a simple way what you are doing or comment on what your child is doing. For example: 'This brick's too big – I'm looking for a smaller one'; 'You're trying some blue in your picture now? That's a lovely bright blue'; 'You've got the firefighters in their fire engine. They all look ready to zoom off.'

Some questions have an obvious 'Yes' or 'No' one-word answer but you can often just as easily ask open-ended questions that encourage your child to think further. These kind of questions can start in several different ways. For instance: 'How did you make that lovely shape in your painting?'; 'I wonder if your boat can take another brick? Or will it sink?'; 'What's going to happen if we … ?'; 'Can you think of another way to do it … ?' 'I'm afraid I can't make this work. How did you do it … ?'; 'Now where are we going to find a … ?' 'I bet you can tell me all about … ' Encourage communication.

ENCOURAGING YOUR CHILD

Children blossom with encouragement. Through-out your family life together you will have to tell them off and tell them 'No' many times, so it is important to balance this up with positives. There are many ways that you can act so as to encourage your child as you play together. When he feels that he is included in your activities with pleasure – regardless of what you are doing – it counts as play for him.

Showing your pleasure

You show on your face, particularly by your smiles, that you are pleased with what your child has done, which can encourage him to keep trying on those occasions when an activity is not going easily.

When you play with babies, you show your interest and enjoyment by your physical closeness, an excited or pleased expression on your face or by actions like clapping with pleasure. Once your child has started to understand more language, he will understand the meaning of what previously was communicated just through your body language.

Voicing your pleasure

Toddlers are delighted to be told 'Well done!' about their brick tower, their finished dinner or the fact that this time they made it to the toilet before they wet themselves. Children are encouraged if you notice and comment on what they have done.

Try not use the same words every time. If you always react to any drawing or model by saying 'That's nice', your children will start to wonder if you really mean it – after a while it will not sound sincere. Ring the changes with other phrases that are natural for you to say and suitable for the age of your child.
- 'I do like that.'
- 'Is that for me? Thank you.'
- 'Isn't it long/colourful/unusual/ enormous…?'
- 'Well done.'
- 'You've done a lovely job on that.'
- 'Just look what you've managed.'
- 'Oh great! You've made it work.'
- 'That was difficult, wasn't it? But you kept going.'

Remembering the past

Four- and five-year-olds have a sense of themselves as individuals with a past in memories, a present of the here and now and a future of plans. When your child is having difficulty with something in play you may be able to encourage him through it or to keep trying by reminding him of what he has managed before. You can boost your child's confidence by pointing out how far he has come and what he can now do that was still difficult for him even a few months ago.

Showing your interest

When you are not closely involved in your child's play for the moment, show your interest and admiration by stopping what you are doing and taking a close look at what he has made or listening with your full attention to his story or account of what he has done.

Try to have somewhere that you can fix up his drawings or put his models on display, if only for a short while. And make sure that no adults, or disdainful older siblings, make fun of his efforts.

PHYSICAL PLAY

Children need active physical play. Not only does it use up energy but also enables them to benefit from the opportunity to practise skills and improve physical co-ordination.

Enjoyable physical exercise

Babies, toddlers and children need plenty of practice if they are to be confident in their existing skills and learn new ones. Join in their physical games, such as:
- Crawling, including speedy crawling for sheer fun and crawl-and-chase.
- Walking and running about. You do not have to go anywhere in particular, simply run about for the enjoyment of it. Vary this by chasing and hiding.
- Jumping and hopping.
- Climbing up, round, over and through things. A good play park is extremely useful but a tolerant adult is also an excellent prop. You may get the odd bruise until children recognize that adults can feel pain too.

- Clambering up and sliding or jumping down.
- Spinning round or twisting in circles.
- Dancing to all kinds of music.
- Wrestling and rough and tumble. This is a very natural use of children's physical skills, but take care that it does not get too rough and that smaller or less physically strong children are not getting hurt or squashed.
- Splashing in the swimming pool. Time in the shallow end of a pool can be very enjoyable for your child long before he has learned to swim so long as you or another adult is within reach.

Playing with equipment

Playing with balls, bats, bikes, ropes and similar equipment help children develop their hand–eye co-ordination and use their whole bodies. Once children are about three they begin to appreciate simple rules which come with the concept of taking turns (see p. 227). Sometimes children play happily together but your child will need some help initially to learn how do any of the following:

- Carrying and dropping big balls.
- Rolling balls to each other.
- Throwing and then catching big and small balls or bean bags.
- Jumping rope and trying to skip.
- Playing with balls and wide bats.
- Kicking balls.
- Pushing along wheeled toys, dolls' prams or buggies.
- Riding push-along bikes or sit-in cars, tricycles and then bikes with stabilizers.

It is up to you to decide what you do or do not allow children to play with or do in your home. If space is restricted then you should make sure that your child has access to safe outdoor space for these activities. Apart from any other considerations, the level of traffic and the speed at which it travels on minor as well as major roads means that it is not safe to let under-fives out to play unsupervised.

If you do not have a garden, take your children out to local open spaces – commons, parks, recreation grounds. Even if you live in the country look for stretches of public space, since a lot of the open land in rural areas is not suitable for play or does not have public right of access.

Exploring and building

To your child, the whole world is a playroom and every object he encounters a toy. It is only through looking at and playing with everyday things that he can start to make sense of the world around him.

Playing with everyday objects

Toddlers like a wide variety of objects, not all toys, that can be explored and used in different ways. Parents can get exasperated with under-twos because they are 'into everything'. Yet toddlers do not pull clothes out of low drawers or dive into cupboards or waste bins precisely in order to be naughty. They are utterly fascinated by the contents of mundane parts of your home and they want to explore. The trick for you is to offer toddlers access in a safe way.

Look at the rooms in your house carefully before your baby is mobile (see pp. 169–71).

Toys that last

The range of toys available is vast and their quality and play value vary from excellent to minimal. Think carefully about what your buy: often the least expensive items are the ones that your child will return to time after time.

Wooden bricks

A set of well-made, different coloured and shaped bricks will give your children pleasure for years. You can buy bricks, but the first basic cubes may come with a push-along trolley that you buy for your toddler.

Wooden bricks are more stable than large plastic cubes. They can be used to build anything from the first tower that your child piles up, and immediately knocks down with a delighted laugh, to the more ambitious building projects of your older children – sets of towers, bridges, walls and then buildings.

Lego and its lookalikes

Your children will also get years of satisfaction from a set of interlocking plastic bricks and other compatible shapes such as Lego, the Duplo range or Stickle Bricks. The best value are those sets to which you can add as your child gets older. Some sets have large size pieces suitable for under threes but which are made to scale so that they will fit with the smaller sizes in sets for older children. A plastic, holed foundation sheet is very useful and is often sold with sets, so that any construction can be fixed firmly at the base and can stay assembled until everyone in the family has admired it. There is no need to feel under pressure to get lots of different kinds of construction sets; your child will find plenty at playgroup or nursery.

Children enjoy putting together simple pull-apart toys in these sets and can progress to making all kinds of constructions. Apart from the sheer pleasure of making something, children are learning to look with care, to experiment with how to fit pieces together and they are learning to plan ahead – to think how to make the construction that they want.

Jigsaws

There is a very wide choice of jigsaws. Toddlers need wooden pieces or jigsaws made of thick card, or the kind of jigsaw with little knobs on the pieces which are easier to handle. Jigsaws suitable for young children have only a few pieces but you can also simplify a jigsaw intended for an older child by making part of it for your young child and leaving easily identifiable shapes for him to do.

Some children are more enthusiastic about jigsaws than others but it is worth making this an enjoyable shared activity with young children. If they become interested in the challenge, completing jigsaws can help children to look carefully for details in the partly completed picture and the remaining pieces. Children are also practising their fine motor skills (see pp. 187–8) as they pick up, hold, turn around and try to fit pieces.

AROUND THE HOME

The great advantage of a home is that your child sees you doing normal adult tasks – everything that keeps a household running. Many of these activities are probably boring to you but they are fresh to your child. Toddlers and children can be just as enthusiastic to help you out in domestic tasks as they are to sit and build a brick tower with you. And they will much rather be your welcomed assistant than wait for what seems like ages until you have finished.

If you let them join in, you will be helping your children's learning as they practise their physical skills, talk with you and actually come to understand more

Making a swag bag

Make up a special swag bag with collections of safe objects that your child can tip out and pore over. Use an old, large handbag or a good-sized cloth bag. You might put in any of the following:

- large squares of material that have different textures
- large empty cotton reels
- cardboard inner tubes from kitchen towels or toilet rolls (toddlers can look through these as well as posting smaller wooden or Duplo bricks through them)
- different sized and coloured boxes or plastic containers and cups
- plastic spoons (strong children's ones, not the disposable kind)
- soft foam or fabric balls
- large wooden curtain rings, not the smaller metal ones
- a set of plastic play keys or a small rattle

Make sure that there are no small objects that could go up the nose or be swallowed, such as beads or small buttons, and nothing that would be unsafe to suck, since toddlers still put objects in their mouths.

You may have to check the bag from time to time since toddlers sometimes gather up objects of value that you may be seeking, like your watch or the remote control. Don't be cross, because it will almost certainly have been kept safe.

about how things work. And, since what they do with you will often reappear, in their own version, in their imaginative play, you are helping them with the raw material for other kinds of play.

Washing and cleaning

Although young children cannot do the washing, and you need to warn them from fiddling with the knobs on washers or dryers, they can give you clothes to put into the machine, and hand you wet clothes to peg out, if you have a line. They can help you sort and fold the clean clothes, and carry a pile to put away.

Young children will not clean up to the same standard as an adult. However, they will be keen to help and it is a very good idea to teach them how to be a helpful member of the household when they are willing. Toddlers and children can use a dustpan and brush, do a bit of dusting or polishing, hand you cutlery or plates that you put in the dishwasher and wash up plastic cups, plates and cutlery that is not sharp.

Young children can also help to wipe up after their painting session or help you to put their toys away. Mobile babies and toddlers enjoy putting smaller objects into bigger ones, especially if there is a clunking sound as a result. Your child can help you put any fitting or stacking toys back together. Young children will help search for the last piece of jigsaw, so long as you do not rush and you show genuine pleasure and satisfaction if they find the missing piece.

Preparing food and cooking

Children can be involved in preparing a meal as well as doing some cooking with you. Even young children can pick out vegetables or fruit for you to peel or cut up. It is good for them to learn the names and shapes of different items as their understanding grows, and you can begin to talk about how they grow and where they come from. They will soon be able to do simple preparations such as peeling a banana, spooning out rice or putting a cake on a plate.

Through cooking, children practise the physical skills of stirring, mixing, cutting and shaping; they learn about hygiene; they begin to understand about measuring; and they observe that some food changes colour and texture, and from solid to liquid as it is heated and cooked.

Using heat

If you show them carefully and supervise them closely, four- and five-year-olds will be able to heat up ingredients on a stove or hob. Never turn away from them, even if you have taught them about heat.

- Using dough, let the children shape what they want. Yeast dough, for buns or pizza bases, is more tolerant of handling than pastry which gets tough.
- Cakes and biscuits, made in different shapes, offer a wide range of possibilities. Creaming butter, or margarine, and sugar is difficult for children, so pre-warm the mixing bowl with boiling water, to help soften butter or margarine or use liquid sugar in the form of honey or syrup.
- If your child has trouble holding a mixing bowl steady, put it on a damp cloth or rubber mat. If your child is too young to use heat, try:
- Decorating plain cakes or biscuits with icing.
- Making fruit salad or ice cream sundae.
- Simple recipes that do not need cooking, like peppermint creams or crispy cereal cakes.

Everything has some play value – even dusting and polishing are fun to preschoolers.

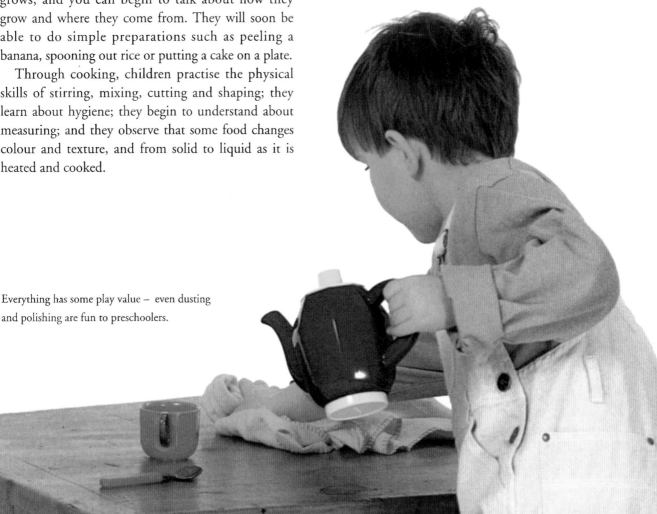

Shopping and other trips

Children obviously enjoy special trips out, puppet shows or the theatre or museums and exhibitions that have displays that they are encouraged to touch. But they can also enjoy local trips, as long as you avoid huge amounts of shopping and chatting with other adults. There are many ways to involve your child in what is going on. Be ready to talk with him about what you see in shops or on the street and spot anything out of the ordinary or of interest – animals, police cars, people that you know.

- Post offices and banks can be interesting if you let your child collect some forms and leaflets. He can use these in his own pretend post office or bank, or put them in his swag bag (see p. 211).
- Make a diversion for shop windows that intrigue your child (this will not necessarily be a toy shop).
- Wherever possible, let children make choices for you in the shops. They can pick out the vegetables in a serve-yourself section, or find the packet or tin that you are seeking. Children who are occupied selecting items that you do want are less likely to make a fuss about sweets and crisps that you don't.

IMAGINATIVE PLAY

Toddlers start to use their imagination in play as soon as they pick up a cup that they know is empty and they pretend to drink from it.

What can you do

Children do not need child versions of everything. In a normal home your child can see some of the actions and responsibilities that are involved in adult life. He does not need a little washing up set if you will let him get up safely at the kitchen sink. But since he cannot play with a real car, provide toy cars or a toy driving wheel and control panel for his play.

Scaled-down domestic equipment
It is worth buying a few plastic saucepans and a tea-set. Your child can use this equipment for cooking on the floor but it will also work well when he is making playdough cakes and playing with sand or water.

Imaginary friends

By the age of three your child will probably be able to play with other children in a pretend sequence. Sometimes part of the play is the involvement of imaginary people. Quite a few children develop and talk about an imaginary friend by name, even blaming this person for wrong-doing. There is usually no need to worry about such a pretence, although you do not have to pretend to see the friend yourself. You would be right to become concerned if play with this imaginary friend was pushing out most other kinds of play for your child, or if your child actually seemed to be frightened by some aspect of the friend. This is something you should talk about to your doctor or health visitor.

You do not have to try to buy a child version of everything in your home. You can, for example, make a believable cooker from an upturned cardboard box with hot rings marked with a thick felt pen. Watch your child and see what interests him before making 'big' purchases.

Pretend child care
Boys and girls equally enjoy playing with cuddly toys and dolls. They enjoy pretend feeding or taking dolls out for a trip, telling them off, taking care of them when they are sick or putting them to bed.

Some children may want a proper doll's cot or a buggy for their birthday or other special occasions. But dolls and teddies can just as easily be put to bed in an box with material cut to size for the bedding.

Dressing-up clothes
A well-stocked dressing-up box can give children a great deal of pleasure and will be used by them for years. There is no need to pay for anything – simply fill a box with adult or older children's cast-offs. You can cut a length off any item that is so long that your children may trip but there is no need to make extensive adjustments.

Miniature size toys
It is worth seeing what kind of setting interests your child most. It might be a garage with cars, a simple

house or similar building with furniture and play people or animals, a farm with animals or a castle.

Flexible props

Three- and four-year-olds can create a pretend setting out of props that need cost you nothing at all. Large cardboard boxes are worth holding on to, since they can become a bus or car, a spaceship or a lion's den. Cushions on the floor may become a castle, and a blue blanket can be a swimming pool. A few basic props and any corner of the room can become a hospital or a shop.

The value of pretence

Your child will not lose sight of the real world if you let his imagination soar in his play. On the contrary it is his chance to explore and try out many of the situations that he sees in your home that you would not let him do in reality – boiling water for a cup of tea, changing the baby's nappy or having lengthy conversations on the telephone.

If your child wants to involve you in his play, take it as seriously as he does. You can follow his lead and still add something yourself. For instance, you can accept a cup of tea and perhaps ask for a (pretend) biscuit or you can watch your child as he swims in a pretend pool and ask him if the water is cold today. In this way, your child is able to practise both the

words that he knows and the physical abilities he possesses as he copies what he has seen you do and adds details and variations of his own.

CREATIVE PLAY

Children love to make things and are delighted when you admire what they have done. Try to display what your child has made, if only for a while – a picture pinned to the kitchen board, a completed jigsaw or a brick tower left for someone else to see as well (do not allow older siblings to mock).

When children go to playgroup or nursery they will be introduced to a very wide variety of arts and crafts. There is no need to try to duplicate every activity these groups can offer, but your child will also enjoy doing simple activities at home with you. You don't need to buy expensive materials; all you need is a few basics plus a selection of those things you would otherwise put in the bin.

What you can do

It is sensible to think carefully where to allow your children to do any activity that involves paint (including some markers), glue or playdough. Tips and spills are likely and you will be less fraught if you, often with your child's help, can clear and wipe up

Play for under fives

Make believe is important to children. Putting teddy to bed if he is tired or unwell encourages emotional development.

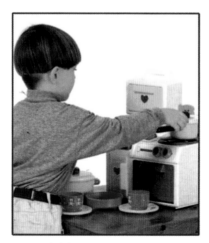

Most children like 'real' cooking, but a play cooker can also give hours of pleasure – mixing, stirring, tasting and serving out.

Painting is very creative – if a little messy. Put a plastic sheet on the floor and get your child a plastic overall.

relatively easily. You do, however, have a wider role than simply mopping up spills; your presence and help will also usually be welcomed.

Making pictures

From as young as 15 or 16 months toddlers relish creating something of their own on paper or card. Pictures do not have to be of anything in particular, although once he gets to three your child will increasingly tell you that he has drawn a person, a house or something else (see pp. 190–1). Sometimes he will enjoy simply making patterns and experimenting with different colours and textures.

Painting and printing
Children can paint on scrap paper, card and the back of leftover wallpaper cut to a manageable size. Under threes really need thick brushes but four- and five-year-olds are ready for slimmer brushes too. Some thicker paint mixes are designed to be used for finger painting or printing with leaves or cut wedges of a firm vegetable such as a potato.

Drawing
Crayons and chalks are less likely to cause damage than paint but drawing still needs supervision. Under threes need non-toxic wax crayons, preferably thick ones which are easier for them to hold. Three- to five-year-olds will still like the wax crayons but will be ready to try some coloured pencils and thick felt tip pens. (Watch out for the tops – younger children put them up their noses and in their mouths and may choke, and if they are not replaced, pens dry out.) Chalks and a chalkboard can work well, especially if you have a garden – chalk dust tends to spread about.

Pre-cut stencils or ready drawn, black outline pictures to colour in help over-threes to practise their control of a crayon or paintbrush and to choose their colours for pictures that they could not yet draw themselves. This kind of material works well for children, but make sure that they also have a chance to make their own drawings and paintings in their own way.

Sticking
As well as drawing and painting children like the possibilities that sticking can give them. You need to buy non-toxic glue that is suitable for children – look carefully on the label, never use glue that contains solvents, or aerosol glue. Plastic spreaders for glue are a good idea – these are easier to clean than brushes, since the glue will dry and then peel off the spreader. Let your child use blunt ended scissors so he can do some cutting himself.

Children can use thick paper, card or little cardboard boxes and experiment with their own collages. Some children like to start a scrap book, perhaps for particular collectables or pictures.

Creative activities

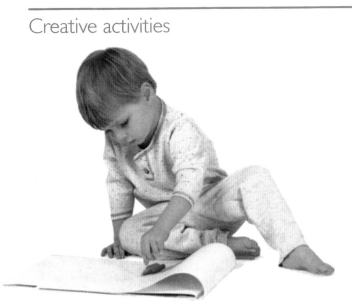

A sketchpad and some crayons will give your child hours of enjoyment as his skills and ability develop.

Sticky shapes – buy packs of precut shapes or sheets of sticky paper to cut yourself – give hours of fun.

Making your own playdough

Most stores sell modelling doughs in different colours, some of them fluorescent, but you can easily make and colour your own (especially if you have run out of yellow when only yellow will do). Mix together in a large saucepan:

2 cups of plain flour
2 cups of water
1 cup of salt
2 tablespoons of cooking oil
2 teaspoons of cream of tartar
food colouring or powder paint

Cook the mixture gently over a low heat and stir continuously. The mixture needs to be well blended and thicken up. Empty on to a plate and let the dough cool before children use it. The salt in the recipe discourages them from eating the dough and it helps to preserve the mixture. You can drop the cream of tartar if you don't have any but the oil is useful because it makes the mixture more pliable.

This dough will keep for several weeks in a plastic bag in the refrigerator.

It is worth keeping items for collage in a box or bag; these include:

- cut-up shapes of felt or any interesting cloth
- lengths of cotton, embroidery silks or wool
- washed and dried milk bottle tops
- dried pasta shapes
- sticky paper shapes
- dried leaves, flowers or grasses
- cut-out pictures from magazines
- old greetings cards

Modelling dough

There are a number of modelling doughs that you can buy, but you can just as easily make up your own.

Playdough is a versatile material for modelling. You can add a small rolling pin and some cutters, which can be small biscuit or pastry shapes. Children can use the dough for pretend cooking, either with toy saucepans or using the plastic trays that supermarkets have for standing yogurts in. Children can shape up animals or snakes and make pretend food. The dough can

The material from which to construct buildings and mould animals, as well as something to squeeze, roll and prod, modelling dough has enormous play value.

Messy play

It is easy to say that a child should be free to explore sand and water, paint and watch the way in which different foodstuffs hit the floor. But allowing a child to go in for messy exploration if you live in a small flat without a garden is difficult and nobody likes clearing up a lot of mess.

It is important for children to be able to make a mess, however. One of the problems nursery schools find is that children who have never been allowed to 'be dirty' develop a fear of messing up their clothes and never choose any of the activities on offer which might involve the possibility of making a mess. Even when they get to nursery or school, they shy away from such materials as paint, glue and modelling clay.

To cope with messy play:
- Find somewhere else to go and play: mother and baby groups often provide messy activities for children; playschool and nursery will provide facilities; parks often have sand pits and paddling pools.
- Keep messy play for a messy hour each day.
- Define a 'messy corner' by putting down a mat: messy play never strays off the mat.
- Use a groundsheet or a piece of polythene (from builders' yards) to protect carpets.
- Sugar in a saucepan can be run through the fingers like dry sand; rice makes even less mess.
- Playdough can be moulded like wet sand.
- The best place for water play is in the bath.
- If you don't have a table for painting, set up an easel in the messy corner or in the bathroom.
- Put a groundsheet or old shower curtain under the coffee table and let him use that for drawing, gluing and sticking.
- Play outside: put on wellingtons and look for puddles to stamp in and mud to walk through.

be rolled back into a big ball at the end or some models can be left to air dry. (On exposure to air, dough starts to harden, which is not a problem when hot little hands are manipulating it. When your children have finished a playdough session, however, encourage them to roll up all the lumps they have finished with and replace them in the containers or in a plastic bag in the fridge.)

If your four- and five-year-olds take to modelling then it may be worth buying some of the modelling clays that are available in a range of colours. The finished models can be baked in a low oven.

SAND AND WATER

Children like natural materials that they can move around and use in many different ways. You may sensibly keep your under-fives away from soil and compost but there is plenty of scope in both sand and water.

Sand

If you have a garden you may have space for either a fixed sand pit or somewhere to put a container that could hold sand – like an old baby bath. Any sand pit or container in the garden needs a secure cover in order to avoid both a rich array of creepy-crawlies and to deter cats from using it as a public convenience.

Use silver sand, obtainable from garden centres. Builders' sand is cheaper but stains hands and clothes and sometimes contains chemicals which irritate skin.

Children will happily play with sand – either sitting in a sand pit or leaning over a container – using buckets, little spades, scoops (like the ones that often come with washing powder), plastic cups and toy saucepans. They like the feel of soft sand and can experiment with filling and emptying and pouring with dry sand. Sand has to be wetted if children want to turn out shapes that will not collapse.

Take care when moving a container – even a small one – full of sand.

Water

There are lots of ways that children can play with water, both indoors and out.

At the sink

Many of the playthings that your child uses in pretend play, like teasets, containers and toy saucepans, will be suitable for playing with in a bowl of warm water at the kitchen sink. He may also like to wash clothes – dolls' and teddies' clothes or something small like face cloths or his own vests.

Your child needs to be safe in how he sits or stands up to the sink, so use a step-stool or a solid chair with the back pushed against the sink. Make sure that the water is not too hot.

Bath time

All you need here is a range of playthings that will survive in the bath. These may be boats and plastic ducks but they can also be any of the playthings your child like using for water play at the sink. He will be able to explore filling and emptying, floating and sinking, and creating bubbles.

Follow the safety guidelines on p. 169 or get in the bath with your child. Apart from the enjoyment of playing with your children, they often chat to you during a relaxing bathtime.

Paddling pools

If you have a garden then warm weather is the time to get out a paddling pool or to fill up child-sized containers like the old baby bath. Children and paddling pools need constant supervision (follow the advice on pp. 169 and 172).

A washing-up bowl at the sink or on the kitchen table allows your child to play with water, but keeps the mess in a limited area. Move breakables and sharp implements from the drainer.

FUN WITH MUSIC AND SONG

When your children are teenagers, you and they may disagree utterly on what constitutes good music. But you have many years to go before then; certainly, during their babyhood and childhood you can enjoy music with your children.

Singing together

Babies and children are simply appreciative if you sing to them. They do not hold up score cards and will enjoy your efforts so long as you look and sound as if you are enjoying yourself too. If you are self-conscious about your singing, then by all means restrict yourself to indoors but do open up this possibility of a shared time with your children.

Songs for young babies

Babies like soft music produced by the human voice. There is evidence that they can hear songs or other

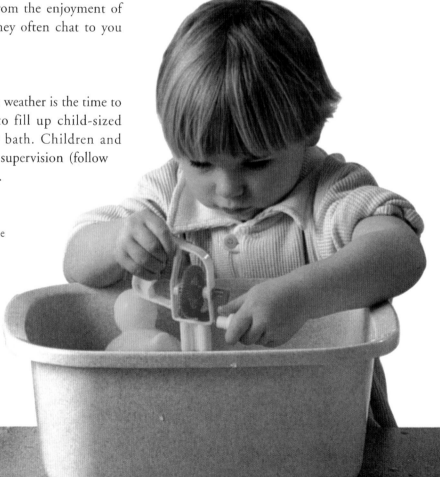

music before they are born and they are able to recognize the pattern of a familiar song.

Babies like and are reassured by the sound of your familiar voice. If he is distressed he can often be calmed by a cuddle, which gives him your familiar feel and smell, and a soft song or lullaby which adds your voice. Lullabies will not automatically send a wakeful baby to sleep, but they are a good and peaceful way of entertaining him in what are going to be longer and longer wakeful periods of his day. (Of course, babies are not interested in songs if they are hungry; basic needs come first.)

If you do not know or cannot remember any lullabies, sound tapes with songs and lullabies will give you more ideas, but do not put on tapes for your baby instead of singing yourself.

You do not have to restrict yourself to lullabies. Try other songs with your baby that you would enjoy singing and see his reaction. Singing is like talking with your baby. It matters less what you sing than how you sing it – with expression, smiles and pleasure.

Songs for toddlers and young children

Once babies are past the early months they will enjoy and begin to recognize songs that you sing regularly. They may also like particular songs from tapes, records or CDs and once they are able to hold themselves up against the furniture they may perhaps bounce up and down in time to the rhythm. There will come a point when your young child will develop a word to request a song and the request may be repeated many, many times.

By the time your baby is two years or more your singing times will become as much singing with him as singing to him. When he goes to playgroup or nursery a whole new source of songs and rhymes will enter your home. However, if you are looking for ideas for your first child, supplement your memory and ideas from within the family by bought tapes and books which give songs with hand movements.

Listening and dancing to music

As well as singing songs to your children, you can enjoy different kinds of music together. This can be selections from your own choice of music – the more varied the better – in addition to music aimed at children. Young children can get the taste for many

Good songs for children

The best songs for children are those that have features that help them to recognize the pattern easily – such as:

- A relatively simple tune which can be sung with lots of expression.
- A small number of words in total.
- Lines or phrases that are repeated in the song.
- A basic verse to which new ideas are added or slight variations made.
- Sounds or perhaps animal noises that accompany the words.
- Hand movements which are part of the song.

kinds of music. If you listen together you will find that even your toddler will develop clear preferences.

Listening to music can be a quiet time of sitting together on a large chair or sofa that has the space for you and one or more children in comfort. Music can also help make a long car journey far more relaxing.

Your children will also enjoy dancing with you to music and not make harsh judgements about your ability. Either both stand and dance together or take your child in your arms (this, too, can be a way to soothe a fretful baby, if you choose something slow and rhythmically rock him). It will not be until they are well into middle childhood that your children will tell you firmly that you are not to dance in front of them, or more importantly, in front of their friends.

Counting the cost

Music can be a potential source of conflict. Children of three or four, or even younger, want to insert cassette or video tapes or CDs themselves. They have seen you do it, it looks easy and children like to do as much as they can for themselves.

Young children sometimes get muddled and may try to insert a sound cassette into a video recorder. They do not know enough to avoid this kind of mistake, and are showing that they have watched you insert a cassette and are trying to do the same. Under other circumstances you would be pleased with your child's willingness to persevere. So try to keep to one side your knowledge of how much this equipment has cost you and the likely bill for possible repairs.

Think about what is best for your household:

- You may decide to keep young children completely away from an expensive system. Your young child will learn to obey a warning look and simple phrase like 'No, not the CD', so long as your family life is not cluttered with masses of 'Nos' and lots of equipment that is out of bounds.
- Teach your child how to use simple controls. Show him carefully how to put in a tape and what controls to use. Stay by him and be prepared to show him as many times as is necessary for him to understand the buttons and the sequence.

If you have taught your child carefully, by the time he is five or six years old he may be more reliable with the controls of your equipment – sound or video – than adult relatives who do not know your system.

Consider buying your child a portable cassette recorder and his own tapes. Show him how to work the buttons and controls. Teach him that this kind of equipment must be treated with care and should neither be bashed nor used with sand or water.

Making music

Babies start to make rhythmic sounds as soon as they can bang a spoon or their mug on the tray of their highchair. They enjoy making the noise and the way in which it gets your attention. Babies and toddlers like exploring the sounds they can make with objects that can be hit, shaken or squeezed. They also get a thrill out of trying to repeat similar sounds by using toys that are designed to make sounds, like rattles. This is the beginning of making music.

You may not have a musical instrument, but this is not a problem since most young children are quite happy with basic instruments such as:

- drums or simple xylophones – or anything that they can bang in rhythm;
- bells – either little hand bells or toys with bells fitted inside;
- all kinds of shakers – you can make effective shakers from an empty plastic bottle half filled with something like lentils, with the top screwed back tightly, or two empty yogurt cartons filled with lentils or beads and then taped together.

Children enjoy the pattern of sounds that these objects make and the physical movements are not too difficult for little fingers and hands.

LEARNING TO LOVE BOOKS

Looking at books, reading and telling stories can be introduced from the early months of life. These activities help to stimulate your child's imagination, develop listening skills and the patterns of speech. Your child will also learn to associate books with interesting information, an essential step towards learning to read. You can enjoy books with your child from his early months. Babies and young children like simple pictures and the sound of your voice as you talk to them about the picture long before they are able to listen to a lengthy story. The range and quality of books for babies and children has dramatically improved over the past 20 years – although classic stories and nursery rhymes still have a place – so you can find something suitable for all ages and interests.

Books for babies and toddlers

Very young children tend to grasp and scrabble at books partly because they are fascinated by the pictures, and partly because they like to explore the physical texture of any object, so pages tend to get torn too easily, or get chewed or sucked. It makes sense not to leave them in a toy basket or put them in your baby's cot. Show your child how to turn pages with care, but try not to worry about torn pages.

Reading to your toddler

If you spend time looking at books with your baby, before he is two he will show that he has favourites and will clearly want to have book time with you. This can be a special time, when he has your full attention.

By about two years of age young children are able to attend, with pleasure, through books of 10–12 pages with maybe a dozen lines on each page. This kind of absorbed interest does not happen automatically with the second birthday; it will have developed in part through the time you have put in during the previous months. However the pleasure small children derive from stories makes reading time a rewarding, shared experience for both adult and child.

Reading to one or more children is not a complicated technique but it is one that deserves your full attention.

- Make the tale sound interesting by reading with plenty of expression in your voice. Sound as if you are enjoying the story, even if this seems like the hundredth time you have read it.
- Go at a steady pace, not too fast, and leave pauses for you and the children to look at the pictures. Some stories have suitable places for a tense pause, or even an excited 'What's going to happen next?'
- It is best to sit very close to your child so you can both see the book clearly and from the same angle. He could be on your lap. If you are reading to several children make sure they can all see – you may need to be on the sofa or even on the floor to do this.
- You can look together and perhaps point sometimes to a picture. But, if it is a story book, do not take long breaks in the story to talk about a picture or your child may lose concentration.
- When children are able, let them turn the pages.

Learning by repetition

Older babies and toddlers will like you to say the same, or a very similar, sequence of words as you talk your way through a picture book. They enjoy the repetition and may well start to repeat words at the right moment, or even correct you if you make a mistake or, worse still, try to skip a section! If books do not come with a story line, you can always make one up around a set of pictures that your child likes.

Once you have created a story around the pictures your toddler will want the book this way each time, so explain it to others who may be 'reading' it to him.

Choosing books to suit your child

To get to know the kind of book that most interests your child so that you do not spend money on a book that is only opened once, try out books first from your local library and then buy your child's favourites, or contact the Young Book Trust for a list of titles. Children's libraries have a welcoming atmosphere, usually with a book box and reading area for young children to encourage them to feel at home.

Try for a range of stories:
- some with people as well as animals as characters;
- some storylines with repeating phrases, since your young child will recognize and start to join in;
- books with good, clear pictures;
- books that have a range of people, including some that look like your family and who do things that your family does, and others that are different.

Books for under-twos

Do not be afraid to buy books for your baby. While it is true that beautifully illustrated hardback stories can be expensive, these are not the best for a small child in any case. There are plenty of inexpensive books that are suitable for even the youngest of children.

- **Thick board books**
  These stand up to tough handling and page turning. You can buy picture books with drawings or photos. Some board books are designed with an extra interest, for example, holes to look through. Some will stand up like a cardboard frieze.
- **Cloth or wipeable plastic books**
  Your baby may like the feel of cloth books since babies go through a stage of stroking and rubbing soft things. Some plastic books are designed to survive in the bath.

- **Clear and brightly coloured picture books**
  Babies and toddlers often like a shiny surface to books. The best pictures are visually interesting but not too crammed full of detail. Young children are still learning to scan pictures and too much on one page can simply confuse them. You can make up your own picture books by putting drawings, cut out pictures and photos in a small pocket album or a photo cube.
- **Books with a simple storyline**
  There are plenty of books that tell a story by no more than a line or two on each page. Reading this kind of book allows you to pace the story for a young child and to spend as much time on the pictures as the tale. It also enables children to begin to recognize simple words because of their association with a clear picture – 'cat', 'dog', 'car', 'boy', 'girl', 'baby', 'cup'.

Making up a story

Suppose your toddler really likes a set of photos of a young child going swimming. There is no text except for the book title, so you made up your own. Perhaps it will go something like this.

- Picture of little girl in her costume: 'There's Martha now. What's she doing? She's going swimming. Going swimming with Daddy.'
- Picture of girl being lifted into pool by her Daddy: 'In she goes. Daddy's got her safe. Into the water. Will it be cold – brrr?'
- Picture of a girl splashing in the water: 'No, it's not cold. Look at her splashing Daddy. Poor old Daddy. Just like you splash your Daddy.' And so on …

Books for twos to fives

Children do not become ready for a different kind of book by their second or third birthday. It is a steady development. You will also find that older children still want to pore over much-loved baby books.

Your child's attention will be held by longer stories and he will be ready to hear new stories rather than always wanting the old favourites. He will still want you to read to him and to look at picture books together but, if you have introduced him to the enjoyment of books when he was young, he will also like to look at books on his own.

Different kinds of stories

You can meet your child's interests as well as extending them. Try for a range of different books.

- Ones about people like yourselves.
- Stories that are out of your own experience, set in other countries or times.
- Fairy stories or myths retold for children.
- Stories in a series about a character your child likes.

Poetry and rhymes

Some very good poetry is now written for children and you can introduce your under-fives to the feel of poetry through rhymes that you chant or sing. Traditional nursery rhymes are particularly good for this – they originate from a time when stories were passed on through the oral tradition, so they had to

have easily memorable themes and rhythms. Pick some books that also have good or amusing pictures.

Books about topics

You will also see many, well-produced books designed for under-fives that have several easily accessible pictures around a specific theme – perhaps cats, life on a farm, dinosaurs, space or another subject – with some text; these are your child's introduction to reference books.

Libraries are an excellent source of this kind of informative book and your child may well begin to develop special interests in one or two topics and be pleased to look for books in order to find out more.

Novelty books

Technical advances in paper engineering have released some very creative books on to the market. You will see pop-up books ranging in design from the very simple to the extremely complex. Books may have:

- flaps to lift or windows to look through;
- parts to feel or to smell;
- items threaded through the book;
- a story that unfolds through additional illustrations on the page as another item is added to the picture;
- pockets or envelopes which hold something else to look at and for you to read out loud.

You will discover which of these books your child likes but remember that novelty books do not survive fierce handling. You may want to keep such books out of reach, for looking at with adult supervision.

Bilingual families

If your family is bilingual you will be talking to your child in the two languages that he needs to speak and you will want to extend this to books as well.

You can use the children's books that are now published in a range of languages, or try a dual-language version with two languages on the same or opposite pages in the same book.

Your two, or more, family languages may follow a different direction of writing and/or a different alphabet. Be ready to point this out to your child so that he associates the different ways of presenting text in the two languages right from the start.

Stories on tapes and television

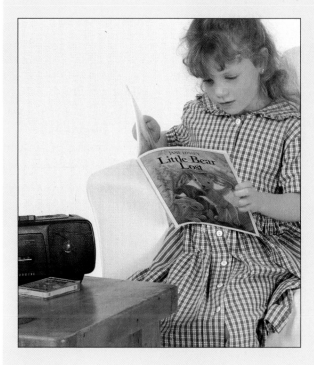

Many children's books are now available on cassette or may be read on television in the morning or afternoon children's slots. You can buy cassettes but, of course, you could tape-record yourself reading books.

It is not a good idea for you to get your children to listen to tapes so that you can give up reading to them yourself. But listening to a new story or an old favourite professionally read can be another way of enjoying books. There is every reason to sit down with your child and enjoy a tape with her. You can look at the book at the same time, or simply relax together and let your imagination create the illustrations.

Cassettes of stories can be especially useful to put on the car tape deck for longer journeys. This can be a real boon if your children start to feel sick when they look at books in a moving car.

Story telling

Before books were widely available tales were passed on by word of mouth, by story tellers. This skill is being revived to an extent and a local story teller may visit your child's playgroup or nursery. You may never wish to tell stories to groups of children, but it is a skill worth acquiring for use with your family.

If you have made up a storyline for picture books, you are well on the way to becoming a story teller. If you read a great deal to your child you will know some stories by heart and may remember favourites from your own childhood. It can be useful to tell stories when you are waiting with your children to be called in to an appointment or on a train, coach or plane journey. Again the same story may have to be told in exactly the same way if you repeat it.

Pre-reading skills

Children often learn favourite stories by heart. They start by joining in but move on to knowing a story so well that they can repeat the words to themselves as they turn the pages appropriately. This is not yet reading but it gives an idea of the pattern of reading and they learn that words and pictures go together.

If your child wants to know what words say or starts to recognize and read words, help him. Show him the letters of the alphabet and their sounds. But don't push him into being a preschool reader for the sake of it. The best help you can give is to build the basic skills which put him on the path to reading.

A positive view of books

If you have taken time and given your attention in enjoying books with your child, you will have taught him a genuine love of books and an interest in what you can find out from them. He will also learn to take care of books.

Helping concentration and observation

Your child will have developed his ability to attend well for periods of time, even to settle back with his books if he is interrupted. He will have learned how to look at a book, scanning the pictures, noticing the details and working through page by page.

Understanding about reading

You will have shown your child how people read so he is not puzzled about the process of reading itself. He can understand how the words tell the story, how you are reading the words and how you stop and turn the page when you have read the last one. Point with your finger to show how you move along the line, or hold back his hand on the page and say, 'I've got one more sentence to go. Look, I'm up to this bit.'

As you share books with your children they have been learning the rules that apply in your written language. English is written and read from left to right and from the top of the page to the bottom. This order is not obvious to children, nor is it a universal way of organizing writing. For instance, Arabic is written from right to left, as is Urdu.

Other reading material

Books are not the only source of written material. You may have shown your child handwriting, and the written instructions to the construction toys you put together and on the board games you play. Advertisement hoardings, cereal packets, road signs, shop fronts, the sides of buses or trucks, all use words and provide your child with a different view of writing and reading, which may encourage him to go back to books and match the words he notices in the wider world.

Relaxing with books

If you take time to enjoy all kinds of books with your child you will help his ability to concentrate, his interests and general knowledge and you will provide him with a head start in learning to read. All these are very valuable, but, in a busy life with children, never underestimate the advantage of a relaxed 'sit-down' time with your child. Reading a book at bedtime is an excellent routine to establish as it relaxes your child and prepares him for sleep. When you look at books with your toddler or read a story to your four-year-old, you can relax for ten minutes and there are not many kinds of play with a child where that is possible!

PLAY AND TECHNOLOGY

There are three important areas where you can help and guide your child as he plays with the technology available to him. These are:

- Developing the habit of making a choice about switching on a piece of technology – and switching it off in order to do an alternative activity.

- Finding out what a set of controls will do and how you work it.
- Taking care of equipment like remote controls, keyboards and control panels of appliances or music systems.

Television

There is a positive side to having a television in your home. You and your children can watch excellent programmes designed specifically to inform and entertain children. You can also enjoy together some of the broader interest programmes that will bring into your living room parts of the world or aspects of nature that you may never otherwise get to see.

But in order to enjoy the benefits, it is wise to establish some ground rules about the television set.

Make a choice about switching it on

Once young children know how to work the television you will need to discourage them from putting it on and cruising the channels, with no idea of what they are going to watch. (It is very unwise to put a television in a small child's bedroom for the precise reason that it is even more difficult to keep track of his viewing.)

You can develop the habit of checking the daily programmes with your child, long before he can do the reading. Make a decision about what he will watch and watch with him sometimes. Offer something else to do with you, if there is nothing of interest on and your child complains, 'But I'm bored!'

Watch programmes with your child

Watching selected programmes with your child has the following advantages:

- You keep each other company: this can be a relaxing time spent sitting together with your child and enjoying something on his terms.
- Some of the children's general interest programmes come up with good suggestions for activities to do with your child at home, so you gain a source of play ideas.
- It provides a chance to talk together. Your child will probably not want you to chat throughout a programme, but, as you watch, you may point things out to each other or comment briefly on what is going on. After you have finished watching

a good programme, talk with your child about what you have watched together. A particularly funny, unusual or interesting programme may be a source of happy reminiscences for some time.

Keep a limit on total hours

Even if your child is watching something good, you do not want him glued to the television for hours at a time. The main problems with television and children come from all the activities that they do not do simply because they are watching so much.

Children need physical activity that uses energy and gives them the opportunity to develop and practise all their skills. If they are sitting slumped or lolling on the floor then they are not running about in lively activity. Nor are they using other physical skills that get practice when they are building, drawing or playing with a bowl of sand or water.

One possibility of sitting around for too long, whether he has been watching television or indeed reading books, is that some children have a burst of wild energy at a really inconvenient time for you. Even more worrying, in the long term, is if children lose the motivation to play in a lively way and slip into a sedentary life style. So think about the balance of active and quiet play in your child's day.

Video

The main difference between television and video is that a video can be played at any time, rewound, sped through and replayed again. You will need to establish limits to how long children watch videos, perhaps confining replays to one a day and making sure that any video within reach is suitable for young children.

Electronic toys

Technology is now applied to toys, but just because a toy uses up-to-date technology, it does not necessarily mean that it will offer the best way for your child to play or the best value financially for you.

It is as well to be wary of expensive electronic 'educational' toys that claim to teach your child all about shapes or numbers. Children learn these concepts through experience and not from a control panel of just half a dozen fixed examples. Your child may enjoy having a toy like this, but it will not take

the place of a helpful and attentive adult and play materials that offer lots of examples of the concept.

Some sound-making control panel toys claim to teach your child his first words. No toy can teach your child to talk. Children learn to communicate with other human beings and they should be learning from the real thing. Other toys claim to teach your child the basics of reading. Again, they cannot take the place of the ideas described on pp. 220–4. They are generally repetitive and of limited interest, and fortunately children get bored with them quickly.

Computers

Many computer games and CD-roms are now designed to be suitable for young children. However, it can be difficult to prise even a small child away from repetitive computer games or hand-held units, so you will need to keep track of the time your children spend playing with them in much the same way as with television and video.

It is useful, indeed essential, for children to develop confidence with computers. Your child's nursery class will probably have at least one computer and, if you have a personal computer at home, you can introduce your child to what it will do – even young children become adept very quickly. If you're connected to the internet, it's worth looking for an internet server that offers a child-safe system in order avoid exposing your child inadvertently to unsuitable material on the web. In any event, technological hardware available at home should not take the place of interested and involved parents who play with their children.

PLAYING WITH OTHER CHILDREN

Children younger than three do not play in a co-operative way, but play alongside others (see pp. 201–2). But that is only half the story. Research into play is often based on observation of pairs or groups of similar-aged children. A group of two- or three-year-olds, with no older children present, may play in parallel rather than together. Children of this age often watch each other and copy what the other one is doing. They may exchange a few words and gestures, but their language and social skills are not sophisticated enough to deal with the give and take in play or with starting and holding on to sequences of play together.

The other half of the story can be seen when there are more children in the family, or the children of two or more families come together. Then the four- and five-year-olds may include the younger ones, once they are mobile and can follow simple instructions, in play. As a result, young children do have a role in pretend play and are tolerated in physical games.

Brothers and sisters do not always get along and older ones will not be pleased if they can never escape from the younger ones. Yet a genuine 'playing together' can develop when siblings are young.

What you can do

There are many things you can do to help children to play together, whether they are your own or other children come to your house.

Adults remain responsible

Adults are the ones who keep everyone safe, especially babies and toddlers. Older children may need to be warned that they cannot treat the baby like a doll or teddy. Even placid babies should not be used as props.

Babies of a few months can be interested in older children, who may be prepared to take part in the kind of repetitive play that babies relish, such as shaking rattles, dropping and fetching and making faces. But older ones cannot be expected always to take younger ones into their play and should never be left with sole responsibility while adults do something else.

Be an available umpire

Children often cannot sort out disagreements beyond one or two attempts and under-fives do not have the same array of strategies for resolving people problems as you do.

If you stay within sight or easy earshot, you can swiftly intervene if tempers seem to be frayed. Do not assume it is always the youngest who are hard done by or the boys who started the hitting.

Child needs and adult needs

Children from different families may not always want to play together for the same length of time as their parents want to socialize. Be sensitive to their needs as well as your own and give the children time apart.

Give children time apart

Even children who get on well together get jaded if they never have a break, or a chance to be alone for a while. Children also get fed up if they always seem to have to share you with another child and never, ever have time just for themselves with you.

Children of different ages will play with different toys and the older ones will be distressed and angry if their painting is destroyed by a crawling brother or if an unsteady sister crashes into their tallest tower before you have seen it. A first child will have become used to playing on the floor and you will need to protect his play area from his naturally curious younger brother or sister. In addition, the older child's little toys, like plastic bricks and crayons, need to be kept away from the baby's or toddler's mouth.

By three or four years children may get breaks in their family day offered by playgroup or nursery. But at home, it helps to give the older child special attention in a quiet time with you when the younger one is having a daytime nap.

Sharing

Life is easier and more enjoyable for everyone if children learn to share. But sharing is one of those areas in which adults expect a great deal more from children than they would from adults.

Parents often say 'Go on, share your toy with your friend' even when the other child is not a close friend, or is a well-known wrecker, or the toy in question is brand new, or all three. Would those same adults hand over something equally precious of their own – a brand new item of clothing, the keys to the family car or a book or CD in the same circumstances?

You can take practical steps to help your children to share, without demanding an unrealistic standard of selflessness.

Know what you are asking

Adults tend to use the single word 'sharing' to cover several slightly different kinds of behaviour. All have their place and can be learned by children if they are not put under unreasonable pressure.

Borrowing and lending

This is the kind of sharing of toys that probably goes on in your own home. The original owner is not in doubt, nor is the fact that the toy should be returned. Borrowers should ask first and be willing to lend in return and those who do not return toys or books in a reasonable state will not be able to borrow again in the near future and may have to make recompense.

Giving

A limited quantity of anything is given. Children learn that it is selfish to have more than your fair share or tuck into something that is not available for all.

Taking turns

Being able to take turns is vital when play materials – the roller for the playdough, the pot of red paint, the swing in the garden, the bikes at playgroup – are limited. Children learn that no one child has the right to hang on to the paint or sit tight on the bike and prevent other children having their go.

Be reasonable

It is fair that your child can put precious possessions to one side when other children visit. A new toy or something that would be devastating if it were broken can stay in the cupboard. A child's toys are not his own if you overrule his wish to keep them safe.

You may have a longer list of toys put to one side if a visitor is known to be careless or a deliberate breaker. But it is not fair for your child to bring out something that he will not then share.

Impose your house rules

As awkward as it may feel sometimes, you have the right to impose your own house rules on child guests. Often children simply assume that fairly wild behaviour is allowed, unless told specifically not to do something. More often than not, once you say, 'Nobody is allowed to throw toys down the stairs in this home', the child will stop.

Learning to follow rules

Four- and five-year-olds devise and impose rules on each other in their play and by this age children are ready for simple games with built-in rules. With you as a teacher and umpire, they will enjoy board and card games.

Suitable board games include those based on pictures. (There may be writing or numbers as well but under-fives need the additional help of illustrations.) Picture dominoes help children to look carefully and to match like with like. You can buy lotto games that depend on matching pictures. Some four- and five-year-olds are ready to match numbers, shapes or even simple words to pictures, but make sure that they have first understood the idea of a board game with pictures. Playing 'Pairs' with illustrated cards helps children to remember and match similar pictures. Snap cards with pictures and card games like Happy Families are possible for four- and five-year-olds who have learned to look carefully.

If you have children older than five, they may be keen on a range of board games that involve counting or following written instructions or illustrations (like snakes and ladders). Younger children may take part in such games so long as you play as their partner.

WHY PLAY COUNTS

Play is a social activity and, although children can be happily absorbed for some time playing on their own, they also want company. If you are willing to get involved in your child's play you will be a real help to him in all the different areas of development in which he is learning so fast. You will miss far too many opportunities if you hold back, feeling that play is not for adults. So don't always expect your child to 'go away and play', or tell him 'play nicely, be quiet I'm talking' or keep saying 'later, later'.

Children do not take a narrow view of play, so you need not either. Play is whatever activity absorbs them. In a sense, the most important aspect to play is that the activity is started, seen through and finished because it is of interest in its own right. There may be an end product but the actual result may be more of a warm glow that comes from having a good time.

Playing with your children need not stop when they go to school. You will enjoy advanced versions of games with your older children and their own play, alone or with friends, will be more complex. The way that you play with your under-fives can build up interests which will develop into hobbies and absorbing leisure activities later on in his life.

Through spending time together, enjoying play and communicating through play activities, you will be creating a close and caring relationship with your child. Not least of all, you will also have fun.

CHAPTER NINE

Help With Your Child

Sooner or later, you are going to have to leave your child, whether for a couple of hours or a full working day. Although handing your baby or small child over to someone else is always difficult, good, reliable child care can both enrich your child's life and make your own life easier.

Sharing the care

Babies and children are social beings. They like and want contact with other people of different genders and ages. And although they need some level of predictability and familiarity in their lives, it is not necessary, or even beneficial, for a baby or young child to be cared for by one person alone.

WHAT BABIES NEED

In the first months of their lives, babies become attached to a few key people. One person may be the most important, or at least the most important for a while. This key person is often the baby's mother but this particularly close attachment tends to come about because in most societies women do most of the child care, and especially the baby care.

Very young babies are still building their knowledge of how to tell one person from another. But older babies and young children show clearly that they are happy with, and would choose the company of, several different people that they know well – father as well as mother, an older brother or sister, a grandparent or other close relative. With a proper chance to settle, they are also able to form a good relationship with a carer who is not a member of the immediate family.

If you are a first-time mother, it is understandable that you might feel concerned that nobody else, even within the family, can take proper care of your baby, because nobody else will do it exactly the way you do. There are great advantages, however, in sharing your baby and allowing other members of the family, especially her father, to become expert. Not only will you be overwhelmed if you cannot get any break at all, but your baby needs to get to know other people in her life and to have this experience in a way that helps her to sort out the familiar from the unfamiliar.

What fathers can do

Fathers can perform every aspect of baby care, except breastfeeding. Mothers are not born knowing what to do with babies. They learn from the experience of having a baby of their own, and from others who are already experienced, often fellow parents or members of the family. It takes time to build a personal relationship with an individual baby, with the result that some mothers find that they get along more easily with one of their children than another.

The point is that 'mothering' does not unfold automatically, so as a father, you do not need to feel that your partner was born to be a better parent. In a family in which you are involved from the outset in her care, your baby will be as happy with you as she is with her mother, and as pleased to see you and conscious of your absence, in the same way too.

Apart from finding out what you need to know about good baby and child care, the most important step for you as a father is to give time to your babies and children so that your experience and confidence grow. If you have not spent much time with your baby, it is easy to think that anything that goes less than smoothly is your fault. But remember, your baby yells at her mother sometimes and is hard to comfort for no obvious reason with her too.

Other contacts

Through becoming attached to a small number of people, your baby will develop a secure base on which to build future relationships. Initially, she will make these relationships, which will not always be peaceful, with her brothers and sisters and through them find her position in the family. Once she has this measure of a social life, supported by you, she can begin to 'broaden her circle' and choose her own friends.

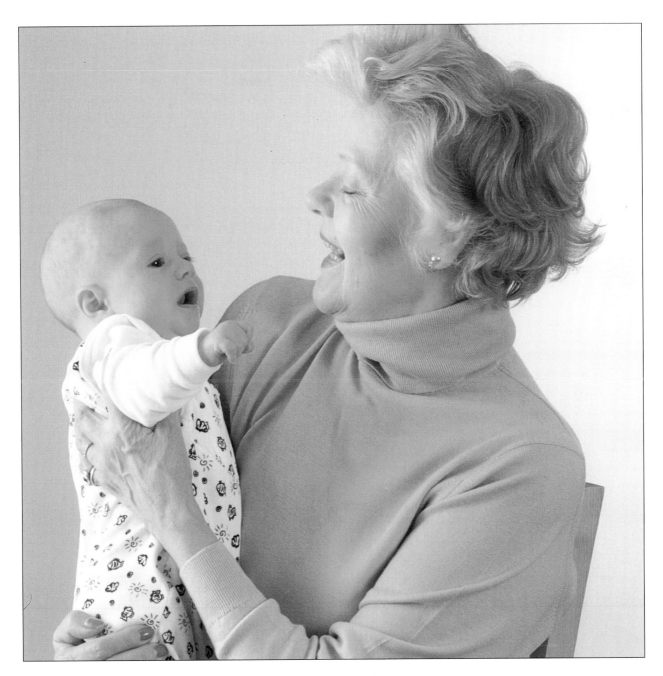

Grandparents can play a very special role in the lives of babies and young children, often developing strong and lasting bonds with their grandchildren.

These developments should be a steady process rather than sudden big changes. In order to develop socially and learn how to relate to different adults and a range of other children, your child has to have the opportunity to make friends. You may give her this through links with other families and later through preschool groups. And, if you have to organize child care to cover for your paid work, a good arrangement can also open up your child's social world.

TAKING A BREAK

From the start, get your baby used to being with other people in the family. This can be for very short periods of time and sometimes you can also be in the same room. Among the possibilities are:

- Stand back and let a grandparent cuddle or sing to your baby, without your hovering close.
- If you are a mother, then let your baby go to her father sooner rather than later. Trust him with her.
- Let a grandparent or aunt or uncle hold and play with your baby while you cook a meal, pop out to the shops or take a much-needed nap.

- If you have close friends who have babies or children of a similar age, spend time together – a social time for the children as well as for you.

If your older babies or young children are happy, you may be able to arrange part of each week in which, for short periods of time, you take turns in having a friend's children and he or she yours. This might allow you to do something you would enjoy just for yourself – a fitness session, a trip to the shops or just a chance to sit and read a book.

There is no reason why swapping arrangements with friends should not work just as well for fathers as for mothers. If you are a father and your baby's prime carer, think about its benefits for both of you.

Time off during the day

However much you love your baby, you will get depressed if you and she scarcely leave the four walls of home. Try to get some variety into your days and include trips out within easy travelling distance. If you know people locally who also have children, get together in each other's houses. Local groups of the National Childbirth Trust are sometimes lively social networks and can put you in touch with other parents with children of a similar age to your own. Consider, too, any drop-in facilities for parents and children. Your local library or GP's surgery may have posters or leaflets, or contact the children's department at your local Social Services. There are several options:

- Parent and child groups at which you stay with your child. These groups may be called drop-ins, one o'clock clubs, toddler groups or parent-and-child clubs. There may be a small fee.
- Some local playgroups or community nurseries may have a special afternoon when local parents are invited to drop in and stay with their children.
- Special parent and baby, or toddler, sessions at local leisure centres or swimming pools.

Groups of this kind can be very enjoyable: you get some adult company and a change of scene and your child gets a different choice of toys and play materials and perhaps some open space. Sessions at leisure centres can ensure that your young child gets to use the facilities in a suitable environment, without older and larger children moving at speed. Your child may start to make friends and you may also find that some of the other parents become your friends.

Group experiences introduce your child to the ground rules of groups of children, including the need to share and take turns. You remain present, so your child can let go of you to an extent, but has the choice of staying by your side and playing with you if she prefers. This experience can mean that playgroup or nursery school, when you do leave your child, may be less of a wrench – although it will not ensure that there are no tears at all later.

If you are a full-time father, it is inevitable that you will be out-numbered at coffee mornings and drop-ins. Take the line that you know exactly what you are doing with your baby or young child – as indeed you do – and you are seeking social contact, not advice. You may meet the suggestion that you have simply stepped in temporarily: ignore it or dispel the misconception as you see fit.

Your agreement with a babysitter

A number of considerations apply to your relationship with any sitter, although some are more crucial if you are using paid sitters. You can reasonably expect a sitter to:

- arrive on time and stay in your house for the whole duration of the sit;
- follow your house rules on habits such as smoking;
- not use alcohol or other recreational drugs while sitting for you;
- arrive in person and not send a deputy, except in case of illness when he or she should let you know in advance;
- not arrive with a friend in tow unless agreed in advance with you;
- focus on your children: he or she should be able to hear the children when they have gone to bed, so there should be no loud music and the television should be low; some sitters arrive with a bag of homework or a book, which is fine so long as it does not come out until the children have gone to bed;
- use your telephone only to call you in an emergency; if you are going to leave other people in charge in your home, get an itemized phone bill;
- not 'nose' about your house.

Getting out in the evening

Children are all different, so you will have to make a decision with each one about when it is feasible to go out in the evening and leave your baby or toddler with a sitter. You may find that your first baby's sleeping pattern is reasonably predictable after only a few months, or that she is happy for a familiar sitter to bottlefeed her if she wakes. Yet your second child may develop an uncanny ability to know when you are going out and either refuse to settle to sleep or wake during the evening and reduce a sitter to a wreck.

If your baby becomes so distressed at your absence that the sitter has to phone you to return, or you arrive home to a desperate child, you may have to take her with you until she is a little older. This, obviously, is probably reasonable if you are going to dinner at a friend's house, but not an option in a cinema or the vast majority of restaurants. It also does not get round the fact that you need time with your partner, without your baby: in a very short time, you can get out of the habit of talking to each other on topics that have nothing to do with children. It is also important to get out if you are a single parent, or if your partner is frequently away on business and just wants to sit in when he or she is at home.

Once you can reasonably organize it, therefore, try to get a reliable baby-sitting arrangement. If you are handing over responsibility, even for short periods of time, you need to pass over any important information about the care of your baby or child and where important equipment is kept. Always leave a number where you can be contacted.

There are several potential choices:
- Sitting arrangements without payment. A relative may be able, and happy, to sit for you.
- Friends with children who also need sitters may be pleased to sit for you and you sit in return, for equivalent amounts of time.
- You may find an organized circle in your area. Such circles usually include at least a dozen or so local families. Each month someone in the circle keeps a record of everyone's name, address, phone number, the children and the sits requested and done. Sitting works on a credit–debit system so if you want a lot of sits or long evening sits, you will have to be prepared to sit to this extent for other families. A circle can work well, and avoids payment, if you are a two-parent family with conventional hours – one of you has to be home with your children while the other is out sitting.
- A paid sitter may suit you better, or be your only option. You may have friends or neighbours with teenagers who would like to earn money by sitting. Meet a potential sitter before you use him or her for the first time to assure yourself that he or she is reliable. Some agencies will provide sitters but you may not know in advance who is coming. If you approach an agency, then find out all the details on fees, any other expectations and how the agency finds and vets its sitters. Try to use an agency that allows you to book a particular person whom you have met, like and trust.

Sitting is a two-way relationship and babysitters can give as many stories of lack of consideration or exploitation as parents can of sitters. It is reasonable for a sitter to expect that the evening is spent sitting, not bathing or feeding the children unless you want him or her there early and agree this in advance. Obviously when your children are older, the sitter cannot expect them to be in bed, but he or she can expect them to go to bed when asked without a big fuss. Sitters should not be expected to do any domestic chores, except perhaps take a message if there is a telephone call and clear up their own cups or snacks.

What a sitter will expect

- that you sort out in advance what the rate is, any increases for time after midnight or at bank holidays, and pay up in full and in cash on your return;
- that you do not cancel arranged sits at very short notice unless you are prepared to pay, because the sitter may well have turned down other families for you;
- that you are home at or close to the time you have promised;
- that if the sitter does not have transport, you either take her or him home or pay for a cab; if your sitter lives close by, walk or watch him or her home.

CHILD CARE

If you want or need to hold down a paid job as well as being a parent, you will have to organize reliable child care. Even if you work from home it is most unlikely that you will be able to fit in your working commitments around caring for your children. Babies and young children need plenty of attention, as well as safe supervision, from a caring adult. They will not be happy to wait while you complete your paid work.

If you are able to pay for a nanny or an au pair to help you in the absorbing task of full-time child care, you are in a minority. The majority of families seeking child care want cover for the time that both parents, or the only parent, are working. The advice here is written from that perspective.

Making the decision

For some families there is no real decision about whether one or both of you continues to hold down a job. Family finances may mean that the income of a single parent, or incomes from both parents, are essential. For some parents anything more than a short break from their profession will have serious consequences on their future career.

Regardless of your initial impulses, however, it is worth thinking about jobs in relation to child care. Talk over the realities with parents who are combining family and careers. Having one or more children is a life change that requires compromises – decide for yourself what these are going to be for your family.

Balance the following important issues:

Income
What do you really need? There comes a point in most families at which basic necessities are covered and your child may prefer your presence to expensive toys or the treats for which your working hours pay. Might part-time working or an ordinary working week, rather than overtime, meet your needs?

Career compromise
What level of compromise are you allowing in your, perfectly reasonable, wish to have the satisfaction of a job or to maintain continuity in your chosen career? Some leeway will be necessary. It is simply not possible to 'have it all' – very involved parenthood and a highly absorbing job – and anyone who claims it is either possible or easy is talking nonsense. A close relationship with children takes time to build and dedication to an ambitious professional career ladder does not leave enough hours in the day, or physical and emotional stamina, to go round. You may have to accept that a refusal to work the elastic hours you managed before your children were born results in a quieter period in your career.

If one or both of you finds that your career suffers in this way, remember that this is certainly not something for which your children can be blamed.

Needs of children
What do your children need and want from you? Many parents who work do succeed in giving their children their full attention when they are all at home together. Family life is organized around providing what children want and family agendas are deliberately child-focused. You will probably find that you wave goodbye to any time dedicated to what you, as an adult, might wish to do, while your children are younger. But do try to get some time alone or with your partner when you can (see pp. 118–20).

Options in child care

A major part of dealing with the feelings and pressures of combining child care and paid work and shifting your focus from job to home and back again, is to make the best child-care arrangements that you can with time to spare. Find out about possible arrangements well before you need care. You may have to get your name on a waiting list for some kinds of care. You can, of course, leave final details until closer to the time that you actually need cover.

Even a good arrangement will not last for ever. Sometimes you and your child will have to deal with change, sometimes with less notice than you would like. The best organized lives and excellent arrangements have an unfortunate tendency to collapse, sometimes with the most inopportune timing.

The law and child care
Although many of the decisions about child care are personal, you are affected by the law of the land. It is against the law in Scotland to leave any child under

12 years of age unattended at home. There is no equivalent law in England and Wales but you can be prosecuted for neglect if a case can be made that by leaving your child or children unattended you are acting irresponsibly or endangering their safety. Factors taken into account are the age of the children, the length of time they are left alone and conditions in the home, including anything hazardous to a child.

In addition, the law does not recognize that it is possible to hand over responsibility to anyone outside the family who is under 16. So if you leave your child with someone under 16, you remain fully responsible for whatever happens in your absence.

Certain kinds of facilities for children must be registered and inspected by the local Social Services under the Children Act of 1989. This law is applied when the children are under eight years of age and the facility is open for more than two hours a day. With few exceptions, this legislation covers childminders, day nurseries (private, workplace or local authority), private nursery schools which take only under fives, playgroups and after-school or holiday schemes.

State-run nursery schools and classes are the responsibility of the Department for Education and Employment. Private nursery schools which have older, school-age children on the premises also fall under the jurisdiction of the DfEE.

The law does not apply to child-care arrangements made within the family with close relatives. But most other arrangements with carers who are not relatives are governed by the same registration and inspection provisions as childminders since carers are judged to be acting as such. These arrangements include nannies who are working for three or more families (but not a nanny employed exclusively by you) and friends who have regular arrangements involving payment. Payment does not, strictly speaking, have to be money. Handing over bags of shopping that you had paid for could be judged as payment in kind.

If you are in any doubt about an arrangement, contact your local Social Services department. Names vary, but look for something like 'day care for under eights' or 'registration and inspection of day care'. Under the Children Act this department has to keep an up-to-date register of child-care services, so it will be a source of the registered childminders in your area, private day nurseries, playgroups and any other schemes for children governed by the Children Act.

Weighing up the issues

When you are trying to decide what kind of child care could suit you, your child and the rest of the family, consider the following factors:

Your child

How old is your child? Babies and toddlers need to be able to relate on a predictable basis to a small number of carers. They will almost certainly become distressed if carers change without warning in a day nursery, or if a nanny or childminder insists on fitting them into a busy social round.

What kind of person or place do you think would suit your child? You may not get your ideal but at least be clear about what you believe would benefit your child.

How many children do you have? Kinds of child care (and the travel involved) which seem manageable with one child may not be the best choice for two or more. The cost of any type of care involving a fee per child may start to rival more expensive forms of care like employing a nanny.

Timing

When will you need care for your child? How many hours of the day do you need and is any of this time during antisocial hours – do you work shifts, evenings or weekends, for example?

Do you work the same days of the week or are you looking for a person or place that could take your child for a different pattern each week?

Do you need child care that will dovetail with your child's preschool playgroup or nursery – taking and pick-ups as well as providing the emergency contact if your child becomes ill or has an accident during playgroup or nursery hours? These provisions will also be important when your child starts primary school.

Location

Where do you want care for your child? Is it easier to have her cared for at, or close to, home or near your or your partner's workplace?

Type of care

What sort of care do you ideally want for your child? Would you rather an individual carer or introduce your child to group care? Does your child have special needs that may require a particular setting or expertise in the carer? Do you have twins?

Cost

How much are you able to pay for care? Costs of the different types of care vary widely. You will usually pay money, although arrangements between friends may be in terms of favours or hours returned. You pay for child care out of your net income. The cost has not so far been allowed as a deductible expense for income tax purposes. You should not normally pay tax on the value of a place in a nursery provided by your employer, but you will have to pay tax on any cash allowance or voucher given to you by your employer to help toward the costs of child care.

Availability

Being clear about what you would like ideally is a good start, but the reality is that sometimes there are more families seeking child care, and particular kinds of child care, than are available in an area. You will need to weigh your preferences with your constraints to select the best out of what is actually available.

Family and friends

You may be able to get the help you need without looking beyond the confines of your immediate circle of family and friends. It is worth investigating the possibilities before you start trying to find an outsider.

Between two parents

If you are a two-parent family, you and your partner may be able to arrange your working hours so that you are never both at work at the same time. This can be successful if you both have predictable hours and you either work part-time or in staggered shifts. Your child care is free and your children get to spend time with each of you. A potential disadvantage is that you and your partner may not get to see each other much as one of you tends to go out as the other comes in. It also means that the times you spend together as a family may be more limited.

Other family members

A relative may be able to care for your child. This can work well if your relative lives nearby or with you, and the number of hours involved do not seem burdensome. The care is probably free and your child knows her carer already. The relative may enjoy the regular contact. Be honest about what is expected and for how many hours. Family relationships are more likely to stay happy if you discuss changes in arrangements and do not simply assume that your relative will do more hours or change days without warning. Relatives need to be able to end the arrangement when they wish, rather than feeling obliged to continue for ever, although you must have sufficient warning to make other arrangements.

Arrangements with friends

If you are seeking cover for only a few hours, you may be able to develop a barter system with a friend. Your friend takes your child or children for agreed times and you do something in return. You may be both fitting working hours into this arrangement. Some people take on job shares with the understanding that the person who is not working takes responsibility for the children from both families.

The advantage of this kind of arrangement is that your child care is free but, of course, your week is fully committed either to your paid work or to the shared child care. It is an arrangement that can work well if the children get on well together and do not mind being in either of the family homes. Young children do, however, sometimes become irritated or sad at always having to share you.

Think carefully about a friend caring for your child for nothing in return. This may work in an emergency until you have a longer term arrangement, but it is inequitable and may affect your friendship in the longer term. And remember if any form of payment passes between friends for child care, the arrangement may bring you under the requirements of the Children Act of 1989 (see p. 233).

Home-based help

If you want your children cared for at home, and none of the 'within-the-family' arrangements is possible, you will have to look for a nanny or an au pair.

The major advantage of home-based child care is that your children stay in their own home, which may be very important to them. You may also get some housework done for you, if you make that part of the agreement. The success of the arrangement depends

Making time to talk

For care within the family or with friends to work well, both parties involved need to make time for conversation. Although an arrangement of this kind is less formal than if you are employing someone or taking your child to a nursery or childminder, you still need to have reasonable consistency between the different people who are caring for a child.

It can be more difficult talking to a member of your family about how he or she is spending the day with your child, but you need to be as sure with a family member as you are with a nanny or nursery that your child is getting the love, care and stimulation that she needs.

It is also important that you and your child's carer are taking a similar line on such developments as toilet training, mealtimes or handling tantrums. The way Grandma brought up her children may not be exactly the way you want her to help bring up yours!

on whether you, your children and the carer get on well. Although a nanny or au pair may be very competent, you may find a clash of child-care style or temperament. You should also consider how tolerable or stressful you will find having someone living in your home, or at least spending long periods of every day there.

Nannies

Nannies are employed by you to take sole responsibility for your children in your home, for agreed hours and conditions. Some nannies have completed training in child care and, unless you are their first family, they will have some experience to offer. Less experienced or untrained carers used to be called mother's helps, but the dividing line has become blurred. It is still the case that the majority of nannies are female.

Employing a nanny is the most expensive form of home child care since you are paying for the exclusive use of a nanny's time for your family. You can try to reduce this by sharing a nanny with another family, but, if the nanny-share involves three or more families, then the nanny must register with the local Social Services department, since she, or he, is judged to be working in the same way as a childminder (see p. 240) and must fulfil the same conditions.

Daily or live-in?

A nanny who leaves home to seek work at a distance will almost certainly want accommodation with the job, otherwise your choice will be based on the hours for which you need care. You will almost certainly need a live-in nanny if your working hours are long or erratic, or if you have business trips that take you away overnight. If you are a single parent, or if your partner has similar working conditions, then you will need total cover.

Cost

The wages that you should expect to pay vary according to where you live and are related to whether the local demand for nannies is outstripping the supply. Other families you know, who are currently employing nannies, or an agency specializing in matching families with nannies, should be able to give you an idea of the going rate in your area. If you choose to have a live-in nanny, you may pay less, but you must consider the cost of additional food and unpredictable items such as use of the telephone and, perhaps, the car.

You are the nanny's employer, so you will have to cover net wages, plus income tax and two kinds of national insurance – employee's and employer's. Some nannies used to operate as if they were self-employed, especially if they worked for more than one family, but the Inland Revenue no longer regards this as a grey area: nannies are definitely employees. Contact your local income tax office and ask for the New Employers' department. You will be sent a starter pack for small employers which will contain all the information and the forms that you need. If anything is not clear, contact the local tax office for advice. There is also a freephone line on National Insurance (see Useful Contacts, pp. 248–51).

In 1998, a daily nanny with experience would expect at least £250 a week in her hand (more in some areas, less if she were less experienced); this means that your outlay could be as much as £400. A live-in nanny might expect around £150–£200, again with you paying tax and N.I.

Choosing a nanny

You can place an advertisement for a nanny in magazines such as *Nursery World* and *The Lady* which also have regular advertisements from people seeking such work and from agencies. An agency will find you someone for a fee. (If you use an agency, pick one by word of mouth and always ask how it vets its nannies, whether it checks their qualifications and so on.)

Always interview a prospective nanny, even if he or she has been found by an agency. Consider having your child with you: she may well have an opinion and you will also have an opportunity to see how the nanny reacts to your child. Do not feel uneasy about asking searching questions of any prospective carer. Do not feel grateful to have found anyone at all. (Mothers can be vulnerable to feeling that child care is a favour, since mothers are more likely than fathers to feel a mixture of emotions about whether they should be working at all.) When you interview a prospective nanny, cover the following areas.

Training and experience

Reliable courses in child care are the NNEB, the more recent NNEB–CACCE diploma, BTEC, NVQ and GNVQ in child care and education. This area is in a state of change so other courses may evolve. Someone holding one of these qualifications will have studied child development up to seven, play and learning and the ups and downs of being with children; she should have had practical experience in different settings. She may not have covered special needs. Always ask what the course involved. (Only private nursery colleges train specifically for nannying.) Ask a nanny to bring certificates to the interview and follow up references, preferably by phone.

Fitting in

You need to gain a reliable sense of how any nanny would relate to your child and to you. If you are going to be at home at the same time as the nanny, it is going to make life easier if you get along.

Your contract with a nanny

A working agreement should cover:

- Normal hours and extra duties, for which a nanny would get additional wages or time off in lieu. Live-in nannies in particular can get caught with being potentially on duty whenever they are in the house.
- Wages and when they are paid. It is the nanny's right to be paid in full and on time.
- Living conditions. A live-in nanny is joining your family and your home. She will, quite reasonably, expect her own room and full board. (A daily nanny should also have her meals as part of her normal day.) However, since a nanny is living in your home it is reasonable for you to set ground rules, when friends can visit, for example, and whether you are willing to have a partner sleep over.
- Notice. An agreed period of notice that either of you has to give in order to end the arrangement may be four weeks once the nanny is settled and you are happy, but make it a shorter period, perhaps a week, within the first month. If at any point you are seriously dissatisfied with a nanny,

pay her the notice period and tell her to go immediately – a disaffected nanny is a potential danger firstly to your child and also, perhaps, to your home.
- Activities and trips. You want your nanny to have initiative but it is preferable to discuss what your child's days will be like. A nanny's responsibility is to organize the day around your child. Trips out should be for your child's interest and enjoyment and any visiting must be focused on your child's enjoyment with other children, not your nanny's with other nannies.
- Consistency. You and your nanny must be consistent in your treatment of such issues as your child's behaviour or eating sweets. Changes like weaning or toilet training should also be joint decisions.
- Housework. Traditionally, nannies will only cook and clean for your child. If, however, there are times of the working day when all the children are out of the house, perhaps at nursery or playgroup, and you want her to do other domestic chores, discuss it with her.

Ask how she would organize a day, given the age of your children. Put a few common ups and downs of life with children to her – arguments over toys, not wanting a nap – and ask her what she would do.

The terms of the job

Make sure that the nanny knows and understands your terms, including wages, hours of work and any other important parts of the working day as you envisage it. Do not leave out any item that is central to the job you want done – such as the ability to drive, that the nanny is a non-smoker, or that you want a certain amount of evening babysitting.

Be clear about whether you want her to take sole charge for all her working hours or whether you, or your partner, will sometimes be in the home and want to spend time with your child.

Give her an opportunity to ask questions; if she looks doubtful or puzzled, ask her about it.

The contract

Organize at least a couple of days when you will be at home with the new nanny. This is your chance to show her the ropes and to discuss details of the arrangement now that she is in your employ. Then, to make misunderstandings less likely, finalize a contract. (You can get examples of contracts from Parents at Work, see Useful Contacts, pp. 248–51.)

Reviewing the arrangement

It is important to get your working relationship as clear as possible from the outset. Make a time to review how things are going after your nanny has been in the job a week or so. Apart from the regular conversations that should be a part of sharing care of children, you may need to have a definite discussion if your nanny is not working in the way that you want or expected. Some give and take is necessary in shared care but it would not, for example, be acceptable to find that a daily nanny took your child back to her own home each day or that a daily or live-in nanny organized trips around her own shopping, friends or leisure interests.

Once your child can talk, she will tell you honestly about what she thinks of a nanny and what they all do each day. Your child's opinion – volunteered or requested – will be an important source of information for you on any care arrangement.

Au pairs

A male or female au pair joins your family from abroad. In exchange for help with child care and light housework, you give the au pair board and lodging and regular payment – currently about £40 per week – to help with living costs. Those whose first language is not English should be given time off for study. Technically, au pairs are aged between 18 and 27 and from Europe; if you employ anyone outside these limits, he or she is not legally an au pair.

An au pair is likely to be with you only for a year, so this form of child care inevitably involves change. Au pairs are also untrained, so it is not fair on them, you or your children to expect them to have sole care of young babies.

Finding an au pair

To the extent that you have any choice in the person who joins your household as an au pair, you are balancing up the same issues as with nannies.

Decide first whether nationality is important: you may, for example, want an English speaker (someone who is bilingual rather than learning English), especially if your children are still in the early stages of learning to talk. If you are bilingual yourself, it will be an advantage to seek an au pair who shares one, if not both, of your languages and can support you in helping your children to grow up bilingual.

Contact the relevant embassy: you can get a number from Directory Enquiries. The embassy will give you the address of the organization that makes contacts for that country. This organization will also be experienced in the paperwork, such as visas. Alternatively, make contact with local networks abroad: your community association may have international links. Agencies (nanny or au pair) will make introductions for a fee, but they are only using the same channels that you can. A good agency will try to match your family with prospective au pairs, and then send you the details of several young people from whom to choose. An agency that offers this kind of service may be worth the fee to get you started.

Once you have had one happy relationship with an au pair, you may find that this contact leads to another. Your au pair may have a friend at home who would like the place or help you to contact a school or a community group in his or her area at home.

Setting up the arrangement

Since au pairs are essentially young people who want to spend a year in England they will not necessarily be experienced with children. For this reason an au pair is unlikely to be a good choice to care for a baby, if you wish to leave him or her in sole charge. Neither is an au pair likely to be suitable for a child with special needs.

Spend time with the au pair, explaining how you wish him or her to work with your children. And make your expectations clear on most of the issues that apply to nannies (see box on p. 238).

Cost

This varies, but in 1995 you could expect to pay around £40 a week for up to 25 hours' help with housework and child care, no more than five hours of which should be in any one day. You are responsible for his or her board and lodging, although au pairs are not liable to pay tax and National Insurance.

CARE OUTSIDE YOUR HOME

If you are seeking care outside your home, all your options will be registered and inspected by your local authority. The possibilities are individual care from childminders or group care in a day nursery or children's centre. Your local Social Services under-eights department will give you a list of registered minders and groups. It may also produce a booklet explaining the standards that the department expects of anyone who offers child care. (Childminders and nurseries are usually inspected yearly.) This material may give you some guidance on the kind of questions that it is sensible to ask a prospective carer.

The officers of the under-eights department will not make specific recommendations for a minder or a group unless your child has special needs which require additional experience or adapted surroundings.

Childminders

Childminders are people who take other families' children into their own home; sometimes a minder also has a child at home. The majority of registered childminders are women, although there are a few men and couples registered together. All childminders

have limits on how many children they can take at any one time, so not all the local minders will have vacancies. Including his or her own children, minders can have only three children under the age of five, only one of whom can be less than 15 months.

There are several potential advantages in taking your child to a childminder. The arrangement is more personal and your child is with a relatively small number of children in a home setting. If your child likes the minder and the other children he or she looks after, this can be a happy form of child care. Your child has 'instant' friends and, for only children, this can be an excellent way of learning what siblings learn naturally: that some toys are for sharing; that babies need looking after; and so on.

The disadvantage is that if your child does not like either the minder or the other children, she does not have the same choice of others to play with that she would find in a group.

Nurseries and day-care centres

Any good nursery or centre will be organized so that children spend much of their time with a small group of children and relating to one, or two, members of staff. Your child should not be trying to make a relationship with many adults or other children. The aim of keeping groups small is also that staff and parents can get to know each other and have opportunities for conversations about the children.

There are many kinds of group care, not all of which will either be available or possible for your family:

Local authority day nurseries

In your area the Social Services department may run its own nurseries, which may be called children's centres or family centres. Although these nurseries may be open for a long day, it is very unlikely that they will offer places solely on the basis that a parent needs day care in order to work. Most local authority nurseries offer a place, which may be part-time, to families who are under stress or to children who need specific help with their development.

Private day nurseries

These are run as businesses, either on an individual basis or as part of a group. A nursery may follow a particular philosophy of care or early education, such

Is it working?

Child care inevitably involves making allowances for differences in style, but these should not be great, nor should your child be unhappy. If an arrangement does not seem to be working, as hard as it can be, you need to look at alternatives.

A good test of whether you should be concerned can be to imagine a friend describing to you what you are currently feeling or have seen going on at your child's minder's or the nursery. What would you advise your friend?

You know how difficult it was to find your child a place to begin with and are almost certainly weighed down with the worry of making alternative arrangements. If you were freed of this anxiety, what would you be saying to a friend? Would it be to think first of the child and take her out of this arrangement? Then do it!

as the Montessori method. Some private groups call themselves day nursery schools. This should mean that there are some qualified teachers on the staff and that an early years curriculum is followed, but check any written material and ask when you visit. If there are school-age children on the premises, a nursery will not be inspected by Social Services, but come under the jurisdiction of the DfEE (see pp. 234–5).

Community nurseries

Community nurseries or centres are usually set up by a children's charity or as a joint enterprise between a children's organization and the local authority. Such nurseries usually offer places to local families.

Workplace nurseries

Some companies or large organizations have established on-site nurseries or made arrangements for places with local private day nurseries. These nurseries help employees who could not accept a job without reliable child care. A place in a workplace nursery will be tied to your job, so bear that in mind if you are not sure about the job in the first place.

After-school and holiday clubs

Once your children are of primary school age, check if your area has schemes for children after school and in school holidays. Some schools offer this facility on site, others have arrangements with clubs that pick up the children from school and take responsibility for them until you pick them up at an agreed time. In some cases you must put your child's name down in advance for a place on a holiday scheme, others operate on an open-access policy. Schemes offer a range of activities and are run in different locations – schools, parks, leisure centres and so on.

Any after-school club or scheme that takes under eights for more than two hours daily must be registered and inspected by the local Social Services department.

Be prepared: in some areas, virtually nothing of this kind of care for over fives exists.

Other groups or centres

State nursery schools or classes, private nursery classes and many playgroups are not set up with the objective of providing child care. They are offering children a preschool experience with the result that unless you work part-time hours that conveniently fit a playgroup or nursery school session or day, these groups will not in themselves offer the child care you need. Even if they do, you will still need cover during the holidays (nurseries and playgroups often take school holidays). Such groups may fit your arrangements if someone else takes your child to and fro and covers the hours that you are at work, plus school holidays.

Deciding on care outside your home

Visit any childminder or group and make your own decision. Try to take your child with you and, if you have more than one potential choice, visit them all. Your priority should be to discover whether the kind and style of child care will suit you and your child. A responsible minder or group leader will be open with you about the general pattern of their days with children and the extent to which they can, or cannot, be flexible to specific requests.

During your visit, and in looking at anything written that is given to you, you need answers to the following kinds of questions:.

Cost

How much will your child's place cost? Minders' fees vary around the country; the cost of a place in a nursery depends on the extent to which it is subsidized or has to make a profit. You also need to know what happens about payment if your child does not attend, for instance, if you are on holiday. Since neither a minder nor a group can slot another child temporarily into your child's place, it is likely that you will have to pay something to hold the place, probably half or perhaps even full fees (ask the Social Services department what is normal in your area). In 1995, minders' fees were £55 to £85 per week per child; nurseries anything between £70 and £125 per week (ask what is included in the fees since low fees may mean restricted hours).

You are not a childminder's employer. You pay the agreed fees, but childminders deal with their own tax and National Insurance since they are self-employed.

Notice to end the arrangement

It is unreasonable for either a parent or a minder, or a group for that matter, to give only days' notice. Check what is expected by both a minder and group.

What will your child be offered?

What do childminders do with the children? A minder should organize her day around them; they should not take second place to her domestic routines. A good minder will take account of the ages and interests of the children in her care.

What plans and programmes does a group offer? Although any group worker should also be flexible to the children, you can expect a nursery to have some clear plans for each day and the pattern of a week. Look for a range of activities that includes some quiet play but also physical games and the chance to run around in a safe outdoor space. Are trips regularly offered – to the local park? the market? the library?

What toys are available?

What kinds of toys and equipment are available in the minder's home or laid out in the group? What can you see that is stored away and when does it come out? Are there signs of children's work around: paintings fixed to the wall or on a minder's fridge? Lego models or playdough figures left on display to be admired?

Ideally visit a minder or nursery at a time when other children are present. Do the children there at the moment look happy? What are they doing? How are any adults spending time with them? How does the minder balance up her conversation with you and attention to other children, including to your own? What kind of indoor and outdoor play space is there? How safe does it look?

How are the children treated?

How does the minder or the group leader react to your questions on common dilemmas? You want a sense of how they deal with the ups and downs of time with children. Does the minder or group worker ask about your child and what she might like or enjoy? How has your child reacted to the minder and her home, or to the nursery or play scheme?

How have you been treated?

Were you welcome? Were you given answers to your questions in an open and friendly way? Minders and groups cannot agree to change their way of working for one parent, but they should be flexible to family preferences. Overall, do you get the impression that you will be able to have a conversation in the future about your child and how everything is going?

Settling in

Settle your child into an arrangement as well as you can. A childminder should be willing to invite you to part of her day or to have your child start with a couple of shorter sessions. A group should be flexible, since its aim is to settle new children calmly.

Some minders and groups have an agreement to go through with each parent. Such agreements or contracts lay out what is expected of you and what you can expect of them. The pattern of rights and responsibilities should be reasonably equitable, not one-sided. Read any agreement carefully before you sign and ask any questions you wish. In order to retain her registration a minder will need your work telephone number so that you can be reached easily if your child has an accident or becomes ill. A group will also need this. When your child starts, you should also cover:

- the name and address of your child's doctor
- any childhood diseases that your child has had and a record of vaccinations
- any individual health conditions that mean that your child needs either special care, adjustments to her diet or the circumstances under which you must be called

Discipline

In December 1994, the Department of Health stated that childminders should not normally smack children, but that parents could give a minder (but not staff in a nursery or other group) written permission to smack 'as a last resort'. Even if you agree with smacking, think carefully about giving such permission which could then be applied under circumstances of which you would not approve.

- personal information: correct pronunciation of her name, or any shortened form by which she is known; whether she has a comfort blanket or her teddy when she goes for a nap; and so on.

Reviewing the arrangement

Once you have made your decision and your arrangement has started, be alert to your child's feelings. If possible, talk with her about her time with her carer. If she is used to communicating with you, she will give you her opinion and

Many playgroups follow a nursery-school approach with children working on a specific theme and several activities geared to that theme.

tell you about her day, even if she does not yet have large numbers of words. If you talk with your child, you will help her to make the link between her child-care setting and her life at home. You show that you are interested and care very much about what happens while you are apart. You will also pick up on anything that might concern you.

A period of settling in is inevitable but do not carry on with any group or individual who is not offering good care to your child. Try to weigh up whether your child's complaint or unhappiness is a temporary matter – an argument with one of the other children over a toy, for example. Take seriously any continuing concerns and raise them with a minder or the group worker who is responsible for your child.

If your child spends a lot of time with another person – whether that is an individual childminder or nanny, or in a group – you have to accept that she will be influenced by the other people. The effects can be positive in that children are learning that not every adult behaves in exactly the same way and adults all have different interests and skills. Yet it is

Providing nursery education

Since 1997 the nursery voucher system, that provided a lump sum for parents to use for private or local authority-run nursery education, has been abandoned. Local authorities are now looking at early childhood education alongside provision for the out-of-school care of all children from 0–14. New partnerships are being forged for the provision of nursery education for all four-year-olds, and over time for at least two-thirds of all three-year-olds, whose parents want them to have it. This nursery provision may be school-based (many four-year-olds are now in school reception classes) or privately run.

important that all the key adults in a child's life work together in a consistent way on key issues and do not complain about other adults' styles in front of children. Talk with your child's carer if there seem to be differences in your approaches to sweets and crisps consumption, for example, or acceptable table manners.

It is reasonable to expect a carer to acknowledge your family's religious beliefs, or lack of commitment to any faith, and not impose other views on your child. Many groups introduce children to some aspects of a range of world faiths, through festivals and stories, but this is undertaken with respect for all the faiths.

Time with your child

Life can be very demanding if you are a parent who is a full-time homemaker. If you have a paid job on top of your family responsibilities, then you may have a limited amount of time to spend with your child. It is important to use whatever time you do have to give your child your full attention when you are home together. Different patterns work better for different people but the following ideas are a good guide:

- Try to have a space between coming home from work and any home responsibilities and make this time available to your child. You can be guided by your child and what she would like. She may not want to play, but simply to be with you.
- If you are tired, activities that involve sitting down may be best. Look at books together, or watch your

child's favourite programme, or video. Just sit and be together.

- On pleasant days and light evenings go for a walk together, or to the local park. You can talk and enjoy the sights without being tempted to start the evening meal or fret over the bills that have arrived.
- If you cook the evening meal, have your kitchen organized so that your child can be with you. Talk together about your respective days. Most working days produce something of interest to a child.
- Don't get into the habit of bringing something home for your children from work or business trips. It is better if, tired as you may be, you give children your time and attention. Presents or sweets are not substitutes for your presence and will soon be expected as a matter of right, with only the absence of anything special being noticed.

When you are short on time, play games and introduce activities that your child does not do with whoever looks after her in your absence. Then, whatever you do will be special, marked by a cuddle that says, 'I'm so pleased to see you.' Children often like homecoming rituals – perhaps she picks up the mail, chooses the vegetables for dinner, or puts fresh milk in the cat's bowl.

PRESCHOOL ACTIVITIES

There are a range of facilities that offer children the opportunity to interact with others before they reach the age at which they start primary school.

State nursery schools and classes

A nursery school is a separate entity from a primary school, while a nursery class is part of a primary school. Both offer a similar curriculum. Places in state nursery schools or classes are free and your local education department will give you information. Alternatively, telephone the nearest schools or classes and talk with the head teacher. Find out the procedure for getting your child's name down well before she is old enough. A state nursery is unlikely to take a child who is less than three years and in some areas children may be close to four. Most offer half-day places (two to three hours), perhaps extended to a whole school day in the last term before your child enters the reception class of the primary school.

Provision varies widely and nursery places may be restricted. Find out what the priorities are in your area: sometimes children with special needs are given priority; local residents may be close to the top of the list; and so on. It is reasonable to want to choose which school or class you would like your child to attend but be realistic. If priority is given to local residents, it is probably not worth applying to a school that is miles away (or be prepared to be turned down).

The emphasis in nurseries is on learning through play. The staff will have a plan for what they offer to the children and a variety of activities within each session. The aim of an early years curriculum is for children to extend their skills and knowledge in all aspects of their development. In the broadest sense they are being prepared for school. Children are not usually taught specifically to read, write and do number work. But the activities that they are offered and the help that the staff provide can be effective in building up the skills that must be in place before a child can read, write or understand numbers.

Private nursery schools

The choice in private education extends to the nursery age group. You pay fees for a private nursery place and the cost varies. Find out the individual details of any nursery school – the age that they will accept children, the size of the school, whether it prepares children for a particular preparatory school, the length of the daily sessions and the school term.

The curriculum followed by private nursery schools varies according to the philosophy of the school and head. Some have a learning through play approach that is similar to state nurseries, some opt for a more formal curriculum with emphasis on literacy and numeracy skills. Others may follow a specific educational philosophy.

Playgroups

The playgroup movement developed as a response to the lack of nursery education. Playgroups are now established as a form of preschool provision and many are affiliated to the Preschool Learning Alliance (PLA). They are now sometimes known as preschools, but not all operate in the same way.

Most charge a fee per session, which is usually low, but bear in mind that over a ten-week term two or three sessions a week can mount up. Groups tend to be run on a sessional basis and some have no facilities for offering anything more than a simple snack. Groups that can offer lunch may have some full day places, with hours rather like a nursery school. There will be some permanent playgroup staff but many groups are dependent on parents' commitment to help in the group on a rota basis. Children usually have to be at least three years old to attend and it is worth finding out in advance what the enrolment procedure is: some playgroups are better than others and you may have to wait for a place.

The playgroup movement has a learning through play approach and some groups offer a daily programme that is very similar to a nursery school curriculum. When the playgroup movement started, a strong part of the philosophy was that parents had a great deal to offer and should be involved in their children's preschool experience. Although this was a novel philosophy in the 1960s, schools have changed tremendously in the subsequent decades and you will probably find less of a contrast today between playgroups and nursery schools.

Choosing a preschool group

Any choice that you make will be shaped by what, exactly, is on offer in your area and then by any vacancies. Since some have long waiting lists, it is sensible to make enquiries at least a year before you would ideally like a place. Talk to other parents with older children, and find out their opinions and information about the ease, or not, of getting your child into a particular group.

Once you have some ideas, visit possible nursery schools or playgroups with your child. If your child's friends are attending, or about to attend a group, she may want to go as well. If you want your child to go to a particular primary school then it would be wise, although not essential, to get her into the nursery class, if there is one (a place in the nursery class does not necessarily guarantee your child a place at the school, so check this too).

Apart from gaining any practical information you need, look and listen, so that you have a feel of the place and people.

Cost

What are the fees, if any? Are parents expected to provide their children with any special clothing, uniform or equipment? Will you have to offer your time on a rota to help out as a condition of a place?

What activities are on offer?

What kind of programme does this group set out to offer and what seems to happen in practice? A plan, or a curriculum layout, can look good on paper but is worthless if staff lack the enthusiasm to bring it alive. Alternatively, a rather general outline can be delivered with energy and lots of attention to each child.

What is the overall feel of the group?

Is it calm without being over-controlled? Do the children – both those on the climbing equipment and those painting quietly – look happy? Do the adults look involved? Is the children's work on display?

What qualifications do the staff have?

State nursery schools and classes have qualified teachers, usually supported by nursery assistants who may have the NNEB certificate. Play-groups should have one adult with the PLA leader qualification. Private nursery schools should have some trained teachers and some staff with child-care qualifications and experience.

What are the group's aims and policies?

A responsible and effective preschool group will have ideas not only on the programme of activities or early years curriculum, but also on its overall philosophy. Ask the group leader or the member of staff who shows you around to give coherent answers to your questions about how they handle children's behaviour and in what ways they keep in contact with parents. Many produce newsletters to keep you in touch with what they are doing with the children, and give details of forthcoming outings, and so on.

What does your child think?

Children vary in temperament so your child may not actually want to join in any of the activities on offer during your visit. What does she say later? How do the staff react to her? Do they talk to her?

Try to spend a little time with your child when you get home from work. Coming-home routines can be very special times to relax with your child.

Settling in

You can help to prepare your child to join a preschool group and, if you think broadly, you may realize that you have already done a lot of groundwork. If you have already given your child experience of time away from you, this will help but will not always smooth the way completely. Ideally coach your child in the ability to take care of herself. Review what she can already do and where she needs more help. In any preschool group no worker should get irritated at being asked for help. Three- and four-year olds are not yet fully competent.

- Can she manage her own clothes and shoes? If some clothes are harder to do up, perhaps she should not wear them to the group initially.
- Can she manage in the toilet – actually going to the toilet, getting clothes up and down and washing hands afterward?
- Is she confident to ask for help if she needs it, not only for her own care but in her play?
- Is she used to dealing with other children?

A responsible preschool group will suggest ways in which you can help to ease your child into the group. Perhaps initially they may want you to stay with your child or suggest that she attend a couple of short sessions to begin with. No group should be inflexible about this, since children vary. A young child who knows a group from visiting to drop off an older sibling may well be counting the days until this is her group too. She may wave you goodbye with a flourish within five minutes. Another child may be extremely wary and need careful settling over several weeks. Some children are keen on the idea of playgroup or nursery until they realize that you are going to leave. It may be a very welcoming group but at the moment your child would rather you stayed. Playgroup and nursery staff are experienced in comforting children who are temporarily upset and should give priority to a cuddle for new arrivals.

You may decide, with the agreement of a worker, that after a long attempt to settle your child, you will say an affectionate and firm goodbye and leave, even if your child cries. All parents find this hard but you may decide it is necessary. It is unwise to simply slip out without saying goodbye to your child – this will shake her trust in you.

THE IMPORTANCE OF HOME

Some aspects of group life will not make sense to your child until she has attended a playgroup or nursery. She may need to learn that adults have to share themselves out and that part of group life is waiting for attention and accepting that her idea for a book or a song will not always be the one taken up.

Your child will be coming into contact with other children whose approach to play or conflict may not be your family's way. If the situation sounds out of hand to you, or your child seems distressed, talk to a member of staff. Your child should not be hit or bitten by another child, but remember that some things would happen even if you were there. It is reasonable for you to be told about accidents when you pick your child up, not find scrapes and bruises later.

Changes for you

You may be excited that your child is going to a preschool group, yet also find yourself feeling sad. The preschool experience is a broadening of your child's horizons, more evidence of the changing of your relationship and your place in her life.

If she settles quickly and with few tears, part of you will be relieved. Yet parents usually admit that they want the best of both worlds – a child who seems happy to spend time without you, but misses you while she is doing so and is pleased to see you again. Be pleased for your child and show interest in what she has done, but do not feel that the value of her group means that you are no longer important.

Your child may enjoy playgroup and look back in later years with nostalgia to her time at nursery, but time there does pass: home and family provide her continuity. You are your child's first playmate – the person she will stare at and try to grab, the person whom she will copy and want to make smile. You will get to know your child with a knowledge that will never be equalled by anybody else who passes through her life and that knowledge will help you to support her as she builds one skill upon another and adds today's discoveries to what she worked out yesterday. You will still be her parent, her continuity and the one who is there for her, when nannies, minders or nurseries are a memory. Your aim should be to help make that memory a happy one.

USEFUL CONTACTS

The following is a list of useful organizations: some are large national charities, others are small local groups run by volunteers. Information may be provided over the phone, in the form of leaflets or in person by attending a counselling session or a self-help group.

GENERAL INFORMATION AND SUPPORT

ACAS (Advisory, Conciliation and Arbitration Service)
Clifton House, 83 Euston Road
London NW1 2RB
0171 396 5100
Advice and information on maternity leave and such matters as unfair dismissal.

Active Birth Centre
25 Bickerton Road, London N19 5JT
0171 561 9006
Information and advice.

Association of Breastfeeding Mothers
PO Box 441, St Albans, AL4 0AS
0181 778 4769
Advice line for breastfeeding mothers and those with breastfeeding problems. Also runs support groups.

Association for Improvements in the Maternity Services (AIMS)
40 Kingswood Avenue, London NW6 6LS
0181 960 5585

Scotland
40 Leamington Terrace, Edinburgh EH10 4JL
0131 229 6259

Voluntary group offering support and advice on parents' rights and choices in maternity care.

Association for Postnatal Illness (APNI)
25 Jerdan Place, London SW6 1BE
0171 386 0868
Network of volunteers, all of whom have recovered from postnatal illness, offering information, support and encouragement.

Caesarean Support Network
55 Cooil Drive
Douglas, Isle of Man
01624 661269 (after 6pm)
Information and support for those who have had or will have a caesarean delivery. Can put you in touch with someone local who has had a caesarean and understands the problems.

Child
Caledonian House, 98 The Centre
Feltham, Middlesex
01424 732361
Self-help organization for people with fertility problems. Helplines for specific problems such as IVF, ectopic pregnancies, miscarriages etc.

Child Poverty Action Group (CPAG)
4th Floor, 1–5 Bath Street, London EC1V 9PY
0171 253 3406
Information on benefits.

Citizens Advice Bureau (CAB)
Free and confidential advice on topics including maternity rights, debts, housing, employment, legal problems as well as personal difficulties. Look in your phone book for your local branch.

CRY-SIS
Serene CRY-SIS, London WC1N 3XX
0171 404 5011

Scotland
21 Falkland Gardens, Edinburgh EH12 6UW
0131 334 5317

Self-help and support group for parents of excessively crying, sleepless or demanding babies and young children. National network of volunteers, who may or not have been parents of such babies.

DSS Helpline
0800 393539
A helpful organization run by people with considerable knowledge of and experience in both tax and national insurance.

Equal Opportunities Commission
Overseas House, Quay Street
Manchester M3 3HN
0161 833 9244
Information and advice on issues of discrimination and equal opportunities.

Family Fund
PO Box 50, York YO1 22X
01904 621115
A government fund administered by the Rowntree Trust, which gives cash grants to families caring for severely disabled children under 16.

Family Health Services Authorities (FHSAs)
If you are new to an area your FHSA can give you a list of local doctors with whom you may be able to register, including those with a special interest in pregnancy, childbirth and family health. Look in the phone book under your local health authority.

Northern Ireland
Central Services Agency for Health and Personal Social Services (CSA)
25 Adelaide Street
Belfast BT2 8FH
01232 321313

Family Welfare Association
501–505 Kingsland Road
London E8 4AU
0171 254 6251
National charity providing free counselling for those who are experiencing relationship difficulties and advice on many other family-related problems.

Gingerbread
16–17 Clerkenwell Close
London EC1R 0AA
0171 336 8183

Scotland
Gingerbread Scotland
304 Maryhill Road, Glasgow G20 7YE
0141 353 0953

Northern Ireland
Gingerbread Northern Ireland
169 University Street, Belfast BT7 1HR
01232 231417

Wales
Gingerbread Wales
Room 16, Albion Chambers, Swansea SA1 1RN
01792 648728

Countrywide network of local groups providing advice and support for lone parents on everything from child care to returning to work and benefits.

Health Search Scotland
The Priory, Canaan Lane
Edinburgh EH10 4SG
0131 452 8666
Information on local self-help groups in Scotland.

Homestart
2 Salisbury Road, Leicester LE1 7QR
01533 554988
Offers support, friendship and help for families temporarily under stress in their own homes. You can refer yourself, or may be referred by your health visitor, midwife or any other health professional.

Independent Midwives Association
94 Auckland Road, London SE19 2DB
0181 406 3172
Offers advice, support and information to women considering a home birth and full care to those women who book a member for a home birth.

Institute for Complementary Medicine
PO Box 194, London SE16 1QZ
0171 237 5165
Charity providing information on complementary medicine and referrals to qualified practitioners.

Labour Relations Agency
Windsor House, 9–15 Bedford Street
Belfast BT2 7NU
01232 321442
Advice on maternity rights in Northern Ireland.

Life
Life House, Newbold Terrace
Leamington Spa, Warwickshire CV32 4EA
01926 421587
Advice and information on pregnancy, miscarriage, abortion and stillbirth.

MAMA (Meet-A-Mum Association)
Cornerstone House,
14 Willes Road
Croydon, CRO 2XX
0181 655 0357
Support groups for new mums and for mothers suffering from postnatal depression.

Maternity Alliance
45 Beech Street
London EC2P 2AX
0171 588 8582
Advice on employment and maternity rights for expectant mothers.

National Association for Maternal and Child Welfare
1st Floor, 40–42 Osnaburgh Street
London NW1 3ND
0171 383 4115
Helpline offering advice on child care.

National Childbirth Trust (NCT)
Alexandra House, Oldham Terrace
London W3 6NH
0181 992 8637
Charity with branches nationwide. Runs antenatal classes to help expectant mothers with labour and birth. Also offers help with breastfeeding.

National Council for One Parent Families
255 Kentish Town Road
London NW5 2LX
0171 267 1361

Scotland
Scottish Council for Single Parents
13 Gayfield Square, Edinburgh EH1 3NX
0131 556 3899

Provides information on all aspects of coping alone. Also runs local groups.

National Society for the Prevention of Cruelty to Children (NSPCC)
42 Curtain Road
London EC2A 3NH
0171 825 2500

Northern Ireland
16 Rosemary Street, Belfast BT1 1QD
01232 240311

Publishes a range of free booklets, and offers counselling and advice to those who feel they may be in danger of harming a child. Aims to protect children from abuse and neglect.

The Parenting Forum
National Children's Bureau
8 Wakley Street
London EC1V 7QE
0171 843 6000
Umbrella group that brings toghether organisations that promote and develop parenting education and support.

Parentline
Endway House, The Endway
Hadleigh, Essex SS7 2AN
01702 559900
Support for parents of children of any age under stress. Confidential telephone helplines are manned by trained parents.

Parents Advice Centre
Room 1, Bryson House
28 Bedford Street, Belfast BT2 7FE
(01232) 238800
Confidential, 24-hour advice service offering support and guidance to parents under stress.

Parents Anonymous
6–9 Manor Gardens
London N7 6LA
0171 263 8918
Helpline for parents who feel they can't cope or might abuse their children.

Parents at Work
45 Beech Street, Barbican
London EC2Y 8AD
0171 628 3578
Rights and options for all working parents.

Also aims to promote the development of workplace nurseries.

Patients' Association
8 Guilford Street, London WC1N 1DT
0171 242 3460
Advice for people who are experiencing difficulties with their doctor.

Relate: Marriage Guidance
Herbert Gray College
Little Church Street, Rugby CV21 3AP
01788 573241
Professional family relationship counsellors nationwide. Fees based on ability to pay.

Relate Northern Ireland
76 Dublin Road, Belfast BT2 7HP
01232 323454
A confidential counselling service for people with relationship problems.

Shelter: National Campaign for the Homeless
88 Old Street, London EC1V 9HU
0171 253 0202

Northern Ireland
165 University Street, Belfast BT7 1HR
01232 247752

Wales
25 Walter Road, Swansea SA1 5NN
01792 469400

Information and advice on all housing matters, including tenants' rights, grants etc.

Social Security
For general advice on all social security benefits, Income Support, pensions etc., call Freeline Social Security on 0800 666555

Social Services
Your area office will give you information on benefits, housing employment, childcare and useful organizations. See phone book under the name of your local authority.

Twins and Multiple Births Association (TAMBA)
PO Box 30, Little Sutton
S. Wirral L66 1TH
0151 348 0020
Helpline: 01732 868000 (7pm-11pm weekdays; 10am-11pm weekends)
Advice on all aspects of twins from pregnancy to breastfeeding to sleep problems.

Women's Aid Federation
PO Box 391, Bristol BS99 7WS
0117 963 3542

Northern Ireland
129 University Street, Belfast BT7 1HP
01232 249041

Scotland
Scottish Women's Aid
12 Torphichen Street, Edinburgh EH3 8IQ
0131 221 0401

Advice, support and refuge to women who have been abused.

ALCOHOL, SMOKING AND DRUG ABUSE

Alcohol Concern
Waterbridge House, 32–36 Loman Street
London SE1 0EE
0171 928 7377

Wales
Alcohol Concern Wales
4 Dock Chambers, Bute Street
Cardiff CF1 6AG
01222 488000

Scotland
Scottish Council on Alcohol
166 Buchanan Street, Glasgow G1 2NH
0141 333 9677

Northern Ireland
Council on Alcohol
40 Elmswood Avenue, Belfast BT9 6AZ
(01232) 664434

Information on alcohol-related problems and where you can get help locally.

Dunlewy Substance Advice Centre
1a Dunlewy Street, Belfast BT13 2QU
01232 324197
Offers help and counselling on alcohol, drug and solvent abuse.

SCODA (The Standing Conference on Drug Abuse)
Waterbridge House, 32–34 Loman Street
London SE1 0EE
0171 430 2341

Scotland
Scottish Drug Forum
5 Oswald Street, Glasgow G1 4QR
0141 221 1175

Information on local treatment and services for drug users and their families.

Smokers' Quitline
0800 002200

Ulster Cancer Foundation
40 Eglantine Place, Belfast BT9 6DX
01232 663281/2/3
Carries out cancer research and education programmes in Northern Ireland. Gives information on the dangers of smoking.

CHILD CARE

Daycare Trust/National Childcare Campaign
Wesley House, 4 Wild Court
London WC2B 4AU
0171 405 5617/8
Advice on obtaining suitable daycare.

National Childminding Association
8 Masons Hill, Bromley BR2 9EY
0181 464 6164

Scotland
Scottish Childminding Association
Room 15, Stirling Business Centre
Wellgreen, Stirling SK8 2DZ
01786 445377

Northern Ireland
Northern Ireland Childminding Association
17a Court Street, Newtonnards
Co Down BT23 3NX
01247 811015

Association for parents, childminders and others with an interest in improving daycare.

New Ways to Work
309 Upper Street, London N1 2TY
0171 226 4026
Information on flexible working hours and job sharing.

Working for Childcare
77 Holloway Road, London N7 8JZ
0181 700 0281
Advice and information for employers, trades
unions and parents on developing childcare
facilities at work.

EDUCATION AND SCHOOLING

Advisory Centre for Education (ACE)
1b Aberdeen Studios
22 Highbury Grove
London N5 2DQ
0171 354 8318
Advice and information for parents of children
in state schools and nurseries. Issues books and
periodicals and runs an Advice Line 0171 354
8321 (2–5pm Mon–Fri)

**British Association for Early Childhood
Education (BAECE)**
111 Cityview House
463 Bethnal Green Road
Lodnon E2 9QY
0171 739 7595

British Dyslexia Association
01734 668271
Offers a helpline which is open 10am–5pm
Mondays to Fridays. They can also send you
an information pack.

Campaign for State Education (CASE)
158 Durham Road
London SW20 0DG
0181 944 8206
Publishes a newsletter and briefing papers to
help parents and others campaign for a better
deal for all state educated children.

The Child Accident Prevention Trust
18–20 Farringdon Lane, London EC1R 3AU
0171 608 3828
An educational charity which researches and
provides information on child safety.

**The Independent Schools Information
Service (ISIS)**
56 Buckingham Gate, London SW1E 6AG
0171 630 8793
Provides a handbook giving information on
independent schools.

Kidscape
0171 730 3300
Publishes a 'Stop Bullying' leaflet and operates
a Parents Bullying Line on Mondays and
Wednesdays 9am–5pm.

Lucid Systems
26 Tunis Sreet, Sculcoates Lane
Hull HU5 1EZ
01482 465589
Information for parents with dyslexic children.

National Association for Gifted Children
Park Campus, Boughton Green Road
Northampton, NN2 7AL
01604 792300

**National Confederation of Parent Teacher
Associations (NCPTA)**
2 Ebbsfleet Industrial Estate
Stonebridge Road
Gravesend , Kent DA11 9DZ
01474 560618
Offers advice and insurance schemes for PTAs.

**The National Association of Toy and Leisure
Libraries**
68 Churchway, London NW1 1LT
0171 387 9592
Provides support for toy libraries, advice on
toys and a range of publications relating to
child development.

The Parents' Charter Unit
Department for Education and Employment
Sanctuary Buildings, Great Smith Street
London SW1P 3BT
0171 925 6155

Preschool Learning Alliance
69 Kings Cross Road, London WC1X 9LL
0171 833 0991
Can provide information about preschool
playgroups in your area. Formerly known as
the Preschool Playgroups Association.

**Royal Society for the Prevention of Accidents
(ROSPA)**
Cannon House, The Priory
Queensway, Birmingham B4 6BS
0121 200 2461

Department for Education and Employment
Sanctuary Buildings, Great Smith Street
London SW1P 3BT

Scottish Education Department
New St Andrew's House
Edinburgh EH1 3TG
0131 244 4440

*The following organizations may be useful in
giving advice on finding a qualified teacher for
your child.*

The Amateur Swimming Association
Harold Fern House
Derby Square, Loughborough
Leicestershire LE11 0AL
01509 230431

British Amateur Gymnastics Association
Lilleshall Hall, Shropshire
01952 820330

Incorporated Society of Musicians
10 Stratford Place
London W1N 9AE
0171 629 4413

Sports Council
16 Upper Woburn Place
London WC1H 0QP
0171 388 1277

FAMILY PLANNING

Family Planning Association
27 Mortimer Street, London W1N 7RJ
0171 636 7866

Northern Ireland
113 University Street, Belfast BT7 1HP
01232 325488

Wales
4 Museum Place, Cardiff CF1 3BG
01222 644034

Information on all aspects of family planning
and contraception.

Family Planning Brook Advisory Centres
Brook Central Office, 153a East Street
London SE17 2SD
0171 708 1234

Advice and practical help with contraception
and unplanned pregnancies. Free and
confidential.

Marie Stopes Clinic
Marie Stopes House
108 Whitfield Street, London W1P 6BE
0171 388 0662
Registered charity providing family planning,
women's health centres, pregnancy testing and
counselling. A charge is made to cover costs.

ILLNESS, DISABILITY AND SPECIAL NEEDS

**AFASIC (Association for All Speech Impaired
Children)**
347 Central Markets, Smithfield
London EC1A 9NH
0171 236 3632
Campaigns and provides advice and
information service etc. for children with
speech and language disorders.

**Association for Spina Bifida and
Hydrocephalus (ASBAH)**
ASBAH House, 42 Park Road
Peterborough PE1 2UQ
01733 555988

Scotland
Scottish Spina Bifida Association
190 Queensferry Road, Edinburgh EH4 2BW
0131 332 0743

Northern Ireland
**Northern Ireland Spina Bifida and
Hydrocephalus Association**
75 New Row, Coleraine BT52 1EJ
01265 51522
Information and counselling for parents.

BLISSLINK
17–21 Emerald Street, London WC1N 3QL
Freephone: 0500 151617
Provides support and information to parents
with a baby in special care.

British Chiropractic Association
Equity House, 59 Whitley Street
Reading RG2 0E6
01734 757557
Publishes an annual register of members. Call
0800 212618 for your nearest chiropractor.

British Diabetic Association
10 Queen Anne Street
London W1M 0BD
0171 323 1531

Northern Ireland
31 Grange Park, Belfast BT17 0AN
01232 610630

National charity which offers advice and
support.

Children's Liver Disease Foundation
138 Digbeth Street
Birmingham B5 6DR
0121 643 7282
Offers information on various aspects of the
disease. Can provide leaflets.

Cleft Lip and Palate Association (CLAPA)
1 Eastwood Gardens, Kenton
Newcastle-upon-Tyne NE3 3DQ
0191 285 9396
Gives support to parents of children with cleft
lip and/or palate.

Contact a Family
170 Tottenham Court Road
LondonW1P 0HA
0171 383 3555
Links families who have children with
disabilities or special needs through self-help
groups.

Council for Disabled Children
8 Wakley Street, London EC1V 7QE
0171 843 6000
Details of organizations offering help for
children and families with special disabilities.

Cystic Fibrosis Trust
11 London Road
Bromley BR1 1BY
0181 464 7211

Northern Ireland
1 Circular Road East, Cultra
Co Down BT18 0HA
01247 272781

Wales
3 Aberfour, Newport, Gwent NP9 9QA
01633 277663

Scotland
Inverallan, 26 West Argyle Street
Helensburgh, Dunbartonshire G84 8DB
01436 676791

Information and support for parents of
children with cystic fibrosis. Local groups.

Disability Information Trust
Mary Marlborough Centre
Nuffield Orthopaedic Centre
Headington, Oxford OX3 7LD
01865 227592
Assesses and tests equipment for people with
disabilities.

Down's Syndrome Association
155 Mitcham Road, Tooting
London SW17 9PG
0181 682 4001

Scotland
Scottish Down's Syndrome Association
158 Balgreen Road, Edinburgh EH11 3AU
0131 313 4225

Northern Ireland
3rd Floor, Bryson House
28 Bedford Street, Belfast BT2 7FE
01232 243266

Support for parents of children with Down's
Syndrome. Runs a 24-hour helpline.

Endometriosis Society
33 Belgrave Sqaure, London SW1
0171 235 4137
Provides information about the condition.

Haemophilia Society
123 Westminster Bridge Road
London SE1 7HR
0171 928 2020

Northern Ireland
67 Woodvale Road, Belfast BT13 3BM

Practical help for families affected by the
disease.

KIDS
80 Waynflete Square
London W1D 6UD
0181 969 2817

A small national organization set up to help
families with children with special needs.
Contact their head office to find out if KIDS
operates in your area.

**MENCAP (Royal Society for Mentally
Handicapped Children and Adults)**
MENCAP National Centre
123 Golden Lane, London EC1Y 0RT
0171 454 0454

Scotland
**Scottish Society for the Mentally
Handicapped**
7 Buchanan Street, Glasgow G1 3HL
0141 226 4541

Northern Ireland
Segal House, 44 Annadale Avenue
Belfast BT7 3JH
01232 691351

Advice and information for parents with
mentally handicapped children.

Meningitis Research Foundation
13 High Street, Thornbury
Bristol BS12 2AC
01454 413344

Northern Ireland
29 Springwell Street, Belfast BT43 6AT
01266 652060

Counselling for bereaved parents and families
and support for parents with children in
hospital.

National AIDS Helpline
0800 567123
Confidential, free helpline which is available
24 hours a day. Information in other languages
is available as follows: *Bengali* on Tuesday
6pm–10pm on 0800 371132; *Punjabi* on
Wednesday 6pm–10pm on 0800 371133;
Gujerati on Wednesday 6pm–10pm on 0800
371134; *Urdu* on Wednesday 6pm–10pm on
0800 371135; *Hindi* on Wednesday
6pm–10pm on 0800 371136; *Arabic* on
Tuesday 6pm–10pm on 0800 282447;
Cantonese on Monday 6pm–10pm on 0800
371137.

**National Association for the Welfare of
Children in Hospital (NAWCH)**
Argyle House, 29–31 Euston Road
London NW1 2SD
0171 833 2041

Scotland
Action for Sick Children
15 Smith Place, Edinburgh EH6 8HT
0131 553 6553

Advice and emotional support for families
with sick children. Local groups.

National Deaf Children's Society
15 Dufferin Street
London EC1Y 8PD
0171 250 0123
Advice and information on all aspects of
childhood deafness. Supports parents through
self-help groups.

National Eczema Society
163 Eversholt Street
London NW1 1BU
0171 388 4097
Advice and support for eczema sufferers.

Royal National Institute for the Blind
224 Great Portland Street
London W1N 6AA
0171 388 1266
Provides information and support for all types
sight impairment

SCOPE
12 Park Crescent, London W1N 4EQ
0171 636 5020
Provides a range of services for people with
cerebral palsy and their families.

**SENSE (National Deaf-Blind and Rubella
Association)**
11–13 Clifton Terrace, London N4 3SR
0171 272 7774
Advice and support for families of deaf–blind
and rubella handicapped children.

Sickle Cell Society
54 Station Road, Harlesden
London NW10 4UA
0181 961 7795
Information and counselling.

Toxoplasmosis Trust
61–71 Collier Street
London N1 9BE
0171 713 0663
Information and counselling for pregnant
women with toxoplasmosis and parents of
infected children.

LOSS AND BEREAVEMENT

England and Wales
**Foundation for the Study of Infant Deaths
(Cot Death Research and Support)**
14 Halkin Street, London SW1X 7DP
0171 235 1721

Northern Ireland
**Friends of the Foundation for the Study of
Infant Deaths**
7 Glennan Avenue, Belfast BT17 9HT
01232 622688

Scotland
Scottish Cot Death Trust
Royal Hospital for Sick Children
Yorkhill, Glasgow G3 8SJ
0141 357 3946

Provides information and support for parents
who are coping with sudden infant death. Can
put you in touch with local groups and other
bereaved parents and provides advice on
prevention. Responsible for the 'Back to Sleep'
campaign.

**SATFA (Support after Termination for
Abnormality)**
73 Charlotte Street
London W1P 1LB
0171 631 0285
Self-help charity offering support to parents
who have had a termination due to a
diagnosed foetal abnormality. Support given
by parents who have also terminated a
pregnancy in such circumstances.

**Stillbirth and Neonatal Death Society
(SANDS)**
28 Portland Place
London W1N 4DE
0171 436 5881
National network of support groups for
bereaved parents.

INDEX

A

abnormalities, congenital 24, 59
  and termination 41
abortion see termination
AFP (alphafetoprotein) tests 24
afterpains 109
after-school clubs 241
AIDS see HIV
air travel: and pregnancy 18
alcohol: and fertility 10
  during pregnancy 28
allergies 84, 160-1
amniocentesis 24, 38, 349
amniotic fluid 17, 24, 38, 46, 58
anaemia: postnatal 117
  in pregnancy 34
anaphylactic reactions 157
animals, allergies to 161
antenatal appointments 16, 17, 20-4, 29
antenatal classes 16, 18, 25, 29
  and single women 14
antibiotics: and fertility 11
  APGAR scores 58
arms: at birth 60
  and startle reflex 62, 63
asthma 160, 161
attachment 144
attention, development of 148-9, 196-7
au pairs, employing 239-40

B

Babinski reflex 63
baby carriers 32, 32
babysitters, employing 232, 233
backache in pregnancy 17, 28, 34, 41
Bart's tests 24
bathing babies 92, 96-7, 97, 98, 99, 169
beds and bedding: for babies 30, 33, 40, 168-9, 371
  bunk 170
  and house dust mites 161
bedtime routines: babies 66, 107
bed wetting 190
benefits, state 28-9, 30
bickering 179, 203
bilingual families 222, 239
bilirubin 359
birth (see labour): emergency 52
  at home 20-1
  in hospital 20
  planning 21
bleeding, vaginal:

after conception 13
  in labour 46-7
  in pregnancy 37, 38, 41
blood pressure (in pregnancy) 23, 35, 38
blood tests (in pregnancy) 22-3
'blues', postnatal 108, 111, 120
bonding 62
bones, growth of 124, 127, 185
books 220-2
bottlefeeding (see also formula milk) 77, 80, 82, 111, 168
  after caesarean 115
  changing to 82-3
  and crying babies 78
  equipment 32, 78, 79, 179, 80
  nighttime 65-6, 72-3, 107
  and regurgitation 164
  stopping 89
bouncing chairs 169
boys and girls (developmental differences) 127
brain, growth of 124, 125-7, 186
  see intelligence
bras, maternity 15, 32, 33
Braxton-Hicks contractions 18
breastfeeding 70-2, 72-3, 74
  after caesareans 115
  and afterpains 109
  and changing to bottlefeeding 82-3
  clothes for 32, 33, 71
  and contraceptive pills 119
  and crying babies 78
  and diet 76-7
  difficulties with 73-6
  and making love 118, 119
  and medication 70, 77
  and milk supply 71, 72, 75, 76
  nighttime 65-6, 72-3, 107
  of older babies 81-2, 87-8
  and ovulation 87
  in public 71
  and regurgitation 164
  resistance of baby to 75-6, 88
  returning to 82
  stopping (weaning) 88, 89
  of twins 176-0
  and working mothers 87, 88
breast pads 32
breast pumps 32
breasts (see also breastfeeding):
  after giving birth 108, 111
  changes in pregnancy 15, 16
  engorgement of 71, 73
  leaking milk from 71
  and mastitis 75

at puberty 303, 304, 305
  sore 72, 73-4, 111
  swollen (of newborn) 60
breath-holding attacks 340
breathing (babies) 124, 128
breech deliveries 55-6
bruising, postnatal 109
  see also haematoma
buggies 31, 40
burns 169

C

caesareans 21, 37, 38, 56, 66, 114-16
  epidural 40, 54, 56-7
candida albicans see thrush
cannabis 11
card games 196, 197, 227
carriers, baby 32, 32
carrycots 30, 31, 169
car seats 31, 32, 33, 172, 172
cats: allergy to 161
  and toxoplasmosis 11
caul 60
CE mark 168, 168
cervix 45, 47, 48, 109
chairs, baby 32, 32, 33, 33
chalazion 344
changing babies see nappies
changing mats 32
changing tables 98
check-ups see examinations and check-ups
child benefit 28
child care 230, 231
  assessing your needs 234, 235
  by au pairs 236-7, 239-40
  by childminders 235, 240-4
  costs of 235, 236, 237, 240
  by family and friends 236, 237
  legal aspects of 234-5
  by nannies 235, 237-9
  at nurseries and day-care centres 240-1
  qualifications in 239
child-health clinics 153-4
childminders 235, 240-4
chlamydia 10
choking 168-9
chorionic villus sampling 24
chromosomes 13
cleft lip and palate 173
climbing frames 187
clinics, child-health 153-4
clothes: baby 30, 31, 131, 32, 40, 100, 169

children's 188-9, 247, 261
  dressing-up 213
  maternity 33
coeliac disease 84, 160
colic 72, 77, 104, 161-2
  and crying 101, 102, 103
collage 215-16
collections, making 197
colostrum 71
comfort objects 144
'community units' 20, 21
competitiveness 198-9
computers 225
concentration 206, 223, 224
conception 12-13
  and pre-conceptual care 10-12
constipation: babies 162
  after childbirth 109-10
  during pregnancy 13, 28, 35
construction sets 187, 210-11
Contact a Family 174
contact lenses 315
contraception: and conception 11
  postnatal 119
contractions 45, 46, 47, 48, 49,50
  Braxton-Hicks 18
  after orgasm 15
  and relaxation techniques 26
cooking: and children 212
  pretend 213, 214
co-operation, learning 198-9
cot bumpers 165, 168
cot death see sudden infant death syndrome
cots 30, 33, 40
  toys for 135, 136
coughs 162-3
cradle cap 163, 368
cramps (in pregnancy) 34, 41
crawling 130, 131-3, 132, 134
  reflex after birth 63
  and safety precautions 169-72
'cruising' 133, 134, 178
crying (babies) 78, 92, 101-4, 107-8, 178-9
CRY-SIS 102, 107
cups, using (babies) 85, 88, 89
CVS see chorionic villus sampling
curl ups (exercise) 112
cystic fibrosis 24, 347, 353, 356

D

dancing 187, 219, 290
day-care centres see nurseries
deafness 140, 143, 154, 195,

testing for 67, 140, 155-6
and toys 175
death *see* stillbirth; sudden infant
death syndrome
dehydration 167
dental care *see* teeth
depression, postnatal 66, 108, 120
diabetes (in pregnancy) 23, 37-8
diarrhoea 163
diet (*see also* food):
before conception 11
when breastfeeding 76-7
in pregnancy 12, 27-8, 34, 35
and teeth 129
and twin pregnancies 40
digestion, babies' 124, 127
diphtheria immunization 157,
159
dismissal, unfair 29
doctors *see* GPs
dogs, allergy to 161
domino deliveries 20
dominoes, picture 227
dough, modelling 216-17
Down's syndrome 24, 166
drawings, children's 188, 190-1,
215, *215*
dressing (of children) 188-9
dressing babies *100*
dressing dolls 188, *188*
dressing-up clothes 213
drinks (for babies) 72, 80, 85-6
dropping things (of babies) 136,
138, 139
drowning 169
drugs: and fertility 10, 11
DTP vaccine 157-8, 159
dummies 89, 129, 138, 168

E
earache 103
ear drops, giving *164*
ears, development of 15, 17, 60
ectopic pregnancy 37
ECV 55
eczema 106, 163, 164
eggs 85, 89, 159
electronic toys 225
embryo 12, 14
emergency delivery 52
emotional development 146-7,
180, 181, 182, 183, 184, 198,
see also jealousy; tantrums
'engagement' 18, 45
engorgement 71, 73, 83
Entonox 53
epidural blocks 21, *54*
caesareans by 40, *54*, 56-7
epilepsy 166
episiotomy 19, 49, 53-4, *54*,
109-10
sex after 118-19

examinations and check-ups:
antenatal 22-4
of babies and children:
preliminary 66-7
at 6 weeks 116, 117
developmental 153, 154-7
postnatal 117
exercise:
after caesareans 114-15
before conception 11
and play 186, 187, 209-10
postnatal 111, *112-13*, 114,
118
in pregnancy 25-6, *26-7*
expressing milk 66, 75, 77, 88
eye drops, giving *164*
eyes (*see also* sight; squint):
of newborn 59-60, *61*
'sticky' 165

F
faeces: of newborn 60, 127
see also constipation
falls, precautions against 169
Family Credit 29
fathers (*see also* conception) 44
at the birth 50-1, *51*, *52*, *53*,
57-8, *59*
and paternity leave 29
reactions to pregnancy 13-14
and sex after childbirth 118-20
sharing care 65, 66, *80*, 103,
107, 230, 231, 232
feeding *see* bottlefeeding;
breastfeeding
feet: of babies 63
swollen (in pregnancy) 23
fertility 10, 11, 12
financial aspects 14
see also benefits; child care
finger foods *85*, 86, 168
fingernails, cutting babies' *99*
finger painting 215
fingers, extra 59, 60
fires: and safety 169
floors: and safety 169
fluid retention (in pregnancy) 35
fluoride supplements 129, 166
foetus, development of 14-18
folic acid 11
fontanelle 59, 185
food (*see also* diet):
allergies to 84, 160-1, 252
baby 83-6, 89
and development of taste 191
and safety precautions 168
forceps deliveries 48, 53, 54-5, 59,
101
foreskin: care of 99-100
formula milk 77-8, 79, *179*, 85
soya 161
stage two ('follow-on') 82, 86

friendships 202, 230-1
imaginary 213
furniture: and safety 169-70

G
games: board and card 196, 197,
227
clapping *145*
computer and video 225
hide-and-seek 133, 138, 139
jigsaws 187, *188*, 211
'peek-a-boo' 138, 139, 145
see also play; swag bags
garden, safety in the 172
gas and air 53
gastroenteritis 80, 167
general practitioners *see* GPs
genitals: at birth 60
see also foreskin; testes
German measles *see* rubella
gluten, allergy to 84, *see* coeliac
disease
GPs (general practitioners) 153
and antenatal care 20, 21
grandparents 231, *231*
growth (babies') 67, 124, *125*
'gumming' 129
gums: care of (in pregnancy) 34
and disease 166
Guthrie test 67

H
haematoma 110, 111
haemolytic disease 38, 59
haemophilia 24, 166
haemorrhoids 35, 110-11
hair: at birth 61
in pregnancy 27
washing babies' *96*
hands, babies': and dexterity
135, 136, *136*, 137, *155*, 156,
180, 181, 182, 184, 187-8
extra fingers on 59, 60
grasping reflex *62*, 63
harnesses, safety 168, 169
head: at birth 59, 63
control of *130*
headaches: in pregnancy 38
health checks *see* examinations
health record books 153
health visitors 152-3
hearing: development of 139-40
problems *see* deafness
heartburn (in pregnancy) 35
heat rash 165
helpfulness (children) 198-9, 278
heredity 160, 185
hernias 67
umbilical 60, 167
Hib immunization 158, 159
hips: 'clicky' 59, 60, 67, 155

HIV, testing for 22-3
holiday clubs 241
home alone, leaving a child 234-5,
home births 19, 20-1, 44, 48
home learning services 174
homelessness 121
homeopathic immunization 158
hospital: packing bag for 19
security in 64
house dust mites 161
housework, children and 211-12
Housing Benefit 29
human chorionic gonadotrophin
13
hyperventilation (in labour) 51
hypothermia (in newborn) 64

I
immunization 153, 154, 157-9
Income Support 28, 29
incontinence, stress 18, 26, 35
infertility 12; *see also* fertility
injections, reactions to 157
insomnia: in pregnancy 36
intelligence 124, 143, 146, 149,
269, *see also* brain, growth of;
memory; think, learning to
intensive care *see* special care unit
internet 225
itching *see* eczema; rashes
IUCD (intra-uterine contraceptive
device) 11, 119 see also
contraception
IVF (in vitro fertilization) 12

J
jaundice 59, 64-5, 67
jealousy 203
jigsaws 187, *188*, 211

K
'kicking' (of foetus) 16, 18
kitchens, 'babyproofing' 170, *170*
Kitemark 168, *168*

L
labour 45, 46-50
breathing for 52, *53*
pain control in 51-3
positions for 49, *50-1*, *52*
serious symptoms in 46-7
lactose intolerance 161
language, development of 140-3,
180, 181, 182, 183, 184, 185,
192-4, 195
lanugo 16, 18, 60
laughing (of babies) 146, 147
legs: at birth 60
swollen (in pregnancy) 23

leg slides (exercise) *112*
'let down' reflex 49, 71
libraries, children's 221, 222
lifting (when pregnant) 34, *137*
'lightening' 45
linguistic development *see* language, development of
Lionmark 168, *168*
lisps 156
listeria 12
living rooms 169-70, *170*
lochia 108
locks, childproof 170
love, showing 146
lying down (in pregnancy) *34-5*

M

manual dexterity *see* hands
mastitis 75, 83
maternity allowance 30
maternity leave 17-18, 29-30
maternity payments 29
mattresses 168-9, 371
measles immunization 158, 159
meconium 46, 60
medicines, giving *164*
   sugar-free 166
memory, development of 148-9, 196-7, 264
meningitis 163-4
   immunization against 158
'messy play' 217
midwives 20, 21
milia ('milk spots') 60, 165
miliaria 165
miscarriage 10, 11, 12, 41
   signs of 37, 41
   tests and 24
   and twins 40
MMR vaccine 158, 159
mobiles 135, 148
modelling dough 216-17
monitoring, foetal 48
'morning sickness' *see* nausea
Moro reflex *162*, 63
mother and toddler groups 153
   see also playgroups
mouth, putting things in 137
mumps immunization 158, 159
muscles 124, 127
muscular dystrophy 24
music 187, 191, 218-20
myelination 186

N

nails *see* fingernails
nannies 235, 237-9
nappies: changing 32, 93, *94*, 96
   disposables 93, 96
   reusables 93, 95, 96
   terry cloth 95, *95*, 96

trainer 93
nappy rash 93, 96, 100, 106, 164
nappy services 95
National Childbirth Trust (NCT) 25, 74, 232
nausea: in pregnancy 13, 14, 15, 16, 36
newborn babies 58-9
   appearance of 58, 60, 61
   breathing of 59, 128
   first days with 65-6, 67, 92
   minor problems 59-60, 66, 67
   premature *see* premature babies
   size (weight) of 61, 63-4
   skills of 61
nightmares 198
nipples, sore/cracked 72, 73-4
nipple shields 75
nose drops, giving *164*
nuchal scan 24
nurseries, nursery schools 232, 235, 240-1, 242, 244-5, 246, 247
nursery rhymes 222
nuts 85, 89, 168

O

obstacle courses, making 187
oedema *see* swelling
one o'clock clubs 232
one-parent family benefit 28
only children 202
oxytocin 49, 71, 72

P

paddling pools 218
pain control (in labour) 51-3
painting, children's 188, 214, *214*, 215
palate, cleft *see* cleft lip
parent-and-child clubs 232
Parentline 102
parents, types of 146, 179-80, Patient's Charter, the 20
pelvic floor exercises 26, 119
pelvic pain (during pregnancy) 36
penis: care of foreskin 99-100
perception, developments in 138-9
pertussis *see* whooping cough
Pethidine 53
pets, allergy to 161
phenylketonuria (PKU) 67
physical development 130-4, 180, 181, 182, 183, 184, 186-7
   see also walk, learning to
piles (haemorrhoids) 35, 110-11
Pill, the: and breastfeeding 119
pillows, use of 168
placenta, delivery of 47, 49
placental abruption 38
placenta praevia 38
plants, poisonous 172

play (*see also* games): creative 214-17, *see* drawing; painting
   and exercise 186, 187, 209-10
   importance of 149, 187, 201-2, 206-8
   'messy' 217-18
   parental involvement in 207-8, 209, 227
   pretend 196, 213-14, *214*
   and technology 224-5
   with other children 201-2, 225-7
playdough 216-17
playgroups 232, 241, *243*, 245, 246, 247
poisoning 171, 172
polio immunization 157, 158, 159
polyhydramnios 38
Portage 174
possetting 124, 127, 164
potty training 189-90
prams 30-1, *31*, 33, 40
pre-eclampsia 38
pregnancy 12-13, 14-19
   assessing due dates 14, 22, 24
   diet in 12, 27-8
   discomforts in 34-7
   emotional reactions to 13-14
   exercise and 25-6, *26-7*
   first signs of 13
   problems in early 37-8
   problems in later 38
   and sex 15
   testing for 13
   and work 28, 29-30
premature (pre-term) babies 63
   and crying 102
   development of 125, 155
   feeding 64, 75
   in intensive care 64-5
   twins 40
prescriptions, free 28, 34
pressurizing children 149
pretend play 196, 213-14, *214*
prickly heat 165
progesterone 13
prolactin 71, 82
pudendal blocks 54
pushchairs 30, 31, 33
pyloric stenosis 167

Q

quarrelling 179, 203

R

rashes 165
   and food allergies 160, 161
   and teething 166
rattles 137
read, learning to: and pre-reading skills 223-4
reading to children 220-1, 223,

224
reflexes, babies' *62*, 62-3, 148
regression 125
regurgitating food 124, 127, 165
rehydration therapy, oral 167,
relactation 82
Relate 116, 120
relating to others (babies) 144-6
relaxation exercises 26-7, 35, 36
   and pain control 25, 51
respiratory distress syndrome 64
resuscitation of newborn 64
rhesus incompatibility 38, 59
rice, baby 84
riding 25
rivalry, sibling 203
rooting reflex 62
rubella (German measles) 11
   immunization against 158, 159

S

safety: in the car 172
   in the garden 172
   at home 134, 168-71
   outside the home 171
salt 89
sand, playing with 217
scalds 169
scans *see* ultrasound
school, preparing child for 202
   see also nurseries
Scope 174
second children, having 202-3
self-awareness 180, 181, 182, 183, 184, 197
self-mutilation 199
separation anxiety 144
serum screening 24
sex (of baby) 13, 15, 24
sexism 197
sexual intercourse: after caesareans 115-16
   after childbirth 118-20
   in pregnancy 15
share, learning to 226-7
'shared care' 21
shoes: in pregnancy 17, 33
   putting on 189
shopping, children and 213
'show', the 45, 46, 47
sibling rivalry 203
sickness benefit 30
sight: development of 135-9, 190-1
   testing 137, 155, 315
signs, making (babies) *142*
singing 218-19
single parents 14, 120-1
sit, learning to 131, *131*
sitting in pregnancy *36*
skin: at birth 60, 61

in pregnancy 16, 27, 36, *see also* stretch marks
problems *see* eczema; rashes
sleep (*see also* insomnia):
  babies 65, 66, 83, 106
    changes in patterns 107
    and checking routine 107-8
    fighting 104
    forming good habits 107
  lack of: effect on babies 104
    effect on parents 105-6
smacking 243
'small-for-dates' babies 63-4
smiling (of babies) 146, 147
smoke alarms 170
smoking:
  and asthma 161
  and cot deaths 165
  and fertility 10
sneezing: of babies 163
social skills, development of 180, 181, 182, 183, 184, 201
  see also friendships; relating
solids (food) 83-5, *184*
songs 218-19
special care unit (intensive care) 63, 64-5, 66, 75
special needs, children with 173
  and play 207
speech *see* language development
  disorders 156, 195
sperm production, healthy 10, 11
spina bifida 11, 24, 173
sport 292-3, 312-13
  in pregnancy 25
spots 165
squints 59, 155, 165
stammering 156, 195
startle reflex *62*, 63
statutory maternity pay (SMP) 30
stencilling 215
step reflex *62*, 63
'sticky eye' 165
stillbirth 41

stitches *see* episiotomy
stories, telling 222, 223
strangers, fear of 138, 144, 145
stress incontinence 18, 26, 35
stretch marks 17, 36, 118
stretchsuits 31, *31*
stuttering *see* stammering
sucking, comfort 89
sucking reflex 15, 62
suction deliveries 48, 55
sudden infant death syndrome (cot death) 70, 165
suffocation 168-9
'superbaby syndrome' 149
swag bags, making 138, 139, 211
swallowing: of small objects 169
swallowing reflex 63
swelling: in pregnancy 23, 27, 38
swimming 25, 34, 35, 37

T

talk, learning to *see* language
tantrums 199-201
taste, learning about 191
TB *see* tuberculosis
teats 78
teeth: babies' 60, 124, 129, *167*,
  see also teething
  care in pregnancy 28, 34
  and fluoride supplements 166
teething 83, 107, 128-9, *129*, 166, *167*
television 223, 224-5
temperament, children's 146, 185
temperature, babies' body 127-8
  and cot death 165
TENS machines 53, 115
termination 24, 41
testes (testicles): at birth 60
  care of 11
  examinations of 67, 155
tetanus immunization 157, 158, 159

'theory of mind' 195-6
thigh lifts (exercise) *113*
think, learning to 180, 181, 182, 183, 184, 194-7
  see also intelligence; memory
thrush (*candida albicans*) 36-7, 60, 74, 164, 166
thyroid function, testing 67
toddler group 232, *see also* playgroups
toenails: cutting babies' *99*
toes, extra 60
toilet training 93, 189-90, 247
'topping and tailing' 98, *98-9*
toxoplasmosis 11
toys: baby 33, 135, 136, 137, 138, 175, 187-8, *188*, 195
  construction 187, 210-11
  electronic 225
  and pretend games 196, 213-14
  safety and 168, *168*, 169
  and sexism 197
transfusion, blood 64-5
'triple tests' 24
tubal pregnancy 37
tuberculosis (TB), immunization against 158-9
twins 39-40, 57, 160, 185
  breastfeeding *76*

U

ultrasound scans 16, *23*, 24
umbilical cord, prolapse of 46
umbilical hernia 60, 167
umbilicus, cleaning 98-9, 167
understanding 156, 157, *see* think, learning to
urine: leaking *see* stress incontinence
  testing (in pregnancy) 23
urticaria 60

V

vaccination *see* immunization
vagina:
  after childbirth 119
  bleeding from *see* bleeding, vaginal
  discharge from 60
vandalism 267, 277
ventouse deliveries 48, 55
vernix caseosa 16, 60
video games 225
videos, watching 225
vision *see* sight
vitamin supplements 29
vomiting 167 *see also* gastroenteritis; nausea; pyloric stenosis

W

waist twists (exercise) *113*
walk, learning to 125, 127, 130, *133*, 134, 156, 178, 186
  safety precautions and 169-72
walkers, baby 130, 134, 169
water, playing with 217, 218
waters, breaking of 15, 46
weaning 88, 89
  and food allergies 160-1
weight: of babies 61, 63-4, 85
  in pregnancy 23
whooping cough immunization 157-8, 159
wind 72, *81*
  and crying 101, 102, 103
window locks, fitting 169
work: when pregnant 28-9
  and separation anxiety 144
  single parents and 120, 121
  and time with child 244, *246*

X

X-rays: and pregnancy 11-12

ACKNOWLEDGMENTS

The publishers would like to thank the following for helping with photography:

Akousa Adom; Ben Alexander; Husnara Begum; Chelsea and Jade Bess; Hal and Anabel Briggs; Rosie Callery; Sandra Chambers; Niccy Cowen; Ben Dawes; James, Simon and Joanna Drayson; Julia Eastell; Julie and Liam Fitzgerald; Xanthe and Robert Gwyn Palmer; Rosy and Angus Halfyard; Sophie and Melanie Hoare; Fran Hollywood; Alexander Jesson; Henri Lanson; Jason and Lucy Lubbock; Josh and Connor Lynch; Daisy and Anne King; Jamie MacIntyre; Jamille Malcolm; Shannon and Debbie Mitchell; Oliver, Max and Sally Nield; Linda Ogden; Oscar Price; Ben, Joe and Cindy Richards; Victoria Salentino; Ben and Edward Sanderson; Max Schofield; Sebastian and Rosemary Tusa; Nigel Waters; Armand Weeresinge; Nicholas West; Caitlin and Jenny Wheeler; Jack and Emma Windsor; Julia Yelland.

Thank you to the following for kind permission to reproduce photographs:

page 23 Custom Medical Stock Photo/Science Photo Library
pages 42-43 Collections/Sandra Lousada

Thank you to the following experts who were consulted on sections of the book:

Clare Brown, Information Services Co-ordinator, CHILD; Professor Geoffrey Chamberlain, Head of Obstetrics and Gynaecology, St George's Medical School, London; Mary Daly, The Health Visitors' Association; Clare Delpach, Director of the Association for Post Natal Illness; Joanie Diamavicius, Director of Support for Termination around Fetal Abnormality; Foresight; Gingerbread; Ruth Grigg and Jane Owen, Medical Information Officer, The Family Planning Association; Sarah Harvey, former midwife and health visitor; Dr David Haslam, GP, patron of CRY-SIS, Chairman of the Examining Board of the Royal College of General Practitioners; The Miscarriage Association; Professor Peter Hepper, Department of Psychiatry, Queen's University, Belfast; Annette Spence, Psychosexual Counsellor, and Fran Godfrey, Advice Sister, Marie Stopes Clinics; Sheila Tunstall, The Caesarean Support Network; Professor James Walker, Department of Obstetrics and Gynaecology, St James's Hospital, Leeds.